*Public Access CD-ROMs
in Libraries: Case Studies*

Supplements to
COMPUTERS IN LIBRARIES

1. Essential Guide to dBase III+ in Libraries
   Karl Beiser
   ISBN 0-88736-064-5   1987 CIP

2. Essential Guide to Bulletin Board Systems
   Patrick R. Dewey
   ISBN 0-88736-066-1   1987 CIP

3. Microcomputers for the Online Searcher
   Ralph Alberico
   ISBN 0-88736-093-9   1987 CIP

4. Printers for Use with OCLC Workstations
   James Speed Hensinger
   ISBN 0-88736-180-3   1987 CIP

5. Developing Microcomputer Work Areas
   in Academic Libraries
   Jeannine Uppgard
   ISBN 0-88736-233-8   1988 CIP
   ISBN 0-88736-354-7 (softcover)

6. Microcomputers and the
   Reference Librarian
   Patrick R. Dewey
   ISBN 0-88736-234-6   1988 CIP
   ISBN 0-88736-353-9 (softcover)

7. Retrospective Conversion:
   A Practical Guide for Libraries
   Jane Beaumont and Joseph P. Cox
   ISBN 0-88736-352-0   1988 CIP

8. Connecting with Technology 1988:
   Microcomputers in Libraries
   Nancy Melin Nelson, ed.
   ISBN 0-88736-330-X   1989 CIP

9. The Macintosh ® Press: Desktop
   Publishing for Libraries
   *Richard D. Johnson and
   Harriett H. Johnson*
   ISBN 0-88736-287-7   1989 CIP

10. Expert Systems for Reference and
    Information Retrieval
    Ralph Alberico and Mary Micco
    ISBN 0-88736-232-X   1990 CIP

11. EMail for Libraries
    Patrick R. Dewey
    ISBN 0-88736-327-X   1989 CIP

12. 101 Uses of dBase in Libraries
    Lynne Hayman, ed.
    ISBN 0-88736-427-6   1990 CIP

13. FAX for Libraries
    Patrick R. Dewey
    ISBN 0-88736-480-2   1990 CIP

14. The Librarian's Guide to
    WordPerfect 5.0
    Cynthia LaPier
    ISBN 0-88736-493-4   1990 CIP

15. Technology for the 90's
    Nancy Melin Nelson, ed.
    ISBN 0-88736-487-X   1990 CIP

16. Microcomputer Management and
    Maintenance for Libraries
    Elizabeth S. Lane
    ISBN 0-88736-522-1   1990 CIP

17. Public Access CD-ROMS in Libraries:
    Case Studies
    *Linda Stewart, Kathy Chiang,
    Bill Coons, eds.*
    ISBN 0-88736-516-7   1990 CIP

18. The Systems Librarian's
    Guide to Computers
    Michael Schuyler, ed.
    ISBN 0-88736-580-9   1990 CIP

19. Essential Guide to dBase IV in
    Libraries
    Karl Beiser
    ISBN 0-88736-530-2   1990 CIP

20. Essential Guide to UNIX in Libraries
    D. Scott Brandt
    ISBN 0-88736-541-8   1990 CIP

21. Integrated Online Library Catalogs
    Jennifer Cargill, ed.
    ISBN 0-88736-675-9   1990 CIP

Public Access CD-ROMs in Libraries: Case Studies

edited by
Linda Stewart
Katherine S. Chiang
Bill Coons

Meckler
Westport • London

Library of Congress Cataloging-in-Publication Data

Stewart, Linda, 1950 -
    Public Access CD-ROMs in libraries : case studies / Linda Stewart,
Katherine S. Chiang, Bill Coons.
       p. cm. -- (Supplements to Computers in libraries ; 17)
    Includes bibliographical references.
    ISBN 0-88736-516-7 (alk. paper) : $
    1. Reference services (Libraries) -- Automation -- Case studies.
2. Optical disks -- Library applications -- Case studies.
3. Information retrieval -- Case studies. 4. Data base searching -
- Case studies. 5. End-user computing -- Case studies. 6. CD-ROM -
- Case studies. I. Chiang, Katherine S. II. Coons, Bill. III. Title.
IV. Series.
Z711. S83   1990   89-49459
025.5'24--dc20   CIP

British Library Cataloguing in Publication Data

Stewart, Linda   *1950* -
    Public access CD-ROMs in libraries : case studies
    (Supplements to computers in libraries v 17).
    1. Libraries. Applications of computer systems. Read only memory.
    Compact discs
    I. Title II. Chiang, Katherine S. III. Coons, Bill IV. Series
    025.00285456

    ISBN 0-88736-516-7

Meckler Corporation, 11 Ferry Lane West, Westport, CT 06880.
Meckler Ltd., Grosvenor Gardens House, Grosvenor Gardens,
   London SW1W 0BS, U.K.

Printed on acid free paper.
Printed and bound in the United States of America.

To whom, or what, shall this book be dedicated?

Individually, Bill would like to recognize his mom — for her guidance,
support, love, and courage; Kathy acknowledges her family;
and Linda would like to thank her husband, Ed, for his cooperation,
understanding, and willingness to listen.

Collectively, this book requires a dedication which transcends the lives
and hopes of the editors.
It was, after all, written with thirty-six other individuals.
So it is to them, and the spirits of cooperation, professional growth, and
better service, that this book is ultimately dedicated.

Table of Contents

Introduction

CD-ROM combines massive storage space, small size, and durability with the capability for random access, inexpensive duplication and mass distribution. Large databases can be held locally, without the need for mainframe computers, and local access obviates the need to pay telecommunications costs or any other time-based use charges. CD-ROM reference tools, in particular, have changed the library's public image.

The educational level of the public has evolved to the level of their wanting a more active role in the selection and retrieval of the information they will use. CD-ROM reference tools, which become more cost-effective the more they are used, are ideally suited for exploration by the public. It is now the responsibility of libraries to provide the access and the necessary assistance.

The story of how libraries have reacted to CD-ROMs is recorded in the archives of our profession. The first articles on CD-ROM concentrated on explanations of the technology and paeans to its potential. Articles by CD-ROM producers and, later, product reviews, dominated the early literature. Librarians relied on a combination of their own ingenuity and policies established for other media to make decisions regarding CD-ROM implementation. We also made site visits to neighboring libraries and telephone calls to distant ones. The first case studies were published in diverse journals, sometimes too late to help the early innovator.

Now literature on CD-ROM applications in libraries is consolidating. Specialized journals, such as *Laserdisk Professional, CD-ROM Librarian* and *CD-ROM EndUser,* compile articles of interest, while monographs have been written to explain various facets of the technology and to serve as manuals. One book, *CD-ROM and Other Optical Information Systems* (Eaton, MacDonald and Saule, 1989), specializes in the public services implications of CD-ROM technology.

Several bibliographies on the subject of CD-ROMs have been published, for example:

Elshami, Ahmed M. 1988. *CD-ROM: An Annotated Bibliography.* Englewood, Colorado: Libraries Unlimited.

Motley, Susan A. 1989. "Optical Disc Technology and Libraries: A Review of the 1988 Literature." *CD-ROM Librarian* 4(5): 8,10,12,14–30.

Fox, Edward A. 1989. "Optical Disks and CD-ROM: Publishing and Access." *Annual Review of Information Science and Technology* 23:85–124.

The goal of this book is to present case studies of libraries which have installed CD-ROM workstations in public access areas. We have provided this compilation of examples as a source of ideas. The primary audience is librarians planning to purchase CD-ROMs or manage their use by the public. This volume should serve as an aid to planning and decision-making.

We solicited contributions from various types of libraries and information centers, contacting public, academic, school and special libraries. Our aim was to concentrate on libraries offering access to commercially produced databases, both bibliographic and non-bibliographic; therefore, we have not included sites offering only public access catalogs or locally produced databases. Several institutions offer these resources in addition to commercial products, and their chapters discuss the types of CD-ROMs provided.

We have included libraries which have only one workstation as well as those having entire information retrieval centers housing their CD-ROMs. We were also interested in unusual or innovative services, workstations in non-traditional locations, fee-based access, training programs for staff or patrons, and networking arrangements.

Finally, since we were interested in hearing from libraries which had not been described in the mainstream media sources, we employed several methods of seeking contributors. We compiled a list of sites we had learned about through both published and non-published sources (such as ERIC documents and NLM reports) and contacted libraries of different types. We called other libraries looking for verbal recommendations and issued a public call for contributions. As a result, this collection contains case studies from such diverse and unpublicized sites as the University of Milan and the Union-Endicott School District, as well as such well-known sites as Texas A & M University and Vanderbilt University.

The first chapter presents an overview of our contributors' experiences in implementing CD-ROMs for public use. This chapter is also meant to serve as a finding aid so that readers interested in a particular issue can determine which libraries are working on that issue and read those case studies first. The body of the book is devoted to the case studies themselves, grouped into two parts. The first part presents case studies grouped into sections by type of library:

—Academic

—Medical and Health Sciences

—School

—Public

The second part presents sections which profile libraries dealing with particular aspects of implementation:

—Separate Facilities

—Charging User Fees

—Networking

—Remote Access

—When CDs are not enough: Magnetic Tapes plus CDs

Those libraries which could be logically placed in more than one section have been placed in the appropriate "implementation" section, with a cross reference from the "type of library" section.

The authors whose manuscripts comprise this book of case studies represent the strength of this work. It has been their energy, dedication and interest, guided by the suggestions, advice and experience of the editors, which have made this work possible. Thanks to the proofreading by our colleague, Susan Szasz, there are not as many errors as there might have been in this book.

We hope that our readers will discover personally and professionally useful information from within these case studies, and learn and apply to their institutions the experiences and suggestions of individual authors. While CD-ROM may prove to be a transitional medium and not a permanent solution to information storage, access and retrieval issues, it has unquestionable potential and definite value. It is in the spirit of demonstrating this potential and sharing its value that we share this book of CD-ROM case studies with you.

Linda Stewart, Katherine Chiang and Bill Coons
Ithaca, New York
November 1989

1

An Overview of Public Access Issues

Linda Stewart

This overview chapter highlights issues introduced in the case studies in an attempt to summarize the common or unique approaches of each of these institutions. The following sections include a review of the goals and roles of CD-ROM, funding and selection, access issues, staff support and training, user awareness, evaluation, impact, problems and future plans. The chapter ends with a brief description of each library, its collections, and CD-ROM products.

Goals and Roles

A number of the goals mentioned by the authors in this book relate to the effect CDs will have on their users. A common aim is to offer expanded service— improved search capabilities at no cost (Auburn, Chapter 5). In some cases, CDs, because of their one-time subscription costs which encourage unlimited searching, are seen as a way of introducing patrons to end-user searching (Boston, Chapter 19; Vanderbilt, Chapter 3; UCLA, Chapter 21). Library staff in the Union-Endicott School District (Chapter 11) want students to learn skills they will need after high school and to be impressed by the library as a place to seek information later in life. Rutgers University at Newark has adopted a new undergraduate curriculum with an interdisciplinary orientation emphasizing problem-solving and the research process (Chapter 17). Its staff sees CDs as a way of encouraging students to use library resources in this program. Howard County Public Library (Chapter 18) had the specific service goal of developing a network so that users could access all databases from any workstation and several users could access one database simultaneously.

Other libraries have goals relating to staff. Brock University (Chapter 2) sees the DIALOG OnDisc products as a medium for training staff in DIALOG online searching. The Schuyler-Chemung-Tioga BOCES School Library Systems Library (Chapter 12) has as one goal informing school library media specialists of advances in educational media; for them, collecting CD-ROMs is a way of promoting teacher awareness, emulating online systems for training purposes, and providing holdings information for interlibrary loan use.

Libraries often use CD-ROM products to maximize otherwise limited facilities. The Hereford Branch of the Baltimore County Library (Chapter 13) is small and geographically isolated. CD-ROM reference tools preclude the need for multiple printed volumes, and references obtained from CD databases can be submitted to the parent library and the full articles sent by telefacsimile. The Carnegie Mellon Libraries, with limited collections in subjects outside the University's expertise, use CD-ROM databases to make patrons aware of materials not held locally (Chapter 22).

Some libraries see exploration of the technology as a goal in itself. For Oregon State University, this is part of the University's research mission, and CD-ROM is a library research project (Chapter 15). The Library for the Department of Information Science at the University of Milan shares this view (Chapter 7), which is particularly appropriate since the Library's primary clientele are computer science students. The medical and health sciences libraries tested MEDLINE products as part of a collective research/evaluation project designed by the National Library of Medicine (Chapters 8, 9, 10, 21).

Several authors describe the roles their CD-ROM products are expected to play and how they fit in with the libraries' other electronic information services. Mann (Chapter 6) sees CDs as part of the product mix eventually leading to the establishment of an "electronic library." Boston (Chapter 19) and Texas (Chapter 14) see them as an extension of existing end-user programs. The Broome-Delaware-Tioga BOCES (Chapter 12) considers them as a next step after their videodisc awareness program. Many libraries have access to electronic information by multiple means. CDs at Carnegie Mellon (Chapter 22) co-exist with the LIS system of locally mounted files—public access catalog, reference tools and bibliographic databases—to which patrons have dial-up access. Libraries in the Union-Endicott School District (Chapter 11) provide access to hard-disk-resident databases, remote online databases and satellite-based databases (offered through a local cable company), as well as CDs. Medical and health sciences libraries often have several ways of accessing MEDLINE.

Funding and Selection
Funding

CD-ROM products are usually much more expensive than similar print products—in some cases, costing over $10,000 per year per disk. A variety of funding mechanisms has been employed for their procurement. St. Louis (Chapter 8) and Oregon State (Chapter 15) use their general acquisitions budget. Boston purchased monograph counterparts such as the Oxford English Dictionary and Books in Print out of its book fund, and paid for others from its Computer Search Service budget (Chapter 19). Auburn (Chapter 5) and Vanderbilt (Chapter 3) changed funding sources over time; Vanderbilt used grant funding to start the service, and now charges subscription costs to departmental library budgets. Auburn funded subscriptions from the reference serials fund during the first year and from the general serials budget thereafter. Brock (Chapter 2) supplemented other sources with money saved by canceling some print indexes duplicated by CD-

ROM. Three libraries mentioned receiving additional funding from students—Kent (Chapter 16) directly by assessing user fees, Utah (Chapter 9) by using monies obtained by a tuition surcharge designed to fund the University's computing program, and Erindale (Chapter 4) from a student vote to pledge $10.00 per year per student to support the library.

Non-library sources are also used for funding. School libraries (Schuyler-Chemung-Tioga BOCES, Chapter 12, and Swift Current Comprehensive, Chapter 20) received money from the state or province, as did the Hereford Branch of the Baltimore County Public Library (Chapter 13), which also received some Title I money under the federal Library Services and Construction Act. Texas received a gift of $100,000 from an alumnus who was impressed by student response to InfoTrac (Chapter 14). Carnegie Mellon (Chapter 22) received a grant from the Pew Memorial Trust, and Howard County (Chapter 18) sought and obtained two corporate grants.

Selection

The selection process involves finding out about available products and applying criteria to determine which products to acquire. Milan (Chapter 7), like other libraries, learns about possible CDs from directories, optical information magazines, promotional materials and product demonstrations. Vanderbilt (Chapter 3) was in the fortunate position of beta-testing three versions of the ERIC database and was able to compare products. The medical and health sciences libraries were given different versions of MEDLINE, and so were able to test and compare them as a group. Kent (Chapter 16) has an in-house trial of each product considered for purchase. Staff there have a practice of returning each product to the publisher before making a final decision so they are not overly influenced by having the product in-hand.

Libraries have a variety of written and unwritten selection criteria, some related to policies in force for other formats. Carnegie Mellon (Chapter 22) added a section for optical disks to its selection policy for electronic media, because the optimal mix of remote online, locally mounted, and compact disk files had to be considered. At Auburn (Chapter 5) staff selecting CD-ROMs must submit the same justification form used for requesting periodicals in print format.

Libraries may add specific selection criteria to the nearly universal requirements of appropriate subject matter and high quality. Brock (Chapter 2) looks at online statistics to determine which databases are most likely to be used. An effort is also made both to support disciplines which rely heavily on online searching and to attract other disciplines to the advantages of computerized searching. Erindale and Rutgers-Newark (Chapters 4 and 17) select easy-to-use databases likely to appeal to undergraduates.

Mann (Chapter 6) looks for search software similar in capability to BRS and DIALOG remote access databases. Libraries with networks, such as Howard County and Rutgers-Newark (Chapters 18 and 17), have special requirements. CD-ROMs must be licensed for networking, they must not require too much memory relative to other products and software residing on the network, and they must be compatible with the network hardware and software.

Access

Patrons

Libraries generally target their CD-ROM services to a particular audience. Sometimes they also restrict CD access to specific user groups. Public libraries, of course, have a mandate to serve the general public. At Howard County (Chapter 18) access to CDs is unrestricted, although librarians often conduct a reference interview with patrons in order to determine whether a CD-ROM product is likely to answer their questions. School libraries are designed for a more specific group; patrons in the Union-Endicott School District (Chapter 11) include students at one high school, one middle school and six elementary schools. The two School Library Systems Libraries (Chapter 12), on the other hand, have as patrons library media staff from individual schools and the occasional teacher or administrator. Within individual schools, access is variable. Sometimes only the librarian searches databases; sometimes the workstations are located in a public area and students are permitted to search. Swift Current Comprehensive (Chapter 20), also a school library, makes its databases available to students at school and in the community. Mann Library (Chapter 6), as part of a land-grant institution, has as its mission the provision of library services to New York State residents, so access to CD-ROM products is not restricted. In the Education Library at Vanderbilt (Chapter 3), area teachers and principals, as well as members of the Vanderbilt community, have access to the CDs. Parties unaffiliated with Vanderbilt must purchase a library card. The Health Sciences Library at Utah (Chapter 9) serves physicians, hospital staff and patients as well as University faculty, staff and students. These patrons all have access to the CD-ROMs. Some libraries are relatively unrestricted, but members of the primary clientele are given priority. In some departments at Auburn (Chapter 5), patrons not affiliated with Auburn are asked to step to the back of the line when people are waiting to use CD databases. At Maryland (Chapter 10), only faculty, staff and students are permitted to make appointments to use the CDs. Others are limited to first-come, first-served access. Other libraries such as UCLA and Carnegie Mellon (Chapters 21 and 22) restrict access to their primary clientele. Finally, some CDs are limited to staff use, such as the Missouri Union List at St. Louis (Chapter 8).

Location

The location of the CD workstations is an important determinant of the services which will be provided and of patron awareness of the system. Several libraries (Kent, Brock, Hereford Branch, Vanderbilt, Carnegie, Mann; Chapters 16, 2, 13, 3, 22, 6) locate the workstations near, or within sight of, the reference or information desk. Rutgers-Newark staff (Chapter 17), wanting students to see the relationship between the CD-ROMs and other reference tools, have integrated them with print periodical indexes. Auburn (Chapter 3) has located them in the reference areas of subject collections; in some areas, they are nearer the reference desk than in others.

In small libraries, such as the school libraries in the Union-Endicott School District (Chapter 11), there may be few options for locations. The placement of electric outlets, or a desire to make the equipment visible to the lone staff member, may determine location. Large libraries, such as the ones at Texas and at Oregon (Chapters 14, 15), have set up separate areas for CD-ROMs and other end-user searching. At UCLA (Chapter 21), because there was insufficient space in the reference area, CDs have been moved into the library's Instructional Media Facility which contains microcomputers used for other purposes. Two health sciences libraries have tried placing CD-ROM workstations in areas outside the main library. St. Louis (Chapter 8) located one MEDLINE station in a conference room in the University Hospital for a three-week evaluation period, and Utah (Chapter 9) has a MEDLINE CD-ROM in its clinical library in the affiliated hospital. Finally, for Swift Current Comprehensive, the location of workstations is now of secondary importance (Chapter 20), since remote bulletin board software permits dial-in access from any nearby school or home computer.

Multiple-User, Multiple-Disk Access

Since CD-ROM products were developed, librarians have been eager to make several disks available at one station and to make the same database accessible to several patrons at once. Equipment is now available to perform these tasks. Brock (Chapter 2) and Milan (Chapter 7) have both connected CD-ROM drives in a daisy-chain configuration to allow several disks to be accessed from the same station. Other libraries have experimented with local area networks so that several users can search the same databases. Boston was a test site for the MultiPlatter CD-ROM network (Chapter 19), and Rutgers-Newark (Chapter 17) has either tested or instituted several different configurations, including a Wilson network running IBM PC LAN software on IBM Token-Ring hardware, a network using Meridian Data's file server, and a network of SilverPlatter products using LANtastic's Network Operating Software. Howard County (Chapter 18) has implemented a Novell network and Swift Current (Chapter 20) uses the Remote Bulletin Board System software to enable patrons to access their CDs both remotely and simultaneously.

Added Software

Software, besides networking and bulletin board software, may be added to perform such functions as security, menu access and transaction logs. Howard County (Chapter 18) has added the Direct Access Menu software to keep use statistics and safeguard the operating system. Rutgers-Newark (Chapter 17) added Automenu to protect DOS and to permit patrons to format blank diskettes on the A drive for downloading purposes. Vanderbilt (Chapter 3) uses Sidekick to provide a menu so patrons can switch databases without exiting to DOS. Programmers at Mann (Chapter 6) have created batch programs that permit any one of several CD-ROMs to be used on a machine without rebooting.

Hours of Availability

Many libraries make their CD-ROMs available whenever the library is open, but others, for security reasons or to ensure adequate staff assistance, limit hours of availability. At Carnegie Mellon and at Maryland (Chapters 22, 10) CDs may be used only when librarians are scheduled at the reference desk, and at Texas (Chapter 14) "when service desks are staffed for full-service operations." Remote access can enable CDs to be searched even during hours when the library is not open (Swift Current, Chapter 20).

Time Limits

Where CD-ROMs are in high demand, it is common to restrict use by a single patron to a specific length of time. A 30-minute limit when other users are waiting is the rule at Brock, Texas, Carnegie Mellon, Oregon State, and Vanderbilt (Chapters 2, 14, 22, 15, and 3). At Utah (Chapter 9) the academic health sciences library also has a 30-minute limit, but at the clinical library, there are no such limits. The longest time limit mentioned—two consecutive hours—is at Mann (Chapter 6). Fifteen minutes is the rule at Auburn and at Swift Current, where searches are automatically cut off by the remote access software (Chapters 5 and 20). At the Hereford Branch, if someone searches for more than fifteen minutes while others are waiting, library staff ask the patron if he needs help, and he is reminded that others need to use the system (Chapter 13). At libraries with network arrangements, time limits are less necessary, because more than one person may search the same product at once. According to a survey at Rutgers-Newark, where no restrictions on time are imposed, the average search lasted twenty minutes, while the longest session required about two hours (Chapter 17).

Scheduling and Advance Reservations

Several libraries, including Maryland, Brock, Milan, the academic health sciences library at Utah, Mann, and Texas (Chapters 10, 2, 7, 9, 6 and 14), permit patrons to sign up in advance to use a CD-ROM. Texas adds that patrons may arrive up to five minutes late for their appointments, but will lose their turns if they are later. At the clinical library at Utah (Chapter 9), there is less interest in reserving appointments because hospital personnel cannot count on being available at a specific time. Staff at St Louis (Chapter 8) prefer not to institute sign-up sheets because of the problems of policing and of handling no-shows and late arrivals. Carnegie and Vanderbilt (Chapters 22 and 3) do not have sign-up sheets either.

The Schuyler-Chemung-Tioga BOCES School Library Systems Library has another approach to ensuring equity; since the Library serves many schools, the CD-ROMs themselves circulate to different sites (Chapter 12).

Fees

Only two libraries mentioned charging user fees. Brock charges from $5.00 to $10.00 for a search on a CD database, if the search is performed by a librarian (Chapter 2) while searches performed by patrons are free. Kent charged $0.15 per minute using a debit card system in order to pay initial subscription costs; charges will be discontinued after Summer 1989 (Chapter 16).

Printing and Downloading

The costs of supplies needed for printing have induced some libraries to either limit printing by patrons or charge for it. Utah (Chapter 9) limits free citations to 200 in the academic health sciences library and to 25 in the clinical library, where patrons may be in a hurry for information. At Brock (Chapter 2) users may print 50 citations free at one time (printing defaults may be set on the SilverPlatter software). Extensions may be granted by staff if the topic warrants.

Although all the libraries permit printing, downloading policies vary. Downloading is not permitted at Hereford Branch (Chapter 13) because the plexiglass panel used to protect the system from tampering also prevents access to the floppy drive. Downloading is not permitted at Carnegie Mellon (Chapter 22), but, since most patrons use Macintosh computers instead of the IBMs or compatibles used as the CD workstations, this is not perceived as a problem. At Maryland (Chapter 10), users may download if they supply a formatted disk, do not need assistance from staff, and have read the PsycLIT permission policy if they are using PsycLIT. Vanderbilt (Chapter 3) encourages downloading to conserve resources, and Brock, which has set limits on printing (Chapter 2), sees downloading as a way of accommodating users wishing to record large numbers of citations.

Staff Support and Training
Staffing

Staffing arrangements across the libraries are so diverse that it is difficult to generalize. Some libraries have designated particular individuals or departments to be responsible for CD-ROM service. At Carnegie Mellon (Chapter 22), these are the database service coordinators, who provide staff training and documentation and ensure system upkeep. Brock (Chapter 2) also assigns responsibility to the computer search service, and Oregon has created a new position, that of CD-ROM Librarian (Chapter 15). At Vanderbilt (Chapter 3), responsibility is divided among the several subject libraries, but the Automation Project Librarian serves as a resource person and coordinates activities among the libraries.

In almost all libraries, user assistance is provided at least some of the time. Libraries assigning CD-ROMs to separate areas in the library must designate staff accordingly. At Oregon (Chapter 15) an administrative assistant supervises the CD-ROM area, with students as the primary staff answering basic questions and loading disks. They refer reference-type questions to the reference desk and difficult technical questions to automation support staff. The compact disk service at Texas (Chapter 14) is also staffed by students. At UCLA, CD products are available in the Instructional Media Facility, along with public access microcomputers and machine-readable materials (Chapter 21). This area includes a division head, a library assistant and several students, all knowledgeable in microcomputer technology. It is felt that, since most questions about the products concern mechanics, this type of staffing is appropriate. Reference questions are referred to the reference desk.

Libraries where CD-ROMS are housed in the reference area normally have staff already available to assist users; CD-ROMs are integrated with their regular duties. At Kent and Auburn (Chapters 16 and 5), these staff are a combination of librarians, support staff and student assistants. At Brock (Chapter 2), CDs are normally supported by Public Services librarians, but there are some hours when no assistance is available. At St. Louis (Chapter 8), circulation staff serve as a back-up to resolve basic problems when reference staff are not available.

Some libraries designate particular staff to handle technical issues. At Carnegie Mellon (Chapter 22) the database services coordinators are responsible for maintaining the hard disks and writing programs for switching from one system to another. At Kent (Chapter 16), the Systems Office installs and maintains CD-ROMs; printers, paper and ribbons are maintained by the library unit in charge of photocopiers. At Mann (Chapter 6), the staff of the Information Technology Section, which is responsible for staff and public access computing, installs the software, resolves technical problems and maintains the workstations. A student employee of the section periodically checks paper and ink supplies and cleans the disks. Reference staff and, when the reference desk is unstaffed, circulation staff, handle paper jams and ink cartridge replacements. At Texas, a special role is given to Computer Sciences students employed by the library (Chapter 14); they repair equipment, perform routine maintenance, install new software and write screen-save and menu programs. At Howard County, one staff member was designated LAN Administrator (Chapter 18). This individual was trained by a consultant to install new databases and troubleshoot system problems. Dealing with vendors, training other staff and writing publicity and search guides are also the responsibility of this individual.

Staff Training

Many methods of training are employed. In-house training sessions are held at Howard County, Auburn and the Hereford Branch (Chapters 18, 5 and 13). At Maryland (Chapter 10), the two-hour introductory course for patrons is also attended by new staff. Since the primary clientele of Broome-Delaware-Tioga BOCES (Chapter 12) consists of school library media staff who are not normally on the premises, this group is invited to tour the facility and observe a demonstration of CD-ROM technology. Product demonstrations are also used for training at Kent and UCLA (Chapters 16 and 21). Sample questions or exercises have been devised for staff training at Howard County, Vanderbilt, Auburn and the Hereford Branch (Chapters 18, 3, 5 and 13). At Utah and Vanderbilt (Chapters 9 and 3) individual hands-on training is provided. Staff are expected to read the documentation and experiment on their own at Boston and Texas (Chapters 19 and 14); students at Texas have a training manual written especially for them. "Cheat sheets" have been written to assist staff at UCLA (Chapter 21); at Utah staff work through the on-screen tutorials (Chapter 9). At Vanderbilt, student assistants observe trained staff as they respond to patron requests; they have a checklist of skills which must be mastered (Chapter 3). At Oregon and Kent (Chapters 15 and 16) machines are located in staff areas to permit advance practice; at Boston (Chapter 19), products are reserved for staff practice before their introduction to the public.

In some libraries, training is received from outside the library. Howard County staff were trained by their consultant (Chapter 18) and at UCLA (Chapter 21), staff have taken extra classes in DOS, word processing and database management systems in order to advise their patrons.

User Awareness

Publicity, documentation and user training are important ways of communicating with library clientele about CD-ROMs. They can make the difference between a product which is used infrequently or unsuccessfully, and one which patrons compete for and which substantially improves their retrieval of information.

Publicity

Publicity about CD-ROMs ranges from attracting the attention of patrons already in the library, to bringing new users into the library, to encouraging others to remember the library the next time they need information.

Within the library, a central location and prominent signs can be an immediate way of capturing interest (Brock, Chapter 2; Erindale, Chapter 4; Auburn, Chapter 5). Notices next to the equivalent printed media can alert patrons to the alternate format (Erindale, Chapter 4).

Brock points out CD-ROM workstations during library tours and holds open-house product demonstrations to interest patrons both in and outside of the library (Chapter 2). Swift Current demonstrated its CD-ROMs to busloads of elementary school students visiting the library (Chapter 20); Howard County held a reception to introduce INFO-LAN to the general public (Chapter 18); and Utah (Chapter 9) featured CD-ROMs at an INFOFAIR of presentations, workshops and exhibits demonstrating methods of information management technology.

Publicity outside of the library has included announcements sent to faculty and staff (Erindale and Auburn, Chapters 4 and 5), as well as flyers to be carried home from school by children—an interesting initiative from a public library (Hereford Branch, Chapter 13). Kent sent flyers to the appropriate academic departments (Chapter 16), while Hereford, with a growing commercial clientele, sent flyers to local businesses (Chapter 13). Brock posted notices on departmental bulletin boards (Chapter 2), and Hereford put posters on local area public bulletin boards (Chapter 13).

Brock and Boston (Chapters 2 and 19) alerted the media by having articles published in the student press; Brock also included a note in the weekly staff and campus newsletter. Auburn and Vanderbilt (Chapters 5 and 3) used library newsletters to announce CD-ROMs.

Announcement of training sessions is another way to publicize CDs. Vanderbilt mentions specific products in brochures offering workshops (Chapter 3); Hereford (Chapter 13) announces adult training sessions in the newspaper.

Staff at the Broome-Delaware-Tioga BOCES, hoping to increase the awareness of educational media personnel in general, gave a presentation at the New York State Computers and Education Conference. In an effort to gather community support, they have also demonstrated the technology at exhibits for school board members (Chapter 12).

Documentation

For occasions when library staff is unable to assist users with CD-ROMs, or in order to serve the independent learner, documentation is useful. Some libraries supply documentation produced by the product vendor or database producer. Oregon, Utah and Boston (Chapters 15, 9 and 19) use vendor-produced templates; Auburn and Boston (Chapters 5 and 19) provide commercial guides and flipcharts. Utah and Brock (Chapters 9 and 2) supply the systems manuals; so does Milan (Chapter 7)—in the original English. (The staff is considering translating them into Italian, however.) St. Louis, Mann, and Brock (Chapters 8, 6, and 2) shelve database thesauri near workstations.

Many libraries write some form of documentation themselves, although staff at St. Louis and Texas feel that patrons really prefer personal interaction to written instructions (Chapters 8 and 14). Quick help charts or brief reference guides are produced at Carnegie Mellon, Maryland, Hereford, Erindale and Oregon (Chapters 22, 10, 13, 4 and 15). The clinical library at Utah provides a one-page list of examples for busy patrons with no time to read lengthy instructions (Chapter 9), Kent produces a step-by-step search guide (Chapter 16), and Vanderbilt a step-by-step flipchart (Chapter 3). Boston has created instructions for SilverPlatter's SHOW and PRINT commands, complete with sample full records (Chapter 19). Howard also produces a search guide (Chapter 18), and Maryland and Brock (Chapters 10 and 2) make available a search strategy planning form, which they encourage patrons to complete. Oregon, with a large collection of databases (Chapter 15), supplies a subject index to available CD-ROM products.

User Training

Most libraries consider one-on-one point-of-use training primary. At Utah (Chapter 9), some users in the academic library are given a brief introduction, while others are talked through an entire search. In the clinical library, the amount of time a busy patron has available determines how much time is spent on explanations. Staff at Vanderbilt are as generous as possible with their time, believing that users are owed the same amount of instructional time as if they were conducting online searches (Chapter 3). At Boston, patrons arriving for a mediated search sometimes reconsider in favor of searching a CD-ROM (Chapter 19). If they have made an appointment, they are eligible for 30-60 minutes of individualized instruction. At Maryland, patrons are not always aware of the type of help they need (Chapter 10) and a technical question often leads to detailed instructions on search strategies and system capabilities.

Some libraries conduct instructional sessions devoted to CD-ROMs. A two-hour introductory course is offered by Maryland (Chapter 10). In the Union-Endicott School District (Chapter 11), high school students receive instruction in the classroom. St. Louis conducts a weekly workshop, which has evolved from an overview of searching fundamentals to a problem-oriented approach (Chapter 8). Vanderbilt offers two-part instruction—generic search strategy and system-specific information (Chapter 3). Kent and Auburn (Chapters 16 and 5) also offer workshops. Hereford Branch (Chapter 13) brings school groups into the library for instruction. The Schuyler-Chemung-Tioga BOCES trains school librarians at an annual workshop, and the director of the library makes on-site visits to installations on request (Chapter 12).

In some cases, CD-ROM instruction is integrated into course-related bibliographic instruction, as at Kent, Oregon, Mann, Vanderbilt, Rutgers-Newark and Auburn (Chapters 16, 15, 6, 3, 17 and 5). Mann also includes CD-ROM instruction with BRS Menus searching instruction in its database searching workshops.

Instructional media and methods vary. Auburn and Boston offer small-group sessions, with students clustered around the workstations (Chapters 5 and 19). Auburn, Union-Endicott and Rutgers-Newark (Chapters 5, 11 and 17) use computer projection equipment to display searches to a large group. Rutgers-Newark has purchased a portable microcomputer with a built-in CD-ROM drive for presentations outside the library. Maryland (Chapter 10) uses a DataShow projector, and Kent (Chapter 15) uses a video projector to present enlarged screen images.

Boston has produced a videotape on library use which includes a section on searching ERIC on SilverPlatter (Chapter 19). Oregon is considering the production of a tutorial using Hypercard (Chapter 15). Texas has opted for the low-technology solution. Having learned from its end-user program's slide-tape presentations, computer-assisted instruction and written manuals that none of these methods is much better than the others (Chapter 14), staff has created written materials for CD. They are easily updated and do not require the use of equipment.

Evaluation

A number of libraries—Howard, St. Louis, Hereford and Kent (Chapters 18, 8, 13 and 16)—ask users to fill out questionnaires. At Texas (Chapter 14) evaluation forms are filled out during "statistics week" in spring semester. Vanderbilt has run several user surveys (Chapter 3). Users were asked to report their status, purpose of search, ease of search, how they learned to use the system, how long their search lasted and their level of satisfaction. UCLA users were asked to fill out a form in connection with the NLM MEDLINE test (Chapter 21). They described who they were, how much experience they had searching, their opinion of the system and level of satisfaction.

Use data are sometimes used in evaluation. Howard tracks use by means of its Direct Access software (Chapter 18). At Boston, SilverPlatter installed a statistical package which collects daily usage data for each database and workstation. This data can be downloaded and aggregated (Chapter 19). At Utah, use data are collected manually; users fill out a logsheet including their status, department, database searched and comments (Chapter 9).

Several evaluation projects have already taken place. At Swift Current, use data were evaluated in relation to predetermined goals, such as having the system functioning by a particular date and a specific number of students searching it (Chapter 20). UCLA studied print-outs which patrons were asked to attach to their evaluation forms. The staff determined that many search strategies were not refined sufficiently, and that some users did not understand how to combine sets or use Medical Subject Headings (Chapter 21). Utah conducted a study of how long patrons had to wait to use a workstation (Chapter 9), and St. Louis (Chapter 8) looked at the record of problems resolved by staff.

Several libraries estimate the success of their CD-ROMs by examining measures of related services. Hereford looks at the number of article requests filled for its patrons by the parent library (Chapter 13). The Schuyler-Chemung-Tioga BOCES (Chapter 12) bases its evaluation on the number of interlibrary loan transactions, complaints from users, requests for additional training and requests for new products.

Finally, Erindale (Chapter 4) surveyed 40 universities and community colleges in Ontario. Location of services, accessibility, charges, impact on services, problems encountered and staff reaction were examined in this study.

Impact on the Library
Impact on Staff

Both reference staff and other types of staff have been affected by the introduction of CD-ROM services. The workload of on-duty reference staff has increased, but off-duty responsibilities have also grown. Boston and Vanderbilt mention the extra time required to learn each new product (Chapters 19 and 3), and Kent adds that adjustment from traditional command-based online searching to menu-driven systems takes a while (Chapter 16). At Union-Endicott (Chapter 11) the number of classes where searching is taught to students has increased; and other libraries offering special courses on CD-ROM or integrating them into pre-existing classes must devote time to planning and teaching these courses. Vanderbilt mentions time spent training staff, particularly students, who have a high turnover rate (Chapter 3).

On the positive side, having CD-ROMs contributes to professional development. Staff learn new skills. At Kent (Chapter 16), staff unaccustomed to searching have acquired search techniques, and at UCLA staff have increased their knowledge of CDs by evaluating several versions of MEDLINE. They have also developed techniques of offering incremental assistance to patrons and encouraging user self-sufficiency (Chapter 21). Staff may also benefit from an improved image (BOCES, Chapter 12). Carnegie Mellon sees two new perceptions of librarians—as equipment technicians (a sometimes frustrating image) and search system experts (Chapter 22).

Staff in other departments are affected by the implementation of CD-ROMs. At Utah, circulation staff, and at UCLA, the Instructional Media Facility staff, assist users with the products (Chapters 9 and 21). UCLA and Mann (Chapter 6) also mention impact on acquisitions staff, who have to keep track of CD licensing agreements and new procedures. Cataloging staff at both UCLA and Mann must devise cataloging to describe CDs and link the records to their counterparts in other formats.

Impact at the Reference or Information Desk

CD-ROMs have had a tremendous influence on the workload at the reference desk; libraries differ only in emphasizing the scope and level of the impact. Auburn (Chapter 5) calculates that in six months, with three products, staff answered over 5,000 CD questions. Erindale (Chapter 4) also notes an increase in reference questions, and Vanderbilt has identified an increase in students from other colleges (Chapter 3). Brock feels that compact disk databases require more time to explain than printed indexes (Chapter 2), and Utah (Chapter 9) estimates that first-time users require from 5 to 25 minutes of individual assistance. Staff also need extra time to arbitrate between patrons. Kent (Chapter 16) felt added time pressure in assisting users because of the per-minute charge. At Rutgers-Newark (Chapter 17), reference staff replaces paper and ink cartridges and troubleshoots system failures. At libraries without networking arrangements, staff may have to circulate or switch disks as well. At UCLA , traffic became so intensive in one location that the CD-

ROM products were eventually moved to another area of the library to be managed by other staff (Chapter 21).

Impact on Collections

Libraries subscribing to CD-ROM reference tools often have print counterparts to these materials. At Oregon at least four and at Brock five print equivalents have been canceled (Chapters 15 and 4). Auburn, Howard County and Carnegie Mellon, on the other hand, have not canceled any print counterparts (Chapters 5, 18 and 22). Vanderbilt and Boston have each canceled one subscription for which there was more than one print copy on campus (Chapters 3 and 19). At Hereford the practice was proactive; fewer print reference tools were purchased than would have been the case without acquisition of their CD-ROM equivalents (Chapter 13). Libraries are often concerned, however, that unless network arrangements are made, only one user can search a CD-ROM database at once. In addition, these databases are often leased instead of purchased. If the CD-ROM subscription had to be canceled, the library would be left with no copy of the information if the print subscriptions had been canceled.

Patrons at Carnegie Mellon have asked the library to subscribe to journals which are unavailable on campus but indexed by their CD-ROM databases (Chapter 22). Interlibrary loan requests have also increased, as they have at Vanderbilt, Erindale, Mann and the BOCES libraries (Chapters 3, 4, 6 and 12). Carnegie Mellon has seen an increase in circulation of materials already owned, although it is difficult to attribute this to CD-ROMs alone, since other self-service databases are also offered. Vanderbilt and Union-Endicott note an increase in journal use (Chapters 3 and 11). Addition of the ERIC database at Mann led to a large increase in use of the ERIC microfiche collection.

Spatial arrangements in libraries are also affected. The clinical library at Utah has removed the print indexes and reallocated the space (Chapter 9). Rutgers-Newark, locating its CD-ROMs among the periodical indexes, has redesigned the reference area (Chapter 17).

Impact on Online Reference Services

Carnegie Mellon, Oregon, Brock, Mann and Kent have all noticed a drop in searching online databases which are also available on CD-ROM (Chapters 22, 15, 2, 6 and 16). Vanderbilt's online searching in general has dropped 58 percent over the last two years (Chapter 3). The clinical library at Utah has also seen a drop in its mediated search services, leaving staff with more time to perfect the searches that are performed (Chapter 9). Drops in online searching are not universal, however. At Brock (Chapter 2) searches on databases with no CD-ROM counterpart have increased; at the academic library at Utah (Chapter 9), there has been little change in fee-based mediated searches, but there has been a drop in fee-based end-user searches. The mediated searches seem to be serving a different clientele than the CD-ROMs.

In some cases the presence of CD-ROMs has occasioned a change in policy. Texas no longer subsidizes online searches in databases which are on campus in CD-ROM format (Chapter 14). At Kent (Chapter 16) online searching staff was reassigned to assist in the CD-ROM area, although this practice was later discontinued.

Problems

Problems which arise in connection with implementing CD-ROM services center on user behavior, products and equipment. St. Louis mentions the difficulty of persuading patrons to set up efficient search strategies (Chapter 8), and Utah (Chapter 9) notes user dependency on the CD-ROM databases; patrons refuse to use printed indexes, even when they are more appropriate.

St. Louis mentions the problem of not receiving updates on time (Chapter 8). At Texas (Chapter 14), discs handled by patrons become scratched. Hereford (Chapter 13) received a defective disc, and had to reduce service during the lengthy wait for a replacement. Many products are unavailable for network use, according to Rutgers-Newark (Chapter 17). Brock (Chapter 2) finds that some search manuals are not useful.

Utah mentions software limitations and problems when patrons exit to the DOS level (Chapter 9). Printers cause difficulties at Auburn (Chapter 5), and paper jams are common at Utah (Chapter 9). Hereford complains of unreliable hardware (Chapter 13). The Schuyler-Chemung-Tioga BOCES (Chapter 12) found compatibility problems at various school libraries when CD-ROM readers were added to existing workstations; Howard had to resolve incompatibilities between different components of networking software (Chapter 18). In other cases, individual products were not compatible with the networks, and vendors, when called, were inexperienced with the complexities of running the products on networks. Finally, Rutgers-Newark is concerned about running products with different retrieval software on the same network (Chapter 17). Many libraries express the desire for more standardization of product software and hardware.

Future Plans

Libraries are enthusiastic about providing cost-free end-user searching, and almost all hope to expand their services. St. Louis, Union-Endicott, Brock, Hereford, and Howard plan to add new databases soon (Chapters 8, 11, 2, 13 and 18). Carnegie Mellon, which has already mounted bibliographic databases on the campus mainframe, hopes to add full-text reference works and numeric data on CD-ROM—products with insufficient demand to mount on the mainframe (Chapter 22). Auburn will be a participant in a collective project sponsored by the National Agricultural Library to text-digitize information for storage on optical disk (Chapter 5).

Maryland plans to develop more courses to train its clientele (Chapter 10). St. Louis is considering the addition of a user-education position (Chapter 8); they would also like to upgrade to faster microcomputers.

Many projects call for improving multiple-disk or multiple-user access. Maryland (Chapter 10) hopes to connect more products in daisy-chain configurations. Howard County and Union-Endicott hope to provide remote, dial-in access (Chapters 18 and 11). One solution desired by several libraries is a Local Area Network. Hereford and Mann (Chapters 13 and 6) would like to implement a LAN; Oregon (Chapter 15) has ordered a 21-drive Meridian system; and Auburn has plans for a Wilson/IBM token-ring configuration to add four more databases (Chapter 5).

Boston (Chapter 19) would like to increase the number of databases in its existing MultiPlatter LAN. Another solution involves using larger computers to provide multiple-user access. Mann hopes to eventually link CDs accessible by LAN to the Cornell backbone computer network (Chapter 6). Milan is designing a system to integrate CD-ROMs with a Unix system (Chapter 7). The entire campus at Utah hopes to connect several dozen CD-ROM databases for a mainframe-based, campus wide system (Chapter 9). Three libraries, Carnegie Mellon, UCLA and Mann, supplement their CD-ROM offerings with locally loaded databases on magnetic tape through campus mainframe computers (Chapters 22, 21, 6); Boston and Auburn may eventually do the same, using NOTIS as a gateway in the case of Boston (Chapters 19 and 5). Future arrangements may involve replacing databases currently held on CD-ROM with magnetic tapes.

CD-ROM reference tools, as they have been designed and marketed commercially, have obvious advantages and disadvantages. CD databases present all the benefits of online searching over print—speed combined with the capability to specify topics in detail, scan many fields of a record, and search multiple years. With CDs there is no dependence on external computers or telephone lines, and hence no need for a modem. Pricing mechanisms currently in practice involve known, budgetable costs. Libraries can make products available directly to patrons without incurring additional costs for each use. The result is a democratization of access which runs counter to the current trend of increased user charges.

Difficulties encountered with CD-ROM result from lack of standardization of interfaces, high start-up costs, awkward leasing arrangements, and lack of multi-user access without extensive investment in technology. Democratization of access leads to attempts to steer user behavior: patrons must be made aware of the products and trained to use them effectively, but discouraged from excessive dependence on them and from ignorance of other formats. Limits may need to be set to equalize access. Staff must be trained and allocated to provide support. Departments not directly providing support will still need to design new procedures and may experience an increase in workload. Careful planning is necessary to ensure a lasting enhancement of the library's image.

CD-ROMs are an important component of the mix of information resources and services which libraries offer. This information mix is dynamic and there is a constant ebb and flow of new products. As information technologies develop, the role of CD-ROM may change. Until that day, there are many libraries for whom CD-ROM represents a bright new feature. It is these libraries, and those who are just beginning to grapple with CD-ROM, who will benefit most from the lessons and advice offered by these case studies.

Library Profiles

2: Brock University Library
Brock University
550 Glenridge St.
St. Catharines, Ontario
CANADA, L2S 3A1
(416) 688-5550 extension 3231
Type of library: academic
Size of collection: 300,000 circulating books, 5,854 serial titles (2,763 current), 200,000 government documents
Size of population served: 10,000 undergraduate students, 700 graduate students, 307 faculty, 370 staff
CD-ROM Products owned: Business Periodicals Index (Wilson), Canadian Business and Current Affairs (Dialog), ERIC (SilverPlatter), General Science Index (Wilson), PsycLIT (SilverPlatter)

3: Education Library
Box 325 Peabody
Vanderbilt University
Nashville, TN 37203
Type of library: research
Size of collection: 217,000
Size of population served: 1,200 Peabody College students, 9,000 Vanderbilt students
Subject specialties: Education, psychology, child study
CD-ROM Products owned: Dissertation Abstracts (UMI), ERIC (DIALOG OnDisc), ERIC (SilverPlatter), GPO (SilverPlatter), PsycLIT (SilverPlatter)

4: Erindale Campus Library
University of Toronto
3359 Mississauga Road
Mississauga, Ontario
CANADA L5L 1C6
(416) 828-5237
Type of library: suburban campus of the University of Toronto
Size of collection: 250,000
Size of population served: 5,300 students
Subject specialties: faculty of arts and sciences
CD-ROM Products owned: General Science Index, Humanities Index, Social Science Index

5: Ralph Brown Draughon Library, Auburn University Libraries

Auburn University
Auburn, AL 36849-5606
(205) 844-4500
Type of library: academic
Size of collection: 1.5 million volumes, 1 million government publications, 1.73 million microforms, 117,000 maps, 19,000 current serials, 150 newspapers
Size of population served: 20,553 students, 1,174 faculty, 3,424 staff
Subject specialties: forestry, fisheries, textiles, aerospace and aviation history, Alabamiana
CD-ROM Products owned: Compact Disclosure, NewsBank, PsycLIT, Readers' Guide to Periodical Literature

6: Albert R. Mann Library

Cornell University
Ithaca, NY 14853-4301
(607) 255-7731
Type of library: academic research library, land grant library for the State of New York, unit of the Cornell University Library, and part of the State University of New York
Size of collection: 590,000 volumes
Size of population served: 8,000 primary users
Subject specialties: agriculture, life sciences, social sciences
CD-ROM Products owned: Agricola (SilverPlatter), Census of Agriculture 1982 (Slater Hall), ERIC (SilverPlatter), Fedstat County Demographic and Economic Databases, GPO (SilverPlatter), Life Sciences (Compact Cambridge), MEDLINE (SilverPlatter), Popline (SilverPlatter), and Test Disc No. 2 (U.S. Bureau of the Census)

7: Biblioteca di Informatica

University of Milan
via Moretta da Brescia n. 9
20133 Milano, Italy
(02)-7575.237
Type of library: academic
Size of collection: 16,642 volumes (218 current subscriptions)
Size of population served: 6,000 students, 50 faculty
Subject specialties: Information and computer science
CD-ROM Products owned: CD-ROM Multilingua : video dizionario (Zanichelli), Dissertation Abstracts OnDisc (UMI), McGraw-Hill Science and Technical Reference Set (McGraw-Hill), Leggi d'Italia (De Agostini), Videoenciclopedia Einaudi (Kronos Europea), Catalogo delle Biblioteche Scientifiche (University of Milan in collaboration with De Agostini publisher), MathSci Disc (SilverPlatter), and The business of CD-ROM: Conference Proceedings, Roma 1987 (Eikon)

8: St. Louis University Medical Center Library
St. Louis University
1402 S. Grand St.
St. Louis, MO 63104
(314) 577-8605
Type of library: academic
Size of collection: 127,000 volumes (50,000 monograph, 3,900 serial titles)
Size of population served: 4,200
Subject specialties: health sciences
CD-ROM Products owned: BRS Colleague MEDLINE, Intelligent Catalog, Missouri Union List

9: Spencer S. Eccles Health Sciences Library, Hope Fox Eccles Clinical Library
Bldg 589
University of Utah
Salt Lake City, UT 84112
(801) 581-8771
Type of library: academic/medical/hospital
Size of collection: 140,000
Size of population served: 25,000
Subject specialties: medicine, pharmacy, nursing & allied health
CD-ROM Products owned: MEDLINE (SilverPlatter)

10: Health Sciences Library
University of Maryland
111 S. Greene St.
Baltimore, MD 21201
(301) 328-7373
Type of library: academic library
Size of population served: 4,600 students, 8,000 faculty and staff
Subject specialties: biomedicine, dentistry, nursing, pharmacy, social work
CD-ROM Products owned: PsycLIT

11: Union Endicott Central School District
1200 E. Main
Endicott, NY 13760
(607) 785-6640
Type of library: district school
Size of population served: 5,300 students
CD-ROM Products owned: Grolier's Electronic Encyclopedia, McGraw-Hill CD-ROM Science and Technical Reference Set, Readers' Guide to Periodical Literature

12: Broome-Delaware-Tioga BOCES School Library System
Broome-Delaware-Tioga BOCES
421 Upper Glenwood Road
Binghamton, NY 13905
(607) 729-9301, extension 603
Type of library: school library system
Size of collection: 8,000
Size of population served: 38,000 students
CD-ROM Products owned: Broome BOCES LePac, Electronic Encyclopedia, ERIC (SilverPlatter),McGraw-Hill Science and Technical Reference Set, Microsoft Bookshelf, SCOOLS Brodart LePac

12: Schuyler-Chemung-Tioga County BOCES
School Library System
431 Philo Road
Elmira, NY 14903
(607) 739-3581
Type of library: school library system
Size of population served: 40 schools
Subject specialties: education
CD-ROM Products owned: Bibliofile, Brodart LePac, Electronic Encyclopedia, EMIL, ERIC (CD450), K–8 Science Helper, McGraw-Hill Science and Technical Reference Set, Microsoft Bookshelf

13: Baltimore County Public Library
Hereford Branch
16940 York Road
P.O. Box 489
Monkton, MD 21111
(301) 887-1919
Type of library: public
Size of collection: @14,000
Size of population served: 21,000
Subject specialties: general
CD-ROM Products owned: InfoTrac II, McGraw-Hill Science and Technical Reference Set, Microsoft Bookshelf, Electronic Encyclopedia

14: Sterling C. Evans Library
Texas A&M University
College Station, TX 77843-5000
(409) 845-5741
Type of library: academic
Size of collection: 1,700,000 physical volumes, 3,300,000 microforms
Size of population served: 39,000 students, 3,000 faculty
Subject specialties: Engineering, agriculture, science

CD-ROM Products owned: ABI/Inform (UMI), Agricola (SilverPlatter), Applied Science and Technology Index (Wilson), Books-in-Print-Plus and Books-out-of-Print-Plus (Bowker), Dissertation Abstracts Ondisc (UMI), Electronic Encyclopedia (Grolier), GPI (Government Publications Index from IAC), Humanities Index (Wilson), InfoTrac (IAC), Kirk-Othmer Encyclopedia of Chemical Technology, LegalTrac (IAC), Life Sciences Collection (Compact Cambridge), Lotus One Source (formerly Datext), Periodical Abstracts Ondisc (UMI), PsycLIT (SilverPlatter), Science Citation Index Compact Disc Edition (ISI), SocioFile (SilverPlatter)

15: William Jasper Kerr Library
Oregon State University
Corvallis, OR 97331
(503) 754-3260 extension 34
Type of library: university
Size of collection: 1,000,000
Size of population served: 15,000 students
Subject specialties: agriculture, life sciences, engineering, forestry, oceanography, home economics, education, pharmacy
CD-ROM Products owned: Agricola (SilverPlatter), Applied Science & Technology Index (Wilsondisc), Aquatic Sciences & Fisheries Abstract (Cambridge), Biological and Agricultural Index (Wilsondisc), Business Periodicals Index (Wilsondisc), Cumulative Book Index (Wilsondisc), Dissertation Abstracts (UMI), Education Index (Wilsondisc), ERIC (SilverPlatter), General Science Index (Wilsondisc), Humanities Index (Wilsondisc), Life Sciences Collection (Cambridge), Medline (Cambridge), MLA International Bibliography (Wilsondisc), NTIS (SilverPlatter), PsycLIT (SilverPlatter), Reader's Guide to Periodical Literature (Wilsondisc), Science Citation Index (ISI), Social Sciences Index (Wilsondisc)

16: Kent State University Libraries
Kent State University
Kent, OH 44242
(216) 672-3045
Type of library: academic
Size of collection: 1,700,000 volumes, 12,000 active serials
Size of population served: 20,000 students, 700 faculty
CD-ROM Products owned: Compact Disclosure (Disclosure), ERIC (DIALOG), Impact (Autographics), PsycLIT (SilverPlatter)

17: John Cotton Dana Library
Rutgers—The State University of New Jersey
185 University Ave.
Newark, NJ 07102
(201) 648-5910
Type of library: Academic

Size of collection: 353,000 books and bound periodicals, 2,400 subscriptions, 516 microform items, 150,000 government documents
Size of population served: 9,500 students, 500 faculty
Subject specialties: Business research, behavioral and neural sciences, biology, chemistry, criminal justice, management, nursing, and psychology
CD-ROM Products owned: API/Inform OnDisc, Applied Science and Technology Index, Biological and Agricultural Index, Business Indicators, Business Periodicals Index, Compact Disclosure, Corporate and Industry Research Reports Index, County Statistics, Essay and General Literature Index, General Periodicals Index, Government Publications Index, Humanities Index, MLA International Bibliography, MEDLINE, National Newspaper Index, Nursing and Allied Health, PsycLIT, Social Sciences Index

18: Howard County Library
10375 Little Patuxent Parkway
Columbia, MD 21044
(301) 997-8000
Type of library: county public
Size of collection: 479,656
Size of population served: 172,000
Subject specialties: business, literacy, local history
CD-ROM Products owned: CIRR OnDisc, Computer Library, ERIC, Grolier's New Electronic Encyclopedia, MEDLINE, Microsoft Bookshelf, Microsoft Small Business Consultant, Newspaper Abstracts, PDR Direct Access, Periodical Abstracts, Peterson's College Database

19: Thomas P. O'Neill, Jr. Library
Boston College
Chestnut Hill, MA 02167
(617) 552-4452
Type of library: academic
Size of collection: O'Neill Library: 802,809 books, 1,053,954 microforms, 7,900 periodical subscriptions, 115,926 government documents, 10,161 media units
Size of population served: 14,561 students, 572 faculty, 554 professional and administrative staff, 944 support staff
Subject specialties: humanities, social sciences, business, sciences, nursing and health sciences
CD-ROM Products owned: ABI/INFORM (UMI), Books in Print (Bowker), CINAHL (SilverPlatter), CIRR (SilverPlatter), Dissertation Abstracts (UMI), ERIC (SilverPlatter), MEDLINE (SilverPlatter), Oxford English Dictionary (Tri-Star Publishing), PsycLIT (SilverPlatter), Sociofile (SilverPlatter)

20: Swift Current Comprehensive High School
1100—11th Ave., N.E.
Swift Current, SK
CANADA S9H 2V6
Type of library: high school
Size of collection: 15,000
Size of population served: 1,000 students
Subject specialties: high school curriculum
CD-ROM Products owned: Bibliofile LC MARC, ERIC, Grolier's Electronic Encyclopedia, McGraw-Hill CD-ROM Science and Technical Reference Set, PC-SIG Library

21: Louise Darling Biomedical Library
University of California, Los Angeles
10833 Le Conte Avenue
Los Angeles, CA 90024-1798
Type of library: academic
Size of collection: 440,000 volumes, @6,000 journal subscriptions
Size of population served: 8,140
Subject specialties: health and life sciences
CD-ROM Products owned: Cambridge Life Sciences Collection, Science Citation Index, Cancer-CD, CHEM-BANK, PsycLIT

22: Hunt Library
Carnegie Mellon University
Frew St.
Pittsburgh, PA 15213
(412) 268-8896
Type of library: academic
Size of collection: 700,000 volumes
Size of population served: 7,000
Subject specialties: humanities, social sciences, industrial management, urban and public affairs, fine arts, music
CD-ROM Products owned: ABI/INFORM, Dissertation Abstracts, ERIC, Kirk-Othmer Encyclopedia of Chemical Technology

2

CD-ROM at Brock University: Introduction, Integration, Adaptation

Maggie Macdonald, Cathy Maskell, Janette Auer

Introduction to Brock University and Its Libraries

Brock University is a medium-sized teaching and research institution located in the Niagara region of southern Ontario. The campus sits atop the Niagara escarpment in St. Catharines, overlooking Lake Ontario in one direction, and beautiful prime farmland (rapidly turning into industrial park) in the other. In this year of Brock's 25th anniversary, there are 9,048 undergraduate students and 683 graduate students in attendance (full- and part-time).

The University is composed of the Divisions of Humanities, Mathematics and Science, Social Sciences, Education, Administrative Studies, and Physical Education and Recreation. An affiliate college, the Concordia Lutheran Theological Seminary, is located on campus.

The University Library is located on six floors of the central tower. Brock students, faculty and staff form the major part of the Library's patrons, but the Niagara Region community in general is welcome to use the collections and most services. The Library is open 91 hours per week, including evenings and weekends.

The collections comprise: 300,000 circulating books; 5,854 serial titles (of which 2,763 are current subscriptions); 200,000 government documents; Special Collections, housing printed materials relating to the history of the Niagara area; and the Listening Room—housing tapes, records, audio compact discs, listening equipment and the Library's circulating music collection. All areas are open to the public except Special Collections and recordings.

The University Map Library is administered by the University Library, but is located in the Geography Department, where it originated. It contains 50,000 map sheets, 600 atlases, and 15,000 aerial photographs of the Niagara Region.

The Instructional Resource Centre is a separately administered curriculum library in the College of Education, housing specialized materials related to education studies. The University Library, however, houses most of the education monographs, serials, and reference books.

The contents of all of these collections are accessible through an online public catalogue, part of the GEAC integrated online system installed several years ago. There are public access terminals on each floor of the University Library, as well as in the Map Library and the Instructional Resource Centre. On campus, remote access to the public access catalogue is achieved through the university data switch. Off campus access is achieved through direct dial to a dedicated line.

The Information Desk and the Computer Search Service office are located close to each other and are administered by the Head of Public Services. Professional librarians staff both locations, but some of the librarians who staff the Information Desk do not have duty in the Computer Search Service office. The bibliographic databases on CD-ROM and the workstations on which they are mounted are the responsibility of the Computer Search Service.

The CD-ROMs that Brock Library has made available to its clients are: SilverPlatter's ERIC and PsycLIT and Sport Discus; H. W. Wilson's Business Periodicals Index and General Science Index: and DIALOG's CBCA (Canadian Business and Current Affairs). The databases are mounted on four workstations. The two Wilson discs share a workstation, as do PsycLIT and Sport Discus.

Philosophy of CD-ROM Public Workstations

Our basic philosophy underlying the provision of CD-ROM databases is centred on the principle that those databases are reference tools available to all, as are all reference books and periodicals, for no charge. Largely for budgetary reasons, online search services have always been charged back to the user at cost. Compact discs allow us to offer computerized access to databases at a fixed cost. Pricing is similar in concept to traditional subscriptions to print indexes. Specifically, it is possible to budget for subscriptions to CD-ROM databases in a way that is not possible for unlimited online searches.

With the full and continuing support of the library administration, CD-ROM service at Brock has become an integral part of reference service. Both the administration and the public service librarians felt that it was important to make the advanced techniques of computer searching available to all users—not only those who could afford to pay for an online search. In the academic setting in particular, CD-ROM databases offer a relatively inexpensive way for students to experience automated information retrieval beyond the library catalogue. Almost all students would benefit from such knowledge, particularly those who will need to find and use information quickly in their future careers. We have been quick to adopt CD-ROM as a tool to improve our service and also acquaint our students with information technology.

Brock's first acquisition was the ERIC SilverPlatter CD-ROM system. It was chosen because ERIC online searches accounted for some 50 percent of online searches in the Computer Search Service at the time. The large education faculty, as well as many social science students (e.g., child studies, psychology, etc.), found the ERIC materials invaluable. As well, the library holds the ERIC ED microfiche collection (over 300,000 fiche), providing full-text support for the results obtained using the CD-ROM product. The database was immediately popular and has been in constant use.

The obvious success of our first CD-ROM acquisition prompted the coordinators of the Computer Search Service to prepare a proposal for the development of the

Computer Search Service—in particular, further acquisitions of CD-ROM databases. Two principles underlay the proposal: to support, if possible, those disciplines which used online search services most frequently and at the same time to make the new technology available to as many different disciplines as possible. In the proposal, the first major justification for acquiring CD-ROMs involved their enhanced searching capabilities, i.e., a variety of access points, the speed and convenience of searching on a computer, and printing the results. In addition, the general educational value of demonstrating and making available new technologies to students was stressed. The value of CD-ROM databases for staff training and practice in online computer searching was also used as a justification for the addition of more CD-ROM databases. The acquisition of a DIALOG CD-ROM product (CBCA) in particular was projected as a boon to staff training at no additional cost to the library. The majority of the online searching done at Brock is through the DIALOG search service. New reference staff members requiring training in online searching can use the DIALOG CD-ROM product to familiarize themselves with search protocols and to experiment with different search strategies. The CD-ROM provides, at no extra cost to the library, good initial exposure to the computerized bibliographic format, though further practice in specific subject databases would necessitate going online.

Initially the proposal suggested the acquisition of PsycLIT because of the heavy use of that expensive online database and because there was a very large number of social science students who would use the database. In addition, it was suggested that the acquisition of two relatively inexpensive Wilson databases, General Science Index and Business Periodicals Index, would be useful to students in other disciplines. The half-height internal Hitachi CD-ROM drives became available just in time for the Library to daisy-chain the two Wilson CDs at one workstation. After one year, then, the library had acquired four CD-ROM databases which were available to the public at three dedicated, locked, workstations in the public reference area. It was suggested that additional databases be evaluated as they became available with the overall goal of broadening coverage. It was projected that CBCA from DIALOG OnDisc would be an essential purchase as it is a major Canadian interdisciplinary database of value to business, politics and Canadian literature students. CBCA was acquired in the Fall of 1988, as soon as it became available. Subsequently, planning began at that time for funding Sport Discus, which had just been announced. The online version of the *Sport Index* was used frequently in support of various physical education classes, and the CD-ROM version was expected to have many advantages over the unwieldy and poorly indexed print equivalent. Future proposals focus on humanities and pure science databases.

Budget/Funding of the CD-ROMs

The system of budget allocation for the CD-ROMs has not yet been completed. Funding has come from various sources: the relevant department's library allocation, alumni donations, and the serials subscriptions account.

The Faculty of Education funds the purchase of the ERIC CD from its library allocation account. The library purchased the workstation and is responsible for the ongoing costs of maintenance and supplies. In support of the CD-ROM, the Faculty of Education also funds the acquisition of the ERIC ED microfiche collection.

Sport Discus, our most recent purchase, is paid for alternately by the Physical Education Department and the Recreation and Leisure Department, from their library allocation accounts. Since the CD-ROM drive it will be installed on is already owned by the library, the acquisition of this CD-ROM is a relatively inexpensive endeavour. The library is responsible only for continuing costs of maintenance, paper, printer ribbons, etc.

There has been no complaint from any of these faculties regarding the use of a portion of their library allocation for CD-ROM purchases. They are very appreciative that the library has a CD-ROM in their subject area.

In an effort to obtain some support for the purchase of the PsycLIT CD-ROM, the University solicited donations from the Psychology Department alumni. Any donation was acknowledged with thanks and an offer of a free search on the PsycLIT CD. Although the total received did not entirely cover the CD-ROM's cost, the donations were certainly most welcome.

In some cases, cancellation of the print version of an index provided funding support. For Wilson's Business Periodicals Index and General Science Index, and DIALOG's Canadian Business and Current Affairs, the respective print indexes were cancelled to support funding of the CD-ROM product. In addition, the ERIC print index was cancelled and funds liberated to support other reference purchases. There has been no complaint from faculty regarding the cancellation of any of these indexes. This may change in the future as print volumes become further and further out of date, but judging from the enthusiasm with which the CD-ROMs have been embraced, it is unlikely that this will occur.

For those CD-ROMs funded by the library, in either Public Services or Technical Services, the subscriptions account is, at present, considered the appropriate place to allocate the funds to cover their acquisition. The microcomputer workstations are purchased separately from the equipment account.

It is hoped that as the CD-ROMs grow in popularity and use they will be the best advertisement for acquisition of new databases. To this end the library is continually advertising their advantages and merits. The central location of the CD-ROM workstation area and the large, clear sign readily identifying the service are also a form of publicity. To supplement this high-profile location and visibility, publicity notices have been published in the weekly campus newsletter for faculty and staff and in the student press. (The library has a regular column in the weekly student newspaper, to which an item on CD-ROMs is submitted at least once a year.) Posters and notices on bulletin boards have been displayed in central areas and in the relevant teaching departments. In addition, as new CD-ROMs are obtained, the Library has issued invitations to faculty, staff, graduate students and others to attend open house demonstrations (with free coffee and doughnuts served as an added incentive)! General library tours and special subject seminars have been good opportunities for publicity about the CD-ROMs. This form of publicity ranges from a general mention and description of the CDs to in-depth instruction on one or more of the CD-ROM databases.

All of the librarians appreciate the value a CD-ROM database can add to the research efforts of students, faculty and staff. As new CD-ROMs are advertised in the library literature, librarians will often apprise appropriate faculty that a CD-ROM product is available in their subject area. If there is enough interest (as there was with Sport Discus and ERIC), the faculty may find the funds necessary for its purchase.

Other Costs Associated with CD-ROMs

The library absorbs the costs of the paper and printer ribbons used for the CD-ROMs. At this time the four CD-ROM stations require approximately three boxes of paper and four ribbons per month. This amounts to an average annual cost of $1,600. The library also absorbs the cost of any repairs that may need to be done on the workstations, the cost of any maintenance supplies, and the associated costs of maintaining and supplying user aids and signs.

Charges for CD-ROM Use

As mentioned previously, the CD-ROMs are available for use free of charge for any patron who will come to the library to use them. However, because of the need for efficiency and availability, we have instituted a policy that librarians will perform searches for those who prefer not to do their own. This policy originated because many Masters of Education students were off campus and often out of town, and therefore found it difficult to come to the campus to do their own searches. Also, of course, many faculty had become used to having searches done for them. The library currently charges $10 for a search on ERIC and PsycLIT and $5 for a search done on the two Wilson databases or on CBCA. The charge for ERIC and PsycLIT is higher because the records for both of these databases contain abstracts and generally require more complex search strategies and more time to perform.

In the last budget year (1988/1989) charged CD-ROM searches accounted for $2,170 in revenue to the library. This income is used to pay for paper, printer ribbons and other costs associated with the CD-ROMs. This practice of charging for some CD-ROM searches is a notable change from the previous philosophy of charging only for direct costs to the Library such as telecommunications, royalties and print fees. Librarians do not search print indexes because it would take too much time. However, the efficiency and availability of CD-ROM databases allows us to offer this service to those who do not have the time to do their own searching or who wish to avail themselves of a librarian's expertise.

Hardware/Software/Maintenance

All of our CD-ROMs are mounted on IBM-compatible microcomputers with attached 2400 baud Epson-compatible printers. Two workstations were purchased with hard drives and the remaining two were recently upgraded to hard drive capacity to accommodate new releases of software and to allow the installation of MS-DOS extensions. Initial problems modifying the autoexec.bat and config.sys files were overcome with patient determination, and subsequent releases of software have given us few problems. Overall, we have had very few problems with the software necessary to run each of our CD-ROM databases.

The most persistent problem we have is with the printers. Patrons consistently switch the settings and move the paper about in the printers so that they often jam. This problem has been partially solved by placing book binding tape over the switches with appropriate "Do Not Touch Switches" signs attached. One printer has broken down, apparently from overuse. Taking this printer out of service for repair caused some frustration for patrons and staff so a backup printer was ordered and is available when required.

At present, every CD-ROM database the library carries has its own drive (current discs only, retrospective discs are installed as required). The two Wilson CDs are installed at one workstation containing two half-height internal CD-ROM drives. (Because of shorter citations and the absence of abstracts it was deemed that less time would be needed to search the Wilson indexes and therefore one workstation would be sufficient.) The PsycLIT workstation, also equipped with two internal drives, houses PsycLIT and Sport Discus. ERIC runs alone on one workstation, as does CBCA. Because each CD has its own drive it is always mounted at a workstation. This may change in the future should more CDs be purchased than workstations. It is probable that, should the library's collection of CD-ROM titles grow to the point where we are unable to provide a dedicated drive for each title, a sign-out policy would be established for the CD-ROMs. This could be combined with a front-end menu for each workstation which would allow the user to select the CD desired. Once the selected CD-ROM is signed-out and inserted into the correct drive the appropriate programs necessary to run that CD would be invisibly loaded by a batch file and the patron could proceed with the search. Another solution would be to consider some type of network. This would not only solve the problem of buying one workstation for each one or two CD-ROMs, but it could make it possible for more than one patron to search a database at the same time. At this point the network systems that are available, though attractive, are too expensive for consideration.

Access/Location/Restriction on Use

The CD-ROM workstations are located on the main services floor of the library. They are situated in an open area near the reference monographs and reference periodicals collections, the Information Desk, and the Reference Office. The CD-ROM workstations are also within sight of the Computer Search Service office. The Information Desk and the Search Office are staffed by Public Service librarians, who divide their scheduled desk time between the two areas.

The main rationale for locating the workstations in this open area is to integrate them with the rest of the reference collection. It was decided from the outset that they would be available to the public free of charge and at all times the library was open. This means that the CD-ROMs are available even at times when there is no Reference or Search Office assistance available (approximately 23 to 25 hours per week). Just as the print indexes are accessible at all times, so are the CD-ROMs. If patrons are having trouble using them when there is no reference librarian on duty they must either puzzle the problem out alone or return to use the CD-ROM at a time when there is assistance available. As is the case with in-depth reference questions, the circulation staff, the only library staff on hand in the late evening and parts of the weekend, are not trained for answering CD-ROM questions and thus are instructed to refer patrons having difficulty to return when a librarian will be available to help them.

On the main floor, the CD-ROMs are located within sight of the circulation desk, which is manned at all times the library is open. Also, because the workstations are able to accommodate all of the databases, there is no need to change CDs or software unless patrons wish to search the retrospective PsycLIT or ERIC discs which must be retrieved from the circulation desk and inserted by staff. The disc and CD-ROM drive area of each workstation is locked so patrons cannot tamper with, or mistakenly harm, any workstation.

The only restrictions we have made with the CD-ROMs relate to limiting the time that can be spent at a workstation and the number of citations that can be printed. The compact discs have proven to be so popular that they are constantly in demand. Thus it has been necessary to impose a time limit on their use so that the maximum number of patrons has access to each database with enough time to perform a reasonably sophisticated search and print the results. For all of the CD-ROM databases the time limit has been set at one-half hour. Sign-up sheets are posted near the workstations. No student may sign up for more than one slot per database per day. The system is loosely monitored by the Search Service librarians but is expected to be essentially self-monitored by students. For the most part it works. Only occasionally have librarians had to intervene to request that one user make way for another.

It has also become necessary to limit the number of citations that can be printed from one search. In general, the limit is 50 citations with or without abstracts. However, an informal extension to 100 citations is allowed. It was necessary to impose this limit because it became apparent that many patrons, once they had put in their major topic and received several hundred or several thousand hits, were unaware of how to narrow their search down to a specific aspect of their topic and retrieve a more reasonable number of citations. As a result, they would attempt to print the large number of citations retrieved from their first few search statements. In a few cases patrons were simply unwilling to spend the time at the machine to limit their search to a reasonable number. They would rather print everything in a large set and select relevant citations at their own leisure. To paraphrase one patron: "I would rather print out all 250 and pick out the useful ones at home, sitting in a comfortable chair with my feet up, than sit here and pick them out."

The SilverPlatter software for ERIC and PsycLIT allows a print limit to be set as part of the setup procedure of the database. This can be overridden during any search by tabbing over to the RECORDS section of the print request screen and specifying a range of numbers, (e.g., 1–50, 51–100, etc.). Usually, though, when the printer stops after 50 citations patrons accept that number as all they will get. As patrons become familiar with the databases, they learn to scan the citations retrieved and print only those that are relevant.

The most recent release of the Wilson software (version 2.2) also allows us to set a print limit. We have chosen a limit of 75 citations, but again the patrons can bypass this by printing 1–75, 76–150, etc.

For the DIALOG CD-ROM database there is no way to set a print limit. However, regular monitoring by the librarians is an effective method of ensuring that a patron is not trying to print an inordinate number of citations.

Patrons who insist on printing all citations in a large set may download their results to their own floppy disks. The patrons must then print the downloaded information elsewhere. Generally, when a patron is spending a long time at the workstation, or trying to print hundreds of citations, some assistance is required with the search strategy or in entering terms according to the particular system protocols. Once a librarian proffers assistance the patron is usually more than happy with 30–50 relevant citations than with hundreds of citations, of which only a portion relate to the topic.

Impact on Staff and the Library

The impact of the CD-ROMs on the library and its staff can be discussed with respect to the following areas: increased workload on reference staff; concern about user support and instruction; concern about the impact of cancelling the respective paper indexes; impact of the CD-ROMs on the online Computer Search Service; impact on other library services such as interlibrary loan and photoduplication.

Increased Workload

It is apparent that the CD-ROMs have resulted in an increased workload for reference staff. Although the service point for the CD-ROMs at Brock is designated as the Computer Search Service office, the workstations are situated closer to the Information Desk. Thus, when patrons are having problems they tend to approach the librarians at the Information Desk first. It is the decision of the librarian staffing this desk whether to help these patrons or, if the Information Desk is busy or if patrons need an in-depth, time consuming introduction to the CD-ROM, they may be directed back to the Search office. Providing assistance for the CDs can and does take more time than providing assistance in using a print index. CD-ROM users require instruction not only on the specifics of the particular database but also on the use of the keyboard and printer. Therefore, not only is the Information Desk receiving more questions concerning the CD-ROMs but these questions generally take longer to answer. So far the increased load on the Information Desk has been effectively handled through the normal practice of having two librarians staff the Information Desk throughout the day and also by having the person staffing the Computer Search Service office take a more active role in assisting CD-ROM users. This is accomplished by the Search office person taking periodic strolls past the workstations to in effect "peek" over the shoulders of those using the CDs. If they look like they are having trouble, an offer of assistance is made. Even if they do not appear to be in difficulty, a casual inquiry as to "how is the search going?" will often elicit questions or comments.

User Support/Education

Generally the approach taken with instruction for the CD-ROMs is an individualized one. With two librarians staffing the Information Desk, and the Computer Search Service office person more actively monitoring CD-ROM activity, we are able to handle instruction on a one-to-one basis. This has certain advantages. It allows the librarian to interact directly with the person having difficulty and to use that person's topic as the example as they are guided through the use of the CD-ROM. It also allows librarians to tailor their comments to the patron's level of knowledge. Some patrons have never used a CD-ROM or even a printed journal index and require an in-depth introduction to the contents and functioning of a CD-ROM. Some patrons are computer illiterate or computerphobic and need to be instructed on the use of the keyboard or to be reassured that they cannot break the machine. Other patrons, reasonably familiar with the CD-ROM in that they know how to enter terms and combine sets, have difficulty selecting the index terms available for their topics. These patrons would benefit from the librarians' knowledge of the database, how materials are indexed and how terms are likely to be combined. For those times when there are no librarians present to give instruction, or for patrons who like to teach themselves, there are several options. There is a worktable next to the workstations with system manuals, thesauri and manuals for topic analysis and search preparation. The table also has handouts for each of the systems to help with the specifics of term entry, citation display and printing, etc., as well as a search preparation form and worksheets (Appendix).

There is some concern that the individualized approach does not reach all of those who could benefit from instruction in using CD-ROMs. Many patrons search the CD-ROMs, print out some citations and believe they have used the system effectively. They never ask for help and are not aware that they may have missed many relevant citations. Also, the individualized approach is very reactive. Instruction is given when it is requested and is concerned only with the CD-ROM being used. The patron could possibly benefit more from an instruction program which introduces not only a specific CD-ROM but also other sources that could be of value. Instruction could also describe how all of these sources, (journal indexes, bibliographies, monographs, online, etc.), interrelate. For these reasons, adoption of a more formalized instruction program for use of the CD-ROMs and other reference sources is being considered. This may take the form of regularly scheduled sessions throughout the year, each covering a different subject area; or it may be in the form of a multi-part workshop at the beginning of each term. The workshop format would compare to the type offered through the University's counselling centre to teach effective study or writing skills. For the library's purpose the workshop would teach effective research skills, of which using the CD-ROM sources available would be part.

Cancellation of Print Indexes

To obtain the funds to purchase some of the CD-ROM databases, it was necessary to cancel the respective paper indexes. To this end, the *Business Periodicals Index*, the *General Science Index*, the *Canadian Magazine Index*, *Canadian Newspaper Index*, and *Canadian Business Periodicals Index* were cancelled. There has been considerable concern and discussion among the librarians as to the effect these cancellations may have on reference service. The CD-ROMs accommodate only one user at a time whereas the print index will accommodate several. Also, the print indexes are generally easier to teach patrons to use; the time it takes to show someone how to use the CD-ROM may frustrate some patrons and turn them away from valuable sources. Conversely, the CD-ROM allows greater flexibility in retrieval, with several access points, and the capability of printing proper and complete citations once identified.

Since the print indexes have just been cancelled it is too early to tell if there will be any negative effect. Once several years have passed with no print copies available, the effect of the cancellations may be more apparent. To obtain more information about patron use and impressions of the CD-ROMs, as well as to clarify the effect the cancellation of the print indexes has had on patrons' use of a source, we hope to carry out a user survey in the fall of 1989.

Now that the library carries both print and CD-ROM formats of some journal indexes, it is imperative that instruction techniques encompass both print and CD-ROM sources and that the librarians giving the instruction be as at ease teaching the use of a CD-ROM index as they are in teaching a print index. The patron should be instilled with the idea that the appropriate source, in whatever format, should be used, and should not be guided by whether it is a print, CD-ROM, or online version.

Impact on the Computer Search Service

It was expected that the number of online searches performed through the Computer Search Service would decrease substantially with the installation of the CD-ROM databases, especially since online searches on ERIC and Psychological Abstracts (the first two CD-ROMs acquired) have consistently accounted for over fifty percent of online searches. The number of searches performed has decreased, but not by the fifty percent or more which constituted the number of ERIC and PsycLIT searches done. Generally, the number of online searches done on databases other than those the library has on CD-ROM has increased. In addition, the Search Service handles the requests for librarian performed CD-ROM searches. These two factors, combined with the more active role the Search Service is taking with respect to CD-ROM instruction, have meant not a decreased workload for the Computer Search Service, but an increased one. It is not always the case, for example, that searching the CD-ROM is faster than doing an online search. Several librarians have noted differences between the CD-ROM product and the online equivalent. Sometimes a CD-ROM search can be longer and more convoluted than performing that same search in the online database. For example, on the ERIC and PsycLIT CD-ROMs it is not possible to search selected fields all at once. They must be searched one at a time, (i.e., "anorexia in de or anorexia in id or anorexia in ti" rather than "anorexia/de,id,ti"). This results in more keystrokes, more set numbers, and generally much more time to do the search. Some librarians have had difficulty with the difference in print commands between the Wilson online databases and the respective Wilson CD-ROM product. There is also general frustration that there is no adjacency search capability for the Wilson CDs. These frustrations aside, all of the librarians agree that performing CD-ROM searches for patrons gives them an excellent opportunity to maintain their online search skills and to become very familiar with database structure and content. Online search requests come into the Computer Search Service office at an irregular rate. A librarian can receive several requests while on duty or none at all. There are times during the year when very few online search requests are received at all. Performing mediated searches on the CD-ROMs allows the librarian to maintain and refine search skills despite the irregular activity of the online end of the Computer Search Service. Another advantage to note is that performing CD-ROM searches for patrons gives those librarians who do no online searching a chance to keep up-to-date with CD-ROM technology and search techniques.

Impact on Other Library Services

Although there are no specific statistics, it is apparent that the CD-ROMs have resulted in an increase in interlibrary loan requests for materials, mainly journal articles, from other institutions. Brock Library's first CD-ROM was installed in the fall of 1987. In 1988 four more CD-ROM titles were obtained. In the budget year 1987/1988 interlibrary loans increased six percent, and in 1988/1989 they increased eighteen percent.

The Photoduplication Office of the library processes faculty and staff copying requests (there is one machine where students make their own copies), as well as any requests from off-campus Faculty of Education students, who submit them by mail and have them returned in the same manner. General impressions are that the CD-ROMs have resulted in an increase in the volume of copying done through this office. On a library-wide scale, photoduplication has increased substantially year after year. It is impossible to determine how much, if any, of this increase is because of the CD-ROMs. It may have occurred anyway due to an increased use of paper journal indexes, or it may be attributable to changes in university population or level of photocopying in general.

Reflections on the Program

Problems with the CD-ROM databases are frequently more related to general concerns with end-user searching than with the specifics of the various databases. Such problems include the need to clarify and define one's topic, the need to use a controlled vocabulary in certain indexes, the need to enter (or look up) terms in a system-specific manner, the need to understand Boolean logic, and the lack of control over the quality of search results (something too easily blamed on the system rather than the searcher). These problems, however, are not necessarily restricted to computerized searching of indexes, though they may be more visible when a patron is using a computerized index. It is hoped that, as with general library searching, users unsatisfied with their search results will read the available supporting material and/or ask a librarian for help. However, these problems may also point out the need to improve our methods of instruction so that the concepts of searching are better understood by library users.

Student, faculty and library staff response to the CD-ROM databases has been overwhelmingly positive. The only reservation could probably be summarized as "Why aren't there more of these available?" It can be said with confidence that the

CD-ROMs are an important part of the library's service which will continue to develop and expand.

Our policies concerning sign-up times and number of prints allowed have evolved over two years in response to the needs of users and the facilities of the library. For example, it became necessary to develop print limits when, among other abuses, one person tried to print over 1,000 citations based on one search term in the PsycLIT database. Further, in response to such problems, the Search office developed a recommendation for a proactive service to the CD-ROM users. It was proposed that the designated Search Office librarian monitor searchers informally on a regular (15–20 minutes) basis and intervene without waiting to be asked whenever the searchers' screens indicate a problem with search terms or search strategy. This would also allow us to monitor the use of both print and display.

Another aspect of the service which has been continually evolving is the design of printed guides to help users with the various systems. The system manuals are not particularly useful for end-users because of either length or complexity. The goal of our CD-ROM guides has been to make the most elementary steps available to users and to suggest they ask for expert assistance when the basic steps are insufficient. They explain how to prepare for a computer search and provide system-specific guidance for each database. In addition, we continually adapt our signs on the bulletin boards at the workstations as we attempt to find effective methods to reach users.

Training in the use of CD-ROM databases has been incorporated into the well-established library instruction programs when appropriate. In addition, much direct training is provided to users on a request basis by librarians from the Computer Search Service or from the Information Desk. This style of service is in keeping with the philosophy of treating CD-ROM databases as reference tools.

CD-ROM service has resulted in significant savings of time and money for library users. Although it is not possible to know whether every user of the system is deriving full benefits from it, librarians feel that, in general, search results and service are definitely enhanced by providing access to databases on compact disc. Our long-range goal is to provide computerized access to a wide variety of disciplines through the use of CD-ROM technology, thus providing superior access to bibliographic literature through the speed and increased manipulability of the data.

Maggie Macdonald has a variety of experience in corporate, special and academic libraries in three Canadian provinces. She has a B.A. (Queen's University, 1972), an M.L.S. (University of Toronto, 1975), and an M.A. in Canadian History (York University, 1976). She joined Brock University as a Reference Librarian in 1984 and became Co-coordinator of the Computer Search Service in 1987. Maggie now lives in Lethbridge, Alberta.

Cathy Maskell is currently Coordinator of the Computer Search Service of the Brock University Library, St. Catharines, Ontario, as well as Science Librarian concentrating on the subjects of Chemistry, Biology and Computer Science. Cathy received a Bachelor of Science degree from McMaster University in 1979, and a second B.Sc. degree from McMaster in 1980. She obtained her Masters degree in Library and Information Science from the University of Western Ontario in 1987 and joined the Brock Library immediately thereafter.

Janette Auer joined Brock University Library in 1973 as a Bibliographic Assistant. She received her Bachelor of Arts degree from Brock University and, in 1975, her Master's degree in Library Science from the University of Toronto. At that time she was assigned the position of Reference Librarian. In 1987 she became Co-coordinator of the Computer Search Service in the library. Janette is presently the Director of the Mathews Library at Ridley College in St. Catharines.

Appendix

COMPACT DISC
SEARCH PREPARATION

STEP 1

Describe your research topic

_____

_____

_____

STEP 2

Divide your topic into major concepts or variables.

CONCEPT A   CONCEPT B   CONCEPT C

_____   _____   _____

_____   _____   _____

_____   _____   _____

_____   _____   _____

STEP 3

Choose the appropriate database for your subject. Note that different databases have different search techniques.

ERIC	PSYCLIT	GSI
Education	Psychology	all sciences
Child Studies	Child Studies	Medical
Sociology	Education	Sports-medicine
Psychology	Sociology	
Physical Education		

CBCA	BPI
Canadian Politics	Business
Canadian Current Affairs	Company Information
Canadian Foreign Affairs	Recreation & Leisure
General Topics	
Canadian Business	

STEP 4   Note that there are different methods of entering terms for the different databases. There is a separate CD ROM Search guide for each database. (e.g. yellow <u>ERIC on CDROM:Search Guide</u>; blue <u>PsycLit on CD ROM: Search Guide</u> etc.) Use the guide for the database you have chosen for directions on the correct method of searching and combining concepts.

STEP 5   Combine your concepts using Boolean logic as explained on the database Guide. Terms combined with OR will broaden a set to include all of either a or b etc. Terms combined with AND will narrow a set to only those items containing both a and b.

STEP 6   Display or print your results using the method on the CDROM guide for your database.

STEP 7   For further help ask a librarian to review your search strategy or choice of database.

Definitions:

Database:

A collection of information stored in computer readable form.

Boolean logic:

A form of computer logic which must be used to specify how the computer should combine sets. (see individual database guide for details).

Descriptor:

Subject index terms taken from a thesaurus and assigned to articles on specific topics.

Search Strategy:

The choice of descriptors and their combination to produce a set of search results on a specific topic.

January 1989   Maggie Macdonald
                                          Computer Search Service

3

CD-ROM: A Successful Format in the Education Library

Jean Reese

Introduction

Vanderbilt University is home to approximately 5,500 undergraduate and 3,500 graduate or professional students within ten schools and colleges. The Jean and Alexander Heard Library, a member of the Association of Research Libraries, serves the Vanderbilt community and holds over 1.7 million volumes with a staff of 235 in its twelve different locations in nine different buildings. Vanderbilt's library system includes seven main divisional libraries—Central/Science, Divinity, Education, Law, Management, Medical and Music libraries. Special Collections and the Television News Archives are considered special units. Among all the libraries, there are 45 CD-ROM titles. The following section contains a brief description of each library division and its CD-ROM holdings. Since the Education Library is the focus of this case study, a more detailed description of that library is included.

The Central Library: located in the General Library Building, contains over 760,000 volumes in the fields of humanities and social sciences. It is supported by the College of Arts and Sciences. The main area of the reference department houses six CD workstations networked in a MultiPlatter configuration containing Books in Print Plus, Dissertation Abstracts OnDisc, Essay and General Literature Index, Humanities Index, MLA International Bibliography, Oxford English Dictionary, PAIS, PsycLIT, Readers' Guide to Periodical Literature, Sociofile, Social Sciences Index, and Newspaper Abstracts. The Government Documents Unit, located on the same level, contains GPO on SilverPlatter. On the eighth floor is the Arts Library with one workstation containing Art Index.

The Divinity Library: located in the General Library Building as well, supports the teaching and research needs of the Divinity School, the Graduate Department of Religion and the Religious Studies Department. The library has CCAT CD-ROM Text Sampler, Religion Index, REX on CD-ROM and the Thesaurus Linguae Graecae.

The Sara Shannon Stevenson Science Library: under the overall directorship and budget of the Central Library, is in a separate building and contains materials in the science and engineering subject areas. All fields of science, mathematics, engineering, and physics, as well as an extensive map collection are located here. Science has three CD-ROM workstations providing access to Applied Science and Technology Index, CASSIS/CD-ROM, Compact Cambridge/Life Sciences Collection, Earth Sciences, General Science Index, MathSci Disc, and Selected Water Resources Abstracts.

The Alyne Queener Massey Law Library: located in the Law School Building, contains in-depth research materials in foreign and international law as well as the standard holdings contained in all major law libraries. GPO on SilverPlatter and Microsoft Bookshelf are the two CD-ROM products which are set up. InfoTrac is also available.

The Walker Management Library: in the Owen Graduate School of Management, supports the research and teaching needs of the school in the areas of general management, finance, marketing, human resources, operations research, international commerce and business. Currently, there are three CD workstations with the products ABI/INFORM OnDisc, Books in Print Plus, Business Periodicals Index, CD/Banking, and CD/Corporate (2 copies).

The Medical Center Library: located in the Medical Center North building, supports the informational needs of the Vanderbilt medical community in research, patient care, and health education. The collection contains 150,000 volumes. The MultiPlatter configuration there includes CANCER-CD and MEDLINE on SilverPlatter, Nursing and Allied Health (CINAHL) CD, PC-SIG Library, and the Physician's Desk Reference.

The Education Library: located on the Peabody College campus of Vanderbilt University, contains materials which support the school of education and human development. Peabody offers a wide range of undergraduate programs including degrees in elementary education, early childhood education, physical education, secondary education, special education, and human development. Peabody has an enrollment of approximately 1,200 students with about two-thirds in post-baccalaureate professional degree programs. The Education Library holds over 217,000 volumes in the fields of education, psychology related to education, child study, library and information science, literature for children and adolescents, and curriculum materials. Formerly the Peabody College Library, it was renamed the Education Library in 1974 when Peabody College became a professional school of education. As a subscriber to the Educational Resources Information Center (ERIC), the library contains the microfiche copies of more than 307,000 ERIC reports and documents in education. The Curriculum Laboratory, another part of the Education Library, is designed to aid programs in teacher education with sources of instructional materials such as textbooks, curriculum guides, educational games, multimedia kits, and microcomputers. The library supports the programs offered by Peabody through the Ph.D. and Ed.D., as well as research by faculty. The staff of the Education Library is small—six full-time and four part-time positions. There are three professional positions, the Director of the Library, Co-ordinator of Information Services, and Reference Librarian. Except for department supervisors, much of the staffing needs must be met by employing student workers.

The Education library serves primarily students, faculty, and staff of Vanderbilt University. Educators in the community and Ph.D candidates from other schools are allowed to use the facilities, but not to borrow books.

The Enhanced Information Access Project and the Beginning of CD-ROM

During the last three years, the library system has taken major steps in the computerization of services. September of 1985 saw the implementation of NOTIS as its online catalog. Called ACORN, it has dedicated terminals available in each of the seven divisional libraries, as well as multi-purpose microcomputer workstations for staff use. Circulation procedures were automated in January 1986. In August 1986, Vanderbilt extended its electronic environment with the implementation of its first optical product. Funding for the Enhanced Information Access Project was received and goals centered on providing broader access to electronic information to the academic community. The grant allowed exploration of the use of automation and other new technological developments to provide access to information beyond the traditional online catalog. The two-year project received $750,000 from the Pew Charitable Trusts with additional funds of $100,000 from the Vanderbilt University Medical Center and $100,000 from the University Reassessment Funds. Installing optical products was a large part of the project, and approximately $200,000 was budgeted for CD-ROM. The decision of how to divide the grant was done on a proportional basis. Consideration was given to supplying those products requested by libraries, but the size of each library and the scope of its collection also played a part in the distribution of products. The greatest effort was made to be equitable. All hardware for workstations also came from the grant.

The Central Library is much larger than the others and serves a larger and more diverse population, thus requiring more products, but the Education Library was chosen as the first of the division libraries to be involved with CD-ROMs. Prior to this, the reference staff offered librarian-mediated online searching. We searched ERIC, PsycINFO, Dissertation Abstracts, and Exceptional Child Educational Resources more than any other databases, but searched others in related areas. Since we obtained the former three on compact disc, we have seen a dramatic drop in librarian-mediated searches. End-user searching was never explored, thus the association with CD-ROMs and involvement with end-users as searchers was completely new.

Today, libraries at Vanderbilt have 45 products on 29 workstations in 10 locations, and there is no uniform service policy across the divisional libraries. For example, at the Education Library we leave our compact discs out during all hours the library is open. There is no check-out procedure. By contrast, at one time the Medical Library had a check-out procedure and left discs at the Circulation Desk when reference staff was unavailable. Each library sets its own policies.

The Education Library has six products on three workstations. CD-ROMs are viewed as an enhancement to the reference services already provided by the Education Library. We want to make sure that patrons know about CD-ROM as well as other sources in the library. Keeping CD-ROM in context does not de-emphasize its importance, but merely serves to put it in perspective with other services.

Access Issues

As part of the grant, Vanderbilt signed an agreement with the OCLC company to test its first CD-ROM product, the CIJE portion of ERIC. We received two workstations on August 20, 1986, which were set up in the Reference Department. Our original hardware configuration consisted of two IBM PC/ATs with IBM display monitors, two Hitachi CD-ROM drives, and two NEC Pinwriter printers. Except for the printers, OCLC provided all the original equipment. The software was OCLC's CD/Search package, and the discs contained the CIJE file from 1969 to May 1986.

Both the Reference and Circulation departments occupy the main floor of the Education Library. The Reference Department assumed responsibility for managing the two CD-ROM workstations. At the time, with a full-time staff of only two, we knew it meant a great deal of work on our part to successfully manage them. In the beginning library staff learned by doing. Initial instruction from the OCLC representative consisted of demonstrations, question and answer sessions, and a great deal of hands-on practice. Upon his departure, we were left with the equipment, two rough user manuals and a toll-free number. Since classes were due to begin in about a week, staff members spent much time learning the system by practicing searches of all kinds. This helped us to familiarize ourselves with features, response time, and some of the problems which might occur.

User reaction was overwhelmingly positive. We opened the service a week after setting up the workstations. We had very few problems with installation. Part of the grant money covered an Automation Project Librarian position. Ramona Steffey was hired and was responsible for most of the installation. She continues to work with the division libraries when questions and concerns arise. This is a rather unique situation. Having a specific person to handle CD-ROM matters eases our load. It is nice to know there is someone to turn to for help.

Products Available

Eventually, during the year, the decision was made to add additional optical products. We purchased ERIC from SilverPlatter and DIALOG OnDisc's ERIC. At one point we had three versions of ERIC available. We made the decision to add additional versions of ERIC for several reasons. DIALOG OnDisc's version offers a nice combination of menu approach for novices and a command search for experts. It is handy for us to be able to use the Command Search mode to do a ready reference question. We also felt such a feature might help students in online search classes practice commands without the cost of going online. Librarians can also use the Online Search mode to update a search for a patron. Also, DIALOG's product allows a very easy means of printing records as you go, which some people prefer. We have since dropped OCLC's Search CD450. In looking at the three products and the features offered, we felt the characteristics of SilverPlatter and DIALOG offered more of what we wanted. We also subscribed to SilverPlatter's PsycLIT and have since added GPO on SilverPlatter and UMI's Dissertation Abstracts Ondisc, which also has its own search language. We now have the three most used indexes in our library—ERIC, Psychological Abstracts and Dissertation Abstracts—available on compact disc. In addition, SilverPlatter's GPO will help us make use of our government documents collection in a much more efficient manner.

Currently, we have six products on three workstations. It is unlikely that the Reference Department will purchase additional CD-ROMs at this point. We would have to invest in more hardware for another workstation, so the product would have to be heavily used to warrant the expenditure. As far as buying new products, we will keep our eyes open for others which suit our needs and fit our budget. There are some school-related products which might be attractive additions to the Curriculum Laboratory. The library will probably purchase Alde's Science Helper K–8 for the Lab. Presently, there is no workstation available in the Curriculum Lab, so the database would have to be added to an existing workstation in Reference. If the purchase of other similar products looks likely, the library will buy a workstation to go in the Curriculum Lab.

CD-ROM Equipment and Location

The CD-ROM workstations sit on three 48-inch x 29-inch tables. Our hardware now includes three Zenith Z-248 microcomputers with two Philips and one Hitachi CD-ROM drive, and three NEC P6 Pinwriter printers. NEC Pinwriter printers are the choice for printing, costing considerably less in supplies than the quieter, but more expensive, Thinkjets. There are two monochrome monitors and one color monitor.

The three workstations are located in the middle of the reference area, visible from both the Reference Assistant's Desk and the Information Desk in front. Thus, any activity involving the computers can be monitored. We really did not have much choice about where to put the equipment due to limited space, but this location turned out for the best. We always intended the workstations to be an end-user product, and with this arrangement the staff can easily observe and offer assistance to patrons using all terminals. Because the workstations are near our online catalogs, we have labeled each computer with a sign indicating whether it is a CD-ROM or public catalog. The workstations are arranged as follows:

Workstation 1: ERIC-SilverPlatter, GPO-SilverPlatter
Workstation 2: ERIC-SilverPlatter, PsycLIT-SilverPlatter
Workstation 3: ERIC DIALOG OnDisc, Dissertation Abstracts

Software or Programming Needs

The workstation on which Dissertation Abstracts and DIALOG OnDisc are loaded has a menu system so users do not have to learn DOS commands for switching directories (figure 1). Marshall Breeding and Ramona Steffey used Sidekick to create a text file which is displayed whenever the computer is turned on, rebooted, or after any program is run. Batch files were written to switch the user seamlessly to the correct directory, execute the program for the CD-ROM product of his/her choice, then re-display the menu for the next user. The CONFIG.SYS file required for Dissertation Abstracts is compatible with DIALOG OnDisc ERIC, which does not require, but can operate under, MS-DOS Extensions.

Availability

The CD-ROM service is available during all hours the library is open. The workstations are turned on in the morning by a member of the Reference Department and turned off at night by an Access Services Department staff member. The discs are left in containers next to the computers. There is no checkout system and patrons may exchange discs themselves. So far, we have had no problem with security, except for one occasion when a compact disc was damaged by being mistakenly placed into a floppy disk drive. Signs now warn patrons not to insert compact discs into floppy drives and we have labeled the compact disc drive. We will monitor such situations, and if this continues to be a problem, will re-evaluate a checkout procedure. However, this would be a last resort since such a procedure would be time-consuming and difficult to manage with limited staff.

```
┌─────────────────────────────────────────────────────────────────┐
│         ┌─────────────────────────────────────────────┐         │
│         │  EDUCATION LIBRARY   CD-ROM WORKSTATION      │         │
│         └─────────────────────────────────────────────┘         │
│  ┌───────────────────────────────────────────────────────────┐  │
│  │ The following CD-ROM databases are available at this      │  │
│  │ workstation for the retrieval of  citations to journal    │  │
│  │ articles,  research   reports, and dissertations:         │  │
│  │                                                           │  │
│  │ (1) DIALOG OnDisc ERIC (1980 -  ):  an index to journal   │  │
│  │     articles and research reports in education and        │  │
│  │     related fields. Corresponds to printed indexes        │  │
│  │     Current Index to  Journals in  Education (CIJE)       │  │
│  │     and Resources in Education (RIE).                     │  │
│  │                                                           │  │
│  │ (2) Dissertation  Abstracts OnDisc (1984 -  ):  a         │  │
│  │     multidisciplinary index to American doctoral          │  │
│  │     dissertations.                                        │  │
│  │                                                           │  │
│  │ (3) DIALOG OnDisc Tutorial: Demonstration of  DIALOG      │  │
│  │     features and modes of searching for novice and        │  │
│  │     expert users.                                         │  │
│  │                                                           │  │
│  │ Be  sure  the  correct disc  is in  the CD-ROM drive,     │  │
│  │ then type the number for the index you wish to search     │  │
│  │ and press ENTER.                                          │  │
│  └───────────────────────────────────────────────────────────┘  │
└─────────────────────────────────────────────────────────────────┘
```

figure 1. Menu screen

Monitoring CD-ROMs

Use of the CD-ROMs is on a first-come, first-served basis. We do not charge for the service, but do expect the patrons to perform their own searches. The computers have become so popular that at one time we instituted a sign-up procedure. However, after a short trial period, we found it to be more trouble than it was worth. Instead, a more casual thirty-minute time limit is in effect when someone is waiting (figure 2). When patrons sign the logbook, they are told about the thirty-minute limit possibility. We try to make sure all users sign the logbook when they first sit down. Patrons can use the logbook to check the amount of time they have spent at a computer and determine if the thirty-minute time limit is up. Users are encouraged to be considerate and check to see if someone is waiting to use the CD-ROMs.

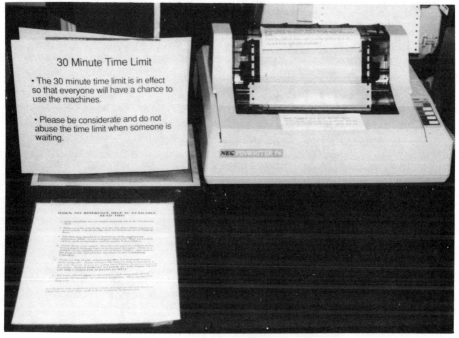

figure 2. Sign for 30-minute time limit.

We recently implemented a procedure to help monitor activity. During the busy part of the day, from 1:00 p.m to 4:00 p.m., we have one student who acts as CD-ROM monitor. His primary function is to watch and take care of CD-ROM activities (figure 3). During these times we are able to enforce the time limit more effectively. We've tried to think of some ways to help this situation, but we have no way of knowing how many people leave because they do not want to wait. It would be nice if a voice could announce, "Your thirty minutes are up. Please check to see if someone is waiting."

Printing vs. Downloading

There are no formal restrictions on printing at this point, but users are encouraged to download as often as possible. Nonetheless, most still print their results. We continue to emphasize the time savings with downloading, but so far the "printers" outweigh the "downloaders." If someone is about to print hundreds of records we certainly encourage them to look through them first.

Multi-User/Multi-Disc Workstations

One recurring problem is the one person per workstation set-up. Ours are still single-user workstations. Multi-user equipment is expensive and right now we cannot afford it. At the Medical Library and the Central Library, the MultiPlatter arrangement for their CD-ROMs seems to be working well.

figure 3. CD-ROM monitor.

Training and Instruction
Staff Training

Student workers help fill in to provide reference assistance during the daytime, and they are our mainstay evenings and weekends. Reference service in the Education Library is available for only 69 of the 92 hours a week the library is open, so there are times when no one is in Reference.

Our first experience in training student workers on CD-ROM was with the OCLC product. We chose students carefully, since they would be responsible for instructing users on the systems. They needed to be able to grasp the elements of Boolean logic and the distinct features of each system as well as to handle somewhat technical questions about hardware problems, software features, printing problems and downloading to disks.

We do not have a formal structure for training staff. Presently we are evaluating our methods of instruction in order to work toward a more uniform method for all staff. A graduate student, Virginia Morgan, who has been working in Reference, wrote an instruction manual which we plan to implement. It provides an overview of the responsibilities and includes exercises on CD-ROM.

Generally speaking, training involves one-on-one instruction between a staff member and the student. Time is spent on each of the systems, in order for trainees to practice and ask questions. Exercises are provided, and students must watch a staff member help patrons to hear the kinds of questions that come up and the appropriate responses to give. The student assistant learns a certain protocol when helping users. A checklist of hardware and software skills must be learned before working alone (Appendix 1). Training students is time-consuming but, due to our staffing pattern, we must deal with it on an ongoing basis. The amount of time needed to train students depends on their work schedules, and generally several weeks is necessary to train them adequately. Training, obviously, will require less time in libraries with more permanent staff members.

User Support and Training

Our goal in obtaining the systems was for the patrons to perform their own searches. Since we are a service-oriented library, the addition of CD-ROM has increased our instruction time, and while CD-ROM help theoretically is no more important than instruction on a printed index, the high visibility and popularity of the workstations have made training end-users extremely time-consuming.

The Challenge

For the patrons, the challenge lies in mastering not only the individual commands and content of a system, but the concepts of online searching as well. They may also need guidance in locating the identified citations. Our staff takes this challenge seriously. We do not believe in offering a service such as this and then letting people fend for themselves (unless they request it!). Regardless of what producers advertise, some kind of preliminary training is necessary on almost all systems for effective results. Most of our users are graduate students working on theses, dissertations, or research papers. It is not enough to show them a few keys and say "O.K., you're on your own."

Given the wide range of users and experience level, instruction has been a challenge. It is on a point-of-use basis for the most part, with whatever time is needed to get the patron started. Some considerations included overcoming patrons' reluctance to ask for help, their early unease in using a computer and their fear of breaking the machine. An initial one-on-one session might include learning the keys on the computer, system commands, and Boolean logic. In the beginning, all of this was done at the computer. Now that we are completing our second year, word has spread, demand has increased and we are busier than ever. This has meant some restructuring in training end-users.

Search Forms as User Aids

We now offer a search strategy form for people to use (Appendix 2). It really helps them to focus their thoughts in writing, find terms in the appropriate thesaurus, and combine them effectively on paper. Staff can work with patrons on their strategies while they wait to use a computer, or patrons may take a form with them and work on a search. This preparation helps make their actual time at the computer more effective and we've found it decreases the amount of instruction actually done at the computers. Instead of describing "and", "or" and "not" as well as equipment use, we now divide the instruction into two parts: search strategy and system-specific information.

Classroom Instruction

We realized the need to offer more organized instruction and designed a general class separate from formal college classes. The purpose of the class is to provide information and practice in putting together an effective search strategy. We also hold a separate session on SilverPlatter since that is our most heavily used system. The area where our workstations are located is not effective for teaching larger groups, so we hold classes away from the reference area. Classes were offered at various times during the last Spring semester, but the response was disappointing. We averaged anywhere from two to fifteen attendees in our CD-ROM classes. We have been asked to come to a professor's class to talk about CD-ROM on specific systems where we sometimes reach 25 or 30 students.

The summer weeks are the busiest time of the year at the Education Library, and many students are here for only a short time. We sent out brochures to faculty members as well as a flyer to each student registered for the summer announcing times of classes and a brief description of the class. We hoped to get summer students to sign up by offering classes at a variety of times. We had a good response for our 6:00 p.m. classes with the number of sign-ups as high as sixteen to eighteen. Some sign-ups do not show up for the class, but turnout has been better than at other times during the year. We have not had a heavy response from faculty, however. We may look at the possibility of developing a library research methods class to be added to the curriculum, but this is now just in the planning stages.

Even with group sessions, we still find ourselves busy on a daily basis answering questions, instructing individuals, and fixing minor problems. While patrons usually remember what they learn about printed indexes, this is not so with the CD-ROMs. If patrons do not use one again for a week, it may be necessary to refresh their memories the next time they come in.

Flip Charts and Written Materials

We have made individual flip charts for SilverPlatter ERIC, PsycLIT and Dissertation Abstracts. These contain step-by-step instructions. A person can go through them and get started on a basic search when help is unavailable. There are brief guides and helpful hints placed next to the computers as well. Preparing and updating these materials takes time, but we feel they offer an alternative and help support point-of-use instruction.

While training staff and end-users has added to our duties, we feel the service requires effective instruction, and is worth the effort. Patrons can learn to use the machines properly and effectively, which will improve their research results. While other libraries offer only a five- or ten-minute instruction session, we believe that since many of our graduate students are now doing their own searches, we owe them the same amount of time we would have spent with them if we did online searches.

CD-ROM Impact

The focus of reference services has changed since the addition of optical products. They have affected the workload of reference staff in several ways:

—increasing time needed to learn new sources

—learning distinct search commands for each system

—more time in training of students

—daily help with end-user questions and problems

While they represent only a portion of our resources, the CD-ROMs have become an integral part of the services we offer. The increase in CD-ROM users has influenced other areas of the Reference Department as well.

Number of Users

A logbook was kept to try to find out a rough figure of how many CD-ROM searches were performed in a semester. (Actual numbers are probably higher, since we could not make sure everyone who used the workstations signed in.) From August 27 through December 18, 1987, there were 1,489 ERIC searches, 693 PsycLIT searches, and 114 Dissertation Abstracts searches for a total of 2,296 CD-ROM searches. The shortest search averaged 16 minutes, while the longest averaged 53 minutes. In the Spring semester, from January 14 through April 27, 1988, CD-ROM searches numbered 2,469, with the shortest averaging 17 minutes and the longest averaging 59.2 minutes. To give you a further idea of the popularity and impact of CD-ROM, we added a separate category for CD-ROMs to our reference statistics. The total number of CD-ROM questions for 1988 was 7,301 (Reese, 1989).

Online Searching

The amount of online searching we do has been cut dramatically with the introduction of optical products. Librarian-mediated online searching has decreased at least 58 percent during a two year period. From July 1985–June 1986 there were 493 online searches; from July 1986–June 1987, 203; and from July 1987–June 1988 there were only 85. Recording logbook statistics for two semesters provides figures which indicate that the CD-ROM workstations must have had an impact on our online searches. This trend has been particularly noticeable during the summer session. Many school administrators, teachers and other educational personnel return to work on their advanced degrees. In the past, conducting several online searches each day was common. The last two summers we have noticed a drastic drop in search requests. While other libraries report no change, or even an increase, this is not true for us. The availability of databases now on compact disc which can be searched free by end-users has influenced the number of requests for fee-based online searches.

Interlibrary Loans

In 1985–86, we had 281 interlibrary loan requests. The next year there were 473, and in 1987/88 the number increased to 892. We have not done a scientific study to determine whether the use of optical databases has been responsible for the increase, but we believe they are correlated.

Periodicals Use

The Periodicals Department has noticed an increase in the use of journals due to CD-ROMs. Generally, if there has been heavy use of the CDs in Reference, that night or the next day will show a heavy demand for journal articles from Periodicals. We are lucky to be able to have a great many of those journals which are indexed by our compact disc products.

Outside Students

We have noted an increase in students from other area colleges coming specifically to use our CD-ROM products. Vanderbilt's libraries are no longer open to the public, but the Education Library allows area teachers, principals, and doctoral students to use the library without charge. It is possible to purchase a Library Use Card if you do not fit any of the "free" categories.

Hidden and Ongoing Costs

All libraries have had to purchase their own supplies such as paper and ribbons. Printing records is so popular that last summer we had to change printer ribbons almost every two weeks. Ribbons cost about $5.00 each and we use three a month for the most part. We try to purchase the least expensive paper.

Deciding whether to include a modem for end-user searching is problematic. It can be an expensive procedure, including locating the workstation near a telephone line or installing one if necessary, plus the actual expense of searching online. The Education Library has a modem attached to its DIALOG workstation, but only librarians go online.

With any new service there is bound to be an impact on the budget. Since all of our hardware and software were initially obtained from grant money, the Education Library saw no financial impact until 1988 when it came time to renew our subscriptions to the compact disc products. We also had to purchase any new ones with money from our library budget. Our total cost for CD-ROM subscriptions alone is over $7,000. We have cancelled only one print subscription, the *Monthly Catalog*, since obtaining GPO on SilverPlatter. It is duplicated at the Central Library, and was used infrequently here. We do not anticipate cancelling any others at this time.

Publicity

The library did not have an organized publicity campaign. Word of mouth was plenty for us. The workstations are enormously popular with students, faculty, and staff. We find that some faculty members now require students to learn how to use CD-ROM as part of a research assignment. Even novice computer users seem comfortable with them after an instructional session. We do publicize classes offered by sending out brochures. Our Education Library Newsletter contains current information on the status of new products or procedures with CD-ROMs. We also try to include helpful hints on various aspects of CD-ROM searching in each newsletter.

Evaluation and Users of Products

Who uses CD-ROM and what is the impact? To try and obtain some feedback, reference staff sent out two informal surveys. First, a patron survey form was given to anyone using the CD-ROMs from May 9 through August 8, 1988. As the survey was not mandatory, not all persons using the CD-ROMs filled out a form. We wanted to capture user reactions to the CD-ROM workstations as well as opinions about service offered. A second questionnaire was sent to faculty members who were listed as teaching a course during the summer of 1987. This survey sought to determine faculty opinions on the impact of CD-ROM, both personally and on their students. Neither of these surveys was scientific, but they did help us learn more about users' reactions and how optical products affected their research. Besides two internal surveys, a more comprehensive survey was done in October 1988 by the Library Administration office. All three are described here.

The First Education Library Survey: Use of CD-ROMs

The following results were based on 39 completed survey forms. The questions which could have received more than one response contain an asterisk.

How did you learn about the CD-ROM products? Fifty-three percent found out from "library staff," 24% from a "friend," 16% checked "other," and 5% learned about them from "faculty."

Which CD-ROM system did you use? ERIC was the most popular of the CD-ROM databases. The total for the three ERICs was 63%, with 45% of that on SilverPlatter's ERIC, 15% from DIALOG/ERIC, and 3% on OCLC/ERIC. PsycLIT was checked by 32% and Dissertation Abstracts by 2%. There was probably a higher percentage of actual use on Dissertation Abstracts/DIALOG/ERIC than the survey indicates. Because the survey forms were not placed on the Dissertation Abstracts table, it is likely more survey forms were handed out to people sitting at the table next to the forms. The fact that SilverPlatter's ERIC is available on two workstations may account for the difference in which system was used.

What is your experience with computers? Sixty-two percent of the respondents checked "some knowledge," 23% said "very little," 8% said "none" and 5% were "experts." The majority of users had at least a little or some knowledge. There is no way to determine what they meant by their experience; however, the responses indicate that very few consider themselves complete novices.

What is your association with Vanderbilt? By far the most responses came under "Graduate Student" with 68% checking that category. "Other" received the next largest percentage with 15%, saying they were not associated with Vanderbilt. These included a visiting scholar, non-Vanderbilt students such as out of state students, paid users (which means they purchased a Library Use Card), and area teachers. Eight percent checked the "staff" category, 7% checked "faculty," and 3% were "undergraduate" users.

What was the purpose of your search? Responses included 40% who checked "research paper," 28% "thesis or dissertation," 18% "other" (comprehensive exam study, ideas for field work, grant writing, report, pilot study, general knowledge, etc.), and 12% checked "article/book publication." The responses indicate a varied use of the CD-ROMs.

Was the system easy to use? Respondents could circle a number from 1 to 5 with 1 representing "very easy" and 5 indicating "very difficult." The results showed that the majority found the CD-ROMs easy rather than difficult to use. Thirty-eight percent checked "1," 42% "2," 17% "3," and 3% "4." No one checked number "5." It is interesting that no one perceived the systems as "very difficult."

*How did you learn to use the system?** The overwhelming number of responses, 71%, indicated that they learned from the "staff." Eleven percent checked "flipcharts/

manuals," 9% said "tutorial," and 6% specified "other" including, "divine insight," "workshop," "class," and "self."

Would you consider attending an instructional class on CD-ROMs? This question helped us learn more about training possibilities. Fifty-nine percent of respondents indicated they would be willing to attend a class on CD-ROM by checking "yes," while 41% said "no." This would seem to back up our efforts to hold instructional sessions.

How long did you search? Given the choice of from less than 5 minutes up to longer than 60 minutes, the results were as follows: no one checked less than five minutes; 25% checked from "5 to 15 minutes," 29% searched "15 to 30 minutes," 33% took "30 to 60 minutes," and 11% stayed "longer than 60 minutes." It is impossible to determine how accurate these times are, because they are based on the patrons' own perception of the amount of time used. However, during part of the summer, users were asked to sign a log book. Thus, we were able to confirm the amount of time spent.

Were you satisfied with your search results? Respondents were asked to rank their satisfaction with search results on a 1 to 5 scale with "1" as "very satisfied" and "5" "very unsatisfied." The answers showed the following: 50% checked "1," 27% chose "2," 8% selected "3," 7% checked "4," and 6% chose "5." It is interesting that those who expressed dissatisfaction with the results still indicated that they would use the systems again. In the future, it might be useful to include an additional question to find out more; it would be helpful to know reasons for an unsuccessful search.

Do you feel the CD-ROMs have saved you time? and If yes, could you estimate how much time you saved? All of those who responded checked "yes," they had saved time; 90% said they had saved an hour or more and 9% checked "30 to 60 minutes."

Did you spend time on your search strategy before sitting down at the computer? Seventy-three percent said "yes" while 26% checked "no." If we were to do another survey, I would add another question: If yes, how did you formulate your strategy? Then I would offer choices. I really believe that, among those who said "yes," some meant they thought about what they wanted to search, but didn't mean that they actually formulated a search strategy on paper. The results do not provide any really useful information without knowing what was meant by "spent time on your search strategy."

In the final question, all of the responses to: *Would you use the systems again?* were "yes." Patrons were asked to write any "additional comments and suggestions" at the bottom of the form. One feature which especially pleased users was the help they received from library staff members. We have made it a point to be available for help. We provide detailed instruction on search strategy, plus we check periodically with searchers to make sure they are on the right track. While such assistance is time-consuming, we feel patrons deserve to be helped by patient, friendly staff members or left alone if desired. We hope a balance is struck between the two. A typical comment follows: "I found the service person to be very helpful and was able to save me valuable time with understanding a new system." Another said, "very patient, helpful library staff member—good teacher." And finally, the next quote seems to sum up all the comments received. "Before I knew about the CD-ROM I would spend hours in the library often frustrated and exhausted—Thanks!"(Reese, 1989)

The Second Survey: Peabody Faculty

A short, informal questionnaire was sent to 28 faculty members listed as teaching courses during the summer of 1988 at Peabody College. While only 13 completed forms were returned, the surveys did provide some useful feedback from the faculty members. Those questions with the possibility of more than one response include an asterisk.

What is your association with Vanderbilt? All were faculty responses. We knew this would be the case, but wanted to be able to send this form to other educational community members in the future.

Which CD-ROM databases have you used? ERIC received 50% of the responses, PsycLIT was checked by 18% of the faculty, and Dissertation Abstracts was used by 31% of the respondents.

How often have you used them? We were interested in the frequency of use of CD-ROM by faculty. Forty-one percent checked "once a month," 25% marked "once a semester," 16% selected "more than once a week," and 16% checked "once a week." I would have guessed that faculty use was not as often as that of graduate students. In fact, many times faculty send their graduate assistants over to do the actual searching.

Have you ever recommended the CD-ROM databases to your students or graduate assistants? All of the faculty respondents said "yes."

Describe the impact of CD-ROM on your research, class preparation, time etc. The answers were positive in the majority of cases. Replies ranged from a simple "useful" to "very helpful, saves a great deal of time," to detailed answers which express how the systems have saved time and energy. For example, one faculty member stated: "It has 'revolutionized' library searches for me. I can now do several days work in an afternoon," and another replied, "I don't know how I did without it."

Describe any impact on students' papers (better references, more thorough research, etc.) Answers ranged from "Don't know," to "I've noticed an improvement in papers," to "much more thorough." I feel I must mention the sole negative response. One faculty member did not agree with the majority. He/she felt the "databases not the best for my purposes." and that his students' papers were "less thorough" and "slip shod." You can't please everyone all of the time! (Reese, 1989)

The Third Survey: Library Administration

Besides our in-house surveys, the Library Administration Office assigned a committee to implement a study of the impact of CD-ROM technology on users in several libraries at Vanderbilt. Ramona Steffey and Nikki Meyer were the principal investigators. The Central Library, Education Library, Government Documents, and Arts Library were chosen to participate because of the high use of CD-ROM products in each. The survey was conducted during the month of October, 1988. All users of CD-ROM during these four weeks were asked to fill out a survey form. Monitors were provided to facilitate observation of users, and to try to get as many people as possible to respond to the survey. Each patron was approached by the monitor after sitting down at a workstation and asked to participate in the survey. Surveys were handed out from 8:00 a.m. to 5:00 p.m. Monday through Friday and weeknights from 6:00 p.m. until 10:00 p.m. Each division was surveyed at least four nights. Weekends were also included. Surveys were handed out on Saturdays from 10:00 a.m. to 2:00 p.m. and Sundays from 2:00 p.m. to 6:00 p.m.

Six hundred and eleven surveys were completed. (The actual number of users is probably higher since not all patrons who used CD-ROMs wished to participate in the survey.) Twenty compact disc products were used during the survey. PsycLIT on SilverPlatter was the most popular with 120 users.

The conclusions from this survey indicate that patrons liked the products and told their friends about them. User comments helped us focus on areas of concern and praised each of the participating library divisions.

Funding of Products—the Budget Process at Vanderbilt

Because Vanderbilt's library system consists of divisional libraries, each serving a distinct clientele, the question of costs and funding does not necessarily have one single answer. In any funding issue at Vanderbilt, library divisions rely on general university support, grants, income from services, endowments, and operating funds from the colleges and schools. System-wide services are funded from taxes. At this point, funding for the Pew-supported products has moved on to the individual libraries' budgets beginning with the 1988–89 fiscal year; thus, each division has had to find monies to support its own products and maintain the popular CD-ROM service.

There are overall budget guidelines which must be followed. Vanderbilt sets the type of budget—in this case, a line item—and the university informs the library administration of the policies and guidelines. Library directors must work within these policies. Each of the libraries' budgets is, in part, dependent on the school or college with which it is associated. Generally, the Provost is supportive of increases in budgets for materials if at all possible. There is usually an annual increment, but this primarily covers the costs associated with inflation.

The actual increase received by a library depends in part on the expense of the materials purchased. In other words, science materials are generally more costly than education resources. Vanderbilt's expenditures for CD-ROM hardware under the Pew Grant totalled $84,310. Subscriptions to databases came to $64,578. While furniture and hardware are essentially one-time investments, subscriptions must be paid yearly. Optical technology carries a high price tag and it represents a substantial recurring investment.

Reflections on CD-ROM

There seems little doubt that CD-ROM technology has influenced our library, and, for the most part, our experiences with CD-ROM have been positive and rewarding. Offering optical products has added to our work load, but the positive and thankful comments from patrons make it worthwhile. Faculty members seem excited and enthusiastic about the CD-ROM databases because compact discs have saved them time and made research less frustrating and more comprehensive. With all the positive, enthusiastic comments, however, it is important not to overlook other library resources available to the educational community. CD-ROM has become an integral part of the library. Judging by the comments and opinions of faculty and students, it has found a home in the Reference Department.

Our service has not changed much since its inception. We have tried some different approaches as far as availability goes, ranging from no time limit at all to a thirty-minute one if someone is waiting. First-come first-served works for us and we will continue to operate that way, modifying as necessary. We still leave discs out for use any time the library is open, urge users to complete a search form, and have a CD-ROM monitor to help during busy times.

Is it worth the cost and time to staff members? If you ask the end-users who faithfully search the many CD-ROM products on campus, the answer is a resounding "yes!" Library staff members also feel the technology is an essential part of services offered and worth the investment, not only of money, but time, as well.

The decision of whether to offer CD-ROM takes some serious thought. But here at the Education Library the format has proved to be a successful one.

References

Reese, J. and R. Steffey. 1988. "Seven Deadly Sins of CD-ROM." *The Laserdisk Professional* 1(2): 19–24.

Reese, J. 1989. "CD-ROM Technology at Vanderbilt University: Impact on Library Staff and the Educational Community." *Optical Information Systems* 9(1): 38–43.

Reese, J. 1989. "CD-ROM at Vanderbilt University: Continuing Costs and Budget Issues." *The Laserdisk Professional* 2(2): 30–37.

Steffey, R. and N. Meyer. 1989. "Evaluating User Success and Satisfaction with CD-ROM." *The Laserdisk Professional* 2(5):35–45.

Jean Reese joined the Education Library as Public Services Librarian in 1985. She is currently the Coordinator of Information Services. Jean received her B.A. degree in Spanish from Furman University in Greenville, South Carolina and her M.A. in Spanish from the University of Georgia. She received her M.L.S. from Vanderbilt University, Nashville, Tennessee. Prior to working for Vanderbilt University, she was in the education profession.

Appendix 1

STUDENT ASSISTANT RESPONSIBILITIES FOR CD-ROM
Reference Department
Education Library

Terminal Objective: Given patrons, CD-ROM computers, and no help, the student will assist patrons in searching ERIC, PsycLIT, Dissertation Abstracts,and GPO meeting 100% of the criteria established by the Reference Librarian.

Objectives:

1. Given computers and keyboards, the student assistant will "warm boot", turn off computers when needed, and describe location and function of important keys such as ESC, CONTROL, BREAK, RETURN/ENTER, COMMAND

2. Given ERIC, PsycLIT thesauri, and a search form, the student will show patrons how to use both.

3. Given computers and compact discs, the student assistant will change discs on all systems.

4. Given computers, printers, paper, and ribbons, the student assistant will change paper and ribbons on all printers in Reference.

5. Given computers and patron, the student will assist in downloading records to a floppy disk.

6. Given computer keyboards and compact discs, the student will enter and exit each program with no questions.

7. Given computer workstation area and waiting patrons, the student will inform patrons of time limits and alternate methods of searching.

8. Given computers and keyboards, the student will find, show and print a journal article record and ERIC document record.

9. Given ERIC and PsycLIT, the student assistant will inform patrons of the differences between databases and location of additional resources for each.

Appendix 2

EDUCATION LIBRARY
CDROM SEARCH FORM

Purpose and Scope

1. In one or two sentences summarize your search topic.

_____
_____
_____

Main Concepts

2. Circle the main concepts from the statement above.

Subject Terms

3. List terms which describe your main concepts. Include any terms from the appropriate thesaurus, i.e., *Thesaurus of Eric Descriptors* or *Thesaurus of Psychological Index Terms*.

FIRST CONCEPT	SECOND CONCEPT	THIRD CONCEPT
_____	_____	_____
OR_____	_____	_____
OR_____	_____	_____
OR_____	_____	_____
OR_____	_____	_____

4. Write out the search statement you will enter in order to get your first set. Use the terms from above and follow example in Search Sample found on index table. This last section should be written exactly as you wish to enter it on the computer.

1._____
2._____
3._____
4._____

ASK A REFERENCE STAFF MEMBER FOR HELP WITH THIS FORM AND WITH SEARCHING.

4

CD-ROM End-User Searching: Implementation Issues in Ontario

Elaine Goettler, Margaret Hawthorn, Sandra McCaskill

Introduction

Since February 1988, the reference team of four and a half librarians at Erindale College in Ontario has been increasingly absorbed in the exciting process of introducing CD-ROM searching to end-users. Support, both moral and technical, has been given generously by American colleagues as well as those on our side of the border, and it was with an idea of widening our knowledge even further that we initiated a phone survey of all Ontario academic libraries in December 1988.

Not only did we find that our own experience was not unique, but the information we gathered led to some interesting conclusions and speculations which may prove useful to librarians contemplating installation or expansion of compact disc databases. This chapter will first describe Erindale's experiences with CD-ROM and then report on the survey results.

Background

Our library, located on a suburban campus of the University of Toronto, has a collection approaching 250,000 volumes and serves over 5,300 students and 350 faculty and graduate users. Online searching of remote databases is offered only on the main campus because a study completed by Erindale reference staff revealed the budgetary and staffing impracticalities of our library offering this service. The main campus, St. George, is one of Canada's major research centers and provides a complete range of database services. The results of our study were a relief, for we all shared a distaste for the creation of two groups of users—those who could afford information and those who could not—and we were unaware of any single Ontario academic institution that did not charge its clientele for remote database searching.

Off-campus online searching and user fees seemed to be a deterrent to all but the most persistent researchers at our college. Given these considerations and the survey results, compact disc technology with its promise of unlimited "free" end-user access proved irresistible.

With the expansion of the compact disc marketplace following High Sierra standardization, we were determined to offer this service. To keep up-to-date, we scanned every publication we could and enlarged our selection of pertinent journal subscriptions. Telephone conversations with industry personnel also proved to be an invaluable source of information, both for hardware and software questions.

Selection

By the fall of 1987, we knew enough about hardware and discs to be able to select them, and, as is the case in many if not most institutions, funding became the crucial issue. Fortunately, a unique opportunity occurred when student leaders at the College pushed for the creation of a Library Enhancement Fund to alleviate the underfunding experienced by the library in previous years. The students held a referendum and pledged $10.00 each per year. Ultimately, this support led to a campaign that grew to include alumni and community contributors. A presentation to the fund's student spending committee (authorized to allocate half of the yearly student contributions) outlined the potential benefits of CD-ROM searching, and the committee agreed to purchase the Library's first workstation.

We were convinced that if we surrounded this initial workstation with an effective marketing strategy, we would generate demand and support for additional equipment. This goal was never far from our minds as we selected a colour monitor to entice curious users (and, we believed, make it easier to teach and use the databases) and placed the workstation adjacent to the reference desk. Our desk is located near the library entrance so many library users passed the workstation as they proceeded to other areas of the library.

The reference librarians selected three Wilsondisc products: General Science Index, Social Science Index and Humanities Index. These databases were chosen to meet the needs of the largest percentage of our undergraduate users and aimed to provide "something for everyone." The relative ease of use and the uniformity of commands made these discs a natural choice for our pilot project. Once we had made this decision and received the databases, we installed the products following the specifications provided by the software publisher.

Publicity was the next task. Signs and posters were posted throughout the library; notices were placed beside the print equivalents to urge students to try the new databases; announcements were sent to all faculty and staff; and previews were offered to interested faculty and administrators. The system manual and even the posters supplied by H. W. Wilson proved to be too detailed for student use. Simpler instruction sheets were created and tested on inexperienced library staff; a user survey was designed and we were ready to unveil our newest service.

Usage

User response to the CD-ROM service was overwhelmingly positive. When we tabulated our survey results, 86 percent of the users judged the CD-ROM version more useful than the print version. The Wilsondisc screen instructions were rated as clear and easy to use by 96 percent of the participants. As a final point, 99 percent of the users believed the library should acquire additional databases. We also kept a simple tally of users and which database they were using. Disc use was measured by a record sheet, divided by week, on the back of each compact disc container. Also, a user count was added as a separate section of our regular reference question tally sheet. New categories included "CD-ROM Introduction," "CD-ROM Help" and "CD-ROM Users."

These tallies demonstrated the incredible popularity of CD-ROM searching. The survey gave us quantifiable information which we furnished to the student committee with our request for more money and we used it to enlist the support of community organizations as well. By the end of 1988, CD-ROM service had grown to include six workstations and eighteen databases. The student fund continued to be our major source of support; additional funds came from alumni and community groups.

While our knowledge of the technical aspects of compact disc database searching was based on extensive prior research, we could not predict the impact of this new service on library operations. The reference team (4.5 Librarians and 1 Technician), however, expected an additional burden and were willing to shoulder it to provide an improved level of user access to information.

After several months, analysis of our disc use statistics showed the appeal of this new service was not tapering off and indeed, as we reached the end of our first complete academic cycle, the growth was sustained. As the number of workstations and databases increased, the number of questions answered at the reference desk also increased and CD-ROM queries were still forming a large component of our reference service (figure 1). The demand for user training from September to November 1988 increased our orientation session commitments 38 percent, even with a moratorium on sessions to non-university clients. Our instruction program in CD-ROM end-user searching included regularly scheduled half-hour sessions for small groups (no more than five) for which students had to register in advance, self-help handouts and one-on-one instruction. Large classroom groups were given a brief introduction and urged to sign up for a session. This burst of activity was not just confined to the Reference Department. The demand for journals reached new records, and the number of interlibrary loan requests zoomed.

The magnitude of the change and its ability to impose new directions on library operations forced us to search for answers to several pertinent questions. First and foremost: Was our experience a common occurrence with the implementation of CD-ROM searching? If this was the norm, how were our colleagues in other libraries reacting to and coping with Pandora's compact disc box? Our goal was to conduct a broad based impact assessment; it became the impetus for three members of the reference team to survey the development of CD-ROM services in Ontario academic libraries.

Methodology

Post-secondary students in Ontario have two options: two-year community colleges or three- to four-year universities. Hence, a review of the Ontario academic environment has to include both of these groups. We surveyed all 40 universities and community colleges in Ontario. An earlier survey of CD-ROM use in Canadian libraries showed a high rate of implementation in Canadian universities (Fox, 1988). As the Province of Ontario contains the largest concentration of post-secondary institutions in Canada, we knew we would have a wide range of responses

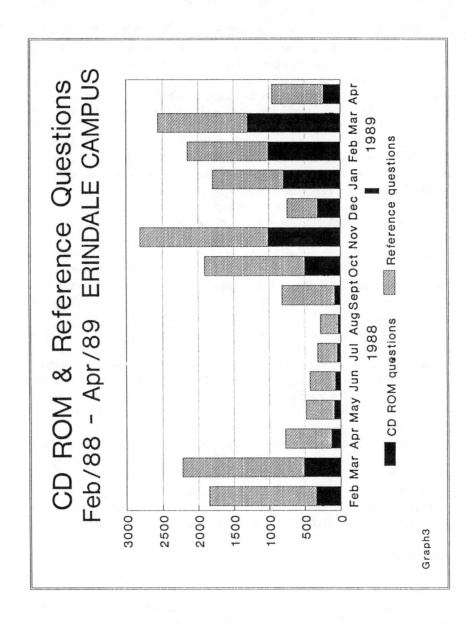

figure 1

and would be able to use our data to provide useful information to colleges and universities across Canada. Previous experiences with the design, administration, and coding of questionnaires caused us to reject a mail survey. Many of the responses could not be anticipated and we would have to be flexible to capture relevant information. In addition, we did not wish to sample the group but to monitor the entire population and ensure a 100 percent response. Hence, we opted for an informal telephone survey directed by a set of questions. We pre-tested the survey at three libraries and it proved to be viable.

In December 1988, and the first week of January 1989, we spoke to 58 respondents at the 18 universities and 22 community colleges in the province. We confined our queries to reference databases (i.e., excluding cataloguing, acquisitions or public access catalogues) and spoke to the librarian providing the service to tally the reaction from the "trenches." For multi-library campuses, all installations were contacted.

The response was phenomenal and a wealth of information poured in. After many hours on the telephone, we realized Erindale was among the academic leaders in the provision of CD-ROM searching in Ontario. Much of the time invested to complete the survey was mutually beneficial. We found ourselves running an ad hoc consulting service but benefitting as well from new insights and information.

Availability

CD-ROM databases were available at 78 percent (14 of 18) of Ontario universities and 41 percent (9 of 22) of the community colleges. Funding was the crucial issue at institutions lacking CDs. In universities without this service 50 percent (2 of 4) cited lack of funds. It was an obstacle for 62 percent (8 of 13) of the community colleges but 31 percent (4 of 13) also stated they had other priorities (i.e., staff, acquisitions or space). This may be explained by the differing aims of these institutions. The community colleges have a mandate to provide technical skills, while the universities foster a broader research-oriented education and have a ready clientele for many research-level databases.

CD-ROMs are an area of growth for Ontario university libraries. Fifty percent (2 of 4) of those libraries without CDs plan to acquire them and 71 percent (10 of 14) plan to expand and upgrade their services. By contrast, for the community colleges, the picture is not as promising: 85 percent (11 of 13) without CD service have no plans to acquire it, and of those with the service, 56 percent (5 of 9) do not intend to expand.

Distribution, Size and Location

Most universities have one or two workstations and there are a few large installations with seven or more products. The community colleges have yet to create a large installation. The reference department predominates as the location of choice for the workstation(s). We asked this question to see if the libraries offering online searching had maintained a territorial relationship vis-a-vis the new CD-ROM service. Only one university library had located its workstation in the online department. The "other" category for workstation location illustrated a wide range of possibilities: serials section; library staff area, not accessible to students; separate room, accessible to students; separate office outside library; and between reference and serials. Several community colleges cited that a variety of uses for their single workstation had led to a location other than reference.

We also tallied the number of unique databases held at each institution. Sixty-four percent of the universities and 89 percent of the community colleges owned four or fewer databases. Large database collections (more than eight) were held in two universities, and one community college had a collection of eight databases. Twenty-nine databases were identified in the survey, but it was unusual to find a title available at more than three institutions (figure 2). ERIC, CCINFO, PsycLIT and CBCA dominate the CD-ROM field in Ontario. Many respondents cited recent legislation requiring onsite knowledge of hazardous materials in the workplace for patrons as the primary reason for the acquisition of the CCINFO disc.

The compact discs were kept at the workstations, except when the reference department used the circulation department to control the discs. Thirty percent of the university reference locations chose to use their circulation department to handle the discs, as did two of the three community college reference locations.

Accessibility

Access policies for non-institutional users differed dramatically between the universities and community colleges. At the universities, 64 percent did not restrict use to institutional members, while 63 percent of the community colleges did restrict access to their own users.

Although university CDs were relatively available to the public, other limitations existed. Many institutions reported queues (42 percent universities and 38 percent community colleges). Hidden access restrictions were also in place at many institutions. These restrictions included: CD-ROM service hours which did not correspond to library hours, unequal access to compact discs in off hours (i.e., leaving what is perceived to be the most popular disc locked in system), and service hours only when reference staff was available. The access profile is outlined below.

Table 1

Limited access (due to hidden access restriction) to workstation and databases?

	Yes	No
Universities	79%	21%
Community Colleges	38%	62%

The configuration of the workstations appears to be a reflection of the need for flexible access to database collections. Many universities (50 percent) and community colleges (86 percent) have chosen not to dedicate their machines to a single database. A combination approach (dedicated and non-dedicated) has been used in 21 percent of the universities in an effort to meet the specialized demands of some locations. The additional expense of acquiring a workstation for each database is not a funding possibility in most Ontario academic libraries, so librarians are eager for multi-user networks to become a reality for libraries. A demonstration disc of the

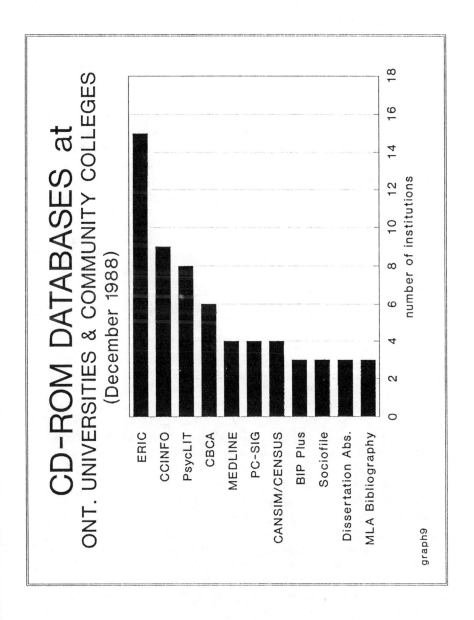

figure 2

PUBLIC ACCESS CD-ROMS IN LIBRARIES: CASE STUDIES

new SilverPlatter MultiPlatter system at the Winterbreak session of the Ontario University and Colleges Library Association meeting in February of 1989 was greeted positively. However, cost quickly became a concern for many and the financial ability of many institutions to purchase network facilities remains doubtful. Recent conversations with a H. W. Wilson representative show promise that this reliable library supplier recognizes this need and intends to market a network within the budgetary grasp of more colleges and universities. It should be available early in 1990.

On an upbeat note, the maintenance attached to the provision of CD-ROM service is not a problem in 71 percent of the universities and 75 percent of the community colleges. Most of the problems were linked to isolated occurrences of a faulty disc/update or incompatibility of hardware and software purchases (Tables 2 and 3). A valuable lesson is to be learned from several institutions where the equipment was purchased by a systems department and the databases by the reference department, only to have the two prove to be incompatible.

Table 2
Hardware Problems

	YES	NO
Universities	43%	57%
Community Colleges	12%	88%

Table 3
Software Problems

	YES	NO
Universities	57%	43%
Community Colleges	38%	62%

Note: It may be hypothesized that the fewer problems reported by the community colleges relate to the smaller number of workstations.

Impact on Related Library Services

The survey highlighted the impact of CD-ROM searching on related library activities (figures 3 and 4). The information from Ontario universities illustrates the realities attached to the provision of this service, while in our community colleges too many factors are unknown to state firm trends, although we have no reason to believe the situation will be radically different from the example of the universities.

Academic libraries introducing this service should expect dramatic changes in online searching, interlibrary loans and serials use. The most substantial impact was on online searching with a decrease of 67 percent experienced by the universities. Few users were interested in online if an equivalent compact disc was available. Recent statistics from the Education Library at Vanderbilt University citing a 59 percent decrease in online searching in each year of the past two years confirm the magnitude of the decline (Reese, 1988). Interlibrary loan requests increased in 42 percent of the universities when CD-ROM service was offered. At Erindale, the

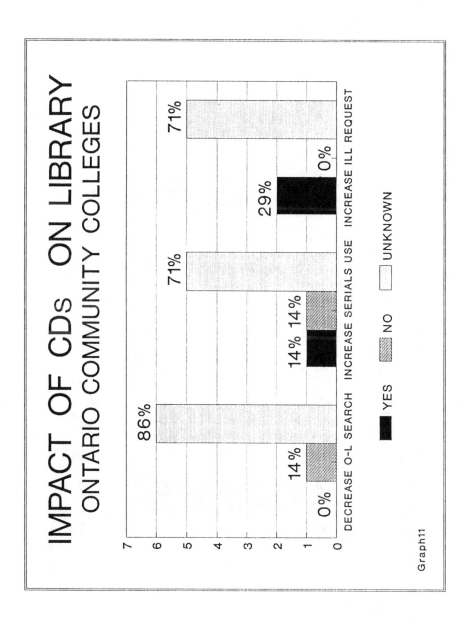

figure 3

PUBLIC ACCESS CD-ROMs IN LIBRARIES: CASE STUDIES

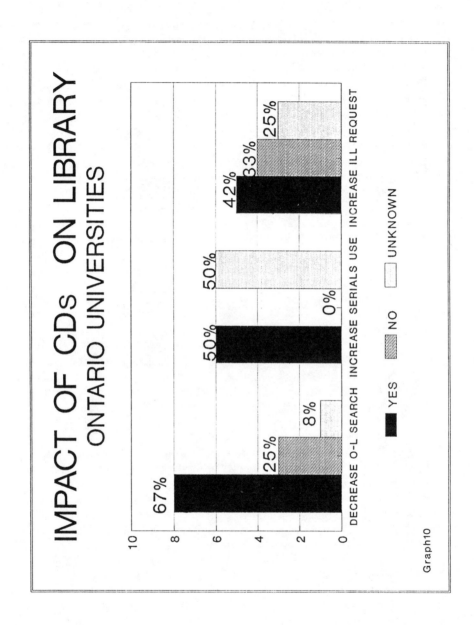

figure 4

interlibrary loan increase is substantial and pinpoints an issue for the future. Interlibrary loans require willing participants, and the ability of our cooperative library systems to handle a spreading demand of this size is a concern which must be addressed.

According to our respondents, libraries should also anticipate an overall increase in workload for reference staff. In the university setting, the acquisition of CD-ROMs carries a high probability of an increase in reference work. If the community colleges follow their existing trend, one could expect an increase in 50 percent of these libraries (Table 4). Indeed, given their early stage of development, it would not be unrealistic to expect the situation to imitate the university experience as they acquire more equipment and databases.

Table 4
Did staff workload increase with CD-ROM service?

	YES	NO	UNKNOWN
Universities	75%	25%	
Community Colleges	38%	38%	25%

At the outset, we decided to survey only those reference staff members actually working with CD-ROM technology, not only to get reactions to hands-on experience, but to see how staff were being utilized to cope with this new development in reference services (Table 5).

Table 5
Was the provision of CD-ROM searching the responsibility of librarians or technicians?

	Librarians Only	Librarians & Technicians
Universities	43%	57%
Community Colleges	11%	89%

Student assistants are used in only fourteen percent of the university libraries and in none of the community colleges. The use of student staff for some of the tasks related to CD-ROMs could be a solution for those libraries which could not otherwise cope with the increased workload.

The provision of end-user education represents a substantial commitment for Ontario academic libraries (Table 6). Most experienced academic researchers have some familiarity with print-format indexes. In contrast, the users of CD-ROM databases are almost always first-time users. Therefore, institutions must make a strong commitment to end-user instruction.

In addition, just over half of the universities (54 percent) have supported their instruction programs with the creation of handouts. It should be noted that many had rejected the manuals offered by the software producers and designed their own.

Table 6
End-User Instruction

	Classes Available	Individual Instruction
Universities	75%	86%
Community Colleges	63%	63%

Planning

The provision of CD-ROM searching represents a major funding commitment for most Ontario institutions. It follows that this investment should be carefully monitored and tracked to plan and direct future management decisions. Unfortunately, in many libraries, the technology has been introduced with few, if any, effective evaluation procedures.

A third of the universities and half of the community colleges do not keep any statistics on their CD-ROM service. Indeed, only 36 percent of the universities (and 43 percent of the community colleges) maintain statistics on the use of their compact disc collections. However, the greatest weakness lies in the area of user surveys. Academic libraries in Ontario have invested thousands of dollars in the provision of a new technology and only seventeen percent of the universities and none of the colleges have conducted user surveys to monitor the effectiveness of, and reaction to, this technology.

Collection Development

Only fourteen percent of the libraries have cancelled or intend to cancel the print version of an index and maintain only a compact disc edition. The need for additional access to indexes was consistently cited as the reason not to cancel. A CD network could alleviate this access issue for those who can afford to purchase one. However, libraries should be monitoring patterns of demand for print and disc versions. Any decision to purchase a network should include a broader definition of costs than the mere price tag for the equipment and license.

At Erindale, we are critically short of space throughout the library but especially in the reference area. The space occupied by existing print indexes has a very high hidden cost in terms of the reality of building costs and funding priorities. We have begun to evaluate the use of the print versions of *Sociological Abstracts* and *Psychological Abstracts*. Preliminary indications show the majority of users are consulting print versions in desperation—an assignment is due and the disc is booked for the rest of the day. During periods of peak-use, students sign up for half-hour time slots to use their choice of CD-ROM databases. They do not prefer the print. Indeed many expressed a strong level of frustration at consulting the print source and the belief that it was a handicap to their studies because they did not believe that their manual search was on par with the search available on disc. Thus, in the future, given the hidden space costs and the reality that print is a second choice for our users, the cost of a network may not be too outrageous in terms of the provision of effective service. At the least, we will gather additional information. We urge other libraries to enter the discussion.

Charging Policies

Only five of the 57 respondents charge for CD-ROM service. Two libraries charge for a search; one charges a flat $10.00 per search done by a librarian. (Note: at that library, students cannot choose to perform the search themselves.) Another charges $6.00 per hour on a credit card. The remaining user charges were related to printing. One installation charges 10 cents per page; another does not charge for the first 25 citations with abstracts or 75 without abstracts. Beyond that limit, there is a charge of 10 cents per reference. This policy was put in place as the result of user abuse of the previous policy of unlimited free printing. One other library has sidestepped the dilemma by allowing its users only to download to disc. These users print the results at one of the campus facilities or on their own equipment.

Reaction to CD-ROM Service

CD-ROM searching has been heartily endorsed and welcomed by users and staff alike in academic libraries in Ontario. An extremely positive reaction from users was cited by 86 percent of the universities offering this service. Many reference staff reported that it was a pleasure to promote a service which encourages journal use and supplies accurate citations. While many community colleges were at an earlier stage in implementing CD-ROM services, 44 percent reported similar reactions from their users. The following comments by the survey respondents describe how this technology satisfies both user and staff needs in many different ways. These sample comments from our survey show the advantages perceived by library staff: it's the first choice of students; staff like new technologies; CDs are more fun and they're easier and more satisfying to teach than print indexes; there is less pressure for staff than doing online searching; they're good for the department's image; patrons' expectations of the library's collection are increased and collection policy will change to meet those needs; CDs get you to information quickly and impressively; CDs make it easier to access journal citations and they make students more aware of journals and indexes; CDs are easier for handicapped students to access and use; and CDs force people to think.

Conclusion

End-user searching on CD-ROM databases has enormous potential to change the shape of reference service and user access to information. Space problems can be alleviated and knowledge increased but, as both our experience at Erindale College and the results of our survey of Ontario academic libraries demonstrate, there are obstacles to be overcome. Based on our data, we recommend careful research and planning before making final decisions on implementation or expansion of this new technology. Overall, our experience has shown that the benefits far outweigh the difficulties!

References

Fox, David. 1988. "CD-ROM Use in Canadian Libraries: A Survey." *CD-ROM Librarian* 3: 23–28.

Reese, Jean. 1989. "CD-ROM Services at Vanderbilt University: The Education Library Experience." *The SilverPlatter Exchange* 2 :10–12.

Elaine Goettler is a Reference Librarian at the Erindale Campus of the University of Toronto. She is an enthusiastic advocate of CD-ROM end-user searching and co-author of several reports and papers on reference services and library instruction. She holds a B.A. and an M.L.S. from the University of Toronto.

Margaret Hawthorn holds a B.A. from the University of British Columbia and an M.L.S. from the University of California, Berkeley. She has co-authored a number of conference papers and reports in the areas of reference and collection management, including a recent presentation on CD-ROMs in reference at the Ontario College and University Librarians' Association Winterbreak Conference, March, 1989. She is currently Reference Librarian at Erindale Campus, University of Toronto, Ontario.

Sandra McCaskill became a Reference Librarian at Erindale Campus, University of Toronto in 1975. Presently, she is the College Archivist and Map Librarian. Sandra received her B.L.S. from the University of Toronto in 1968. She returned to university on a part-time basis to complete her M.L.S. in 1978. Prior to working at Erindale, Sandra was a Reference Librarian at the University of Windsor.

5
Staff and User Training for CD-ROM at Auburn University

Boyd Childress, Marcia L. Boosinger

Introduction

Auburn University is a comprehensive land-grant university located in east central Alabama with an enrollment of approximately 18,000 undergraduate and 2,500 graduate students. The nearly 1,200 faculty and varied curricula are organized into 13 colleges or schools: Agriculture, Architecture, Business, Education, Engineering, Forestry, Human Sciences, Liberal Arts, Nursing, Pharmacy, Sciences and Mathematics, Veterinary Medicine, and the Graduate School. The bachelor's degree is offered in 138 fields in 64 departments, the master's degree in 60 fields, and the doctorate in 38 fields.

The Auburn University Libraries include the Ralph Brown Draughon Library, the central research library of Auburn University, which was constructed in 1962, and two branch libraries, the Architecture Library and the Veterinary Medical Library. A small collection to accommodate the additional evening and late evening study needs of undergraduate students is located in the campus all-night study facility.

Since the beginning of fiscal year 1981–82, the combined collections of the Auburn University Libraries have grown at an average annual rate of 5.1 percent to include over 1.5 million volumes as well as 1 million government documents, 1.73 million microforms, and 117,000 maps. The Libraries subscribe to over 19,000 current serials, nearly 12,300 of which are periodicals and over 200 of which are newspapers. Auburn University Libraries spent a total of $3,208,448 in 1987–88 for library materials and binding. The staff added 67,089 volumes and 891 new serial titles to the collections during that year.

The collections in the Draughon Library are organized with printed material arranged by subject in three departments: Humanities, Social Sciences, and Science and Technology. U.S. government documents and microforms are organized for use in the Microforms and Documents Department. The construction of an addition to Draughon Library, to be completed in mid-1990, is underway; it will more than double currently available space and will address the library's space needs.

Background on CD-ROMs

The Auburn University Libraries have had CD-ROM products available for patron use since 1987, and, as of May 1989, they are: Compact Disclosure, PsycLIT, Readers' Guide to Periodical Literature on Wilsondisc, and NewsBank. Approval of, and funding for, subscriptions to CD-ROM products must follow the same procedures as approval and funding of any other subscription in the Auburn University Libraries. A librarian (to date no faculty members outside the library have done so, although they may) requests the desired product using a Periodicals Review Committee justification form (Appendix). Any additional comments gathered from other librarians and faculty in support of the product are attached. The subscription is reviewed for funding by the Periodicals Review Committee, which consists of the Assistant Librarian for Reference and Information Services, the Serials Acquisitions Librarian, and three faculty from departments outside the library. If approved, the subscription to the CD-ROM, like all other subscriptions, is funded out of the appropriate reference department serial funds for the first year, and out of the general serials budget for every year following. For example, the cost of the first year's subscription to Readers' Guide to Periodical Literature on Wilsondisc was taken out of the Humanities Department funds, since that department requested it, but subsequent years' subscriptions will be funded from the general serials budget of the Libraries.

The initiative for the introduction of CD-ROM was supplied by Disclosure, Inc., which in late summer of 1987 offered to place its product in the Draughon Library on a trial basis. This marketing device, often used with regular customers, was easy to accept since Disclosure would supply the disc, the disc player, the software, and a board to add to the central processing unit—Auburn University Libraries already had the remaining components of the workstation. Since Auburn has a divisional reference arrangement, the patrons accessing the business collections were a ready-made clientele.

It did not take long for students and faculty to discover Compact Disclosure. Faculty members from key departments were notified and, naturally, students were regular patrons. The initial use of Disclosure was a request from an instructor wishing to develop a mailing list for southeastern-based companies. Additional criteria were added to reduce the size of the list (number of employees, total sales, etc.) and the search results were then downloaded.

We were eager to test the level of interest, so users were asked to complete a brief survey. Results were tabulated after a two-week period, and the most telling conclusion was the great interest exhibited by students and their ease in using the system. They used Disclosure to supplement course assignments, explore potential employment possibilities, and satisfy their curiosity about information on disc. After two months of enthusiastic user reaction, the Social Sciences Department staff negotiated with the Dean of the College of Business to provide funding for Compact Disclosure. In the end, the College of Business paid for a complete workstation (CPU with hard disc drive, monitor, keyboard, and printer, minus disc player) and the Auburn University Libraries absorbed the continuing cost of the Disclosure subscription.

The next CD-ROM, PsycLIT, was also a "try and buy" venture, and its reception was highly favorable. A decision to purchase PsycLIT was made after considerable support was expressed by Auburn University faculty. Thus, by the close of 1987, Auburn University Libraries' users were accessing these two CD-ROM products, and the trend to provide information on disc was firmly established.

Auburn was selected as a beta test site for Newspaper Abstracts OnDisc in October, 1987. Housed in the Microforms and Documents Department, this product and all accompanying hardware were returned to UMI with comments after its three-month test. The current version is under consideration for subscription. NewsBank CD-ROM, also housed in Microforms and Documents, was received, complete with workstation, beginning in June 1988, due to the Libraries' subscription to the NewsBank microfiche. When NewsBank made an offer to place its newspaper disc in the Auburn University Libraries, reference librarians readily accepted. The most recent CD-ROM acquisition is Readers' Guide to Periodical Literature on Wilsondisc from the H. W. Wilson Company, first received in October 1988. Because this was the first CD-ROM product subscribed to by the Auburn University Libraries after undergoing recommendation by librarians and consideration by the Periodicals Review Committee, we feel that it firmly established CD-ROMs as a vital part of user services. Readers' Guide was also the first CD-ROM product at Auburn which did not come with at least one piece of donated or loaned equipment. The workstation for Readers' Guide was purchased entirely with a portion of the quarterly instructional materials allocation normally used for bibliographic instruction equipment.

Philosophy

The primary rationale for obtaining the CD-ROM products available at Auburn has been to expand services. The CD-ROMs chosen for trial and subsequent subscription provide large numbers of users with a low-cost and sophisticated means of access to information otherwise difficult or impossible to obtain. This rationale of improved service (coupled with a successful, tempting marketing strategy on the part of the disc producers and vendors) prompted the trial of Compact Disclosure. The demand for company information by a burgeoning College of Business clientele, the expense of searching many business databases online, and the difficulty of manipulating and interpreting the information found in the print and microformat versions of stock ratios and 10-K reports were all problems resolved by the use of Compact Disclosure. The availability of keyword and Boolean strategies for searching fifteen years of psychological literature made a cumbersome and difficult-to-use print tool, *Psychological Abstracts*, much more accessible to less sophisticated patrons such as undergraduates. Underfunded psychology and social sciences graduate students and faculty profited from free searching. Sheer demand for greater accessibility to a print tool already in constant use fueled the subscription to Readers' Guide on Wilsondisc.

Auburn University Libraries' mission and goals statement clearly emphasizes user service, a fact which was supported by reference librarians wanting to expand services to include CD-ROMs. In addition, CD-ROM products are projected to fit into the Auburn University Libraries' strategic plan for the comprehensive bibliographic instruction program. They will provide an introduction to the skills and concepts necessary for database searching, particularly valuable when the keyword and Boolean applications of the NOTIS system are put into use.

Access Issues

CD-ROM products in the Auburn University Libraries have been located following the divisional pattern of the reference departments. The Draughon Library is divided into six main reference departments: Humanities (including General Information), Social Sciences, Science and Technology, Microforms and Documents, Special Collections, and Archives. The various CD-ROM products were viewed on trial and later purchased at the request of the Social Sciences, Microforms and Documents, and Humanities Departments based on the needs of users, as perceived by the reference staffs in each of those departments. In each case, users were best served by locating the CD-ROM in question in the same department as all other materials on the same subject, i.e., Disclosure and PsycLIT were most logically located in the Social Sciences Department with other business and psychology materials. The Readers' Guide was best located in the same department as the two print subscriptions to the index, and NewsBank was most useful and convenient when located in the Microforms and Documents Department along with the NewsBank microfiche.

Draughon Library is undergoing major addition and renovation work, and this additional constraint prevented the development of any sort of central "automated reference center" such as that at the University of Vermont. Each department requesting a CD-ROM product was able to wrestle only enough free space for its own workstation.

Placement of the workstation within the specific reference department was determined by the department staff, given the lack of space available. The Social Sciences Department placed its shared Disclosure-PsycLIT workstation and printer directly on the reference desk, with the CD player located on a shelf just under the counter. This arrangement allows for easy switching of discs, and provides hidden space for the unlocked player. It also allows staff to answer user questions and provide point-of-use training on CD-ROM products without having to leave the reference desk. The Humanities Department placed the workstation for the Readers' Guide on a table about eight feet away from the reference desk, leaving the desk and adjoining counter area free for other inquiries, but in close enough proximity to allow for easy monitoring and instruction. The Microforms and Documents Department located the NewsBank CD-ROM and the second Readers' Guide workstations across the room from the reference desk, in the only available space with electrical outlets. Both the Humanities and Microforms and Documents Departments leave the discs locked in the CD players all the time.

Policies concerning use of CD-ROM have developed in a follow-the-leader fashion, with the Social Sciences Department leading the way with time limitations, patrons served, and permissible printing and downloading of materials. All CD-ROM workstations have a 15-minute per patron per hour time limit clearly posted above each, which must be strictly enforced on certain workstations, and only occasionally invoked on others. Due to the great demand for both Disclosure and PsycLIT, users must strictly observe the limit. Use of Readers' Guide and NewsBank is less, but the time limit is being enforced more frequently with the increased use of both products. Use of Disclosure and PsycLIT by non-Auburn University patrons has grown significantly, thanks to word-of-mouth on neighboring campuses. Currently the Social Sciences staff deal with that problem, not by checking IDs, but by asking those patrons unaffiliated with Auburn to step to the back of the queue when several users are waiting for a CD-ROM. The Microforms and Documents Department has reported using the same process to handle crowds waiting to use the second Readers' Guide in their department, but the Humanities Department has not had a problem with an overabundance of outside users. Some non-Auburn users have shown their displeasure with the informal practice of serving our primary clientele first by expressing themselves rather vocally. A written policy concerning access to outside users and a method of implementing such a policy is currently under consideration.

Fees for printing and downloading have never been seriously considered for two reasons. Increased service to undergraduates is one rationale for CD-ROM subscription, and charging for printing would nullify any cost savings such products afford undergraduates. Also, the collection of revenues generated by such fees, currently handled by a cashier through the Libraries' administrative offices, would involve immense amounts of staff time. It was felt that the cost of the paper used to print citations from any CD-ROM was well worth the staff time saved. As an alternative to printing, downloading has been permitted on any CD-ROM which has that feature and to any user who provides a formatted disc.

Multiple users and multiple disc databases have been accommodated only recently. Because an extra CD workstation and player had been ordered for the Microforms and Documents Department (MADD) in anticipation of a CD product produced by the Government Printing Office, it was possible to provide a second access point to the Readers' Guide by using the most recently superseded disc at this extra workstation. Backfiles of many of the periodicals indexed in the Readers' Guide are stored on microfilm at Auburn; therefore, a second workstation in the Microforms and Documents Department was a logical addition. Because the microfiche copies of company 10K and annual reports received from Disclosure also are stored in MADD, plans are being made to load Compact Disclosure on the same workstation as Readers' Guide.

Staff training for Readers' Guide was informal one-to-one instruction conducted in the two departments concerned. Staff in Humanities were typical in their reactions as they watched with great interest the setup and initial trial of the Readers' Guide. Each staff member had read the instruction booklet prior to setup and then each took a turn at the workstation, trying at least the first two modes under the tutelage of the staff member who had tried the disc just before. Much independent practice ensued in the next several days, accompanied by much consultation of the instruction booklet. While all of the librarians tried all four modes, staff were less likely to venture past WilSearch, even in practice. Graduate and undergraduate student staff were trained according to need; those who had reference desk time received training on Readers' Guide. Training included the maintenance of a rather temperamental and sensitive Fujitsu DL2400 printer which requires frequent reloading of paper. A sign giving printer use instructions is posted at the workstation, along with the flip chart of full instructions.

Staff Training
Philosophy

Training is provided to prepare support staff to serve in a reference capacity. With divisional reference collections, staff necessarily answer queries at the reference desk and need to be able to operate a CD-ROM workstation. Training is necessary, but not mandatory for all staff.

At Auburn University Libraries, the persons responsible for training are the authors of this article, because of their experience with databases and CD-ROMs. Future plans call for more reference librarians to become staff trainers.

The Social Sciences Department has established an informal training program intended both to expose its staff to CD-ROM applications and to train reference staff in the practical use of CD technology. As the use of CD-ROMs is so extensive, new librarians are provided immediate individual instruction, as opposed to training sessions. The training sessions we provide include staff at three other levels— support staff, graduate student assistants, and undergraduate student assistants. Generally support staff provide reference desk coverage an average of only nine to fifteen hours a week. Graduate students may staff the desk up to 20 hours a week, and student assistants, between 10 and 15 hours per week. Often these individuals have no librarians as backup, thus they need enough training to enable them to operate CD-ROM products effectively while on duty alone.

We considered several issues when planning staff training. Initially, we encountered the ever-present resistance to technology, but most staff at all levels were able to conquer their fear of computers. In addition, all staff needed to know what to expect from each database. This pointed out the need for further education of staff as to realistic expectations. Still another consideration was troubleshooting and reacting to the unexpected. Finally, we had to consider the various levels of computer expertise. Many students were already computer literate, while many staff have seldom had a need to access automated information systems. Experience with NOTIS proved to be most beneficial in the last respect.

A decision to limit the length of staff training sessions was made before any training began. Part of the reason was psychological—we hoped to accomplish the objectives in stages. For example, the Social Sciences Department staff required training on Compact Disclosure and PsycLIT, and it was decided that a complete bombardment with database contents and search techniques was too much for one long session. The other reason for limiting training sessions was the demand on staff time. It was difficult to work with four or five individuals together for much more than an hour at any one time. We also had to work around student and faculty use of the compact discs. It is not surprising, then, that a one-hour session is the present practice.

Several compact disc products had been available for up to 18 months before training was considered a necessity. For example, Compact Disclosure and PsycLIT were available in the Social Sciences Department and the staff had some limited experience with these two discs. But training had been established as a goal that year and staff members were being called upon more and more to provide backup reference assistance as the volume of reference activity increased dramatically.

Components of Staff Training

The immediate need, in the first session, was to describe briefly the compact disc—whether it was bibliographic or numeric, what type of questions it had the potential to answer, and what (if any) were the print equivalents. The intent here was to provide the basics of the database without going into lengthy detail. For example, we told staff PsycLIT was psychological in nature, and could be accessed for questions in psychology, education, sociology, business and other related subject areas.

After the briefing on database coverage, practical search techniques were discussed in connection with available database documentation (i.e., the *Thesaurus of Psychological Indexing Terms* for PsycLIT, the *Compact Disclosure Users' Manual* for Compact Disclosure, and the instructional flipchart and user's manual for Wilsondisc). Several examples using the *Psychological Abstracts* thesaurus were used to demonstrate this step:

Women	use	Human Females
Cancer	use	Neoplasms
Locus of Control	use	Internal External Locus of Control

This gave us an opportunity to explain several points, the first of which was using the hyphen when searching. Without adding the burden of understanding precision and recall, the intent was to stress using descriptors. We also mentioned the postings notes and dates the terms were added. These are often useful, even to the novice searcher, and each of these was illustrated with an example on the disc. Instead of having the trainer operate the keyboard, staff members were encouraged to try it themselves. This increased the staff's comfort level with CD-ROM. This session concluded by emphasizing such search basics as combining terms, and displaying and printing search results.

A second session, held a week later, began with a review of the first session. Then we moved to combining terms using the OR operator and continued with several other features such as publication year, language, and population. For example, the topic of adolescents' use of drugs (limited to 1988 publications) was plotted as follows:

#1	Adolescents or adolescence
#2	drug-usage
#3	#1 and #2
#4	#3 and 1988 in PY

The above strategy was introduced before demonstrating that another one-step strategy was an alternative.

> #1   (adolescents or adolescence) and drug-usage and
>   1988 in PY

We made a conscious decision to omit mention of the NOT operator because the database vendor trainers suggested not to make frequent use of it. When staff became successful at executing more detailed searches, the NOT operator was explained, with appropriate warnings.

Questions were encouraged at the sessions, but we asked participants to save questions until the end of the second session. We felt that with two instructional sessions the staff might well be able to answer their own questions, and we wanted them to observe all of the sample searches.

The final concepts in the second session were downloading and the exchange (F8) function. Downloading was introduced as simply an extension of the print command. The exchange feature proved to be more difficult to explain, particularly executing a search strategy with a single command after the exchange of discs.

After the two sessions were completed, each staff member was given a reference question to solve utilizing PsycLIT. These questions were generally not as detailed as identifying a specific article, but included a bibliographic subject listing, an author search, and a disc exchange assignment. A trainer observed each assignment but made no comments nor answered questions until the staff member completed his or her answer. At that point, the trainer made any necessary suggestions and answered questions. The result was that each staff member ended up with a correct or acceptable answer. This was considered a measure of successful training, but a more accurate measure was the staff's new level of confidence.

Disclosure Example

A brief glance at Compact Disclosure training helps to illustrate staff training. Disclosure was the first compact disc introduced to users, and while staff had more exposure to its use, it had only been used to access company-specific information. The prime training objectives included a demonstration of identifying a specific SIC code, searching by SIC code, searching by geographic codes (city, state, etc.), restricting a search to companies in a specific geographic region in a specific industry (airline companies in Georgia, for example), and searching by number of employees, share holders or auditor. The entire session was conducted in the easy menu mode since the staff was unfamiliar with DIALOG command searching.

Two of the functions targeted for special attention were the display feature and the transfer function. The main purpose behind this emphasis was the economy of printing or downloading only the needed fields or groups of fields. This was crucial in downloading since on average only five or six full company records would fit on a single floppy disk. Thus, the company profile, an address, and the text segments were emphasized as print or transfer choices. Staff were encouraged to explain these options to users in order to conserve paper in printing and eliminate user frustration in downloading. Emphasis was placed on downloading to an appropriate disk drive and not to the hard disk, a common error.

Finally, each staff member was assigned a question to search. Staff had more problems with these questions and, although the answers were generally correct, some staff misinterpreted the assignment and provided more information in printing answers than necessary. But in all such instances the trainer was careful to point out how each mistake was made and how to remedy the situation. The staff member was then given a second opportunity to respond to a similar question. This proved partially successful.

User Training and Documentation
Training Individual Users

Several levels of user training are available. Point–of–use training is of course the most frequently used type of instruction on all the CD products, with librarians standing by as coaches, but with the user actually using the keyboard and accessing the information. As with any reference inquiry, the usual procedure is to begin with a brief reference interview to be certain that the tool is actually the best one for the information needed. Next, we walk a first-time user through a search step by step, prompting the user after each command and response from the CD-ROM. Users are told what sort of tool they are using, its scope, and what sort of information they may expect from it.

Readers' Guide Example

When introducing Readers' Guide, for example, we explain to users:
—the database contents (six years of popular magazine article citations, arranged by subject, which are insufficient if specialized or technical information is needed)
—what the user is seeing on the screen (which varies according to what has been left on the screen from the last user)
—browse mode (an alphabetical subject listing of terms used by Wilson to index magazine articles)
—windows
—important keys, such as the return key (The distinction between the return key and the control key are important to our users because our online catalog uses the control key to enter a search.)
—posting numbers
—highlighting to select an item (This emphasis is necessary to avoid confusion with our online catalog which uses line numbers and the control key for the selection of an item on a guide or index list.)
—the asterisk (*) and the F8 function keys
—the parts of the citation
—printing
—scrolling forward and backward

We then usually check to see that the first citation retrieved fits the user's need. We are available to answer any further questions as the search progresses or to solve any problems with the equipment, but frequently, this is sufficient instruction for a user working only in the browse mode. This instruction is followed by exact directions to the specific magazine issues listed on the printout obtained from the CD search.

While this is the general outline of the steps of the point-of-use instruction for a user of Readers' Guide on CD-ROM, this process varies greatly, depending on the user's familiarity with computers, his searching experience with the computer catalog, and the subject being searched.

User support varies from product to product at Auburn. All but one of the workstations are equipped with some sort of brief user guide or summary of commands to supplement the menu-driven systems and built-in help screens. The user guides provided by PsycLIT and Disclosure were laminated and posted at the workstation in Social Sciences, while a more extensive flip chart of instructions for using the Browse Search and Wilsearch modes of the Readers' Guide is available in Humanities and Microforms and Documents, along with large Wilson-provided posters and stand-up signs describing use of the two modes. NewsBank users are provided only the on-screen instructions for its use.

Training Groups of Users

Training of a group of users may take one of three forms: small group instruction, class instruction with CD as one part of an hour-long subject seminar, or class instruction with CD-ROM as the focus of an entire presentation.

Small Group Instruction

Small group instruction on Readers' Guide, Disclosure, or PsycLIT has occurred in classes in Business and Professional Writing, Developmental Studies, Educational Media, Family and Child Development, Speech Communication, and numerous others. In cases where small group instruction has been appropriate, several librarians from different reference departments cooperate in a larger presentation of resources found on various floors of the Draughon Library. In order to get patrons to the actual locations of the various sources, the classes have been divided into groups of eight or less. Librarians were informed of possible paper or project topics ahead of the presentation in order to use relevant searches in their demonstrations. Because the groups are small enough to allow for standing around one terminal, the steps involved in demonstrating Readers' Guide, for example, are very much like those followed when giving point-of-use instruction to an individual, except that the Wilsearch mode is also discussed and the differences between the Browse and Wilsearch modes are demonstrated and stressed. One class member is chosen as searcher for the group. The librarian stands to the side of the workstation and discusses what the student is bringing up on the screen. A comparison of the Wilsearch and Browse Search is made, using a term which may have yielded no exact match in Browse, but which can be manipulated in Wilsearch. Synonymous terms are combined using "any" at the beginning of a subject word, and truncated if possible. A second subject may be added to show a combination of concepts. The Boolean logic in both steps is pointed out. Results are then compared with those found in the Browse Search by examining several actual citations to find search terms within the author and title fields as well as the subject field. Students are then asked to suggest other topics to practice. The CD demonstration is followed by a demonstration of the use of the online catalog for locating the actual magazine article.

Class Presentations

For class-sized presentations we use a Kodak Datashow LCD computer projection panel to display searches on a large screen. Whether the CD product is part of a broader subject seminar or the whole show, the use of this type of projection equipment makes viewing and understanding the information and concepts presented much clearer and more accessible.

All four CD products currently in use have been successfully demonstrated using the LCD projection panel. Hardware requirements include an IBM-compatible microcomputer with 256K of RAM memory, a CGA card and one asynchronous communications port, keyboard, as well a CD controller card, and an overhead projector and screen. A monitor is not necessary because the search is displayed on the LCD panel, which sits on the overhead projector, and the image from the microcomputer to the LCD panel is projected onto the screen using the overhead projector.

Examples of large group presentations in which CD products were only parts of subject seminars include presentations for large (50–60 students) sections of a course entitled, "Man the Consumer." The online catalog, indexes to government publications, the Readers' Guide on CD-ROM, and NewsBank CD-ROM were the primary tools taught. The steps used to teach the two CD products followed very closely those used in teaching the tools to small groups, making use of prepared, relevant subjects for searches. Because this sort of session is held in a large auditorium, however, the keyboard was operated by the librarian rather than a member of the class. This sort of instruction allows the students to see clearly all that appears on the screen and to take notes while following the lecture. Students come away with a completely realistic idea of what they will see and can do when they begin their own searches.

Use of CD-ROM for an entire presentation has been an especially effective way of instructing potential end users who need an in-depth understanding of database construction, controlled vocabulary, and Boolean logic. Worries about online time and cost constraints are alleviated. PsycLIT and Disclosure were very effectively used with a class of Educational Media students who needed to understand how the product and similar databases from other vendors worked, but who did not necessarily need an actual search in either database to satisfy an information need.

Impact

The impact of CD-ROMs has been felt in the entire library program, from staff to collections to equipment. The impact on staff is greater than simply the acquisition of just another index. Staff are called upon to teach users everything from the layout of the keyboard and operation of the printer to Boolean logic and the concept of controlled vocabulary. Great amounts of staff time are spent at a user's side discussing search strategy, downloading capabilities, and where to go after obtaining bibliographic citations from the CD-ROM, as well as unjamming printers, changing ribbons, and switching discs. The impact on reference desk staffing can be measured by numbers of questions related to the use of CD-ROM. These are tallied along with directional and reference questions. For a six-month period beginning October 1988, the Humanities and Social Sciences Departments answered 4,721 questions (13.9 percent, or roughly one-seventh, of the 33,907 total reference inquiries made for the same time period) concerning Readers' Guide, Disclosure, and PsycLIT.

The level of training and education is perhaps the area of least impact— certainly when compared with the impact of CD-ROM aquisitions on the budget. When considering the budgeting for CD-ROMs, the hidden costs are numerous. In the continued process of staff training and user education, the cost of learning to use a CD-ROM product differs little from learning to use a new abstract or index. But with CD-ROMs there are budgetary considerations such as hardware obligations, including maintenance contracts, paper and ribbon costs, and security, to consider. Over an extended period, the costs associated with the increasing number of CD-ROM applications are considerable, though difficult to calculate.

We have not cancelled existing print indexes. Various factors went into this decision, which will be evaluated periodically. The purchase of PsycLIT serves as an example of such decisions. The pricing structure created by the APA and Silver-Platter provides only a small price differential in the subscription of both products compared to the cost of PsycLIT only.

Table 1
Subscription Prices for PsycLIT and Psychological Abstracts:
May 1989

Psychological Abstracts only	$ 750.00
PsycLIT when subscribing to *Psychological Abstracts*	$3595.00
PsycLIT only	$3995.00

After considerable discussion and informal surveys, the decision not to cancel print sources was made. Another example helps to illustrate this point. The Auburn University Libraries subscribe to Disclosure with the Spectrum feature and receive microfiche annual reports for all New York and American Stock Exchange companies as well as 10-Ks for all Fortune 500 and Alabama companies. The use of these microfiche materials was not greatly affected by Compact Disclosure, and all services were maintained. Another decision made was to maintain two subscriptions to the *Readers' Guide* while accessing the same source on Wilsondisc. Since the present configuration allows for only two users to access the CD-ROM at a time, it was considered essential to continue two print subscriptions. In the future, costs will demand that services be reevaluated realistically, and print sources or CD-ROMs may be cut.

Publicity

Initial publicity for each of the workstations consisted of signage, usually located on top of the CRT, announcing the product and urging users to try it, with librarian assistance if desired. Other signs were also posted near the corresponding print or microformat products such as *Psychological Abstracts,* the *Readers' Guide to Periodical Literature,* and the company 10K and annual reports, notifying patrons that a CD equivalent existed elsewhere. Where appropriate, letters were written to teaching faculty, such as those in the College of Business to inform them of the arrival of Disclosure, and those in the Psychology Department to notify them of PsycLIT. Patrons using products initially bought on trial were usually asked to fill out a brief survey which served to collect responses to the product while reinforcing the positive experience of using it. CD-ROMs of a more general nature, such as Readers' Guide and NewsBank, were announced in articles printed in the quarterly newsletter, *Auburn Library Topics.* All CD-ROM products merit separate paragraphs in the library handbook, *A Guide to the Use of the Auburn University Libraries.* The best publicity, however, is word of mouth from satisfied users, who routinely bring fellow students and faculty in to see the "computer with magazine articles," or the "computer with company information on it."

Reflections on the Program

Overall, the use of CD-ROM products at Auburn University Libraries has been a great success. All products are receiving increased use, and are outgrowing the single workstation configurations currently in place. Changes in the service revolve around the budgeting for and acquisitions of such products. Gone are the times of "try and buy" based on user response, because user response to this form of technology has been overwhelmingly positive regardless of the product and difficulty of use involved. Although following the same guidelines for subscription as for any serial has delayed the acquisition of additional CD-ROMs, it has allowed for the prioritization of potential CD purchases and has ensured that continued funding for such acquisitions exists.

Problems with equipment have been minor and include only some recalcitrant printers and bulky printer enclosures which were soon discarded. Social Sciences continues to make use of such a printer enclosure, finding the noise reduction helpful and having easier access than the other two departments to the printer because the workstation is located on the reference desk itself.

The departments are learning ways to make increased use of scarce resources, such as the arrangement to load superseded Readers' Guide and Disclosure discs on the extra workstation in Microforms and Documents in order to double access to both databases. Future plans include a local area network in order to best utilize existing subscriptions, as well as possibly four more: MLA International Bibliography, Newspaper Abstracts on Disk, ABI/Inform OnDisc, and MEDLINE. Ideally, a network will allow multiple workstations to access all available CD-ROMS and will permit several users to use the same CD-ROM simultaneously. In addition, Auburn is participating in the National Agriculture Library's text digitizing project using the aquaculture CD-ROM, and has received the CASSIS CD-ROM. The Census Test Disc 1 has arrived and also will be used.

Ideally, the future holds a multi-database system for the Auburn University Libraries, in cooperation with NOTIS. In a NOTIS-proposed multi-database system, ERIC could be a part of the library subsystem, along with MEDLINE and all the H.W. Wilson indexes, and would be accessible from all university terminals and from remote sites dialing in. Online public access catalog entries and Auburn's periodical holdings would be linked to the various database records. While such a configuration might eliminate the need to purchase numerous individual CD-ROMs, the expense involved in committing to such a system is immense, and not all database vendors will be amenable to such licensing agreements. Some stand-alone CD-ROMs, requiring extensive staff training and use of staff time for user instruction, will most likely continue to be in use even with the implementation of such a system.

Boyd Childress is Social Sciences Reference Librarian and History Bibliographer at Auburn University Libraries, a position he has held since 1981. Prior to that, he was a reference librarian at Western Kentucky University. He received a B.A. in History from Virginia Commonwealth University in 1971 and an M.A. (History, 1974) and M.L.S. (1976) from the University of Alabama. At present, his duties also include those of departmental online search services coordinator.

Marcia L. Boosinger has been Bibliographic Instruction Librarian and Humanities Reference Librarian at Auburn University Libraries since 1986. She received a B.A. in English (1973) and an M.S. in Library, Media, and Instructional Development (1983) from Purdue University and an M.L.S. (1986) from the University of Alabama.

Appendix

AUBURN UNIVERSITY LIBRARIES
JUSTIFICATION FOR NEW SERIAL/PERIODICAL ORDER
(Attatch to regular order request form)

Because the library has a limited budget with which to purchase new serial and periodical titles, it is important that each request be considered carefully. It will be helpful if you can provide appropriate information regarding the usefulness and importance of the requested title to Auburn University's teaching and research program. Some questions may not be applicable. Subject librarians will try to provide any information that may not be available to you.

Requested by: Date:
Department: Phone:
Complete title of the serial/periodical:
Publisher: Date publication began:

FOR FACULTY/REQUESTER USE:

1) This title is important for: (check all as appropriate)
my individual research;   general faculty/dept. research;   graduate research; undergraduate use;   current awareness;   course support - List courses:
2) Indicate approx. number of student/faculty directly affected:
3) List other teaching faculty members who might find this journal important and/or other programs it would benefit:
4) The articles in this journal are in the following languages:
5) Relative to other new periodical/serial requests in this subject area that might be purchased this year, please consider this title: essential;   important;   useful.
6) Please attach any publisher's fliers/brochures/sample issues you may have.
7) Additional comments:
Signature

FOR LIBRARIAN/SUBJECT SPECIALIST USE:

Please provide as much information as appropriate, and as possible, in answering these questions.
RELEVANCE:
      1) Refereed journal?   Article quality?
      2) Other titles on subject in library?
      3) Degree level granted by department or program?
      4) RBD Library collection level status?
      5) Interdisciplinary use?
AVAILABILITY:
      1) Available elsewhere on campus?
      2) Elsewhere in the state?
      3) Number of ILL requests submitted this year?
      4) On microfilm?
      5) Availability & cost of retrospective volumes?

ACCESSIBILITY:
    1) Indexed in major indexing or abstracting services?   If so, which ones?
    2) Does it have its own index?
    3) Listed in Ulrich's?   Katz, 5th ed.?

ADDITIONAL COMMENTS:

PRIORITY GROUPS/RANKING: Relative to other new periodical/serial requests in this subject area that might be purchased this year, please consider this title: essential; important;   useful;   of little value

Signature

(Original version of this form courtesy of the University of Arizona Libraries)

6

CD-ROMs for Public Access: Integral Components of Collections and Services in an Academic Research Library

Susan Barnes, Edwin Spragg

Introduction

Scholars concerned with academic study and research are beginning to rely on electronic information resources. They are sophisticated users of microcomputers for their academic work, and expect to have an equally sophisticated "electronic library" of resources available from their workstations.

The "electronic library" has become a commonplace phrase to describe a collection of computerized information resources, in electronic form, accessed at the workstation, often via telecommunications networks. In order to remain viable into the next century, academic research libraries must take the leadership role in the development of the electronic library to respond to scholars' needs.

Presently, printed resources occupy a key position in the storage and dissemination of scholarly information. However, computerized databases are challenging this position. These electronic resources are being added to academic library collections in a multiplex of formats, including the optical medium known as CD-ROM. Conventional wisdom holds that CD-ROM is a transitional storage technology which will be replaced by some other format. Although CD-ROM does have limitations, it has transformed everyday services in many libraries, and regardless of its future, it typifies the current expansion of storage formats from traditional print to electronic.

CD-ROM is part of the everyday operation of Cornell University's Albert R. Mann Library, mainstreamed into the library's services and processing procedures (Coons, 1988). It is not treated as a special or unusual format. Information stored on CD-ROM is an integral part of the library's collection, which also includes microcomputer software, electronic data files, computerized bibliographic databases, microforms, maps, and printed books and journals.

This chapter describes the philosophical rationale for acquiring CD-ROM at Mann Library, gives details of acquisition and processing, summarizes provisions for access, and reports on the effects these resources have had on library services. First, in order to show CD's place in Mann's collections and services, we present a sketch of the projects moving this academic research library toward its electronic future. This overview will place CD-ROM systems at Mann Library in perspective, as one of a variety of available information resources.

Institutional Context

Cornell University is an unusual combination of a publicly and privately funded research university. It was established in 1868 as a land grant institution, but received its initial endowment from Ezra Cornell. The university's main campus in Ithaca serves a population of approximately 12,000 undergraduates and 6,000 graduate students, along with over 2,000 faculty, researchers, and extension staff.

Albert R. Mann Library

Mann Library is state-supported, as part of the State University of New York system at Cornell. Mann is also the land grant library for New York State. Its primary mission is to serve the 8,000 students, faculty and staff of the New York State College of Agriculture and Life Sciences, and the New York State College of Human Ecology. In addition, it supports the University's Division of Biological Sciences and the Division of Nutritional Sciences. Mann's collection strengths are in the agricultural sciences, life sciences, nutrition, human development and family studies, consumer economics, and related social sciences. After the National Agricultural Library, Mann Library has the nation's strongest collection in agriculture. Its collection numbers 590,000 volumes, including 9,600 serial subscriptions.

The library is organized administratively into three divisions reporting to the library director: Public Services, Collection Development, and Technical Services. These three divisions and the library's administrative staff are served by the Information Technology Section (ITS). The ITS is Mann's systems support group, providing technical and managerial support for selecting, installing, maintaining, and operating computers and telecommunications connections. ITS provides this support for both staff and public computing.

An Electronic Library

The concept of a "scholar's workstation" has its roots in Vannevar Bush's Memex (Bush, 1945). At the workstation, the scholar generates information using word processors, graphics packages, or other software. The scholar uses telecommunications connections and search software to retrieve information, and stores information using database management programs or spreadsheets. The scholar is then able to organize this information, format it, and produce textual documents, charts, or graphs. The equipment and software for accessing and managing information in a scholar's workplace is collectively referred to as the "scholar's workstation."

This vision of scholarly activity requires an electronic library which can provide access at the scholar's workstation to many types of information, in a variety of formats, from multiple locations.

The electronic library brings technological challenges, but does not necessitate a redefinition of an academic library's role. An important new element is the need for the library to work closely with computer professionals who provide the technical infrastructure. This infrastructure includes the necessary hardware, software, and network connections to enable the scholarly information system to function.

Mann Library is conducting a series of projects to evaluate the effects of electronic formats on scholars' use of information. This development of a scholarly information system is a natural extension of Mann's traditional role of selecting, acquiring, organizing, and providing access to printed information.

Mann's electronic library is still under development, so that some electronic resources are available from the scholar's workstation while others must be accessed from within the library. Portions of the scholarly information system available at the workstation include an online catalog with library holdings and circulation information, an electronic reference service, and locally mounted bibliographic databases. In the near future, full text journal articles, and numeric files will also be available. One of the library's conceptualizations of the scholar's workstation is an opening screen for a workstation showing a desk, with icons representing the electronic resources that are available (figure 1).

The electronic information presently available only in the library includes "semi-public" computer access to commercial databases on remote computers, public access computers for use of applications software such as word processors and spreadsheets, and CD-ROM based information systems.

Resources at the Workstation

Mann's online catalog uses the NOTIS system, which provides Cornell library holdings and circulation status information to anyone who can access the university's mainframe computers. An electronic reference service offered through an e-mail system operated by Cornell's central computer support group, Cornell Information Technologies, is available to those who have access to the Cornell network.

Mann is experimenting with access to several locally mounted databases, including Agricola and subsets of BIOSIS in the fields of nutrition, genetics, and entomology. These bibliographic databases, searchable through BRS Search, are at present being used by a test group of almost 200 faculty, researchers, and graduate students. The members of the test group have received training in searching and the use of telecommunications software and protocols. Their database use is being monitored in order to determine whether their use of computerized bibliographic data changes as a result of being able to search from their offices, free of charge.

Access to computerized biological and agricultural numeric files is available through the library, and in the next two years will be expanded to the scholar's workstation, with access via the national network. It is anticipated that access to full-text information will be available in 1990.

Finally, Mann staff are developing a gateway to provide easy selection of resources and effortless switching between resources, regardless of physical location. This gateway program will be the key to tying electronic resources together at the workstation level; it will be the window of entry to the electronic library (figure 2).

Electronic Resources from within the Library

Mann has, since the mid-seventies, provided access to commercial databases located on remote computers. This access has been from terminals or microcomputers in the library, via telephone lines. The staff perform searches of these databases for

The Scholar's Workstation: A Possible Opening Display Screen
Albert R. Mann Library, Cornell University

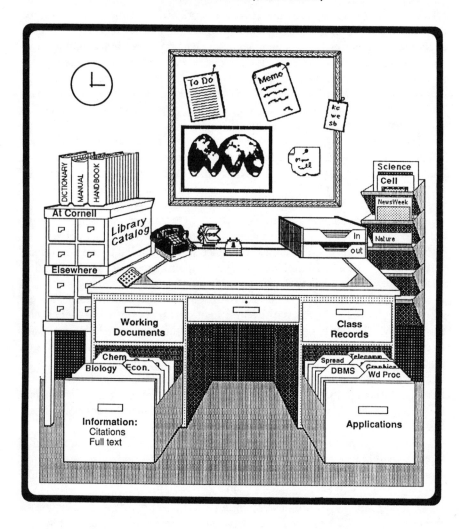

figure 1.

users on a cost-recovery basis. They also encourage use of these remote online resources from within the library by end-users who have had some training. The library is exploring arrangements with commercial vendors in order to provide access to some of their databases at a fixed rate, so that Cornell scholars are not impeded by cost barriers, and so that remote databases can take their place on the menu of choices available at the scholar's workstation.

At present, CD-ROM database use at Mann is limited to one user per workstation. The library plans to develop a networked, multi-user/multi-disk configuration for its CD-ROM systems, so that any CD database can be used at any public-access microcomputer in the library, including those in the library's Microcomputer Center. After implementing this network, the next step will be to connect it to Cornell's backbone network, making the CD-ROM databases available at any scholar's workstation on campus. CD-ROM's place in Mann's electronic library will depend on the success of network options, and on the development of equipment that handles multiple discs smoothly and quickly.

Case Study: CD-ROMs at Mann Library

CD-ROM based services at Mann have been characterized by their integration into existing procedures and services, and by the number and variety of resources on CD-ROM that have been acquired and are being used.

The library provides the following CD products for its users:

    Agricola (SilverPlatter), 1970-present
    Census of Agriculture 1982 (Slater Hall)
    ERIC (SilverPlatter), 1966-present
    Fedstat County Demographic and Economic Databases, 1989
    GPO (SilverPlatter), 1976-present
    Life Sciences (Compact Cambridge), 1986-present
    Medline (SilverPlatter), 1983-present
    Popline (SilverPlatter), 1827-present
    Test Disc No. 2 (U.S. Bureau of the Census), 1988

Mann Library owns about 150 printed indexing and abstracting journals that cover subjects ranging from acid rain to zoology. Until recently, it was not unusual for the large tables in the library's Indexes and Abstracts room to be littered with stacks of heavily used titles: *Bibliography of Agriculture, Index Medicus, Current Index to Journals in Education, Resources in Education,* and *Monthly Catalog of United States Government Publications.* Now that the CD-ROM versions of these indexes are available in Mann Library, this is no longer the case. The print versions are receiving far less use, as shown by decreased shelving and less wear and tear on individual volumes. We believe that this indicates a strong user preference for compact discs.

Why are the CD-ROM systems so popular? For library users, CD-ROM products allow free, self-service access to computerized databases. The users feel free to experiment with their searches since the meter is no longer running. In addition, CD-ROM provides greater retrieval capabilities than do printed works.

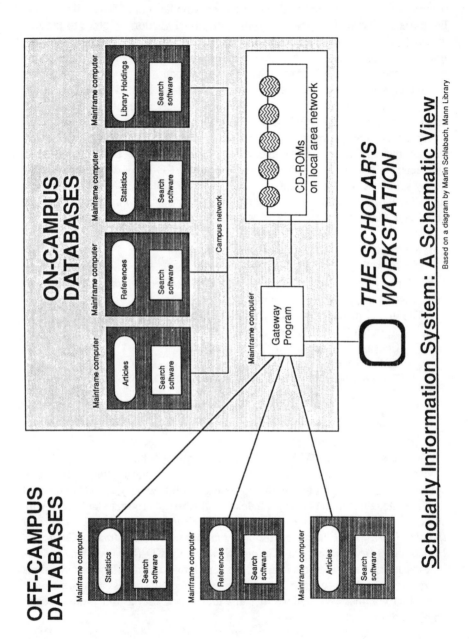

ON-CAMPUS DATABASES

OFF-CAMPUS DATABASES

THE SCHOLAR'S WORKSTATION

Scholarly Information System: A Schematic View

Based on a diagram by Martin Schlabach, Mann Library

figure 2.

The library, by subscribing to these databases, can provide access to electronic information by paying a fixed fee. This pricing structure for CD-ROM products allows the library to control prices, unlike current arrangements with commercial vendors of online databases where the library is charged on a per-use basis.

The CD-ROM systems are used primarily by students. This format meets needs that were difficult to serve with traditional mediated online searches. The CDs provide free immediate access to information, popular options for undergraduates who are often meeting term paper deadlines and who usually are not willing to spend much money for information. Additionally, the CD systems add the glamour of the computer, which is missing in printed indexes. The lure of the computer is powerful among younger users particularly, since they are more likely to have used computers before attending college.

Selection

The philosophy at Mann is to use the same criteria in choosing CD-ROM databases and systems as those used when selecting material in other formats. These include factors such as subject coverage, currency and accuracy of contents, reputation of author and publisher, and price. Overlap with existing resources in Mann and other libraries at Cornell is another consideration; we avoid duplicating subscriptions whenever possible. Some CD-ROM databases such as ABI/INFORM and Sociofile, which are useful to our patrons but not within our primary collection scope, are available in other units of the Cornell University Library.

We have developed the following additional criteria for CD-ROM selection, because CD-ROMs have features that distinguish them from print materials:
—The search features should be similar in power to BRS and DIALOG, if the product is a bibliographic database.
—The software should be easy to use.
—There must be no unreasonable licensing restrictions.

Librarians in public services at Mann obtain trial or demonstration versions of CD-ROM products. After evaluating the products, the librarians decide which products to recommend for purchase. Final purchase decisions are made by the Head of Collection Development.

Acquisitions and Cataloging

Although CD-ROM products are ordered by the Acquisitions Department in much the same way as other materials, checking them in and cataloging them require new procedures and skills. Most items are checked in on the NOTIS serials control system at which time receipt of discs and new search software is indicated and the return of superseded discs is noted. Each CD-ROM product is cataloged according the the 1987 draft Chapter 9 of AACR-2, including classification and subject headings. New considerations are necessary when cataloging CD-ROMs:
—Managing the large number of physical pieces, such as CD-ROM discs, floppy discs, user's manuals, tutorials, thesauri;
—Deciding whether an item is a monograph or a serial: archival database discs could be either; search software in several versions could be an irregular serial;
—Separating information applying to the data from information applying to the program: e.g., the publishers may be different;

—Indicating withdrawal of superseded CD-ROMs.

After installation and cataloging, the product is the joint responsibility of the Information Technology Section, for technical support, and the Public Services Division, for user access.

Technical Support

After the check-in procedure is completed, the product is installed by ITS staff, who also handle machine selection and repair. In addition to the five workstations available for public use, an additional CD station is available in the library's Online Classroom for instruction sessions. All six workstations feature IBM PCs with hard disks, two of the PCs have color monitors. The library has an assortment of CD readers: four Philips readers, one Hitachi, and one Digital. An ink-jet printer is attached to each CD station. The library owns one Apple CD reader; it is presently being used to evaluate patron reaction to Macintosh-based CD systems.

An ITS student employee makes regular maintenance visits to ensure that printers are working and paper supplies are ample. The student also cleans the disks regularly. Without this preventive washing, the heavily used disks (primarily the backfiles of MEDLINE and Agricola) sometimes become unreadable. Ongoing minor problems such as paper jams and printer cartridge replacement are handled by reference desk staff and, after the reference desk is closed after 10 p.m., by circulation desk staff.

The ITS staff have installed batch programs that display menus when the CD workstations are powered up each morning. This introductory screen for CD-ROM selection allows any one of several CD-ROMs to be used on a machine without rebooting. These menus are similar on each machine, and feature the most likely CD systems to be used at each workstation. An ITS programmer is currently developing another program to track the number of uses of each database, duration of use, and time of use. This information will be used in staffing and subscription decisions.

The ITS staff have had to acquire some additional technical knowledge unique to CD systems. On the whole, however, installing and maintaining CD systems has been similar to installing and maintaining staff and public microcomputer workstations.

User Access

Before any CD-ROM systems were installed at Mann, potential sites in the library were evaluated. Four areas were compared for their accessibility and availability of user assistance:

1. The Microcomputer Center. The library's public access Microcomputer Center contains 27 IBM PC-compatibles connected in a LAN, and nine Macintoshes. It was designed to provide equipment and software for information access and management. The Microcomputer Center's hours are the same as those of the rest of the library building. It is located on the first floor, which is a particularly attractive location. It is, however, one floor below the Reference Desk.

2. The online searching office. Located in the public services office area, this room houses the microcomputers that are used to access remote online databases. The office is a semi-public area, staffed by librarians who perform mediated searches and assist with end-user searches. Extensive database documentation is available in this room, and the possibility of using these manuals and thesauri for both remote and CD-ROM database assistance was tempting. However, there is limited space in this office, and additional staff would have been necessary to open it to the public during all library hours.

3. The Indexes and Abstracts Room. This room is on the same floor as the Reference Desk. Placing CD-ROM systems next to analogous print tools would have been logical, but the CD workstations would not have been visible from the Reference Desk.

4. The Reference Desk area. This is the location that was chosen. It is a highly visible area where CD-ROM workstations are available during all library hours. Reference staff can observe the systems' operation and provide assistance to users.

The most frequently used disks are kept in their primary workstations, with backfiles and seldom-used databases stored in a filing cabinet at the reference desk. Desk staff hand out disks when asked, without requiring identification from library patrons. This system works well and no security problems have yet resulted. The library is considering moving toward an "open shelving" arrangement for the disks.

Users are encouraged to sign up in advance although this is not required. There are daily sign-up sheets which allow for up to two consecutive hours of use. Searching is free and available to everyone, and there is no limit on printing or downloading. Users are very pleased with these policies.

CD database availability is publicized in the same manner as mediated and self-service searching of remote online databases. CD database information is included in handouts and educational presentations. Along with word-of-mouth, these methods have made the CDs sufficiently well-known that they are in almost constant use and sign-up sheets are often filled.

User Support

Public services staff assist users with selection and operation of CD systems and with interpretation of search results. Although this is the same level of assistance provided for users working with printed reference tools, the introduction of the CD systems provided some challenges. To assist with the plethora of databases available, reference desk staff have learned database contents and structure, search and display commands, and methods of user instruction. The most frequently used systems and databases are easy to remember, but staff have to relearn the lesser-used files each time they are used.

Tools are placed at each workstation for user support. These include a brief guide explaining important search commands, the producer's search manual, and a thesaurus, if appropriate. However, many users require help in the formulation of sound search strategy and with understanding the bibliographic citations they retrieve from the databases.

Our experience is that CD-ROM products, despite help screens, documentation, and the best efforts of programmers, are not self-explanatory for most users. Efficient search methods need to be taught and misconceptions concerning database content and scope dispelled. These concepts are taught both at the Reference Desk and as part of the library's instruction program. The latter includes both course-related training on individual databases and "open" workshops which cover generic search skills for both CD-ROM and remote databases.

The presence of the CDs has had noticeable effects on services. Users' needs for help with database selection and system operation have led to a steady increase in reference desk traffic. Easy identification of educational documents in the ERIC CD-ROM database can be tied to a large increase in use of the library's ERIC microfiche collection. CD database searching has increased demand for interlibrary loans. Mediated searches of databases now provided on CD-ROM have decreased significantly. The most heavily used databases for mediated searches are now BIOSIS and CAB Abstracts. As these databases are made available on CD-ROM at Mann we expect the level of mediated searches to decrease even more markedly.

CD-ROM Evaluation

Mann Library conducted an evaluation study in April of 1987, in which a CD-ROM system was compared to its printed equivalent, and students who had received formal instruction in CD-ROM use were compared to students who had received no instruction. Test groups performed assigned searches, and their search results were analyzed to determine number of relevant references located and average minutes needed to find each relevant reference. Results indicated that users of ERIC on CD-ROM found more relevant references, more quickly, than users of the printed index. Instruction in the use of ERIC on CD-ROM improved student performance, while instruction in the use of the printed index had little effect. Students expressed an overwhelming preference for the CD-ROM database (Stewart, 1988).

Mann Library is now comparing interfaces to CD-ROM databases. Until recently IBM PC and compatible microcomputers running search-and-retrieval software in a DOS environment have been the standard for CD-ROM searching systems. Lately, CD-ROM search-and-retrieval systems for the Apple Macintosh have begun to appear. As part of a major hardware grant received from Apple Computer in 1988, and with the assistance of SilverPlatter, Mann Library is assessing user response to IBM PC-based and Macintosh-based CD-ROM systems. Our goal in this evaluation is to identify those aspects of a textual interface and those of a combined textual and graphic interface which are preferred by users.

Challenges for the Future

We have summarized the reasons for the appeal of CD-ROM in the academic library: they have powerful search and retrieval capabilities, are relatively easy to use, and are convenient. They enable libraries to offer end-user access to databases for a fixed, or at least predictable, cost. Along with these advantages have come some issues whose resolution will affect the future of CD-ROM in the electronic library. These include:

Access Improvement

Single-user, single database workstations are still the most common access arrangement for CD-ROM resources in academic libraries. Dissatisfaction with this arrangement is growing, however. Users of large databases such as MEDLINE and Agricola have grown weary of the constant need to swap discs and repeat searches in order to search a range of years. In libraries where advance reservations are necessary for the use of popular CD-ROM databases, the need for access by more than one user at a time is acute. Finally, scholars expect electronic resources to be available at their workstations and wonder why trips to the library are necessary to use CD-ROM systems. The development of networked CD-ROM systems, where multiple discs from disparate CD-ROM vendors can be searched by several users at once from scholars' workstations, will allow this format to occupy a niche in the electronic library.

Interface Enhancement

Interfaces to CD-ROM databases have improved markedly over the past four years. Most CD-ROM interfaces now feature powerful search capabilities and built-in user assistance. These interfaces are far from perfect, however. The large number of CD-ROM questions received by reference staff indicates that many users do not find these systems self-explanatory. Users of CD-ROM systems perform better after they have had some instruction (Stewart, 1988). By conducting research in the field on user reaction to these systems, libraries can identify areas most in need of improvement by vendors. At the same time, vendors must continue their efforts to improve CD-ROM interfaces.

Format Selection

One particularly important challenge is choosing the best configuration of resources to meet user needs, as more databases are produced on CD which are also available in magnetic form for local access and as remote online databases. The Agricola database is a good example of this challenge. It is available in CD-ROM format from several competing companies, with interface software for both Apple Macintoshes and IBM PC compatibles. The database can also be acquired on magnetic tape to be installed on local mainframe computers, and is available online from various commercial database vendors. Much of it is also available as the printed *Bibliography of Agriculture*. Which option is best? It is likely that, for a library serving a heterogeneous population, no single option will meet all users' needs.

There seems little doubt that optical discs in some form will continue to increase in importance as storage options. Libraries have come a long way in a short time in their use of this technology. Ten years ago, Charles Goldstein of the National Library of Medicine spoke to a group of medical librarians, discussing the possibility of distributing the MEDLINE database on laser disks. At that time, MEDLINE was available online from two computer vendors: the National Library of Medicine and BRS. The database, like other online bibliographic databases, was searched almost exclusively by search intermediaries, and only via complex command languages.

At that meeting, Mr. Goldstein stood in a spotlight in a darkened room, holding a shiny rainbow-hued laser disk the size of an LP record. He predicted the widespread availability of MEDLINE and other databases on optical disc. The audience was interested by the possibility, but many were unsure of the practicality or the need for this distribution option. Mr. Goldstein's predictions were greeted with general disbelief. Now, a decade later, MEDLINE and a host of other databases, bibliographic, full text, and numeric, are available on small optical discs. End-user access, to these and other formats, has become more common than mediated searches of command-driven systems.

> There is no doubt that the computing environment of the future will consist of workstations on individual desks, linked to a campus network that provides resources to meet most of the general computing and information needs of the scholar. The campus network will also be the gateway to more specialized resources around the country and even across the world. However, in a changing technological context there is no clear pattern as to which resources will be housed on campus, or available through national networks.
>
> (Arms, 1989)

There is also no clear indication as to which will be the primary storage formats in the electronic library. In order for CD-ROM to find a place at the scholar's workstation, technological limitations must be overcome. In any case, Mann will continue its development of an electronic library, in which the CD-ROM format will be evaluated as one option among many.

References

Arms, Caroline. 1989. "Libraries and Electronic Information: The Technological Context, Part Two." *Educom Review* 24 (3):43.

Bush, Vannevar. 1945. "As We May Think." *Atlantic Monthly* 176(1):101–108.

Coons, Bill and Linda Stewart. 1988 "Mainstreaming CD-ROM into Library Operations." *Laserdisk Professional* 1(3)8:29-40.

Stewart, Linda and Jan Olsen. 1988. "Compact Disk Databases: Are They Good for Users?" *Online* 12(3):48-52.

Susan Barnes has been Head of Public Services at Cornell University's Albert R. Mann library since January, 1989. She has also held positions at Columbia University's Augustus C. Long Health Sciences Library, the Louise Darling Biomedical Library at UCLA, and the National Library of Medicine. She has a B.S. in horticulture from Washington State University and received her M.L.S. from the University of Washington School of Librarianship.

Edwin Spragg has been Information Services Coordinator for Mann Library since 1982 and Entomology Librarian since 1983. He received his B.A. degree from Washington and Jefferson College and M.L.S. from the University of Pittsburgh. He also earned an M.A. in history from the University of Pittsburgh. Before joining the Public Services staff Ed was Order Librarian in the Acquisitions Division of Mann Library. Prior to that he was on the staff of the Cornell Law Library.

7

Using Read-Only Optical Media in the Department of Information Science Library, University of Milan, Italy

Gian Carlo Dalto

This case study will describe the library's facilities, its experience with automation, production of a union catalog on CD, the "CD-teca" facility for public access, and experiments in multi-user access.

Institutional Background

In April 1984, the Department of Information Science was founded with the aim of providing coordination and support to the degree program in computer science at the "Università degli Studi" of Milan. The community showed more and more interest in this discipline and the University began to receive applications from outside the university. This led to the establishment of an open enrollment system, with an internal organization which does more than support the exclusive, privileged few of the academic world. Milan's educational opportunities and facilities are also available to the general public, experts in the field, and subject researchers.

Library Facilities

The Library of the Department, the Biblioteca di Informatica, was formally established at the same time as the Department; prior to that date, the library was a small specialized branch of the main Institute. Within a few years it developed into a library that met the instructional and research needs of degree-granting courses, and is the only specialized library in the field of computer science in Milan. At present, it is expanding in terms of both the quality and quantity of available documents.

The Biblioteca Informatica is managed by the Librarian, with the assistance of three colleagues. The Department's Director, Professor G. Degli Antoni, strongly supports the library, and each year several students volunteer their time and expertise to assist with various automation projects. In addition, some dissertations done at the University have focused on library automation.

The library serves the Department's approximately 6,000 students, 50 teaching and research faculty, and many freelance technicians. It has also become an important reference point for everyone in Milan who, at different levels, is interested in computer science. As a consequence of some interesting initiatives—

leadership in the development of a CD-ROM scientific library union catalog and the use of UNIX for the online catalog—the library is recognized as a leading innovator throughout Italy.

These statistics, recorded in May 1989, describe the library's collections: material holdings consist of 9,800 monographs, including 1,118 microfilm dissertations from foreign universities; 1,267 proceedings; 6,842 volumes of periodicals (218 current titles); 11 databases on CD-ROM; and several instructional software packages and self-instructional training courses for IBM PC and Macintosh personal computers.

Services and products offered include mediated online searching of bibliographic databases, personal computer self-instructional training courses, research assistance, an in-house online catalog of 260,000 items, and CD-ROMs, including a union catalog of science library holdings. Research projects underway include a graphics interface between UNIX and Macintosh, and an interface between UNIX and the CD-ROMs.

Philosophy

The activities related to the handling of bibliographic information have to take into consideration the expansion of computer science methodologies and the technological development which is necessary for their achievement. In Italy, however, the few specialized courses in "library science" are based on a substantially humanistic/literary approach, which totally neglects this philosophy.

Support for this philosophy is to be found in the changing information needs of the specialized scientific, technological and industrial communities. As a consequence of the considerable increase in scientific literature, the value of secondary information has increased. Library service has to find the appropriate tools to satisfy these needs.

Failure to apply the appropriate tools means that the profession will run the risk of inadequately addressing and answering users' information needs. It will also favor an ill-aimed policy of self-centered collections and duplication of access, with a resulting waste of financial resources (thus lowering a library's cost/benefit ratio).

Automation within the Library

Since the establishment of the library, we have chosen to automate and experiment with new computer-science technologies—to offer the best possible service, to compensate for the lack of staff and money, and to keep a direct link with the research activities of our Department. Experimentation with CD-ROM and other information technologies naturally falls within this philosophy.

The Electronic Catalog

The library is responsible for its own software development and has developed its own computerized catalog for the management and circulation of materials. This automation project involved creating a 260,000 item database and was completed in-house with the assistance of students who coded the programs. A "mini"

Honeywell-Bull X-40 computer, with 600MB of storage, houses the database and runs under the UNIX System V operating system. The database management software used is UNIFY release 4.0. Two serial ports are available for dial-in connection by users of the Department's local area network.

In the library's reading room, which seats 120, terminals are available for accessing the catalog and for loan or reference requests. All three of these procedures are fully automated and operate without help from the library staff.

The catalog user interface is a "friendly" menu-driven system, with lots of options even novices can use. The procedures relating to circulation are particularly appropriate; they reliably suit a heterogeneous audience and minimize red tape.

At present, the electronic catalog contains 105,320 article and book titles and 161,200 authors (these have been gleaned from collected works, proceedings, and congress papers). To date, we have entered 35,770 headings, and the catalog will soon contain a list of the library's magazines.

Rationale for CDs

Information science methodologies and automated technology can considerably improve information access and retrieval, especially in comparison with traditional paper systems. A good retrieval system, when added to a personal computer, can reduce searching time and increase search efficiency.

Since 1980, technological developments have made the following possible: more powerful, smaller computers at lower prices; high performance peripherals; sophisticated software packages; optical mass storage, which can store, at competitive costs, different kinds of information such as images, text, and sound; and user-friendly interfaces. Rapid technological developments will soon result in optical memories of over 1 terabyte (compared to the present 1 or 2GB).

Small libraries compete directly with vendors or specialized services for end-users. Online information services provide good bibliographic information, and in the last few years some end-users have elected to directly access and use these new technologies.

The use of CD-ROM is not confined to the commercial world. Since CDs are becoming so important for the distribution of bibliographic information, it could be said that the library is becoming the "natural Aristotelian place" for CD-ROMs. In fact, they make it easier for the librarian to solve problems such as space planning and the handling of heterogeneous materials. CD-ROM also promotes the exchange of documents and bibliographic information between different libraries. CD-ROM can solve old problems too, such as aggregating gray literature into one source and substituting for microforms.

For those reasons we chose CD-ROM but we also took into consideration the Italian information marketplace. Italy, unlike many other countries, does not have a long standing tradition of online information systems or library networks. For this reason, and others, Italy is second only to the United States for the production and distribution of material on CD-ROM and for the number of drives sold.

The Union Catalog of the Scientific Libraries

It is possible for the library to use CD-ROM to produce applications in-house, instead of relying on existing market applications. The union catalog was the result of collaboration between the Faculty of Science of the University of Milan and some of the scientific libraries of private research institutes.

Given the high price of an online catalog and its possible incompatibility with the systems of individual libraries, we chose CD-ROM for four main reasons: 1) it uses a well known technology with standard operating systems (which makes it possible to implement database management systems); 2) production costs are low: the price to produce 150 copies of the disc was about 13,000,000 lire (including the costs of pre-mastering and the royalties paid for the utilization of the information retrieval software), and there were no data entry costs, thanks to the cooperation of the participating libraries and their pre-existing machine-readable databases; 3) it operates even on micro-systems used by small libraries, which can afford to pay the low price of the basic workstation; and 4) data are physically impressed on the disc so there is no risk of damaging the data by an improper use of the computer.

Ninety percent of our books are published by American publishers, so we purchased BiblioFile's LC MARC records. To speed the updating and data entry process, we transferred the pertinent bibliographic MARC records from BiblioFile to a hard disk. The remaining records were entered by hand. The MARC format is not compatible, for the moment, with the format of our database; consequently problems with record transfer have temporarily put an end to this process, and BiblioFile is now only used to produce bibliographic cards for the paper catalog, which is still kept in the library as a back-up for bibliographic searches.

We took particular care developing the user interface, omitting tedious manuals and allowing an intermediate approach suitable for novice users. All operations are determined from easily readable menus, with help available at any moment. One key selects the commands to prevent any keying error (mistakes are pointed out by an error message).

The present version was developed for the MS-DOS environment and distributed to various libraries for testing at the beginning of the year. We are also evaluating the costs of conversion to the Apple Macintosh microcomputer environment. Tests have proven the validity of the procedures, and evaluation has shown that the interface is easy to use. Query response times were satisfactory, most being on the order of a few seconds.

Our prototype stores, at the moment, 30,000 records of monographs and periodicals. Organizing the data bank took six months, including the acquisition of the data from the different libraries. The first release is an experiment and will be followed by a second, more complete release (work is presently in progress).

The union catalog has become a useful reference tool for the libraries which are located in different buildings, and it is used by members of the scientific community because of the interdisciplinary nature of their research. Smaller libraries with limited resources are able to use the collective catalog to offer researchers more information than previously possible. It has also been useful for collection development and planning the acquisition of new materials.

The "CD-teca" of the Library

The standardization of file format by the High Sierra Proposal and its subsequent adoption by the International Standards Organization made it possible for us to establish a CD-ROM service. With consistent handling and hardware configurations established, we were ready to acquire products and to establish a new service for our users.

The creation of the CD-teca went through an experimental phase with the purchase of a number of discs in 1986. Prior to that date, we acquired BiblioFile's LC MARC records on CD-ROM; it was seen as an opportunity to get to know this medium and to study the possibility of integration with the library's information system.

Our library owns a considerable number of publications on CD-ROM. The selector reviews bulletins, directories, specialized magazines, and various promotional materials from database producers and distributors for CDs to purchase.

During the experimental period, we purchased our first major database and created the first PC CD-ROM workstation (for the consultation of four databases). Presently, the hardware consists of six Hitachi drives (five are model 1503s and one is a model 1502s), three IBM PC-compatibles (one Olivetti M24, one Unisys 3137 and one Ready 640), and one Macintosh SE. The first dedicated CD-ROM workstation has recently been created and placed in the reading room. It consists of a PC and four CD-ROM drives connected in a daisy-chain configuration.

CD-ROM databases which are currently available include: CD-ROM Multilingua: video dizionario (Zanichelli, 1987), Dissertation Abstracts OnDisc 1985–1988 (UMI, 1988), McGraw-Hill Science and Technical Reference Set (McGraw-Hill, 1988), Leggi d'Italia (De Agostini, 1989), Videoenciclopedia Einaudi (plus updates) (Kronos Europea, 1988), Catalogo delle Biblioteche Scientifiche (University of Milan in collaboration with De Agostini publisher, 1989), MathSci Disc (SilverPlatter, 1989), and The business of CD-ROM: Conference Proceedings, Roma 1987 (Eikon, 1988). Forthcoming CD-ROM titles are: Computer Library Abstracted Periodicals (Computer Library, 1989), The Oxford English Dictionary on CD-ROM (Oxford Electronic Pub., 1989), and the World Atlas (Electromap, 1989). Of all of these tools, the two which are used most often are Dizionario multilingua and Leggi d'Italia. MathSci Disc, a current arrival, is available in both an MS-DOS and Macintosh version. It will probably become one of our most frequently used discs.

Documentation and Instruction

The impact of CDs on the public has not been traumatic, and after patrons' first curious approaches, the obvious usefulness of this medium has become apparent. Certainly the users' behavior has been affected by their prior experiences with computerized systems. Their continued facility with the computer has obviated the need for any form of software or database training. The same applies to library staff. The option of learning the various methodologies through practice has been left to the users, who, in case of need, also had at their disposal the relevant manuals and direct access to the library staff. Very few users have approached staff for assistance, and then only on a few occasions (mainly in the early operative phases). It is our experience that most commercially available CD-ROM products were user-friendly and after a short time of practice it has rarely been necessary for users to use a manual. The English manuals were not a problem; however, in an attempt to assist all kinds of patrons, the tutorial has been translated into Italian.

CD-ROM Administration and Management

Although subscriptions to CD-ROM publications are quite expensive, users are charged only for printing the results of their search. We do not charge for the computer consultation. To consult the CD-ROMs no formalities are needed; it is necessary only to make an appointment for the use of the computer. CD-ROMs connected to the workstation are available to the public whenever the library is open.

For security reasons, the personal computer's system boxes are not kept in the reading room, but are in the office inside the library under the direct control of the staff; users have access only to the keyboard and monitor. An especially adapted keyboard can be used by the public for consultation.

The workstation consists of an IBM PC compatible Ready 640 with a color monitor and 20 MB hard disk, four Hitachi drives and cables, a Hitachi controller card (CDIF 25-A2), a MS-DOS operating system, release 3.1, MS-DOS CD-ROM Extensions, and the juke-box software.

The software for the juke-box installation is a batch file which combines various MS-DOS commands and allows access to the four drives. It retrieves the search software, stored on the hard disk, through a main menu selection of the requested database. This personal computer is dedicated to the CDs; to use the computer for other purposes or to change its configuration, you have to reboot the system.

Multi-User Access: CD-ROM in the Unix Environment

The limitations of CD-ROM's one-disc, one-user environment has promoted the development of numerous applications, mainly in the MS-DOS environment. For the CD-ROM market, the implementation of multi-user access is essential. It would increase the number of potential users and consequently, the spread of CD-ROM technology. This scenario might eventually reduce high purchase and drive prices.

The successful integration of CD-ROMs into a multi-user environment has occurred in our library because of cooperation on a thesis degree project between the BULL Italia and the Department of Computer Science. The objective of the project was to integrate the CD-ROM into a UNIX environment by the creation of a device driver.

The choice of UNIX was deliberate. It is the perfect environment for software development because it is hardware independent and the developed software is easily exported to different machines. For these reasons UNIX is becoming an operating system standard for mini- and micro-computers (and perhaps for the next generation of personal computers). It is a multi-user and multi-tasking system and it has a large variety of applications. These qualities make it one of the most popular operating systems in the university environment. In fact, as already mentioned, our library has its own UNIX machine.

The device driver we have developed is a software module which allows the kernel of UNIX to control the CD-ROM driver. Its main purpose is to perform all the necessary operations so that a peripheral will correctly execute the I/O requests of the kernel. In our case, the CD-ROM drives have to access the stored data as a sequence of blocks. Because of the diversity between the CD-ROM file format (i.e., High Sierra format) and the UNIX file system, the device driver could not read files present on CD-ROM. Therefore it needed an interface tool capable of making the High Sierra file compatible with the peculiarities of the UNIX files. A study of the hardware functions of the drive and of the related controller SCSI was completed to solve the problems of connecting the CD-ROM drive and the UNIX machine.

The device driver was modified by inserting functions which make the CD-ROM file structure look the same as that of a file system of UNIX. In this way, the CD-ROM appears to the kernel of UNIX as a hard disk, allowing applications to use standard UNIX system calls to access files resident on the CD-ROM. This solution means that any ordinary user program can use the CD-ROM in the same way as it uses a normal file system of UNIX.

The test phase used two disks in High Sierra standard with identical information retrieval software. The results confirmed our expectations. It will now be possible to run more and more CD-ROM applications on UNIX machines, opening a new arena for this medium. We will soon analyze the feasibility of integrating the existing UNIX based library information system with CD-ROM, including the CD-ROM multi-user access facility.

Conclusions

Our library's experiments with this new medium have confirmed its value. In our opinion, its application is well suited to the academic world, particularly as a way to distribute bibliographic information that is not time-sensitive. CD-ROM can also help solve space problems and problems in the storage of non-conventional material (e.g., software, technical manuals, and gray literature).

The ability of CDs to handle multimedia, its interactive strengths, and its random access search features make it a valid alternative to micrography. At present, information which is online is an irreplaceable resource. One can hope that the future will deliver more integration between databases on optical disk and those online. Optical media are becoming very important for document delivery, particularly given the possibility of full-text and the projects being promoted and financed by international organizations (e.g., project ADONIS).

The arrival of hypertext further widens the horizon of the optical memories. In particular, the integration between multimedia records, made possible by optical technology, and the linking power of hypertext, offer unexplored prospects. The library can be seen as a huge electronic, interactive book, an artificial reality which allows users to navigate it using associative procedures which partially reproduce mental mechanisms, putting in action semantic links which overcome traditional barriers to knowledge transfer.

Problems with CD-ROM are the issue of standards, the lack of a common interface, and their high subscription costs. While the acceptance of the High Sierra format helps, it will be a number of years before we achieve a truly international, multimedia standard. Very often, users complain about the lack of interface standardization for information retrieval. A good interface should offer, other than a real independence from the existing operating system, the opportunity to use different applications through a single user interface.

There is a controversy of sorts on prices. Producers of CD-ROM drives blame publishers for the high costs; publishers blame the poor distribution of drives for the unexpanding market. These factors should not be ignored, and one can hopefully expect that in the near future publishers of CD-ROM products and producers of hardware will seriously reconsider their economic policies. Government institutions should also show more interest in supporting the production and diffusion of CD-ROM publications.

To get over this impasse and push the publishers in the right direction, it is very important for librarians to overcome their cultural biases and abandon their steadfast reliance on the irreplaceability of the paper document.

Gian Carlo Dalto graduated with a degree in philosophy from the University of Milan. At present he is the Librarian of the Library of the Department of Information Science of the University of Milan. He is the leader of the library automation project and he coordinates the publication of the scientific library's union catalog on CD-ROM.

8

New Approaches to Access: CD-ROM at the St. Louis University Medical Center Library

T. Scott Plutchak

In the spring of 1987, a book titled *CD-ROM, the New Papyrus* (Lambert, 1986) was circulated among several staff members at the St. Louis University Medical Center Library (MCL). For many this was their first in-depth look at a technology that held great promise. Now, two years later, the library has had considerable experience with some CD-ROM based systems, and while the promise of this technology remains great, it is tempered by a healthy dose of realistic skepticism and a clearer understanding of the complex issues involved.

The Environment

The St. Louis University Medical Center Library (MCL) serves all of the programs of the Medical Center including the School of Medicine, School of Nursing, School of Allied Health Professions, Center for Health Services Education and Research, Department of Orthodontics, Center for Health Care Ethics and the University Hospital. The population served includes undergraduate and graduate nursing students, public and allied health students, medical students, researchers in a variety of health care fields (everything from transplantation to AIDS), and clinicians treating patients. These different groups have a wide variety of information needs, but what binds them together is that they need the very latest information and they need it right away.

The MCL's primary service points, along with its book and journal collections, are housed in the Learning Resources Center (LRC) on the Medical Center campus. The MCL's Educational Media Department, which houses audiovisual and microcomputer services, is located in the School of Nursing Building, across the street from the LRC. Since 1985, under the leadership of Judith Messerle, the library has pursued an aggressive strategy aimed at achieving the broadest possible range of cost-effective information access services.

As is the case in many libraries, automation efforts have proceeded piecemeal. Prior to 1988, the MCL had no online public access catalog, no end-user searching of databases, and no automated circulation or acquisitions. Although some planning efforts have been undertaken, the MCL is still several years away from a fully integrated automated library system. Since 1985 the MCL has been cataloging on OCLC. It uses the PHILSOM system (Periodical Holdings in Libraries of Schools of Medicine) for serials control and participates in several online interlibrary loan networks. The reference department accesses a wide variety of databases for its diverse clientele, with MEDLINE use accounting for over ninety percent of all online access.

As CD-ROM products began to be widely available to the library community, the MCL investigated the possibility of applying this technology to some of the library's automation concerns. The MCL sees its mission as involving both the provision of access to information and support for the development of life-long learning skills, and in both of these areas the CD-ROM products coming to market appeared to provide the means for the Library to take concrete steps toward fulfilling its mission. The library has taken advantage of the CD-ROM format to provide access to the MEDLINE database, the public access catalog and the Missouri Union List. The timeline for this process is presented in the Appendix.

The National Library of Medicine's CD-ROM MEDLINE Evaluation

The MCL's first major opportunity to gain hands-on experience with CD-ROM came when it was approached by the National Library of Medicine (NLM) to participate in an evaluation of CD-ROM MEDLINE products. MEDLINE is the most important online information resource in any academic medical library, and online searches account for a substantial portion of the library's budget. Clients are currently charged for searches, but on a sliding scale which provides a substantial subsidy to Medical Center students and faculty.

NLM had been negotiating since 1986 with a number of vendors who were interested in developing CD-ROM versions of the MEDLINE database. The results of these negotiations were a series of leasing agreements which allowed NLM to retain a certain measure of control over the integrity of the database, and which also mandated participation in a systematic evaluation of all the MEDLINE products generated by the different vendors.

In essence, each vendor agreed to place its product in three libraries of NLM's choice for an evaluation to be run by the individual libraries under the guidance of NLM. The libraries invited to participate were chosen in the summer and fall of 1987 and equipment was scheduled to arrive in the spring of 1988.

Between the time that the MCL was initially approached to participate in the NLM study and the time that the equipment and systems arrived, two other CD-ROM products were evaluated: Cambridge Abstracts CD-ROM MEDLINE and MICROMEDEX. Although they were examined for their own sakes, the experience did provide the MCL with some useful experiences prior to the NLM study.

Cambridge and MICROMEDEX

There are a number of significant differences between these two systems. Cambridge MEDLINE is, of course, entirely bibliographic in nature and is a simple extension of the sorts of reference materials libraries have had in place for years. It was possible to explain the system to patrons by referring to *Index Medicus* and other paper indexes with which they were likely to be familiar. MICROMEDEX is a completely different product. The system is composed of three major subsystems, DRUGDEX, POISONDEX and EMERGINDEX, each of which may be obtained separately. These components contain a great deal of information on individual drugs, poison reactions and treatment, and emergency procedures, respectively. Whereas MEDLINE is primarily a research tool, designed to lead the user to particular items in the published literature, MICROMEDEX is an informational tool designed to give specific answers to specific questions, without the questioner needing to go to additional sources.

The library obtained Cambridge Abstracts CD-ROM MEDLINE first, and on a trial basis. (Cambridge was one of the companies participating in the NLM study, but as the first vendor to come to market with a MEDLINE product, it had been making systems available to libraries for evaluation for several months before the NLM study began.) At about the same time, the library also tested the MI-CROMEDEX system. Both systems were made available in the library for walk-up patrons for a period of several weeks. Users of the systems were asked to fill out a brief questionnaire.

Although both systems were well received by the users of the library, neither was purchased. We felt it was premature to select the only MEDLINE system we had looked at when we were getting ready to evaluate another one. In the case of MICROMEDEX, the price alone made it prohibitive, although it continues to occupy a prominent place on our wish list. The Hospital Pharmacy, which got its first exposure to MICROMEDEX through our evaluation, subsequently obtained the system for its own use.

BRS Colleague Disc

In March 1988, the library received the necessary equipment and software from BRS Information Technologies to participate in the NLM study. Full results of the library's study, along with reports from the 20 other test sites, appear in the proceedings of the evaluation forum which was held at the National Library of Medicine in September 1988 (Carlin, 1989). The essential details of the MCL's evaluation are described below.

One workstation was set up in the library near the circulation desk where it was immediately visible to all persons entering. Signs were posted at the entrance to the library announcing: Free MEDLINE Searching! A brief announcement was included in the Library's newsletter.

No instructions were placed at the terminal other than the brief user guide provided by BRS. The CD-ROM discs were placed next to the terminal, as was a box of questionnaires. The Circulation staff, who would be the most likely target for questioners, were instructed to refer questions to the Reference staff or the Associate Director. These individuals maintained a written account of problems and concerns noted by people using the system. All users were encouraged to fill out questionnaires.

As a supplemental study, a workstation was set up in the conference room of the Internal Medicine department in the University Hospital for three weeks. The department is a five-minute walk from the library, so immediate, on-site assistance with the system was not available. As in the library installation, a brief instruction booklet and stack of questionnaires were placed next to the terminal. In addition, a sign was put up encouraging users to call the Reference Department for assistance. We received several calls and, when necessary, someone from the Reference Department would go immediately to the conference room. It is very likely, however, that this arrangement discouraged some people from seeking assistance when they ran into problems.

The results of the study raised a number of questions for the library. Among the 123 people who answered the questionnaire, the level of satisfaction was very high. Although we attempted to correlate level of satisfaction with actual problems encountered while using the system, we could find no significant differences among any groups of users in how they rated satisfaction. It did not seem to matter how well the system met someone's particular needs or even how easy they perceived its use to be—most users loved it.

The experiences of the librarians in helping users, however, made it clear that many people were seriously misusing the system. Inappropriate selection of terms, lack of understanding of the contents of the database, and awkward and excessively time-consuming search strategies were common. It became very clear to us that user satisfaction is not a reasonable guide to gauging whether or not the system is doing a good job of accurately meeting user needs (Plutchak, 1989).

These concerns on the part of the Library staff were even more acute in the case of the Internal Medicine portion of the evaluation. Although resistance to filling out questionnaires made it difficult for us to formally assess the experience of individuals using the system, the information we gathered informally made it clear that users of that system were having the same sorts of problems that we observed in the library. Unfortunately, the distance from the library meant that far fewer of those problems were addressed by librarians. Nonetheless, the indicated level of satisfaction remained high, even while the expressed levels of ease of use and adequate retrieval were lower.

Another interesting aspect of the Internal Medicine study was that we could find no evidence that having the system available in the conference room encouraged anyone to use it who would not have made the trip to the library to use it. Although we suspected that more onsite support would have had a greater effect in this area, we were forced to conclude that proximity alone was not a sufficient inducement to make greater use of the system. We are cautious in making that statement, however, given the short period of time during which our evaluation took place. We suspect that other institutions with similar situations may find very different results.

A great deal of discussion took place among the librarians concerning these issues. We felt that the level of user acceptance made subscription to a MEDLINE system mandatory. However, we also realized that considerable training and interaction with the users would be required for us to be assured that the ease of using the system was not misleading users concerning their results. As the library has moved ahead with CD-ROM applications, the experience gained during the NLM study has guided our thinking and shaped our implementation strategies.

MEDLINE

Configuration and Access Issues

As a result of the NLM evaluation, the library subscribed to two copies of the BRS Colleague Disc products. Two workstations have been set up in a study room near the circulation desk (printer noise made it necessary to isolate the workstations). The workstations consist of Intel 8088-based IBM clones (XT-Class) with monochrome screens, EPSON printers and Hitachi CD-ROM drives. In the study room are two complete sets of CD-ROM discs (1985 to the present) and several copies of the *Medical Subject Headings* (MeSH), the controlled vocabulary thesaurus used to index the MEDLINE database.

Since the MCL's public access computers are housed in the Educational Media Department (as mentioned above), there was some discussion as to the most appropriate location for the CD-ROM workstations. The final determination was that these systems are primarily reference tools and that it was more important that they be near the reference librarians, rather than located with the machines that are used for Computer Assisted Instruction and general computing.

In keeping with the MCL's philosophy of maximum access, we have put as few controls on use as possible. The workstations are available at all hours the library is open (generally 7:30 a.m. to 11:30 p.m.). All discs are kept with the workstations. We are aware that many libraries control access to the discs, for example, by keeping them on reserve. After consulting with BRS and being assured that replacement discs could be obtained at a nominal cost, we decided to leave them out in the open. After nearly a year we have had no problems with discs being damaged or stolen. The increased accessibility to the user makes it well worth the risk. We have experienced occasional problems with patrons putting the CD-ROM discs into the floppy disk drives, but, after putting a warning sign over the floppy drive itself, this problem has been nearly eliminated. (This sign is applied in such a way that the drive can still be used for downloading.)

No fees are charged for use of the systems. The questionnaire used during the NLM evaluation specifically asked about the willingness of users to pay a small fee. Although most users indicated they would be willing to pay a charge, we have determined that the costs of implementing reasonable charges are scarcely worth the increased revenue. The BRS subscription itself has been paid for out of the general acquisitions budget, absorbed by the library as are paper subscriptions. We are concerned about the funding issue, however, and continue to monitor the cost, leaving the possibility open for instituting some sort of charging mechanism in the future.

Use of the systems has been high, although it fluctuates widely and follows the ups and downs of the academic year. During most of the year, two workstations have met the demand fairly well, although there is occasional queuing. Requests for signup sheets occur from time to time, but we have resisted. Signup sheets raise policing problems as well as difficulties in handling no-shows or late arrivals. It has proven more effective to handle the occasional conflicts that arise between people using the systems and people waiting on an ad hoc basis.

The BRS subscription has not been timely. Updates were originally scheduled to be quarterly. The library's subscription was entered in June of 1988 and began with discs for 1985, 1986, 1987 and January–May 1988. In the late Fall of 1988 a January–August disc was received. No further update appeared until February of 1989, when the complete 1988 disc was received.

According to a series of letters from BRS to subscribers in March, April and May 1989, some of the delays were caused by the National Library of Medicine's requirement that each vendor completely remaster all of the CD-ROMs each year in order to account for changes made to the complete database. This last point should be emphasized since it affects all MEDLINE CD-ROM products. The National Library of Medicine goes through a complete "reprocessing" of its entire database every year. This is primarily due to annual changes in the MeSH vocabulary. Appropriate changes are made throughout the database going back to 1966. Additionally, NLM has been engaged in a project to "catch up" on indexing older material that it has missed for one reason or another over the years. When material from earlier years is indexed, the citations are loaded into the current file. At year-end processing, these citations are distributed into the appropriate backfiles. Thus the content and indexing of the entire 20-plus year database changes every year. NLM's insistence that all discs be remastered resulted in delays in BRS product delivery and the necessity that the subscription prices be raised. Notwithstanding this increase in price, the MCL approves strongly of this requirement since it maintains the integrity of the database.

Training and User Support

In general, the MEDLINE installations have been very successful. The biggest problem by far has been the matter of user training. There has been relatively little formal staff training: the Reference staff essentially trains each other, and other staff (principally Circulation staff) have been trained in small groups on an as-needed basis. The library's staff is small enough to make this approach practical. But dealing with user-training is much more complex.

As mentioned above, the MCL considers support of life-long learning skills to be an integral part of the library's mission. Consequently, we are concerned not only with teaching patrons to use a specific system, but with attempting to ensure that they gain some understanding of the fundamental principles involved, so that they will be able to take advantage of future developments throughout their careers.

We have observed that very few users read the online tutorial. Very few understand the structure or content of the database. Very few understand the difference between controlled vocabulary (MeSH) and keywords. These misunderstandings result in poor search strategies, inaccurate retrieval, missed citations and wasted time. Our biggest difficulty, however, has been in getting users to understand the depth of the problem. We are continually beseeched with requests to "tell me how to do it in five minutes" or to "put up a sign with the five steps I need for searching." The majority of people using our systems are health science students, and they seem to have much greater difficulties in this area than practicing health professionals who have a greater understanding of the literature and the terminology in their fields.

The following analogy has proved useful in our thinking about the problem. Consider a standard wordprocessing package like WordPerfect. Compare it to an end-user CD-ROM interface like BRS Colleague. On the software end, both packages consist of a finite number of commands, each of which performs a specific operation. It is possible to learn the use of the primary commands relatively quickly, and to master all of the commands with repeated use over a finite period of time. However, the user of WordPerfect comes to the software already having the ability to write—that is, having the abstract knowledge necessary for putting words into sentences, creating coherent paragraphs, and following a train of thought through a series of expository pages. No one imagines that the wordprocessing package makes this sort of fundamental knowledge unnecessary. On the searching side, we see that there is a similar body of knowledge, principally knowledge of the literature and terminology of the field itself, but also encompassing such principles as database structure, specificity of indexing, appropriate use of controlled vocabulary as opposed to keywords, and the methods a skilled searcher uses to emulate the thinking of the author of a paper in order to find the best way to retrieve it. These skills—the art of searching—are analogous to good writing skills. To think that we can teach good searching skills to someone who lacks an understanding of these areas by teaching them the use of a front-end system is as flawed as to think that an illiterate can write a good short-story simply by being taught the commands of WordPerfect.

The complicating factor, of course, is the question of what level of expertise is really required. Most patrons are able to retrieve useful information on their first try, even without using the "most appropriate" terms (be they keywords or controlled vocabulary), and with practice, they will become more proficient. In light of this, our training efforts concentrate on immediate problems rather than fundamentals. Most assistance to users is provided on a case-by-case basis. The members of the Circulation staff possess a basic knowledge of the system and can handle many queries. More complex questions are referred to the Reference staff who often spend a great deal of time with each user working through the problem.

Based on our observations of our patrons' behavior we have prepared few written training materials, preferring to rely on person-to-person interaction. We have held a series of come-as-you-can workshops designed to provide patrons with some training. Initially the workshops were biweekly, but are now held once each week. Attendance varies from none to five or more. The thrust of the workshops has changed over time, from an overview of fundamentals to a clinic-based approach that addresses specific search problems. Although the workshops are reaching an increasing number of patrons, most assistance is still provided on demand as user problems arise.

Since the systems have been implemented we are finding an increasing number of faculty members requiring their students to use the CDs. Sometimes we find out ahead of time and can arrange group training sessions; sometimes we find out only when the students arrive and start asking for help. We are actively encouraging the faculty to make us aware early in the process of any such plans they have so that we can ensure that the experience is productive and useful for the students.

During the NLM evaluation, we saw that the system appeared to bring in many users who had no previous experience with any sort of online searching. Consistent with that finding we have seen no decrease in the amount of searching being done by the reference librarians using the regular online systems. We have no formal data to explain this, but it appears that the availability of the CD-ROM systems has increased the awareness of online searching among our clientele in general. We found in our formal evaluation that a high percentage of people using the CD-ROM system had never had a mediated search. So while some people are doing more of their own searching, the total volume of all kinds of searching continues to increase, as does the number of searches done by reference staff. We suspect that this will also result in a shift in the kinds of searches being done by reference staff and hope to be able to study that more formally in the near future.

The Intelligent Catalog

While the MEDLINE product has occupied much of the library's attention and is the most obvious use of CD-ROM, it is not the only CD-ROM product in use. In January 1987, as the library was evaluating the results of its experiences with Cambridge MEDLINE and MICROMEDEX in preparation for the NLM evaluation, interest was raised on the St. Louis University campuses concerning the Intelligent Catalog. This is a CD-ROM based public access catalog being marketed by Library Corporation, a firm best known for Bibliofile, its CD-ROM cataloging product. Stimulated by the work of the Law Library, both the Pius XII Library (on the main campus) and the Medical Center Library entered into negotiations with Library Corporation to bring the Intelligent Catalog into all of the campus libraries. As a result of this process, five workstations were provided for the use of the MCL's clientele in February of 1989.

For a variety of reasons, the use of the Intelligent Catalog is significantly different from the MEDLINE product. For one thing, it is utterly inconsequential to the user that the storage medium is CD-ROM. The users have nothing to do with switching discs: they simply interact with a system.

The user-interface itself is relatively independent of the storage medium. One can easily imagine the same sort of user interface being developed for a system that relied on magnetic storage.

The search software used has been designed by Library Corporation strictly for use on its Intelligent Catalog and is relatively user-friendly. That is, most untrained users can get something out of the catalog without assistance, although many of the Catalog's features do require instruction to use well. Patrons can print a list of items found, sorted by call number, author or title. They cannot, however, download the results of their search to a floppy.

For the library, the main consequence of the use of CD-ROM in this product is that it makes it an affordable option. Library Corporation has effectively exploited the particular qualities of CD-ROM to come up with a product that can be successfully marketed to libraries with limited resources and medium-to-large collections. In the standard arrangement with Library Corporation, the library purchases the equipment outright, buying as many workstations as needed. Each workstation consists of an IBM-compatible microcomputer with internal CD-ROM drive, monitor, printer, specially designed keyboard and a cabinet designed to lock the computer away from the user. In the initial mastering process, all of the library's machine-readable records are mastered onto a CD-ROM disc. Since the MCL catalogs on OCLC, it has arranged to have a monthly tape sent directly from OCLC to Library Corporation. Library Corporation reformats the records and loads them onto a magnetic cartridge. The cartridge is sent to the library, which inserts it into the workstation. The software effectively interfiles the records on the cartridge and on the CD-ROM disc so that the newest records are searched along with the records on the CD. If a record has been changed, only the newer record (on the cartridge) is displayed. When the cartridge is full, a new CD-ROM is mastered. For this service the library pays a low monthly charge per workstation. This charge is set at a standard rate and is unaffected by the number of times a new CD-ROM needs to be mastered.

The advantages of this system are several: first and most important is that this technology, because of its relative low expense, enables the library to provide an automated public access catalog to its patrons before the planning for a fully integrated library system has been completed. This system provides the library with considerable flexibility in locating workstations: we currently have two near the Circulation desk adjacent to the card catalog (which will shortly be removed altogether), one near the Reference area, one in Technical Services and one in the Educational Media Department. Since the stations are completely independent and relatively portable, we can change the locations of the stations on a moment's notice. In addition, we can obtain additional workstations without being concerned about reconfiguring the system.

A further advantage is that several of the other campus libraries are now using the same system. Thus, a student who habitually uses the main campus library but has an occasional need to come to the Medical Center Library will find a familiar public access catalog. At present, only the holdings of the particular library in which the workstation is located can be accessed from each workstation. However, we may set up workstations in each library from which the holdings of all libraries can be searched. This will not be a true union catalog; however, it would take us one more step beyond our current capabilities.

From the perspective of integrated library automation, this system has many limitations: it cannot be updated more often than monthly; because the workstations are stand-alone units, they must each be updated individually; the system is not integrated with the rest of the library's operations; and the system does not allow for dial-up access. Library Corporation's long-range plans indicate an intent to develop an integrated library system built around CD-ROM based components. The MCL is currently evaluating the Circulation module. If fully implemented, this system would enable a client at an Intelligent Catalog workstation to retrieve circulation information about a desired item. However, the MCL is not yet convinced that Library Corporation's approach is the best one for all of the MCL's long-term automation needs, and we are aggressively pursuing other options.

Missouri Union List

Library Corporation is not the only vendor exploring the possibilities of a CD-ROM public access catalog, and it is through another product, LePac (by Brodart), that the MCL participates in the Missouri Union List project. The Missouri State Library has contracted with Brodart to produce a set of CD-ROMs which contain the monograph holdings, in union catalog format, of over 200 academic and public libraries from around the state. The CD-ROMs are searchable using the LePac software. The State Library has provided the disc sets and software free-of-charge to each of the participating libraries.

Although the MCL has had the system in-house for several months, it has received very little use for a variety of reasons. The system was designed primarily as an interlibrary loan tool. Medical libraries in the St. Louis area participate in two very sophisticated online interlibrary loan systems: PHILNET, which is run in a consortium-type arrangement through Washington University and serves the greater St. Louis area, and DOCLINE, run by the National Library of Medicine and operating throughout the country. Virtually all of the MCL's interlibrary loan needs can be met through these systems (plus a moderate amount of OCLC ILL subsystem use) and there has therefore been little incentive for the Interlibrary Loan staff to use the Missouri Union List. Secondly, while it would be useful for some of the library's clients to be able to have holdings information for other libraries in the St. Louis area (e.g., Washington University and the University of Missouri-St. Louis), the MCL has been unwilling to make the system publicly accessible. With both the Intelligent Catalog and BRS MEDLINE currently in use, the Missouri Union List would be one more system to learn and would lead to additional confusion on the part of a user population still struggling with the differences between the two systems already available. In addition, the LePac software still suffers from a number of serious bugs that make it potentially frustrating and/or misleading for the user. For these reasons we have tended to make limited use of the system and this use is only by librarians to answer specific questions. We will probably make more extensive use of the system on this basis in the future, but it is still a very open question as to whether we will make it available for patron access at any time in the near future.

Future Plans

CD-ROM planning for the immediate future at the MCL is concentrated into two areas; first, we are continuing to assess the state of the market with regard to MEDLINE products. Currently, there are eight vendors of MEDLINE CD-ROM products, each with a different approach, although none of the systems presents an ideal solution for all of our needs. However, the amount of competition this engenders has led the vendors to be extremely responsive to requests from libraries. Due to the update problems with BRS, the MCL decided to switch systems when the BRS subscription came due in May 1989. We have taken out subscriptions to the CD+ version of MEDLINE which offers a number of advantages over BRS: quicker updates, expert and novice modes, and the fact that the full database goes back to 1966. At the time of this writing we have not received the new software, but are planning for the transition.

One of the great advantages of CD-ROM technology in general is that the financial and equipment considerations are such that one need not be "locked-in" to a particular system once an initial purchase has been made. It is still possible to respond to the rapidly changing environment as necessary.

Secondly, we continue to look at additional products for their potential use in the library. The MCL has ordered the CINAHL (Current Index to Nursing and Allied Health) CD-ROM product and will make that available during early fall of 1989. This system provides access to nursing and allied health literature beyond that provided through MEDLINE.

In evaluating various products, one of the key elements of concern is the disparity of search interfaces. As alluded to in the discussion of both the Intelligent Catalog and the Missouri Union List, the MCL perceives serious problems in introducing multiple products requiring multiple methods of searching. We are acutely aware that many of our library users are very inefficient and ineffective searchers when using the end-user systems that exist. Adding to the number of search interfaces available will only exacerbate our training problems. For this reason, we anticipate mounting the CINAHL system on a separate workstation rather than attempting to set up a menu system that would enable users to switch between it and MEDLINE on the same computer.

On the equipment end, we will be upgrading the workstations for the MEDLINE CD-ROM to Intel 80286-based (AT-Class) computers with EGA color screens. We have found the difference in speed between the machines we are now using and the more powerful computers to be substantial.

Conclusions

CD-ROM technology has enabled the library to make services available in a cost-effective manner. However, we do not see the technology as a panacea. In fact, it has heightened our awareness of the multitude of problems the library faces with the introduction of all end-user systems, whether they make use of CD-ROM technology or not. The fact that this technology seems to encourage "splintering" of services having different user interfaces rather than integration of services with a shared user interface makes our concern even more acute.

The primary impact on the staff has been the increased demand for training and assistance. While the introduction of CD-ROM MEDLINE has not lessened the demand for pre-existing reference services, it has placed a very heavy demand on the reference librarians and the circulation staff to assist users as needed. Occasionally this demand leads to considerable stress and frustration. One of our reference librarians has spoken of the conflict she feels, on occasion, between her desire to help teach someone to make good use of the MEDLINE CD-ROM system and her desire to simply do it herself when she knows she can provide the search much more quickly and accurately. These issues have led the library to serious consideration of establishing user education positions that would enable some of the staff to specialize in training issues.

Continuing advances in computing power and storage media indicate that CD-ROM technology is likely to undergo significant transformations over the next several years. Our interest in total integration of library automation/management has certainly not been decreased by the use of this technology and we are not convinced that CD-ROM has yet established its long-term role in this development. However, CD-ROM technology has allowed us to greatly increase the range of services available while allowing us to retain a great deal of flexibility in planning. The goal of achieving more options for information access continues to drive our decision-making, and CD-ROM is likely to remain a viable option for the immediate future.

References

Carlin, Beth, Suzy Conway, Kathy Gallagher, Linda Hulbert, and T. Scott Plutchak. 1989. "Evaluation of BRS/Colleague CD-ROM MEDLINE in an academic medical center library and in a clinical setting." In *MEDLINE on CD-ROM: National Library of Medicine Evaluation Forum*, ed. Rose Marie Woodsmall, Becky Lyon-Hartmann, and Elliot Siegel. Medford, N.J.: Learned Information.

Lambert, Steve, and Suzanne Ropiequet, eds. 1986. *CD ROM: The new papyrus: The current and future state of the art*. Redmond Wa.: Microsoft.

Plutchak, T. Scott. 1989. "On the Satisfied and Inept End User." *Medical Reference Services Quarterly* 8(1): 45–8.

T. Scott Plutchak has been Associate Director of the Medical Center Library at St. Louis University since 1987. Prior to that he was at the National Library of Medicine, first as an NLM Library Associate and then as a Technical Information Specialist in the Bibliographic Services Division. He received a B.A. in Philosophy from the University of Wisconsin-Milwaukee, and an M.A. in Library Science from the University of Wisconsin-Oshkosh.

Appendix

Timeline:
Introduction of CD-ROM at the St. Louis University Medical Center Library

Mar 87 MCL staff begin gathering information about CD-ROM applications.

May 87 Initial contact from NLM re: willingness to participate in CD-ROM MEDLINE evaluation.

Nov 87 MCL begins six-week evaluation of Cambridge CD-ROM MEDLINE and MICROMEDEX.

Dec 87 Formal invitation from NLM to participate in evaluation.

Feb 88 MCL begins to investigate suitablilty of Library Corporation's Intelligent Catalog.

Mar 88 MCL receives software, discs and equipment from BRS for evaluation.

Apr 88 BRS MEDLINE evaluation begins.

Jun 88   Data-gathering for BRS MEDLINE evaluation is completed. MCL subscribes to BRS MEDLINE.

Sep 88   Report of BRS MEDLINE evaluation is made at NLM's Evaluation Forum. MCL receives software and CD-ROM discs for Missouri Union List.

Dec 88   MCL signs agreement with Library Corporation.

Feb 89   Intelligent Catalog installed for patron use.

Jun 89   MCL cancels BRS subscription; subscribes to CD+ and CINAHL.

9
CD-ROM Utilization in a Health Sciences Setting

Mary E. Youngkin, Kathleen M. McCloskey, Nina E. Dougherty, Wayne J. Peay

Introduction

In keeping with its mission of service and innovation at the University of Utah, the Spencer S. Eccles Health Sciences Library and its clinical branch, the Hope Fox Eccles Clinical Library, are pursuing new applications of technology which enhance library service and access to information. In 1983, the University of Utah was selected by the National Library of Medicine to develop a strategic plan for the implementation of an Integrated Academic Information Management System (IAIMS). The National Library of Medicine's IAIMS initiative is intended to develop institutional models for the organization, access, and utilization of health sciences information.

As part of this planning process, the Eccles Health Sciences Library identified free access to bibliographic databases as a major priority, with the MEDLINE database as the first goal. MEDLINE is the primary database for most health sciences users, but in 1983, dial-up, fee-for-service access was all that was available at Eccles Library. Any charge for information service is an automatic disincentive that essentially excludes students from access to a powerful resource. Free access to MEDLINE addressed this problem. At the time planning began, the distribution of MEDLINE on magnetic tape had just begun. However, the combination of a significant hardware investment, ongoing maintenance and the $12,500 cost to lease the tapes was, and continues to be, an expensive solution. The emergence of compact disc read-only memory (CD-ROM) technology offered an alternative approach to providing free user access to the most heavily used bibliographic databases.

In the fall of 1987 the libraries began testing and evaluating compact disc products, and by December a decision was made. As a result, MEDLINE records from 1983 to the present are now available in the Eccles Libraries through the compact disc product, SilverPlatter MEDLINE. While both libraries offer identical years of coverage, the difference in setting and clientele make their experiences with the system different. The resulting comparison may prove useful to institutions planning CD-ROM services in multiple or diverse settings.

The Libraries

Eccles Library

The Spencer S. Eccles Health Sciences Library serves a clientele of 800 faculty and 2,800 students in the School of Medicine and the Colleges of Health, Nursing, and Pharmacy at the University of Utah. Immediately adjacent to the University Hospital, the library also supports the information needs of its physicians and staff. In addition, as a Resource Library in the National Library of Medicine's Regional Medical Library Program, Eccles Library serves as a primary source of information for health sciences professionals, patients, and the general public in the intermountain region of Utah, southern Idaho, and southwestern Wyoming.

The staff consists of eight professional librarians, 15 full-time staff and 12 FTE hourly student assistants. The 140,000 volumes in the collection, along with audiovisual materials and Clinical Library holdings, are accessible through the library's online catalog, OCLC's LS/2000, on in-house public terminals, by modem, and through the University of Utah Campus Computer Network.

Online reference services include fee-based searches of the NLM, BRS, DIALOG, STN, and WILSONLINE systems. These mediated services are supplemented by strong support for end-user searching. Monthly "Basics of Searching MEDLINE on the NLM System" classes are taught by library faculty. Documentation, passwords, and equipment are also provided for the BRS Colleague, PaperChase, and Grateful Med end-user systems and software.

The University of Utah and the Salt Lake City area have a sophisticated group of computer users. To support their needs, the library and its staff participate actively in the promotion and development of innovative applications of computer technology. For the past seven years, the library has sponsored INFOFAIR, an annual one-day event for end-users which includes presentations, workshops and exhibits focusing on aspects of information technology such as intelligent information retrieval, the Unified Medical Language System, expert systems, reprint file management, hypermedia, and the authoring of CAI programs for medical education. Other library projects include participation on medical expert system knowledge engineering teams, support for the development of hypermedia and interactive videodisc products within Computer & Media Services (Slice of Life III VideoDisc, HyperBrain, HyperHeart, and HyperHistology), the mounting of a state-wide bulletin board and electronic mail service for health professionals for the Utah Health Sciences Library Consortium, the publication of the *IAIMS Newsletter*, and the coordination of the monthly meetings of MCSCUG (Medical Center Small Computer Users Group), "an informal group of computer users who enjoy staying abreast of what's happening in the computer world."

In this environment, the addition of CD-ROM to other reference services needed little intellectual justification. It simply represented the application of a new tool to an old problem, and allowed us to meet our goal of providing free access to information in a timely, easy, and relatively inexpensive fashion. Access to a compact disc version of MEDLINE specifically targets the needs of students who cannot afford to pay for an online search.

The Clinical Library

The Hope Fox Eccles Clinical Library, the clinical branch of the main Eccles Library, is located on the fourth floor of the University Hospital and is open daily from 6:00 a.m. to midnight. Its location places the library in close proximity to the cardiac intensive care unit, patient rooms, nursing stations and the Drug Information Center. The library serves the medical students and staff, clinical faculty, hospital administrative staff, and other patient care staff of the University Hospital. The Clinical Library's print collection offers the most recent five years of 181 clinical journal titles, approximately 450 of the most current clinical and reference books, and a collection of nursing education video tapes. The library also houses two Macintosh computers and a wide range of software for student use. The Clinical Library offers brief online MEDLINE searches without charge to its patrons on topics relating to the direct care of specific patients in the University Hospital as part of its Clinical Medical Librarianship Program (CML). Searches run in preparation for publishing or for presentations made within the hospital for professional staff, such as grand rounds, in addition to those for basic medical research, are fee-based.

The Clinical Library does not have ample staffing (one professional librarian and 3.15 FTE student assistants) to attend rounds with the health care professionals. However, it was felt that the provision of increased access to patient related information could be made possible through an end-user CD-ROM workstation. In this way, the concept of free access to medical information could be expanded beyond patient-specific care to include clinical research and teaching.

The CD-ROM Service

Compact disc service at both libraries currently consists of access to SilverPlatter MEDLINE from 1983 to the present on single workstations. At Eccles, the system runs on a Leading Edge with a hard disk, 640K of RAM, color monitor, a single CM 100 Philips drive, a CM 153 controller, and an Epson compatible dot matrix printer. The Clinical Library station is identical except that the software is run from two 5 1/4 inch floppy disk drives. The systems are accessible whenever the libraries are open, and no fees are charged, regardless of whether citations are printed or downloaded. Documentation and all discs are kept on the table next to the station and patrons are free to change their own discs to search from year to year. Patron assistance is available upon demand at all times. Financial support for the acquisition of the hardware and the annual subscriptions is provided by the University's Instructional and Research Computing Program. This program is funded by a self-imposed tuition surcharge which the students of the university initiated in an effort to ensure student access to computers on campus.

The location of any new end-user service should maximize its use. The location should also allow for the best possible patron assistance feasible given current staffing levels. At Eccles Library a number of policy decisions dictated that the CD-ROM station be located in an area open to the public but behind the main reference desk. The service needed to be highly visible and very accessible, with as few restrictions as possible, and yet equipment security and maintenance needed to be taken into account. Also, while some consideration was given to locating the system in the library's instructional computing facility, we felt strongly that patron assistance for the system ought to be provided by the staff most familiar with MEDLINE and *Index Medicus*. Proximity to the main entrance, current journals, the online catalog, and other printed indexes and abstracts was also important. Moreover, so that we could provide the one-on-one patron assistance we felt the system required, the station needed to be located so that Reference and Circulation staff could easily provide this service without abandoning other responsibilities.

Locating a CD-ROM workstation in the Clinical Library assured system access to residents and medical students who are frequently too busy to venture far from the patient care area. The need for a separate system close at hand and available every day from 6:00 a.m. to midnight for these patrons was deemed essential.

Because student computing fees contribute heavily toward the cost of the system, policy states that first priority will be given to University of Utah students. However, no restrictions have been made on who may use the system, and IDs have never been requested. At Eccles Library patrons are asked, each time they use the system, to fill out a simple log sheet which also doubles as an appointment sheet. The log includes time of day, name, status (student/staff/faculty), department, years searched, and a small space for comments. The current version also includes a place to indicate whether the patron had to wait to use the workstation. Advance appointments may be made in person or by telephone, and patrons are allowed 30 minutes for each search session.

At the Clinical Library, no restrictions are placed on the amount of time a patron can spend on the system. Therefore, the search log does not track time of day or length of searches. As the use of the system increases, time limits may need to be set. At present, patrons have imposed self-limitations on the system out of consideration for others without any intervention by library staff. Patrons of the main library who are accustomed to reserving time slots are now beginning to ask to make reservations in the Clinical Library as well. However, requests for reserved time slots have not been popular in the Clinical Library since patrons working in a hospital/patient-care situation cannot anticipate their schedules and are often unable to count on being available for a prearranged search appointment.

User Support

SilverPlatter MEDLINE was tested prior to purchase for its ease of use. Patrons were given a very brief verbal introduction to the system and then answers to any subsequent questions. We discovered that no amount or variety of printed documentation or onscreen help substituted for personal point-of-need assistance. While we selected SilverPlatter over other systems, it was not judged to be so friendly or transparent that patrons would not need instruction or help. Consequently, at each library, users are provided with one-on-one point-of-need assistance to the level required or requested. Brief aids are provided and an introduction to the use of SilverPlatter MEDLINE is incorporated in tours and classes.

In the past, specific groups of students, such as those in drug information, occupational health, and medical informatics, have been formally trained in searching online MEDLINE through the MEDLARS system. Their training is now focused on searching MEDLINE on the SilverPlatter CD-ROM. Other regularly scheduled bibliographic instruction classes and tours now include an introduction to CD-ROM as well as orientation to online databases and print tools. Special orientations focusing specifically on SilverPlatter have also been given for students and new residents at the request of instructors.

During weekdays the staff members who assist users with CD-ROM include the faculty librarians in the Clinical Library and Reference Department of Eccles Library, the Reference Department Information Associate, who provides much of the user assistance during those hours and is also an experienced search intermediary, and the student assistants from the Reference Department and Clinical Library. During evening and weekend hours, Circulation assistants and supervisors, and the student assistants at the Clinical Library provide support. Those staff members who are not experienced searchers have been trained through a combination of on-screen tutorials and individual hands-on instruction. Most have taken the "Basics of Searching MEDLINE" class, and have reinforced their own knowledge of the system through the experience of teaching it to others. The amount and type of help staff members provide is highly variable and is dictated by a complex combination of factors. Among these factors are the staff member's own level of expertise and perception of the patron's need, the needs of other patrons coming to the desk, and the patron's questions, personality, demand for assistance, experience with computers and the SilverPlatter software, subject expertise, knowledge of the MEDLINE database, and purpose of the search.

At Eccles Library, first-time users are given a brief walk-through of basic system functions, MeSH headings, the structure of the MEDLINE database and, often, advice on search strategy for their individual topic. Then, depending on questions asked and the staff member's perception of style and need, patrons are either left alone with assurances that their questions will be answered, or they are talked through their entire search. Documentation provided includes the MeSH tools (Medical Subject Headings), the system manual, a function key template, and various versions of single sheet handouts.

The Clinical Library's philosophy regarding user support has been to monitor patron behavior while using the computer and to offer assistance at the appropriate time, well in advance of any frustration. The information needs of Clinical Library patrons often differ from those of Eccles Library clients in that rapid retrieval is of crucial importance. It has been standard procedure to ask how much time the individual has to invest at that moment and gauge system introduction/instruction accordingly. For example, the instruction might consist of the Clinical Librarian pointing out the various search steps during the quick retrieval of a review article, or may involve 20 to 30 minutes of instruction on the system and the intricacies of the MEDLINE database. Staff have been trained to be sensitive to the time constraints and needs of the patrons. On many occasions users are interrupted during search sessions to respond to pages on the Clinical Library paging phone. Because patrons infrequently read the system users' manual and often do not seem to read screen messages, in-house printed documentation is limited to a one-page easy-to-read list of examples showing how to input limit features such as review, human only, and words in title.

The Users

Statistics supplied by users about themselves are very incomplete for both libraries. Nevertheless, conclusions can be drawn. While some patrons frequent both libraries, there are significant overall differences between the libraries' patrons and their use of the CD-ROM services.

An accurate analysis of the departmental affiliation of users is difficult because of the broad and nonspecific way in which patrons identify themselves. For example, "Medicine" can mean either the College of Medicine or the Department of Internal Medicine, and "Pharm" could mean the hospital pharmacy, the College of Pharmacy, or the Departments of Pharmacology or Pharmaceutics. At Eccles Library, approximately 34% of CD-ROM users identified themselves as "Pharmacy/ Pharmacology," 25% as "Medicine," and 21% as "Nursing." The remaining 20% listed 50 different departments including dance, law, political science, informatics, biochemistry and women's studies. In contrast, Clinical Library users are more homogeneous. Not surprisingly, 62% of the users identifed themselves as "Medicine." The Departments of Pathology, Pharmacy and Surgery account for 30%, and the "other" category, which includes lower campus/undergraduate students and patients, accounts for the remaining 18%.

A comparison by university status shows a much higher concentration of student use at Eccles Library than at the Clinical Library. Students account for approximately 64% of the total use compared to 35% at the Clinical. At Eccles, staff and faculty use is approximately equal at 16% each, and "unspecified" patrons account for the rest. In addition to the student users at the Clinical Library, who are primarily medical students, 20% of CD-ROM use was by staff, 20% by residents, and 10% by faculty. The remaining 15% gave their names, but not their status.

The marked difference in the total number of searches reported at each library may help explain why appointments have become a necessity in the academic setting. Between August of 1988 and April of 1989 Clinical Library users logged 352 searches. For that same period, Eccles users ran 1,869 searches. Since users do not always log their searches, both statistics are low, but the proportion may be relatively accurate.

In December of 1988, we began tracking how often patrons had to wait in order to use the system at Eccles Library. By April of 1989, 44 percent of the patrons who wanted to use the workstation had to wait. Furthermore, the number of people who have to wait is actually much higher than the statistics reveal, because patrons don't understand that portion of the log form, and rarely fill it in on their own. The station has become so popular that access to it has drastically changed. A year ago virtually all users were walk-ins. Now, they either wait, make advance appointments, are referred to the Clinical Library, or leave. In the last month, there were several days when the log sheets were filled from 7:30 a.m. until 10:30 p.m.

The Clinical Library successfully gathered data on the span of years patrons searched. The 1989, 1984 and 1983 discs were discounted because they were not available during most of the period in which statistics were kept. (The initial subscriptions to MEDLINE at both libraries only included discs from 1985 to the present. The years of coverage were expanded to include 1983–1984 when the subscriptions were renewed for 1989.) The difference in use between the 1988, 1987, 1986 and 1985 discs was minimal. It appears that users are willing to change the discs to look at older citations on a regular basis. This is significant given the fact that clinical searchers are under time constraints and typically perform very quick searches. It may be due to the specificity of their topic or it may be the manifestation of their familiarity with computers, their knowledge of the structure of the MEDLINE database, and their expertise in the subject area. They are able to quickly search and retrieve relevent material.

The number of discs, i.e., years of MEDLINE, searched during a session at Eccles Library relates to what can occur during a 30 minute session and to the search topic, as well as to user expertise. New users and those with broad, general topics typically examine and print large numbers of citations and rarely have the time or inclination to pursue their subject past the current disc. Experienced searchers with specific topics examine multiple discs just as they do at the Clinical Library.

In both libraries, patrons tend to display citations on the screen and then print selectively. Rarely do they download to a floppy disk. Print limits have been stored in the SilverPlatter software for both libraries: 200 for Eccles Library, and 25 for the Clinical Library. Although Clinical Library users may readily print more than the 25 citations, it is atypical for them to print the large numbers of citations with abstracts that Eccles patrons do on a routine basis.

Patrons run searches for a variety of reasons, including student papers, personal information, legal cases, grand rounds, publication, patient care, current awareness, research, and grant proposals. How effectively they perform those searches and how that could be evaluated are questions which remain unanswered. End-user searching, by nature, does not lend itself to intrusive questioning by library staff. Patrons want to be left alone and few will take the time to fill out a log sheet or a questionnaire. Users are generally satisfied with whatever they have retrieved because they have performed the search themselves.

Impact and Evolution

The impact of the CD-ROM service has been significant. On a campus-wide level, CD-ROM seems to have altered the information-seeking habits of library patrons. Abandoning traditional tools and a predisposition toward looking for books as a first step, some patrons seem to view a compact disc database as the beginning and endpoint of their literature search. It may even be that the reputation of CD-ROM has enticed some students into using the resources of the libraries for the first time, for it is apparent that they did not previously know that online databases existed, and despite explanations, patron understanding of the difference between the parent online database and its compact disc versions is still fuzzy. Individuals who had never previously requested an online MEDLINE search think the CD station is the only MEDLINE that exists. Patrons have quickly become dependent and would have difficulty doing without the systems available in the Eccles Libraries and the main university library. To quote a recent letter in the student newspaper, "Life without CD-ROM isn't worth living."

The technology itself is very popular. Patrons tend to use a compact disc database over a printed tool even if the subject coverage is not as appropriate. For example, a graduate bioengineering class camped out at the MEDLINE work-station despite the fact that in some cases their topics would have been better researched in the engineering indexes and abstracts in the science library on lower campus. Satisfaction is partially based on the fact that they perform the search themselves, but "free" is an important word. Also important is the capability of an instant printout.

There is a hidden danger in this popularity. MEDLINE is currently the only CD-ROM database available at the Eccles Libraries and has tended to be used for all information needs whether appropriate or not. Although additional CD-ROM databases of interest to the health sciences will be provided on the university campus in the near future, some of the major basic science information resources will still not be available to the user. Until significant sources such as Biological Abstracts and Chemical Abstracts are available on campus and offered at no charge, it is possible that the glamour of CD technology will continue to dissuade patrons from pursuing alternate or more appropriate sources of information either because the print versions are too tedious to use, or because the online databases are too expensive to search. The research process becomes a question of economics and ease, not of content or validity of information. The ultimate result might be the provision of less, not more, information.

Response to SilverPlatter MEDLINE at Eccles Library has been overwhelmingly enthusiastic even without an active publicity campaign. Announcements were made at the time of initial evaluation and then again at installation, and several small presentations were given. However, word of mouth seems to be the effective communication mode at the University of Utah. Eccles Library consistently has new first-time users. They call and request an appointment on "THE MEDLINE" without really even knowing what it is. A comparison of utilization for January through May of 1988 and 1989 shows a dramatic rise. The total number of searches for that five month period almost tripled, increasing from 551 in 1988 to 1516 in 1989.

All of this popularity is not without consequence. Despite the fact that the system is generally user-friendly, first-time users at Eccles Library require from five to twenty-five minutes of one-on-one instruction from desk staff. This situation has provided the very positive opportunity for a high level of staff/patron interaction and yet those same staff are also responsible for traditional reference, bibliographic instruction, online searching, assistance with five online catalog terminals and a public access workstation. When we initially set up the service we felt disc security warranted that staff members change discs for patrons. That policy was quickly abandoned in order to save both staff and patron time.

The demand for CD assistance has taken its toll on non-reference staff as well. Evening and weekend reference is primarily handled by the Circulation staff, which at most, consists of a supervisor and one desk assistant. While they have been trained in reference services and in searching SilverPlatter MEDLINE, very often the clientele they assist are students and faculty from lower campus or other universities, the general public, and others who are not regular users of the library. The library and computer skills of these patrons vary widely and consequently their need for assistance is, in general, much greater.

The installation of the CD-ROM station has added an intellectually stimulating but time-consuming instructional task to duties which already include circulation, reserve, interlibrary loans, answering phones, quick reference, bibliographic instruction, and online catalog assistance. As the system increased in popularity, the staff's role was further complicated by the need to arbitrate between multiple patrons all competing for the same workstation. The hiring of a part-time Saturday reference assistant alleviated the weekend situation to a certain extent, and a temporary strengthening of policy language resolved the problem of a few individuals who were seriously monopolizing the equipment. The planned installation of more workstations in a network environment will address the problem of the demand on the single workstation, but the problem of providing user support is likely to grow and additional solutions are needed.

Equipment and disc security have never been a problem in our institutions. The discs simply sit out on the table next to the player. Despite the curiosity revealed in the frequent question, "What would happen if I put this in my audio CD at home?" we have never lost a disc to theft or abuse.

The principal difficulties we have encountered relate to printing. Paper jams and the system software's default to printing "all" citations at the carriage return, constitute a significant problem. Patrons who are unfamiliar with hardware don't know how to disable the printer quickly, nor can they find the CTRL/BREAK keys to interrupt the system. Even when they successfully invoke the command to discontinue printing, they are confused by the fact that the printer will continue to print citations until it has emptied its buffer. Problems with the software are being addressed by the vendor, but there are still occasional system freezes and an inability to print or display certain citations. Also, because software for other demo or sample CD systems is stored on the same hard disk, the station at Eccles Library is not dedicated to SilverPlatter. This makes it easy for patrons to accidently "quit" to DOS, thereby wiping out their search strategies and leaving them at a point where they do not know how to reenter the system.

Initially we had expected to reduce the cost of our in-house quick reference searches by doing as many as possible on SilverPlatter. In fiscal year 1987–88, we were able to cut in-house online searches by half, but the reality for 1989 is that we are rarely able to get to the CD-ROM workstation for our own purposes. The same is true in the Clinical Library.

There have been many predictions that CD-ROM would drastically lower the number of mediated online searches performed in libraries. At Eccles Library, at least initially, no such impact was felt. The number of for-fee searches performed was not significantly reduced. Students have historically not been heavy users of for-fee search services. The provision of free access to MEDLINE on compact disc generated a new population of searchers who might otherwise have used traditional printed sources or gone without the information they needed. Faculty and residents continue to request searches from us. As they become more expert with the system, this may change. What has declined markedly as a result of CDs is end-user use of the library's public access workstation for searching remote online databases. CD-ROM now offers free access to the same MEDLINE records they used to access through Grateful Med or Colleague on our equipment. When they search online systems now, they do it from their offices or homes. The impact of CD-ROM upon Clinical Library services has been very interesting and somewhat different. As the popularity of the CD-ROM increased, a noticeable drop in the number of requests for free patient-related (CML) searches was recorded. Although the CD-ROM was only in place for six months of the 1987–1988 year, the number of CML searches dropped by 21 percent from 585 to 458. This is directly attributable to CD-ROM. Residents and medical students who had previously requested numerous searches were learning and using SilverPlatter MEDLINE in lieu of requesting a search from the Clinical Librarian, even though the CML search did not cost them anything. Additionally, the enthusiasm was so high from users that frequently they would recruit new users, bringing in as many as three or four new people to "instruct" them in the use of the system. This opportunity was capitalized upon by Clinical Library staff to interject additional instruction as needed. Often the person who brought the new recruits learned additional information in the process.

The impact of SilverPlatter MEDLINE on staff time is quite different than at Eccles. In the Clinical Library, new users tend to ask questions only as they encounter new information or have a problem, and seem to function without a great deal of additional instruction. Some, of course, are quite intrigued with the system and ask numerous questions relating to the structure of MEDLINE and the use of subheadings. When considered along with the reduced number of CML searches performed, this independence in Clinical Library patrons should result in a reduced workload for staff. In reality, the nature of the work has changed. Even prior to the introduction of the SilverPlatter MEDLINE, *Index Medicus* was so rarely used that student desk assistants had little opportunity to practice their skills instructing patrons in its use. The assistants' knowledge of the database and their role within the library has actually been enhanced by the fact that they now regularly assist patrons in searching MEDLINE on CD-ROM. Furthermore, the requests received by the Clinical Librarian, while reduced in number, are much more complex in nature, demanding more preparation and online time to complete. Nevertheless, the reduced volume has made it possible to spend more time and money on each search and to expand the definition of a CML search to include those run relative to outpatients and discharged or deceased patients.

SilverPlatter MEDLINE has also had an impact on the Clinical Library's collection and physical arrangement. Since it is a no-growth library, space is always at a premium. With the addition of the CD-ROM station, there was justification for cancelling the subscription for the rarely used print *Index Medicus,* housed on the library's large index table. This cancellation allowed us to move the remaining indexes to the journal shelving area and place the heavily used student-funded microcomputers and printer on the index table. Eliminating the two temporary carrels on which the microcomputers and printer resided freed up floor space and gave the library a more spacious and less cluttered appearance. Since the printed copies of *Index Medicus* were removed, there have only been three requests for them, and no complaints regarding their absence.

The Future

Long-range planning is essential in the dynamic environment of CD-ROM technology. While the single drive, single workstation, CD-ROM application has demonstrated its power, it has also demonstrated its limitations. The technology is far from mature, with no standardization of hardware or software. In planning for the future, the evolution of the technology must be anticipated in order to take advantage of significant enhancements.

Multiple drive workstation and database configurations are now entering the market. In some instances, these configurations can also be connected to local area networks. In the very near future, access to these systems will be possible by dial-up and across larger campus-wide networks. This potential for campus-wide access has led to close collaboration between the two Eccles Libraries, the Law Library, and Marriott Library, which is the main university library. During this last year, a committee with representatives from each library evaluated CD-ROM databases and hardware. The goal was to provide a broad selection of databases on campus. The resulting plan is to initially mount 26 CD-ROM databases within the four libraries, with the Eccles Libraries acquiring seven of the databases. In Eccles Health Sciences Library and Marriott Library, the CD-ROM databases that can physically and contractually be networked will be accessible first on networks within the libraries, and then by dial-up and through the campus network.

The first objective in selection of the CD-ROM databases was to acquire the important bibliographic resources for all of the major subject areas of each library from the currently and imminently available and affordable products. In order to limit the number of search interfaces presented to the user, a second objective was to obtain the databases from as few vendors as possible, a goal most easily realized by Eccles Library since all seven of its initially identified databases are offered by SilverPlatter. Even now, however, Eccles Library must plan for a multiple CD-ROM vendor environment as Government Printing Office depository CD-ROM databases are beginning to appear. It is anticipated that additional, specialized CD-ROM databases will be acquired and integrated into the configuration at all of the libraries as both products and funds become available.

With additional user workstations and seven new databases on the horizon and more to come at the Eccles Libraries, search assistance, training and management must be included in the plan. Given current staffing levels, it is clear that optimal user training and individual assistance will be difficult. As a result, new strategies need to be developed. One approach under consideration is to enhance the user-training-user model by identifying and providing special instruction to users who will train other users. Another strategy is to investigate the use and development of front-end programs that would provide uniform database access, gather information on users and their searches, and provide assistance in database selection and searching. Users will need help when confronted with a variety of databases and search interfaces. An attempt to make database access look uniform at some level and to help the user select and effectively search the right databases will alleviate an otherwise confusing and difficult situation. Software that records user characteristics and search performance would provide information to aid in the development of front-end expert assistance software and the design of specialized training programs.

Conclusion

The installation of SilverPlatter MEDLINE in the Eccles Libraries at the University of Utah has been overwhelmingly successful. Our decisions have been validated and rewarded by incredible use of the system and support for new developments. CD-ROM is a valuable and appropriate tool for libraries of all types and sizes, but care should be taken in planning the services to reflect the unique needs of each library's own clientele. In the health sciences setting, both large academic and small hospital libraries can significantly enhance services through the use of this powerful technology.

Mary E. Youngkin joined the staff of the Spencer S. Eccles Health Sciences Library in 1974. In her fifteen years at the library, Mary has worked in both the Public Services and Information Services Departments of the library. In 1987, Mary was appointed to her current position, Head of Reference Services. Mary received her B.S. in English and a teaching certificate from the University of Iowa in 1972, and her M.L.S. from Brigham Young University in 1987.

Kathleen M. McCloskey joined the Spencer S. Eccles Health Sciences Library faculty in 1982 as a Reference Librarian. She became the Head of the Eccles Clinical Library in July of 1987. Kathleen received her B.S. in English Literature from the University of Texas, her M.L.S. from Brigham Young University and a graduate certificate in gerontology from the University of Utah. Prior to working for Eccles Library she was a Special Projects Librarian at the VA Medical Center Library in Salt Lake City.

Nina E. Dougherty is the Assistant Director for Information Services at the Spencer S. Eccles Health Sciences Library. Nina received her B.A. in Anthropology and her M.A. in Library Science from the University of Wisconsin-Madison. Prior to assuming her present position, Nina was Extension Librarian and Head of Reference Services at Eccles Library. She has worked as an EMBASE trainer for Elsevier Science Publishers and in 1986 received an adjunct appointment in the Department of Medical Informatics in the School of Medicine at the University of Utah.

Wayne J. Peay joined the faculty of the Spencer S. Eccles Health Sciences Library in 1977. Wayne was appointed Director of the library in 1984. In 1988 he assumed additional responsibilities as Director of Library Automation for the University of Utah. He graduated with a B.A. in History from the University of Utah and an M.S. with honors from the School of Library Service at Columbia University. While attending library school, Wayne worked at the Medical Library Center of New York.

10
CD-ROM Teaching Techniques: Instructing PsycLIT Users in a Health Sciences Library

Paula G. Raimondo

Background

The staff of the Health Sciences Library, University of Maryland, was introduced to CD-ROM technology in 1986, when it participated in the beta-test phase of PsycLIT. A product of the SilverPlatter company, PsycLIT is the Psychological Abstracts equivalent on compact disc. During the test phase, library patrons rated PsycLIT a friendly and valuable research tool, and urged the library to become a subscriber. The service has been heavily used ever since.

The Health Sciences Library serves the schools of medicine, nursing, dentistry, pharmacy and social work, as well as the Maryland Institute for Emergency Medical Service Systems, the University of Maryland Cancer Center, and the University Hospital. The majority of PsycLIT users are from the schools of social work, nursing, and medicine.

End-User Searching

PsycLIT is seen as a complement to our other in-house database services, MaryMED and HSL/Current Contents. MaryMED, a subset of MEDLINE, covers approximately two years, and includes only English-language biomedical journals held by the Health Sciences Library (about 1,600 titles). HSL/Current Contents covers approximately six months of ISI's Current Contents. MaryMED, HSL/Current Contents, and PsycLIT are all free to users when searched in-house. The Health Sciences Library also offers BRS After Dark at a nominal fee.

PsycLIT has been so well received that a PsycLIT search, as part of the preparation for a term paper, is now required by two faculty members. These individuals, who teach research methods courses in the school of social work, routinely devote about two hours each semester to bibliographic instruction and library orientation. PsycLIT is introduced during bibliographic instruction, but only fifteen to twenty minutes are devoted to it. Forty to fifty students are required to use PsycLIT for their papers after receiving this brief overview. While the Information Services staff is gratified to have introduced such a popular service, the additional pressure of having to schedule, and somehow train, PsycLIT's large audience was felt.

Point of Use Assistance

When PsycLIT was first introduced, users received one-on-one instructional sessions. However, this labor-intensive approach, by far the method of choice with our patrons, could only last during the months of the test phase. Once the product was released commercially, purchased by the library, and incorporated as part of our end-user searching services, patrons were asked to learn to search on their own. To assist them, on-disc help, printed documentation, and a one-page double-sided instruction sheet are available. The proximity of the workstation to the reference desk also allows users to get assistance from the staff. All of these methods are useful to varying degrees.

Although they are encouraged to take a few minutes to plan a search strategy, and to ask for help if needed, most users just sit down and immediately begin typing in terms or sentences. Ironically, it appears that the most consistent way users get help with the conceptual aspect of a search (e.g., choosing terminology, combining concepts, broadening or narrowing results) is when they ask a question involving a mechanical process (e.g., correcting an error, shifting to get the pound sign, or printing abstracts).

In one extreme example, a staff member going to the aid of a patron who asked for help with the SHOW (display on screen) command, discovered the patron browsing through 675 records because he did not know how to combine terms to refine his topic. This situation is not new to reference librarians who frequently find that patrons ask indirectly for the information they need. To determine what it is the patron really wants, the librarian conducts an interview, asking a series of questions which ultimately results in finding the information in an efficient and timely manner. The greatest risk of not finding information in PsycLIT comes when the user does not ask for any assistance.

The Course

After observing how so many patrons approached searching, the staff concluded that while there was no way to force users to learn and apply good search strategies, they might be more open to creating alternative strategies for searching if their concern about mechanics were alleviated. To this end, a structured, two-hour course, entitled "An Introduction to PsycLIT," was developed. It has become a useful mechanism for teaching interested patrons, as well as new staff members, the basics of searching the system.

Preparation

"An Introduction to PsycLIT" is widely publicized on campus. Mechanisms for publicity include the campus newspaper, the bulletin of the school of social work, and the newsletter of the hospital nursing staff. In addition, posters are hung at various locations throughout campus and in the library, and the course is also advertised via CoSY, the campus electronic conferencing system. Typically, attendees are faculty, students and staff from the departments of psychiatry and pediatrics, and the schools of social work and nursing.

The course is offered at least once each semester, at varying times of the day, and on different days of the week. To date it has been offered three times, with an average of eighteen attendees. The session was designed to complement other classes taught by the library staff, where the conceptual/intellectual aspects of database searching are emphasized. The class is held in a room large enough to seat twenty to twenty-five comfortably. The workstation equipment is brought in and hooked up to the Kodak Datashow System (Datashow is a liquid crystal device which, when connected to a microcomputer and placed on an overhead projector, displays whatever can be seen on the computer's monitor). This makes it possible for the entire class to view the PsycLIT screen without having to crowd around the workstation.

Objectives

The course is structured so that by the end of a session, participants are able to: describe the scope and coverage of PsycLIT; identify the advantages and disadvantages of searching the psychological literature on CD-ROM versus online or in print; prepare a search strategy using controlled vocabulary as well as key words; combine terms and sets, using the Boolean operators AND and OR, and perform searches on PsycLIT.

Scope and Coverage of PsycLIT

The course outline calls for these objectives to be presented first, followed by examination of the database. The scope and coverage of PsycLIT are discussed, along with a comparison of *Psychological Abstracts* (in print), PsycINFO (online) and PsycLIT. Emphasis is placed on years of coverage, type of coverage (PsycLIT does not contain citations to books or dissertations), and costs involved. Also included is a brief discussion of the process wherein an article is read, indexed, abstracted, and added to the system. The staff finds this type of overview helpful in de-mystifying literature searching for patrons. Knowledge of the process can be applied to the use of other indexing and abstracting services as well, since many secondary sources, and their online counterparts, are compiled in a similar fashion. For example, once the concept of controlled versus uncontrolled vocabulary is understood, it can easily be transferred to another indexing/abstracting tool, to facilitate use of that tool.

Successful use of PsycLIT depends, among other things, on understanding what a "field" is, and knowing which fields are important in displaying and printing records. A sample record is viewed, the concept of "field" is defined, and the class is asked to identify those fields which are essential for locating an item. Besides author, title and journal name fields, institution, descriptor, and abstract fields are defined and demonstrated. The intention is for users to be able to develop a sense of what the system is doing and where it looks when it searches for a word, a phrase, or a bound descriptor (i.e., a multiple-word subject heading where the words are connected by hyphens, such as internal-external-locus-of-control).

The Mechanics of Searching

Advantages and disadvantages of searching PsycLIT on CD-ROM—as opposed to print or online—are then covered, with emphasis placed on speed of retrieval and flexibility of the system as advantages, and lag time between publication and appearance on disc as a disadvantage. Since so many of PsycLIT's advantages are due at least in part to CD-ROM technology, a discussion of hardware and software is included. The compact discs and floppy disk used for searching are displayed, and the monitor, cpu, printer and disc player are all briefly covered. Considerably more time is given to a discussion of the keyboard as the most important piece of hardware from the new user's perspective. Function keys, shift keys—necessary for typing the requisite pound sign (#)—backspace, tab and control/break keys are emphasized. This brief introduction goes a long way toward reducing the stress experienced by users new to microcomputers, typically about half the class. The reduction of stress in turn leads to an increased ability to concentrate on the contents of the search.

The Intellectual Process

A discussion of the equipment is followed by 45 minutes on the conceptual aspects of searching PsycLIT. This section of the lecture begins with instruction on use of the "Thesaurus of Psychological Index Terms," PsycLIT's controlled vocabulary, and the advantages and disadvantages of using subject headings versus searching with keywords. With the equipment set up for searching it is easy to display examples which illustrate the points made. Attendees are encouraged to ask questions, and to come up with additional examples. Those who have already used PsycLIT usually ask the most questions and volunteer examples based on their experiences.

Following this comes coverage of the Boolean connectors AND and OR. NOT is briefly mentioned, along with warnings of the potential loss of relevant citations when it is used incorrectly. Venn diagrams, as well as live demonstrations, are used to illustrate ways to connect concepts (Appendix 1).

With this information, potential users should be prepared to complete the PsycLIT search form (Appendix 2). This optional form is designed to assist patrons at the PsycLIT workstation, as a way to encourage them to prepare a search strategy before they begin inputting terms. During class each step on the form is covered, with time allotted for questions and additional examples. The instructor then performs the prepared searches on PsycLIT to illustrate using additional subject terms, narrowing to English, or using both singular and plural forms of a word.

Up to now, the instructor has been demonstrating specific points about the search process. Once this has been accomplished the sample search form is completed and a "real" search is performed. To assist in this, every attendee is given a copy of the PsycLIT instruction sheet, the same sheet that is placed at the workstation. It was designed to provide brief, step-by-step assistance, and has proved to be successful, as long as novice users have the presence of mind to read it. The same examples used in the search form are included on the instruction sheet, in an attempt to provide consistency and decrease confusion. The class then goes through the search one step at a time. This allows for an introduction to the mechanics, and a review of the conceptual process. About ten minutes are allotted for questions.

Using the Index

One "step" which is not included on the instruction sheet, but is mentioned on the search form, is use of the index function. Since the index is so important when doing an author search it is demonstrated in class. Examples of the same author using first name only for two articles, first name plus middle initial for two more, and first name, maiden name, and married name for another are displayed, as a way to illustrate the usefulness of the index in achieving comprehensive search results. Use of the index in finding alternative word endings is also briefly covered.

PsycLIT Policies

Discussion of the index is followed by an explanation of the policies of the Health Sciences Library as they relate to PsycLIT. Users are asked to make appointments in advance whenever possible, and due to the popularity of PsycLIT, are limited to a one-hour session per day. The service is available to all faculty and students from other schools, and social services or health care providers who have access to the Health Sciences Library, but priority is given to University of Maryland at Baltimore faculty, staff and students. Only they may make appointments to use the system. Others must come in to the library and take a chance that there will be an opening. No one, however, is restricted from attending the "Introduction to PsycLIT" course.

As previously mentioned, the service is free. No limits are placed on the number of records printed. PsycLIT is available whenever the reference desk is staffed. In general, this is from 8 a.m. to 8 p.m. Monday through Friday, and from 9 a.m. to 5 p.m. on Saturday, as well as during additional Sunday hours throughout the fall and spring semesters. September through November, and February through April are the periods of heaviest PsycLIT use.

Users may download (transfer the records to a floppy disk instead of printing them on paper) under the following conditions:

—The user must supply a formatted disk. The Health Sciences Library does not supply, or assist with formatting, disks.

—The user must be able to follow the instructions for downloading without assistance from the reference staff.

—The staff provides the PsycLIT permissions policy statement, which the user is asked to read before downloading.

Users are reminded that assistance is available in various ways, and are encouraged to refer to the instruction sheet and on-disc help located at the workstation.

Course Evaluation

Finally, everyone is asked to complete an evaluation of the session (Appendix 3). The suggestions made by the class are all given serious consideration and implemented when practical. Generally the users are very pleased with the session, but a few ask that hands-on time be included as well. There is no way to include hands-on practice during the limited amount of time given to the class, and the staff has found that expanding sessions to over two hours significantly decreases the number of attendees. Instead, we respond by reminding everyone that use of PsycLIT is free, and that they are given some guidance by the librarian at the reference desk. While this is not ideal, it does seem to produce excellent results. There is a very high level of satisfaction with the service, and many users return.

The Future

The decision to keep this course at an introductory level, as well as the two-hour time constraint, have dictated that some of the more advanced features of the system be omitted from discussion. There is no demonstration of how to search using AND and OR in the same statement, for example, or of the Boolean operators WITH and SAME.

A demonstration of the index has also had to be reduced to a quick explanation and a few points on its use. Perhaps in the future, if there is sufficient demand, a course for the more advanced user could be added.

Shortly, the library will be linking two compact disc players together (daisy chaining) so that both compact discs (1974–1982, and 1983 to the present) can be searched without the staff having to manually switch discs. This may have some small impact on formal instruction. If and when additional products are introduced, however, significant changes may be necessary. If another SilverPlatter product were to be added, for example, a new course dedicated to that product could be developed, or a system-specific class could be taught. If a new CD-ROM database not produced by SilverPlatter were added to the end-user services offered by the library, a significant amount of change would occur. Different software, probably necessitating different mechanics, would be used. It is likely that an additional course would have to be developed.

In either case, the positive feedback from patrons, and the speed and convenience of the technology, have resulted in making the teaching of PsycLIT, and the provision of compact disc searching service, a pleasure for the staff.

Paula G. Raimondo has been an information specialist at the Health Sciences Library, University of Maryland at Baltimore, since 1980. She is currently coordinator of end-user services. She received her B.A. in English from Livingston College, Rutgers University, and her M.L.S. from Rugers Graduate School of Library and Information Services. From 1977–1980 she was a hospital librarian in Trenton, NJ. From 1975–1977 she was the librarian for the New Jersey Commission for the Blind & Visually Impaired in Newark.

Appendix 1

PsycLIT ON CD-ROM

PsycLIT covers the world's literature in psychology and related disciplines and is compiled from material published in "Psychological Abstracts". It consists of two compact disks, which cover 1974 - 1982, and 1983 to the present. PsycLIT covers over 1400 journals in 29 different languages.

BEGIN by pressing the **F7 (RE-START)** function key, on the left side of the keyboard. This will clear the previous search.

<u>STEP ONE</u>: <u>Plan Your Search</u>. Use the "Thesaurus of Psychological Index Terms", and the PsycLIT Search Form, to assist you in selecting terminology and developing a search strategy.

<u>STEP TWO</u>: <u>To FIND Information</u>. If you are not in the **FIND** mode, press the **F2** key. You are now ready to type in your term(s).

If you choose the option of using the terminology listed in the Thesaurus, connect any multiple-word terms with a hyphen. (Example: Internal-external-locus-of-control).

NARROW your retrieval by using **AND**
INCREASE your retrieval by using **OR** ⟩ See "Combining Terms", below

Be sure to press the **RETURN** key after each line.

Use the **pound sign (#)** when combining search statement numbers.
(Examples: <u>#1 AND #2</u>   <u>#2 OR #3 OR #4</u>)

COMBINING TERMS USING "AND"

USE "AND" TO CONNECT DIFFERENT CONCEPTS. "AND" <u>NARROWS</u> RETRIEVAL. (LINES THROUGH CIRCLES ARE MEANT TO ILLUSTRATE THAT YOU WILL RETRIEVE ONLY THOSE ARTICLES WHICH CONTAIN <u>BOTH</u> THE CONCEPTS <u>APPETITE DISORDERS</u> AND <u>HUMAN MALES</u>)

COMBINING TERMS USING "OR"

USE "OR" TO COMBINE SYNONYMS OR RELATED CONCEPTS. "OR" WILL <u>INCREASE</u> OR <u>BROADEN</u> YOUR RETRIEVAL. (LINES THROUGH CIRCLES ARE MEANT TO ILLUSTRATE THAT YOU WILL RETRIEVE ALL ARTICLES ON <u>APPETITE DISORDERS</u> OR <u>ANOREXIA NERVOSA</u> OR <u>BULMIA</u>.)

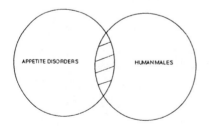

ON THE SCREEN, THE SEARCH LOOKS LIKE THIS:

#1: APPETITE-DISORDERS

#2: HUMAN-MALES

#3: #1 AND #2

USE OF HYPHENS BETWEEN WORDS IN SUBJECT HEADINGS INDICATES THAT THESE TERMS WERE LOCATED IN THE 'THESAURUS OF PSYCHOLOGICAL INDEX TERMS'

ON THE SCREEN THE SEARCH LOOKS LIKE THIS:

#1: APPETITE-DISORDERS

#2: ANOREXIA-NERVOSA

#3: BULIMIA

#4: #1 OR #2 OR #3

USE OF HYPHENS BETWEEN WORDS IN SUBJECT HEADINGS INDICATES THAT THESE TERMS WERE LOCATED IN THE 'THESAURUS OF PSYCHOLOGICAL INDEX TERMS'.

- OVER -

STEP THREE: To Look at (SHOW) the Results of the Search.
*** Note: You will be looking at the results of the **last** search statement you have entered. ***

Look at the results of your search by pressing the **F4** (SHOW) key.

At the FIELDS: prompt, type **TI,AB** (This will give you the **titles** and **abstracts** for the records).

Press the **TAB** key ▇▇ (on the left side of the keyboard) to get to the RECORDS: position

- - Press RETURN to see **Titles** and **Abstracts** of ALL the records
OR
- - Type the **numbers** of the records you would like to see   (Example: 1-30 and RETURN)

Make a note of the individual record numbers you wish to **PRINT** if you are not interested in printing all of them

STEP FOUR: To **Print**
*** Note: You will be printing the results of the **last** search statement you have entered. ***

Press the **F6 (PRINT)** key

The system will automatically provide you with the fields in the **CITN** (citation) format:
    AU = author
    TI = title of article
    JN = journal name, volume, pages, year
    IN = institutional affiliation of the first author

Or, you may instead choose the fields you wish to print, separated by commas. If you want to print the citation and the abstract, for example, type **CITN,AB**

then

Press the **TAB** key ▇▇ to get to the RECORDS: position.

Your three options at this point are

- - ALL - to print all citations (Simply press RETURN)

- - A specific group of citations (Example: 1-30 and RETURN)

- - Numbers of specific records, separated by commas (Example: 1,5,6,9 and RETURN)

REMEMBER TO PRESS THE **F2** KEY, TO RETURN TO THE **FIND** MODE, WHEN YOU WISH
TO REFINE YOUR STRATEGY, OR TO ADD NEW TERMS

Appendix 2

University of Maryland at Baltimore
Health Sciences Library

PsycLIT Search Form

1. Write a summary statement describing what you are researching.
   USE OF BEHAVIOR MODIFICATION IN EATING DISORDERS

2. Divide the statement into separate concepts.
   BEHAVIOR MODIFICATION / EATING DISORDERS

3. List your search terms. Include synonyms and/or subject headings ** for each
   concept.

BEHAVIOR-MODIFICATION	**APPETITE-DISORDERS**
BEHAVIOR-THERAPY	**ANOREXIA-NERVOSA**
	BULIMIA

   _____   _____

   _____   _____

4. **BROADEN** your search by using synonyms, or words similar in meaning, to
   describe your concepts. Use **OR** to combine the synonyms.
   APPETITE-DISORDERS OR ANOREXIA-NERVOSA OR BULIMIA

   _____ OR _____ OR _____

   _____ OR _____ OR _____

5. **NARROW** your search by combining subjects in **AND** search statements.
   Consider limiting retrieval by year, language, age group, sex, population
   (human or animal).
   APPETITE-DISORDERS AND HUMAN-MALE
   (retrieves articles on appetite disorders in men or boys)
   BULIMIA AND PY=1988
   (retrieves everything on bulimia published in 1988)

   _____ AND _____

   _____ AND _____

- over -

** You may use your own terminology, the terminology provided in the "Thesaurus of Psychological Index Terms", or a combination of both. Be sure to **hyphenate** the words in a term listed in the thesaurus.
    Example: **TREATMENT-EFFECTIVENESS-EVALUATION**

When searching by an author's name, use the **INDEX (F5)** as your first step. The **INDEX** will display all variations of an author's name.

Also consider entering singular and plural forms of a word.
    Example: **THERAPIST OR THERAPISTS**
Check the **INDEX (F5)** for all forms of a word.

For additional information, consult the PsycLIT manual, or use the **HELP** function **(F1)** to get more information on the screen.

1989

Appendix 3

EVALUATION
Introduction to PsycLIT

Please evaluate today's seminar so that we can make future sessions more valuable. The scale is as follows:

Strongly disagree	Disagree somewhat	Agree somewhat	Agree	Strongly agree
1	2	3	4	5

1. The seminar objectives were clearly stated.

   1   2   3   4   5   Average score=4.76

2. The handouts/transparencies were helpful.

   1   2   3   4   5   Avg score=4.76

3. The demonstration was helpful.

   1   2   3   4   5   Avg score=4.50

4. The length of the the seminar was adequate to cover the topic.

   1   2   3   4   5   Avg score=4.41

5. The speaker(s) was knowledgeable about the topic.

   1   2   3   4   5   Avg score=4.82

6. I can describe the scope and coverage of PsycLIT

   1   2   3   4   5   Avg score=4.18

7. I can identify the advantages/disadvantages of using PsycLIT.

   1   2   3   4   5   Avg score=4.38

8. I could prepare and conduct an effective search on PsycLIT.

   1   2   3   4   5   Avg score=3.82

9. Other comments or suggestions?

   See next page

Other information
10. _____ Faculty   _____ Staff   _____ Student

11. _____ Dentistry   _____ Medicine   _____ Nursing
    _____ Pharmacy   _____ SSWCP   _____ UMH
    _____ MIEMSS   _____ Other (please specify)
    _____

11

CD-ROMS in the School Library: One District's Experience

Gail K. Dickinson

The Union-Endicott Central School District has over three years of experience in electronic information retrieval. The district has CD-ROM resources in every school, including the elementary level. In addition to CD-ROMs, the district offers other electronic resources such as online searching and an automated catalog. Union-Endicott High School won Honorable Mention in the DIALOG Excellence in Online Education program for the variety of resources it makes available to students, and for its effort to educate teachers in electronic information retrieval.

Institutional Background

The district is located in a suburban area and serves the village of Endicott and the surrounding township of Union, near Binghamton, in south central New York. The district contains one high school, one middle school, and six elementary schools, with a total student population of just under 5,000. The district administrative structure consists of subject supervisors, including the library super-visor who reports to the assistant superintendent (Appendix). The subject supervisor is responsible for the zero-based program budgeting used by Union-Endicott.

The district also has classroom teachers serving as grade level chairs for each grade, K–6. The grade level chair-persons meet with the classroom teachers at their respective grade levels at various times each year and provide important coordination for district-wide curriculum. These grade-level chairs also function to disseminate library media and other information to the classroom teachers.

This structure of subject supervisors and grade level chairs, and the organization of the library media services as a department, all help provide a framework for com-munication, an essential part of any new program. Information about the electronic information retrieval program was disseminated throughout this structure in a number of different ways. At the secondary levels, the subject departments have the opportunity to meet with the subject supervisor twice monthly; grade level chairs meet with them several times each year. The librarians have used these meetings to inform teachers of the resources available to them through their school libraries.

At Union-Endicott the computer services department and library staff have worked together to achieve the kind of electronic information retrieval program that includes skills we felt students would need after graduation. Our philosophy is that the school library is an access point for materials, and students should see the library, not as an end in itself, but as a retrieval system for resources beyond the school. This philosophy seems to have been justified; since we have moved into the electronic information age, not one student has been heard saying "this library doesn't have anything for me."

History of the Program

Our decision to enter into the electronic information retrieval process, and ensuing decisions once the process began, were based on a general idea of what the next step should be, with a firm hope that we were right. Long-range planning was even more vague, with definite plans running no more than one year in advance, and only a general outline for the year after that. We found it very difficult to plan realistically on a long-term basis; the emerging technology of CD-ROM changes rapidly, with new software and new ways to use the hardware listed monthly in the journals. So far, our decisions have been correct, and our mistakes have been ones that have been easily corrected.

In the 1985–86 school year, Elissa D'Elia, then librarian at the Ann G. McGuinness Elementary School, wrote a section of a successful Chapter II Grant. The grant funded the library's purchase of a CD-ROM player and Grolier's Electronic Encyclopedia in 1986. It also provided for the purchase of a Jonathan card, which allowed the CD-ROM player to work with the library's Apple IIe computer.

The Electronic Encyclopedia proved to be very successful in the elementary library media center. It was also determined that the Encyclopedia, because of its low cost and versatility, would be purchased for the high school and middle school library, along with the Wilsondisc Readers' Guide to Periodical Literature. Because of the expense of the Jonathan card (around $2,000), and the necessity for a hard disk drive to run Readers' Guide, it was decided to use IBM computers, rather than Apples, for the high school and middle school. Chapter II funds paid for these additions. About the middle of the year, however, it was apparent that at the high school level one CD-ROM player was insufficient; therefore the high school principal provided funds for an additional CD-ROM player.

In the 1988–89 school year, the elementary libraries, with the exception of one K–3 school, were furnished with IBM PC computers and the Grolier's CD-ROM. These computers were originally to be PS/2 Model 30s, but due to budget restrictions, the libraries received PCs from the principal's office of each school. Only four CD-ROM players were purchased since one elementary school already had a player.

Not all of the hardware or furniture was purchased new, or with library money. Some items were moved from other areas of the school and some were purchased from other departments' funds. CD-ROM was so exciting that the high school principal and the computer services department were ready to push any available funding into these programs. This was especially true after initial implementation, when it was evident that the program was going to be a success. No administrators could look at these products and not want them for their library programs.

Timeline and Budget

1985–86 school year

Information for the Chapter II grant researched.

1986–87 school year

Ann G. McGuinness Elementary School: Purchase of one Jonathan card, Grolier's Electronic Encyclopedia, Apple IIe and printer, Computer table

1987–88 School year

High School: One IBM PS/2 with printer, one Hitachi CD-ROM drive, Readers' Guide to Periodical Literature, Grolier's Electronic Encyclopedia and installation of an outside telephone line.

Middle School: One IBM PS/2 with printer, one Hitachi CD-ROM drive, Grolier's Electronic Encyclopedia, McGraw-Hill CD-ROM Science and Technical Reference Set.

1988–89 School year

Elementary Schools: five IBM PCs with printer, four Hitachi CD-ROM players.

All Schools: seven copies of Grolier's New Electronic Encyclopedia.

When Grolier's New Electronic Encyclopedia was published, copies of that updated resource were purchased for all libraries. Based on the date of original purchase, we paid three different prices for the update. The Ann G. McGuinness Elementary School Library received its update for only $26.95, since it had participated in the earlier distribution of the Electronic Encyclopedia. The high school and middle school libraries had older versions of the product and paid $99.00. The four elementary libraries buying the encyclopedia for the first time paid the full retail price of $299.00. While the product was exactly the same for each library, a distinct advantage of CD-ROM resources is that, after the initial investment, the updated version is frequently quite inexpensive.

Services

There is some discussion in the literature on whether to offer online searching or to purchase CD-ROM databases. At Union-Endicott, we have found that these services are complementary. We offer students the opportunity to use the following variety of resources:

Hard-Disk Resident Databases

The Discover program for career and educational guidance is used by the students to refine their interests in order to choose an educational option, or to find information about a particular occupation or college.

Satellite-Based Databases

The X-press service is a collection of news and information services. The X-press service is provided through a local cable company and is free with basic cable service (a slightly more advanced version is available for a low fee, around $15.00 a month). Students search for current information in categories such as sports, for current scores and stories; news, for headlines, articles, and editorials; and entertainment, which has horoscopes as well as movie reviews and television schedules.

CD-ROM Databases

Our CD-ROM resources are the core of our program. The Readers' Guide is the most used resource. The second most used resource is probably Grolier's. Also available are Facts on File News Digest and Microsoft Bookshelf. Our local Board of Cooperative Educational Services (BOCES) also has produced two CD-ROM databases: the A-V resource catalog, which is the catalog to the film and video library; and the School Library System database, which has the records of the school libraries for 14 counties in our area. [See Chapter 12] We also use Bibliofile for retrospective conversion.

Online Databases

The subscription to the Readers' Guide CD includes a password for its online database, which is free, except for communications network charges. Union-Endicott also offers its students access to databases found in the Classmate network, from DIALOG Information Services. Once a school has a telephone line in place, the selection of databases is amazing; for example, through a long distance telephone number, students can log into the NASA Spacelink database in Huntsville, Alabama, and find updates on the space shuttle, and other space flight news. They can even leave messages for NASA. Nearby universities offer their online public access catalogs for log on also. Union-Endicott students and faculty can use the SUNY-Binghamton and Syracuse University library catalogs without leaving their high school library.

Problems and Solutions

The implementation of electronic information retrieval radically changed the operations of the school library media programs. It was impossible to predict exactly how these resources would be used, or even where to put them to get maximum use, so in the beginning we made several adjustments in the buildings' libraries.

High School

The biggest facility change was in the high school library. The reference area was previously in a balcony on the second floor of the library. The first computer and CD-ROM system were installed there, as well as the telephone line. The X-press system was located in an alcove on the first floor of the library. The problem with both of these systems was that they were not in a direct line of sight and supervision.

To correct this, the entire library floor plan was modified, and the reference section was moved downstairs. By this time, we had added an additional computer and CD-ROM system. We added an electrical strip with outlets six inches apart along the length of the wall, a total of 37 outlets. This was to solve any present or future problem with electricity. The modem phone line and television cable X-press line were also moved to the wall, with cables long enough to be moved to any part of the line in case the computers needed to be switched later. The wall space above the computers was covered with bulletin boards to draw attention to the computers and create a "center" atmosphere.

Middle School

The Jennie F. Snapp Middle School library is located on both sides of a hallway and occupies three separate enclosed rooms. The CD-ROM system was placed on the only available table space in the reference area, near a window. This seemed to be acceptable and even desirable at the time of installation, but the glare on the computer screen caused by the light through the window was such a problem that the curtains had to be closed on all except extremely cloudy days, making the library quite dark.

Furthermore, the computer for online searching had to be placed in the librarian's office to share the telephone line. This inside line goes through a switchboard, which adds some line noise, but not enough to prevent its use. The middle school facilities problem still needs resolution.

Elementary Schools

The elementary libraries of Union-Endicott are, like most elementary libraries, far too small for the kinds of programs that are required by today's guidelines. The computers were placed wherever space could be spared. Where necessary, electrical outlets were added.

When additional computers are placed in each elementary school library during the 1989–90 school year, the space problem will become increasingly severe. But the importance of these products to the elementary library program insures that "somewhere" will always exist.

Supervision

Any time an open telephone line is accessible to students security becomes a concern. This is a continuing issue for us, but we have taken steps to partially allay our fears. We moved the computers nearer the librarians and turned the sound up on the modems. Our final modification was to put a key-lock on the telephone line. The line is locked every afternoon and unlocked in the morning. With these security precautions, we felt secure enough to allow students to freely use the online options on the Readers' Guide, and to teach the online process.

Hardware Problems

Our first mistake in purchasing computer equipment was to buy monochrome monitors, thinking that for text use, with minimal graphics, no color was needed. Most of the reasons currently given for the purchase of color monitors are aesthetic reasons such as: "more attractive to students," "easier on the eye," etc. Our problem with monochrome monitors was much more basic: to teach successfully with a computer one needs a large-screen projection system, and those systems generally require a color monitor.

For high school students, a "live" demonstration is a much more successful way of teaching than using illustrations from previous searches. With the computer actually searching the CD-ROM during the teaching process, students maintain an interest in watching the search unfold, and the librarian can modify the topics according to the students' interests.

We have two large-screen projection systems. The first is a panel which sits on top of an overhead projector. The panel displays whatever is on the computer screen, and the overhead projector enlarges it onto the wall screen. The second system, our preference, is to use two 25 inch television monitors. These monitors, mounted on 48 inch tall carts, keep the students' attention, and allow the librarian to show the search process as it unfolds and to modify it to the students' interest and abilities.

To use either of these two options, the computer must have color capabilities. Our first solution was to call the computer technician each time we needed to teach a class. He would temporarily install an RGB (red, green, blue) card in the computer. After several months of doing this, on a weekly basis, it was decided that henceforth all computers used in the libraries would have color monitors.

This second solution has been very satisfactory and we have learned to make the necessary cable connections to hook and unhook the monitors. The middle and elementary schools are still in the "monochrome monitor" phase, which will be corrected in the 1989–90 school year.

To avoid problems, consider the following: place the computers in a central area that will be supervised; use electrical strips with multi-outlets, and extra-long cables for maximum flexibility; and use color monitors.

Instruction and Resources

Our adoption of electronic information retrieval has had a dramatic effect on the library instructional program. Teachers uniformly saw this as something that their students needed to learn. In some cases students asked for research assignments so they would have a reason to use these resources, and the number of classes that the librarian taught increased tremendously.

In addition, classes that rarely used the library, such as computer classes, now came in, so their students could be introduced to a new type of computer technology. The library orientation classes also had to be lengthened to cover the computerized resources. The students were then given assignments to use the resources, which resulted in instruction that was almost one-on-one.

When classes of 25 or more students came there were lines for the computers. What we have found is that students do not object to waiting, because when their turn arrives, their search takes minutes and sometimes only seconds to complete. Most printers have some amount of memory, so that search results can be printing for one student while the next student is performing his search. Students are even willing to come back after school. Because of this, the library hours were extended from 8:00 a.m.–3:00 p.m. (school hours) to 7:00 a.m.–4:00 p.m.

During the initial phase of CD installation in the high school, it was apparent that one CD-ROM system was not enough. The problem was not the number of students waiting to use the resources, but the variety of resources that were offered. The amount of time needed to load programs made it difficult to change discs mid-way through an instructional period. The high school librarian approached the principal with the problem and was able to purchase another CD-ROM drive to be attached to a computer originally intended for management use. Now the Readers' Guide and Grolier's Encyclopedia can run simultaneously, while other products are loaded as needed. This problem of changing discs in the middle of the instructional period is still a pressing problem for the middle school. There is a real need for the middle school to have another CD-ROM system, which should be obtained in the 1989–90 school year.

The effect of the CD installations on the elementary instructional program has yet to be determined. The elementary instructional schedule will certainly be affected, as there will be additional classes. The elementary librarians each have two buildings to supervise, so the library clerk in each building must be competent in the use of the CD resources.

Effects

The use of the Readers' Guide on CD has doubled the use of magazines at the high school. Previously, students who were told to use three sources of information used the first three print sources they found, regardless of whether they were current or relevant. By using the CD-ROM version, students know how many sources are available on their topic, and usually want to print the entire citation list. Students now use many more than the assigned number of sources for their research.

The BROWSE function, found on most of the CD-ROM products we offer, has an additional benefit. In BROWSE, students input a search term and retrieve an alphabetic list of subjects beginning with that search word. Given the list, students tend to use the main search term first, but will also use the additional subdivisions.

Students are using more sources, using more varied sources, and doing more complete research now with the addition of the electronic resources.

Improving the interlibrary loan service will be a major focus in the next few years. With the addition of the Readers' Guide and the CD library catalogs, teachers and students now have access to citations to a wide variety of materials in a variety of locations. Through our membership in our local BOCES School Library System, we have access to interlibrary loan networks that other school libraries have difficulty accessing. In many areas, the traditional sources for interlibrary loan, such as public and university libraries, are reluctant to loan to school libraries.

Staff Development

Union-Endicott has a Teacher Center which offers short courses on various topics relevant to new developments in instruction. Teachers are paid an hourly rate based on salary for attending these classes, and teachers who are course instructors are paid for teaching them. Since the inception of the electronic information retrieval program, the library staff has been an active participant in the Teacher Center Program. The courses have been divided according to level and the school librarians have been the instructors.

These courses were developed and taught according to grade level. We felt that teachers would obtain maximum benefit from participating in a class that presented instructional uses for the electronic resources at their grade level. The high school, middle school, and elementary school teachers registered for the class taught by their school librarians. We felt the "fear factor" of new technologies would be diminished if the teachers were working with someone they knew. The content of the course was essentially the same at all levels taught. The librarians briefly discussed the technologies and the basic hardware required. The majority of the time was spent on how to use the CDs and ways for teachers to use them with students. This approach has been successful and will be repeated periodically as long as the demand for classess continues.

We are currently planning a new course designed to give teachers an understanding of the interlibrary loan process and how they can use the school library as an access point for instructional materials, supplementary materials for lesson plan preparation, research materials for students, and professional development. The CD-ROM resources will be a major part of that course.

Future Plans

Our future plans focus on increasing the number of students who can use these resources at the same time. A networking system is being planned that will allow students to use various CD-ROMs and the online catalog from a variety of searching stations. In addition, a dial-up system to provide students access to the electronic resources from home is also under study.

During the 1989–90 school year, the elementary libraries are scheduled to receive voice/data telephone lines which will give them online access to back up the CD resources. An additional computer will be added to be used for management purposes, and a budget for the purchase of new CD products and the new editions of the current products has been approved.

Conclusions

Many factors have contributed to the success of the electronic information retrieval program at Union-Endicott. The cooperation between the library department and the computer services department has prevented many problems from happening. Another factor has been the support of the central administration and the building principals. They have been willing to venture into this new program without reassuring answers to questions about how this new step would affect resources, instruction, or budget.

The one factor that has contributed most to the success of our program has been the enthusiasm of the librarians. The use of CD-ROM resources has completely changed the nature of the library program and has created an entirely new area of instruction for librarians. The librarians are able to communicate their enthusiam to classroom teachers, who in turn, transmit this excitement to their students. In the past, students have had to limit their studies to the material that could be found in the school library. With electronic information retrieval, paired with interlibrary loan, students are now limited only by their own imagination and intelligence.

At Union-Endicott we feel that we are preparing students for the world of information technology. Students have accepted these resources as preferred research tools, and teachers have welcomed the opportunity to move beyond the information-locating research process and to spend more time teaching students what to do with the information they find.

Gail K. Dickinson has been Supervisor of Library Media Services for Union-Endicott Central School District since 1987. She received her undergraduate degree from Millersville University and was a school librarian in Virginia for eight years before receiving her M.S. in L.S. degree from the University of North Carolina at Chapel Hill in 1907.

Appendix

Union-Endicott Central School District Staffing

	Grades Served	No. of Students	Prof. Staff	Clerical Staff
District library media services located in the H.S. library			.6	4
Union Endicott High School	9–12	1,400	1.9*	4
Jennie F. Snapp Middle School	7–8	700	1	3
ELEMENTARY SCHOOLS George H. Nichols	K–6	500	.5	1
Thomas J. Watson	K–6	400	.5	1
Charles F. Johnson	K–6	400	.5	1
George W. Johnson	K–6	400	.5	1
Ann G. McGuinness	4–6	300	.5	1
Linnaeus W. West	K–3	500	.5	1

* High School staff is comprised of one full-time librarian, one half time librarian, and .4 of the supervisor's time.

12

CD-ROMs Go to School

Janet M. Bohl, Cynthia B. LaPier

Introduction

Those who have information have power, and it is the responsibility of schools to ensure that their students have the skills necessary to find information in any medium, in any library. Elementary and secondary schools in the United States are using databases on CD-ROM to help meet that responsibility. The skills learned using CD-ROM bibliographic databases can be transferred to online searching of library and vendor databases, and the development of higher level thinking skills (e.g., synthesis, evaluation) can be fostered through the use of CD-ROM software. Students experienced in Boolean search techniques and keyword, truncation, and wildcard searching can use their ability to apply search logic and search techniques to pursue information throughout their lives.

This chapter describes the experiences of two regional education centers in the south central area of New York, where carefully planned programs introduced the CD-ROM format to teachers, administrators, and students.

Background: The Structure of Library Media Support Services for Public Schools in New York

The elementary and secondary schools in New York are funded and admini- stered by school boards. In addition to school boards, 42 Boards of Cooperative Educational Services (BOCES) and five urban school districts provide a wide variety of shared, centralized educational services to kindergarten through twelfth grade schools. The services tend to be those that can be provided more cost- effectively through a shared arrangement. Exceptional child education programs, vocational education, specialized adult education classes, and a myriad of compu- terized services are offered by the BOCES. The BOCES receive funding, appor- tioned by the state, for some of their programs. However, the majority of the programs are funded by the participating school districts.

Each BOCES is composed of several divisions including an Educational Communications and/or an Instructional Support Services Department. Over the past 15 to 25 years either the Division of Educational Communications or an Instructional Support Services Department has provided most BOCES with a film/

video library, an instructional television service, and equipment repair, but until 1979 there was no system for sharing library services and resources.

In 1978 the State of New York legislated the funding for 12 pilot School Library Systems (SLS) within selected BOCES. Their main responsibilities were the coordination of database development and interlibrary loans. The Broome-Delaware-Tioga BOCES was one of the pilot systems. Five years later School Library Systems were given permanent status and started in the 35 remaining Educational Communications/Instructional Support Divisions of BOCES and the urban school districts that function as BOCES. The funding for the Systems is provided by the New York State legislature, but organizationally the Systems fall within the BOCES.

This case study describes the CD-ROM activities in two School Library Systems, Schuyler-Chemung-Tioga (SCT) in Elmira and Broome-Delaware-Tioga (BDT) in Binghamton. Since BOCES are organized around school districts, a county, such as Tioga, can be served by two or more BOCES.

The Schuyler-Chemung-Tioga BOCES SLS is made up of seven districts with a total of 40 public and non-public elementary and secondary schools. The Broome-Delaware-Tioga BOCES serves 15 public school districts and four non–public schools with a total of 75 libraries. The school libraries within both systems are typical as there are no specialty schools (such as arts or science) within the group. All the collections are fairly consistent and the clientele are students (pre-kindergarten through high school seniors), teachers, administrators, and staff. However each of the libraries is unique and is a reflection of the individual librarian, the level of administrative support which it is receives, and the teachers and students that are its clientele.

The School Library System offices are located in each BOCES facility and are primarily administrative, but they do house a small professional school library media collection that serves librarians. Many teachers and administrators also use these resources regularly.

Automation

Prior to the creation of a shared database on CD-ROM, many of the SLSs throughout the BOCES were automating their own catalogs. The first products were Computer Output Microfiche (COM) catalogs, and computer-generated print lists. Using Brodart Automation as the vendor, the Broome-Delaware-Tioga BOCES began developing a database of their schools' library holdings in MARC format in 1980. The original output products were COM catalogs and camera-ready copy. The first input was typed onto scan sheets which were read by optical character recognition (OCR) scanners. As the technology improved, the off-line input was transferred to the Brodart MicroCheck software. In 1987 the Brodart Interactive Access online system was installed and records were input on that system. The SLS provided all the schools in the system with copies of the COM catalog and microfiche readers.

SCT began using Brodart's Online System in 1985. In that same year they explored a variety of methods for providing access to their in-house database of recent acquisitions and materials whose records had been converted. The primary options were microfiche and Brodart's LePac catalog on CD-ROM. The librarians immediately and wholeheartedly chose LePac.

The decision was made easily because not only did most libraries lack microfiche readers, but most librarians (and students) did not want to deal with microfiche. Although little was known then about the potential of a CD-ROM catalog, the librarians instinctively felt it would be a better and more effective format for student use.

There were still a few hand-written cards or cards with abbreviated authors and/ or titles within the card catalogs. In some cases there were no cards for the books in the collections. The librarians realized that by converting and creating records they would be providing students with consistent amounts of information, and by providing keyword access they would be providing flexible entry points to those records, and subsequently, to the items on the shelves.

SCOOLS: South Central Organization of (School) Library Systems

In 1985 the South Central Research Library Council initiated discussions among the seven SLSs in the south central counties in New York, including Broome-Delaware-Tioga and Schuyler-Chemung-Tioga, to see if they could collectively apply for regional automation funds for their libraries. The South Central SLSs proposed the creation of a CD-ROM union catalog, but the proposal was not approved at that time. Instead, in 1986 a merged COM catalog was produced by the seven School Library Systems. Six of the School Library Systems use Brodart as their bibliographic utility; one uses OCLC. Planning continued, however, and in 1988 a second COM catalog and a CD-ROM version were produced. Since the timing did not coincide with OCLC's downloading schedule, only six School Library Systems participated in the merged database CD-ROM.

The database contained the Union Catalog of Books, the Union List of Serials, and a Directory of Librarians. Individual schools had to pay for the hardware to run the CD-ROM, although in some cases the School Library System was able to supply the hardware. Each school had the option to acquire the CD-ROM.

At SCT the greatest problem with implementation was the hardware. In the schools that received hardware purchased and installed by the System there were no problems. When CD-ROM readers were added to existing workstations there were constant compatibility problems, most of which revolved around the monitors.

Meanwhile, school libraries were steadily acquiring commercial CD-ROM products [See Chapter 11] so that by the time the SCOOLS disc was distributed, 14 out of 73 libraries already owned CD-ROM drives in the BDT BOCES area.

CD-ROM Integration into the Library

To foster an awareness of optical technology the BDT SLS purchased four Hitachi CD-ROM drives in September 1987. One drive was reserved for demonstrations and research (mainly ERIC SilverPlatter searches) in the office. The other three drives were circulated to schools that owned appropriate microcomputers. Software purchased for demonstration and circulation included Grolier's Electronic Encyclopedia, the McGraw-Hill CD-ROM Science and Technical Reference Set, the Wilsondisc Demonstration Disc, and Microsoft Bookshelf. Grolier's has been the most popular.

The BDT SLS also received outdated LePac discs of the Finger Lakes Public Library System's catalog of central and member library collections, since three of the BDT BOCES school districts are within the Finger Lakes Library System's area of service.

The excitement over the SCOOLS CD-ROM was still high when the LePac CD-ROM for media in Broome-Delaware-Tioga BOCES arrived. Video, films and multi-media holdings of the BDT BOCES Division of Educational Communications had been incorporated into the BDT BOCES database and COM catalog. Those holdings were not included in the SCOOLS database because those materials were not available for interlibrary loan to other BOCES regions. Instead, in 1989, a separate CD-ROM of those holdings was produced for the BDT schools. The disc contains over 7,000 titles of video recordings, 16 mm films, videodiscs, and multi-media kits. Bibliographic information on those same resources is also available in a print catalog.

In the SCT BOCES, 12 secondary school libraries and nine of the elementary school libraries have CD-ROM readers to access the SCOOLS disc. The System office circulates OCLC CD450 ERIC, and EMIL (Education Materials in Libraries/OCLC), Microsoft Bookshelf, Grolier's Electronic Encyclopedia (both versions of software), McGraw-Hill CD-ROM Science and Technical Reference Set, and Science Helper (K–8).

The Schuyler-Chemung-Tioga School Library System has two CD-ROM readers. One is used by the interlibrary loan clerk to locate items from the SCOOLS disc. The other reader is used by anyone who needs to access the CD-ROM software collection. The System Director searches ERIC, scans the public domain CD-ROM produced by PC SIG, looks up esoteric quotes on Microsoft Bookshelf, searches Bibliofile, and checks the SCOOLS discs. Students have used the station to search the encyclopedia, librarians have used it in online training sessions, and other BOCES staff have examined products within their areas of expertise. For instance, the elementary science specialist was wildly enthusiastic when searching the Science Helper (K–8).

Discs are changed frequently. There has never been a problem jumping from one program to another; usually it is just a matter of exiting one software program and executing the next one. The system does not have to be rebooted between programs.

Access

The philosophy of the SCT School Library System is service on demand, as quickly as possible. The machine is available whenever the building is open, and it is generally always in use. If someone makes a request to use the equipment every effort is made to satisfy the requester. There are no fees, downloading is encouraged, and printing is also supported.

Within SCT schools access is a different situation. The CD-ROM reader is attached to the machine that the librarian also uses for management, word processing, and any other tasks that are automated. The computer is usually located in an office with use generally limited to staff in response to a student's need. In a few instances the machine is in the public service area and student use is not as controlled. Then the librarians encourage the students to use the machine all day. They work with them, helping them make interlibrary loan requests and monitoring the printing. This monitoring is fairly easy to do in a small school library where the reading or work area is visible to all staff.

Probably 95 percent of the searching is done on the SCOOLS disc. Multiple disc access is primitive. Since switching discs is relatively rare, it is usually accomplished by a reboot.

At BDT BOCES and in many of its component schools, the CD-ROM software is loaded on a hard drive and conveniently accessed from a CD-ROM menu, which resides as a sub-menu from the main menu for each microcomputer.

Publicity by the SLS

The library media staff from each BDT BOCES district were invited to BOCES for personal awareness sessions and a tour of the new Educational Communications Center. In the school year prior to the production of the SCOOLS CD-ROM each group was given a demonstration of CD-ROM and videodisc. Visiting administrators and groups of teachers on curriculum writing teams meeting at BOCES were also given demonstrations and the CD-ROMs were the subject of presentations at several conferences, including the New York State Computers and Education conference.

The culminating publicity for the SCOOLS CD-ROM was a celebration on the day the discs were distributed. Over 50 library media specialists and computer staff participated in workshops where both the browse and expert search modes of the LePac disc were demonstrated, as was the interlibrary loan feature. The attendees were particularly impressed by the latter.

The awareness and publicity efforts will continue as long as there are schools which have not yet adopted this technology.

Training

Teachers

At the SCT SLS, staff training for school librarians takes place in the annual workshop session when the updated SCOOLS disc is distributed. The need for training on LePac is minimal since searching is relatively easy, requiring very little time or practice to master. The interlibrary loan module is more complicated so the training session concentrates on the use of this subsystem.

Conversely, at the BDT BOCES, the importance of teaching search techniques is emphasized to librarians and classroom teachers. To endow students with the ability to state a problem, select the appropriate terms to use, and determine the most advantageous search techniques for the occasion is to equip them with a life-long skill. Students who are thus trained will be able to retrieve information from systems that have not yet been invented.

The System provides abbreviated instructions as well as a copy of the Brodart manual with all the discs. The Coordinator/Director makes site visits when librarians are unable to get the program to work. Usually this is the result of a hardware problem, mismatched disc to system, and once in a while an unfamiliarity with the program or computers.

It is important that staff become used to the hardware and software. The staff should feel at ease with the disc: they should understand that it is durable, that it can be written on, that scissors and magnets will not erase the data, and that dust can be removed by simply wiping the disc.

Software training should be extensive and repeated. Unfortunately, it looks as if the CD-ROM software programs will be using different search software for quite a while. Librarians will have to become familiar with all of them. This is asking a lot of librarians in one-person libraries. Until search interfaces develop some consistency, an interim solution to the multiplicity may be for librarians to develop an expertise in the most heavily used systems only.

Training takes a lot of time. After a training session, users should be given an opportunity to practice with an expert to watch and provide support. Even if the menu is right on the screen at all times and seems obvious, there may be a word or command that does not make sense and needs some explanation.

Some librarians have also received training on the ERIC (OCLC) disc. At one point it was thought that online searching would be conducted in the schools, but this has not become commonplace. In most schools mediated searching will probably be on CD-ROM rather than on remote databases.

Students

User training is even more minimal than that given to the librarians. Each librarian determines how the CD-ROM programs will be used within the school. They decide whether the students will have free, unlimited access, or monitored access, or mediated searching. Students are much more comfortable with the computer, and attached CD-ROM reader, than many of the librarians. Some students already take for granted the amount of data stored on the disc, the ability of the software to import data into an interlibrary loan form, or its ability to search using Boolean operators.

Funding

The costs for the production of the CD-ROMs was born by the School Library Systems. The intent is to produce an annual version of the SCOOLS database, at least until all libraries within the System are automated. At that time, the use of CD-ROM as a means of sharing a database will be reevaluated. However, continuing SCOOLS production may be delayed because of a lack of funding, even though when the systems work as a consortium, the CD-ROMs actually cost each of the cooperating school library systems less than microfiche or print versions of the same database.

Hardware cost is a major factor, but not always a deterrent. In the BDT BOCES area, one high school's Student Council provided funds after seeing a demonstration of the SCOOLS disc. In a neighboring district the Library Club raised enough money to purchase the hardware.

In the SCT SLS no print publications were cancelled when the CD-ROM version was introduced. There was no subscription to the ERIC print indexes, and a printed union catalog had never been produced. The union list of serials and the directory of librarians were in-house publications, incorporated into the SCOOLS database.

Impact

CD-ROM databases have had a great impact on interlibrary loans. The SCOOLS catalog has opened up new resources for school libraries. They now have the option to select from the holdings in a region instead of a library. The ERIC CD-ROM retrieves citations available in very few school libraries. These bibliographic CD-ROMs create demands for resources that the SCOOLS discs and the interlibrary loan network allow school libraries to meet. Resources are truly being shared.

Students and faculty have come to understand the potential of the CD-ROM. It enhances the research process, making it easier and faster. However, patrons are not as aware of the drawbacks of CD-ROMs. Because of the ease with which materials can be located, and the success of interlibrary loan, the CD-ROM products encourage uncritical use by patrons and the librarians. Everything comes up on the screen so easily and looks so good that the user does not evaluate the material to determine its real value. The Grolier's Electronic Encyclopedia is very easy to search, and provides better access points than the print volumes. But in the end the articles are still just encyclopedia articles with the same limitations as the print version.

Future/Reflections

When we look back on our choice, four years later, it is obvious that one mission of the School Library Systems was achieved with the introduction of the SCOOLS CD-ROM. We had a sense that by building the union catalog we could help students take advantage of interlibrary loan and networking, a service which academic and public libraries have offered for years. We were right.

We were attuned to computer technology and to the fact that hardware was sometimes difficult to acquire outside of classrooms or labs. We also knew that all too often students were not impressed by libraries. They did not use them effectively and they tended to forget the library skills they did learn. We saw CD-ROM, more broadly, as a way to attract students to the library. The librarians may not have fully grasped the possibilities of CD-ROM, but they knew that something great was about to happen.

CD-ROMs, used as locator tools for resources, may be stepping stones to total online systems, or they may be the final product. In some situations CD-ROMs are more cost-effective than an online system.

Is the time, energy and money expended on the optical format worthwhile? One library media specialist in a small rural school summed it up nicely on an evaluation form, "If it were not for the School Library System, we would not be aware of the exciting capabilities of CD-ROM technology today." Empowered, enthusiastic librarians, teachers and students make it all that much more worthwhile!

Janet M. Bohl has been with the Broome-Delaware-Tioga BOCES Division of Educational Communications since 1979. She is currently the Administrative Coordinator of Instructional Support Services and School Library System Director. Prior positions have been as an elementary school library media specialist, director of a small suburban public library and head of children's services in a medium-sized public library. She holds New York State certification as a school library media specialist, school administrator, supervisor, teacher, and public librarian with degrees from SUNY Geneseo in Geneseo, NY, and SUNY Cortland in Cortland, NY.

Cynthia B. LaPier became the Coordinator/Director of the Schuyler-Chemung-Tioga BOCES School Library System in 1985. Cynthia received her B.A. in English, American Literature from SUNY Albany, and her M.L.S. from SUNY Albany. Prior to working at the SLS, Cynthia was the Head of Reference at Elmira College.

13
Project RFD (Rural Facts Delivery)

Lisa Hughes Peeling

When the decision was made to open a new library branch in the northern area of Maryland's Baltimore County, the challenge facing the administration and staff of the Baltimore County Public Library (BCPL) was how to provide patrons with the widest array of services and materials possible within the constraints of a facility containing 5,000 square feet of working space and an opening day collection of 11,000 items. It was at this juncture that the idea of using CD-ROM databases was proposed as a way of providing many types of current information to a variety of users, thereby maximizing the use of the available library space.

The Library Setting

The Hereford Branch, as the new facility is called, was proposed to serve the 21,000 residents of rural northern Baltimore County, an area encompassing over 220 square miles. Patrons had been clamoring for a facility in the northern area of the county for years. The population growth of seven percent in the years 1980 through 1986, and projections for a further increase of five to seven percent in the next five years, warranted the attention of the Baltimore County Board of Library Trustees, who requested funds for a permanent library facility to be established in the 1987–88 fiscal year. Although the north county area had once been primarily a farming district, the profile of the community had changed rapidly to include many people employed in professional and managerial-level positions. New residential construction permits, which had doubled in the previous five years, produced homes listed in the $150,000 to $200,000 price range. Despite the influx of new residents, no additional schools had been planned to supplement the existing four public elementary schools, one middle school, and one senior high school. However, an increasing number of small and medium-sized businesses had recently moved to or opened in the Hereford area to meet the growing needs of the local consumers there.

Prior to the establishment of the Hereford Branch, patrons traveled to the Cockeysville Area Branch located twelve miles further south. While the Cockeysville Area Branch's collection of 160,000 items, extensive periodical and microfilm holdings, and staff of 16 librarians offered excellent services and materials, library users who came from the farthest north and west areas of the county needed to travel up to 25 miles one-way to reach the Cockeysville Branch. Clearly, a trip to the Hereford Branch would mean a savings in time and fuel, but at what cost in available materials and services? It was decided that the Hereford Branch would, at its inception, be a "satellite" of the Cockeysville Area Branch.

Satellite status meant that the Hereford Branch would be staffed by employees from the Cockeysville Branch and supported by the considerably larger Cockeysville holdings. A "hotline" telephone would be installed, by which a librarian at Hereford could request from the staff at Cockeysville a shelf check for a title or information from one of the reference tools. The needed item would be transferred to Hereford in the next day's delivery of materials, or the information would be photocopied and sent, within 30 minutes, via telefacsimile to the waiting patron at the Hereford Branch. In a similar fashion, the patron at Hereford could obtain a list of periodical citations from Infotrac II and ask the librarian to transmit the list to a clerical staff member at Cockeysville. The staff member would then retrieve the articles from a microfilm bank of periodicals, photocopy them and send the materials, by telefacsimile, back to the patron at the Hereford Branch. There would be no charge to the patron during the period in which a Maryland Department of Education grant would support the service; after the expiration of the grant, the materials sent by telefacsimile could be checked out of the library for the usual three-week loan period, or could be purchased by the patron at the same price per page as the cost of photocopying the material. Using these measures, the patron at Hereford would have access, within a short waiting period, to the much broader collection at Cockeysville, without having to make the longer trip.

Previous Experience with CD-ROM Products

The patrons and staff of Baltimore County Public Library had some limited experience with CD-ROM databases. Not only had the CD-ROM index of periodicals been in use in several branches, including Cockeysville, since March of 1987, but the public catalog had been converted to CD-ROM and placed in each of the branches during August of 1987. Reactions from the public and staff had been mixed, but the majority of users had positive reactions to their experiences with the CD-ROM databases. The staff marvelled at how quickly the public accepted and used the new CD-ROM catalogs.

Based upon these successful experiences, librarians from the Information Services department and administration members planning for the new Hereford Branch decided that other CD-ROM databases might prove helpful to patrons in the north county area, providing them with access to information that might not otherwise be obtained from a limited print collection. Offering online databases directly to patrons as end-users was rejected because of the generally higher costs and amount of time needed to learn how to search the databases.

The key piece to solving the materials and information access puzzle lay in finding the monies to purchase hardware (the greatest expense) and software (the CD-ROM databases), as well as supplies such as printer paper and ink cartridges. The most promising avenue of finance appeared to be grant funds.

Project RFD (Rural Facts Delivery) Grant

An application was written for Project RFD, as the Hereford electronic library project became known, and submitted to the Maryland Department of Education, Division of Library Development and Services, for federal funds awarded under Title I of the Library Services and Construction Act. Baltimore County Public Library had applied previously for project grants, which helped supply "seed money" to establish new programs, the cost of which would be absorbed by the BCPL budget after the grant funds ended.

The Project RFD application stated that the goals and objectives were related to the *Maryland Plan for Libraries 1986–1991* Goal 1, objective 1.7: "By 1991 all users of Maryland libraries should have access to information through a variety of electronic databases or services to meet their needs in the most efficient manner" (Maryland State Department of Education, 1986). The project was secondarily related to Objective 1.1 Sub-Objective 1.1a: "By 1991 users of public libraries will be able to obtain during a visit to their library satisfactory subject materials 75 percent of the time" (Maryland State Department of Education, 1986). Goal III of BCPL's own long range plan *Growth Without Expansion* concurred with the goals of the project: "To improve delivery of information services to library users" (Rodger and Palmour, 1983).

The grant was awarded by the Maryland Department of Education, Division of Library Development and Services, for a two-year period beginning July 1, 1987 and ending June 30, 1989. The greater portion of the project (employees' salaries, building rent, etc.) would be funded locally by Baltimore County. The Project RFD grant supplied the funding for:
—CD-ROM workstations with printers
—a microfilm cartridge reader/printer
—a microfiche reader/printer
—two telefacsimile machines
—telephone lines for the telefacsimile machines and a modem
—a personal computer and printer for online database searches
—online database charges
—furniture
—supplies
—CD-ROM software

In addition to providing electronic information resources to the residents of rural northern Baltimore County, the project was intended to "enable the state to develop a cost effective model for library services to remote, less densely populated areas" which could be "replicated by other public libraries in Maryland" (Baltimore County Public Library, 1987). The objectives of the project included recording the number of users over the two-year period in order to document the increased utilization of the library's resources.

Online Services

The CD-ROM databases and periodical article telefacsimiles would be supplemented by the availability of Vu/Text, an online, full-text database vendor of news and business information.

The Vu/Text database group was selected because it could provide both up-to-the-minute and retrospective business and news information in full text, and the Hereford Branch would have very little storage space for old newspapers, magazines, or standard business reference tools. Based upon the nature of the information needed, the librarian would make a determination as to whether the Vu/Text databases could most completely answer the patron's needs. If that were the case, the librarian, who had been trained in online searching, would perform the search and deliver the full text of the needed articles to the patron as soon as the search could be executed. The idea of training patrons and allowing them to perform their own searches on Vu/Text had been considered but was rejected; it became apparent during the librarians' training that the amount of time needed to learn to execute even basic searches precluded searching by the public as end-users.

CD-ROM Products

Selection

Important factors in the selection of the CD-ROM products were subject content and ease of use. The products chosen were identified through exhibits at the American Library Association conferences and through promotional materials sent by vendors to the coordinators of materials management and information services at the administrative offices of BCPL.

The databases purchased and reasons for selection of each product follows:

InfoTrac II: Already in use in most BCPL branches, this periodical index references Magazine Collection, a microfilm collection of periodical articles; Infotrac II provides the microfilm reel and frame number for most citations. As the Cockeysville Branch owned the microfilms, Hereford could tap into the Magazine Collection through facsimile requests.

Grolier's Electronic Encyclopedia: "All 21 volumes of the *Academic American Encyclopedia* on a single CD-ROM." As the publisher states, this tool provides a wide range of information that could be used by elementary school students through adults. A printout of all or any part of an article that the patron could take home would make information from the source even more accessible than a circulating set of encyclopedias.

McGraw-Hill CD-ROM Science and Technical Reference Set: A CD-ROM edition of the *McGraw-Hill Concise Encyclopedia* and the *McGraw-Hill Dictionary of Scientific and Technical Terms,* this source would be helpful to middle school students through adults (especially during science project season). While the graphics portion of the database would not be accessible to our patrons because of hardware limitations, the database would complement a sparse science collection in the areas of earth sciences, astronomy, biology, and zoology. Again, the availability of a printout for the patron to take home would relieve some of the pressure to build the print collection in the sciences.

Microsoft Bookshelf: A CD-ROM product that contains 10 ready-reference type tools, this database is intended to be used by writers in conjunction with a word-processing program. Some of the tools have print counterparts which are frequently used by librarians and the public: the *American Heritage Dictionary;* an electronic version of *Roget's Thesaurus;* the *World Almanac and Book of Facts; Bartlett's Familiar Quotations;* and the *U.S. ZIP Code Directory.* Other tools, while helpful to a writer, would be less useful to the average patron: the Houghton-Mifflin Spelling Verifier and Corrector; Houghton-Mifflin Usage Alert; a directory of standard business forms and letters; and a bibliography of business information sources.

While the Vu/Text databases could only be accessed with the assistance of a librarian, the other CD-ROM databases were available to the public at all times. Each CD-ROM product was allocated a workstation which included an IBM-compatible microcomputer, a CD player, and a printer. Each workstation was located within 20 feet of the information desk, a vantage point from which a librarian could easily observe patrons needing assistance.

Patron Access to Electronic Technology

Unlimited printing was permitted, and there was no charge for use of the database or printer paper. No limits were placed on the amount of time a patron could occupy a workstation; however, if the librarian was aware that a patron had been using the database for fifteen minutes or more and another patron was waiting, the librarian might approach the patron using the database and ask if any assistance was needed and/or make the patron aware that others were waiting to use the tool. Overall, this procedure has proven effective. The databases most likely to have a patron waiting for use were InfoTrac II, which was heavily used by high school and adult students writing term papers, and Grolier's Electronic Encyclopedia, which was popular with the middle school students.

On occasion, the librarian would need to monitor the use of the printer attached to the Grolier's Electronic Encyclopedia workstation. For example, after one student commented to the librarian that the children compared printout lengths and competed to see whose was longest, it was feared that the paper, and not the information, was most prized.

Downloading of information was not an option available to patrons. In order to protect the CD and drive from tampering, a plexiglass panel was attached to the front of each unit, also preventing access to the floppy disk drive. As printing was unlimited, there were no complaints regarding this policy.

As the grant nears completion, the possibility of installing a local area network is being considered. Once installed, the local area network would allow more than one workstation to access each database, and thereby reduce the amount of time patrons spend waiting to use a particular CD-ROM product. Other CD-ROM products are under consideration for purchase, including Facts on File News Digest and Ebsco's Magazine Article Summaries. Both of these products would broaden the scope of information services available to patrons.

Staff and Patron Training on the CD-ROM Products

Training on the new technology was a two-part enterprise. It was necessary that all librarians assigned to the Cockeysville Branch become familiar with the databases, because any of the staff might be assigned to the Hereford Branch on a particular day. The staff would then be called upon to train and assist members of the public in the use of the CD-ROM databases.

Two librarians from the Cockeysville Branch were given the task of familiarizing themselves with the CD-ROM products and then instructing 21 other Cockeysville staff librarians. The librarians who assumed the "instructor" role developed a checklist of concepts that each librarian needed to learn in order to use the Microsoft Bookshelf, Grolier's Electronic Encyclopedia (Appendix 1) and McGraw-Hill Science and Technical Reference Set. Staff members were then asked to complete a "homework assignment" for each product in which they would practice their new skills in searching the database (Appendix 2). An additional assignment required the librarians to select a CD-ROM product that "fit" the question and state the method by which they found the answer. Initial training sessions lasted one hour for each of the databases, with a follow-up session of one-half hour in order to review the assignments and clarify search techniques.

A group of four librarians attended a one-day training session in the basic techniques of searching the Vu/Text databases. The group condensed the information into a two-and-one-half hour session whereby the other staff members were taught the search protocol for Vu/Text.

All of the software and hardware purchased under the Project RFD grant was installed at the Cockeysville Branch during the one-month training period and then transferred to the Hereford Branch in time for the opening date.

Statistics on the Use of CD-ROM Products

One of the objectives of the grant was that a stipulated number of users would acquire information through the use of the electronic resources. The numbers would increase from Year 1 to Year 2, demonstrating a broadening exposure of the CD-ROM products to the citizens of northern Baltimore County.

Statistics were gathered using several methods:

1. Each time a request was made for information or periodical articles to be transmitted from Cockeysville or Hereford via telefacsimile, a form was filled out by the clerk sending the information. The form recorded the source used (helpful knowledge in developing Hereford's collection), the number of pages transmitted, and the name of the patron, so that participating patrons could be tallied.

2. A supply of questionnaires was placed at each CD-ROM workstation, with a sign requesting patrons to fill out the form and leave it in the marked box. While this was not a consistently reliable source of information, as patrons did not always fill out the forms, it did provide some indication of patrons' attitudes toward the CD-ROM databases.

3. Each time a librarian performed a search using one of the Vu/Text databases he or she recorded the database used, the information needed, the search strategy, the length of time connected, and the results achieved. (A form was created that was

originally intended to be filled out by patrons after using the Vu/Text database, but after the decision was made to limit searching to librarians only, the form was filled out by the librarian after interviewing the patron regarding the information retrieved.)

One of the objectives of Project RFD provided that at least 300 library users were to receive "an in-depth introduction in the use of all the electronic resources located in the Hereford library" (Baltimore County Public Library, 1987) by the closing date of the grant. This objective was met by offering tours to the community at several levels: children from one local elementary school were given tours; adults and senior high school students attended afternoon and evening sessions of instruction on the use of the databases; librarians and administrators from school and public libraries outside of Baltimore County received training in the new technology; and individuals were offered one-on-one training sessions with the librarians as scheduling allowed. Patrons were asked to fill out a training questionnaire following their session, and the responses were used to fine tune the instructional techniques used during the sessions.

When tours or instructional sessions were scheduled, additional staff members had to be sent from the Cockeysville Branch. Meeting the objectives of the grant has required many staff hours; however, the installation of the new technology has provided staff members with the opportunity to develop new skills and to interact with an exciting new genre of information tools.

Evaluation of CD-ROM Products

In the process of purchasing materials for the initial Hereford collection, selections were made with the criterion that the CD-ROM products would provide information that need not be duplicated in print. For example, only one general reference encyclopedia, rather than the usual two, was purchased; the *ZIP Code Directory* and *Bartlett's Familiar Quotations* were not purchased in print form; no additional science encyclopedia was purchased. The impact of these decisions had both positive and negative aspects, and is discussed in the brief reviews of each CD-ROM product below.

InfoTrac II: One of the easiest-to-use of the products selected, the major drawback of this CD-ROM database was the unreliable hardware provided by the vendor. When problems occurred in the operation of the compact disc drive or CPU, as frequently happened, the vendor would send new equipment by air freight to the library. The time during which the database was not available to patrons would sometimes amount to several days or more. Although a subscription to a print index of periodicals had been purchased, the starting date of the subscription was only shortly before the opening date of the Hereford library. Therefore, when InfoTrac II was not in service, no retrospective index to periodicals was available. This situation was frustrating and disappointing to both patrons and librarians.

Grolier's Electronic Encyclopedia: This product was successful with the widest age range of patrons. On-screen prompts gave the user instruction in most instances, with only a few cryptic messages needing translation by the librarian in order for patrons to use the product. The bibliography supplied at the end of most entries was helpful to patrons who desired more information on the subject they were researching.

McGraw-Hill Science and Technical Reference Set: The availability of Boolean logic in this database's software made this CD-ROM product especially helpful in finding science-related information. However, the keystrokes needed to print or access the articles were not apparent to the first-time user, the software needed improvement in the area of on-screen directions, and the greatest difficulty arising from the acquisition of this product was that the original compact disc purchased proved to be defective. The producer promised a replacement disc, which unfortunately could not be supplied until a new issue of discs had been completed. This resulted in a period of several months during which the database was not available to patrons.

Microsoft Bookshelf: As stated previously, this product is intended to be used in conjunction with a word-processing program. The product assumes that the user already knows how to search the database and therefore provides very few on-screen directions. A page of directions to assist the user was written and mounted behind a plexiglass plate attached to the front of the central processing unit. Without training, most patrons found this database very difficult to use. Also, at the time of purchase, the copyright date of the World Almanac and Book of Facts was already one year behind, and the producer's promise of an updated version never materialized.

These descriptions do not take into consideration the excitement and enthusiasm engendered in patrons by the CD-ROM products. While some products were simpler to operate than others, those patrons who had a genuine need for the information contained in the databases were willing to take the time needed to learn the commands necessary to access the data. Once they had become familiar with the databases, patrons required little assistance from the librarian in the use of the CD-ROM products.

Publicity for Project RFD

An effort was made to attract patrons' interest in the CD-ROM products through the publicity surrounding the opening of the Hereford Branch. A flyer was created for this purpose. It was distributed at local businesses, posted on area bulletin boards, and carried home by children with their school bulletins. Notice of the adult training sessions was given in local newspapers and posted at each workstation in the library. Early training sessions were filled to capacity; additional sessions have been offered and community interest is still evident.

Tours of the library and training sessions in the basic use of the new technology were provided for a total of 158 adults and 328 students, from elementary through senior high school. The training provided was a somewhat abbreviated version of the training sessions provided for the librarians, depending on the ages of the group being trained and the group's previous computer experience. The checklists developed for use in the librarians' training were the primary tools used in the public sessions; however, the depth and detail of the search techniques taught was tailored to the group at hand.

Determining the cost of providing CD-ROM products requires a multi-step analysis. A cost analysis has not yet been completed for Project RFD, as the grant has not terminated as of this writing. When this process is undertaken two factors will be considered: 1) the purchase of the hardware needed to run and access the compact discs, 2) the price of the products. The best hardware that can be afforded should be purchased during the initial investment so that inaccessibility due to equipment breakdown is minimized. While the price of a compact disc database may be greater than the print version of the same information, the cost per use decreases each time the product is used. The added convenience of printing the information as many times as necessary to fill the patrons' needs could possibly exceed that of photocopying a print version of the product. The ongoing expense of printer paper and ink cartridges or ribbons is currently paid for by the grant; it may be subsidized by Baltimore County Public Library for a period following the grant. Ultimately, coin-boxes attached to printers may be necessary to recover the printing costs as more CD-ROM products become available throughout the Baltimore County Public Library system. The personnel costs are an additional commitment a library must make in order to implement any new service program.

As databases are updated by the producers, Baltimore County Public Library will purchase the revised editions of the products it already owns—an outdated version is as undesirable on compact disc as it is in print. It has been the experience of the Library that the revisions of CD-ROM products have been offered to current owners at significantly lower prices than the original purchase price of the database.

Future Installations of CD-ROM Products

Project RFD has provided a useful testing ground for future CD-ROM equipped branches of Baltimore County Public Library. Some considerations that will be included for future installations at other BCPL branches are:

—Request a vendor demonstration (by competent personnel) of the operation and features of each database and a 30-day trial period so that staff would have hands-on experience and would be able to carefully evaluate the product in terms of the library's needs.

—The installation of a local area network so that each CD-ROM product can be accessed from any workstation, thereby reducing or eliminating waiting periods.

—Provision for security of the product. This could be accomplished in a number of ways, such as installing the compact discs in a multi-disc server in an area inaccessible to the public, or by installing a locking device that would prevent patron access to the compact disc and the CD drive in the public area.

Patron Response

One of the measures of success of Project RFD is the response of the patrons to the new technology. In the first nine months at the Hereford Branch, the CD-ROM databases were used more than 2,000 times (this number reflects the total number of uses, not unique users). A sample of comments, gathered from patron questionnaires, follows:

—Always ask for help when using the new equipment for the first time. Next time, we'll be able to function alone.

—It was very helpful. It gave me almost all the information I needed for a report.

—Didn't have all the information I needed, but it did have most of it.

—The wait for the computer was the only problem.

—A terrific resource to have in the library.

—This is a good idea. This type of computer should be put in other libraries.

The administration, staff, and many patrons of Baltimore County Public Library agree with this last suggestion. Project RFD has provided both the library staff and the patrons of Baltimore County Public Library with an opportunity to interact with one of the most exciting new resources in the realm of information retrieval. Our experiences will assist us, not only in the future selection of CD-ROM products, but in providing database producers with feedback on how to make their products easier to use and more attractive to potential customers. Project RFD has also demonstrated that a small library in a rural, sparsely populated area can, through the use of new electronic technology, provide its patrons with the information sources previously only available at libraries with greater resources and larger collections.

References

Baltimore County Public Library. 1987. *LSCA Project Application Project RFD (Rural Facts Delivery)*.

Rodger, Eleanor Jo and Vernon E. Palmour. 1983. *Growth Without Expansion Baltimore County Public Library Long Range Plan II 1983–1988*. Towson, Maryland: Baltimore County Public Library.

Maryland State Department of Education, Division of Library Development and Services. 1986. *Maryland Plan for Libraries 1986–1991*. Baltimore, Maryland: Maryland State Department of Education.

Lisa Hughes Peeling has been employed by Baltimore County Public Library since 1986. She is currently assigned to the Cockeysville and Hereford Branches as a Public Services Librarian. Lisa received her B.S. degree in Instructional Technology from Towson State University in Towson, MD and her M.L.S. from the University of Maryland in College Park, MD. Before coming to BCPL, she worked as a medical librarian for St. Joseph Hospital in Towson, MD and as a research assistant for ABC News in Washington, D.C.

Appendix 1

GROLIER ASSIGNMENT

For each question, note the keys you pressed to get the information & print the first paragraph of the article or print the first screen of an article title list where appropriate.

1. Look up the Compromise of 1850.

2. Look up Melvil Dewey.

3. Is there an article on Mohammedanism?

4. What kind of information is available on rugs or carpets?

5. When searching for mentions of Jesus, does it make a difference how you search? Compare your results when searching for simply Jesus, Jesus or Christ and Jesus Christ or Jesus the Christ. Print only the search screen showing the number of occurrences.

6. How would you look up articles on the Stone Age but eliminate references to "man"? Does this give you more or less occurrences of Stone Age than if you searched for Stone Age alone? Print only the search screen for each search showing # of occurrences.

7. How would you get just a bibliography of books about dolphins or porpoises? Include a printout.

8. Was anyone born on October 21?

Appendix 2

GROLIER CHECKLIST

I. Turning machine on
    A. autoexec-type this to reboot or use CTRL-ALT-DEL keys

II. General
    A. Pull-down menus
        1. Many commands we won't use
        2. Some commands available only in word search
            Alt-O, Alt-S, Alt-U
        3. Toggle commands: Alt-O, Alt-M, Alt-Z
        4. Alt-M marks paragraphs at a time or single lines
    B. Arrow/cursor keys on number keypad
        Del key-deletes letter under cursor
        End key-moves cursor to end of line
        Home key-moves cursor to beginning of line
        Ctrl-Pg Up keys-moves to first screen
        Ctrl-Pg Dn keys-moves to last screen
    C. Highlighted choice will be chosen when your press ENTER
    D. ESC takes you back a step at a time

III. Browse Titles
    Takes you to a complete list of article titles starting with A.
    Use this method of searching when you want a complete article on
    a subject.
    A. Insert window for search term(s)
        1. Proper names-type last name first
    B. Cross-references indicated by colon
    C. Terms in capitals (link terms)-corresponding article in
        encyclopedia
        1. Alt-L moves cursor to next link term. Press ENTER to
            get to that article title; ENTER again to see text.
            Press ESC to return to previous article.
    D. Screen numbers
        First number indicates screen you're viewing; second number
        indicates total number of screens. Screens are counted
        based on size of window you're using.
    E. Indication of other features
        Factbox, outline, discography, tables

IV. Printing-Alt-P
    Can change options to print various portions of text. High-
    light; ENTER to choose. Dot indicates active options.
    Highlight "Begin Printing;" ENTER. Changed options remain
    in effect until changed again or you return to title screen
    before beginning a new search.

V. Word Search
    Takes you to a complete list of article titles in which a word
    or combination of words appear. Use this method of searching
    if you don't find a complete article on your subject.
    A. Search logic
        1. "and" search-terms on separate lines
        2. adjacency/phrase search-2 or more words on same line;
            searches for words side by side, in any order
        3. "or" search-terms on same line; comma between terms; no
            space between
        4. truncation-? short truncation; * unlimited truncation

B. Options-Alt-O
    Can change search and relation options. Highlight; ENTER to
    choose. Dot indicates active options. ESC to get to search
    screen. Changed options remain in effect until changed
    again or you return to title screen before beginning new
    search.
    1. Negate words
        Type word to be excluded; change relation option; ENTER
C. Tab key-next occurrence of search term(s);
    Shift-Tab-previous occurrence

VI. Browse Word Index
    Takes you to a complete list of indexed words found in the
    encyclopedia and indicates number of articles in which word
    appears and total number of times it appears in those articles.
    Use this method of searching for the following:
    1. to look up a series of words (e.g., all words begin-
        ning with BIO)
    2. to see if a word appears in the encyclopedia
    3. to check the spelling of a word before beginning search
    4. to search all occurrences of a word

14

The Wiley Laser Disk Service at Evans Library, Texas A&M University

Vicki Anders

Texas A&M University is a major public university, the second largest in Texas, with nearly 3,000 faculty, and a student enrollment of over 39,000 (including over 6,000 graduate students). The University's traditional strengths are engineering, agriculture and science, but in recent years the Business College enrollment has surpassed all but Engineering, and Liberal Arts enrollment is experiencing the fastest growth. Sterling C. Evans Library closely mirrors the emphasis of the University with strong collections in the sciences and the vast majority of the materials budget committed to serials purchases. In 1987 the collection numbered 1.7 million volumes and 3.3 million microforms, and the materials budget was over 3.5 million dollars.

Evans Library has a strong commitment to computer technology. Early in 1967 a "home-grown" circulation system was in use, followed by an automated acquisitions and fund accounting system, and the use of OCLC for cataloging. Since then Evans Library has migrated through the ALIS system to its present NOTIS configuration. The Library began providing online access to databases through its Automated Information Retrieval Service (AIRS) in the early 1970's, and in 1983 began offering online access to end-users.

End-user Searching

End-user searching became a very popular service at the Library. Students lined up at the desk for a chance to access user-friendly BRS/After Dark databases and would wait for hours rather than lose their turn on the one terminal allotted to them. In the first year, end-users racked up 207 hours of connect time. Over the next two years end-user demand caused the Library to upgrade equipment from DECWriter terminals to microcomputers and to add more searching stations, up to our present total of four scheduled searching stations with one backup station to accommodate drop-in patrons or mechanical problems.

End-user searching also forced the Reference Division to examine different methods of teaching patrons how to search, and taught us that no system is user-friendly enough for an inexperienced patron to use without personalized, one-on-one instruction, and no system is so fool-proof that a patron cannot crash it out of ignorance or curiosity. We experimented with a slide-tape presentation, computer-assisted-instruction programs, and a written manual to teach patrons how to search, and we found that none of these methods was significantly better than the other. In essence, first-time users still need a staff member present to answer questions and prompt the user regardless of the original instruction program the user had experienced. We have settled on the written manual because it is easier than the slide-tape program to update, and it does not tie up a precious microcomputer (as a CAI program would) that could be put to better use as a searching station.

At present, the end-user searching service is staffed by two people working together; one worker is drawn from a pool of student assistants trained to work the area, and the other is a regular library employee (non-professional) working half time. They advise end-users on database selection, assist during the online search, handle equipment and supplies problems, write invoices if a patron is to be billed for the service, and keep a statistical log of all searches. The end-user staff is a necessary part of a successful program that now uses 1,176 hours of connect time per year, accounting for nearly 75 percent of the total online time logged by Evans Library.

Our experience with end-user searching in an online environment proved to our satisfaction the need for such a service. Most patrons certainly prefer a computerized literature search to a manual search of printed indexes, and user-friendly search software is easy enough to learn. Although a trained search analyst accustomed to performing mediated searches might shudder at the amount of garbage an end-user retrieves in a typical search, the end-user himself is perfectly happy with a system that produces a printout of a hundred citations, half of which may be relevant.

The only problem is the cost. In the five years of operating a full-scale end-user search service, the total invoiced cost has been $23,000 to $28,000 per year. At first the Library supported all the costs of the service, but since then, as the Library's budget has changed, we have experimented with subsidizing all or part of the connect costs, all of the printing costs up to a certain sum, and various combinations of subsidies of connect and printing costs. The Library's portion of the costs has been paid from the materials budget. No matter what the Library charges, there are always patrons willing to pay for the service, and we have filled at least 80 percent of the available appointments even when the patron was paying half the connect cost and all the printing costs. For the past year and a half, a gift from the Association of Former Students has paid for the connect costs, leaving only the cost of citations from BRS/After Dark databases for the patrons to pay. At present, since most patrons use the Knowledge Index system, which does not charge for citations, they pay nothing for an online end-user search; as a result we frequently book up all available appointments and must turn some patrons away. We have a policy of limiting students to two free searches per week in order to keep a few dedicated end-users from consuming a majority of the available appointments. Once the two free searches are used, the patron must pay half the connect cost—an average of $3.00 per search. On occasion students forget that they have used their two free searches. When they are told they will have to pay for the third search, they go away saying, "I'll wait until next week." Obviously a free search is very attractive to students.

Wiley Laser Disk Service

Unlimited availability, no appointments, user-friendly, free—these are the features end-users want in a database, as our experience with online end-user searching shows. Compact disc technology seemed to promise these features; therefore when the first hints of CD-ROM databases began circulating, Evans Library began investigating. Cost was the main obstacle to establishing a CD-ROM unit, and this obstacle was overcome in the spring of 1986 by a generous gift of $100,000 from a former student, Mr. James E. Wiley.

InfoTrac was the first database to be installed. Information Access Company had set up two demonstration units in the Library before the Wiley gift was finalized, and perhaps it was the comments collected from users of InfoTrac that showed Mr. Wiley how useful and welcome such systems would be. Although frequent crashes caused the Library staff to question the reliability of the system, patrons loved InfoTrac and lined up to use it. Definitely InfoTrac would be one of the databases purchased with the Wiley gift, but several questions had to be answered before the Wiley Laser Disk Service could become a reality, namely: which other databases to buy, what equipment to use, and where to put it?

At the time we began investigating the availability of databases, Digital Equipment Corporation announced that it was bringing out several technical databases on CD-ROM, including portions of Engineering Index and NTIS. This was perfect for us since our statistics from both mediated searches and end-user searches proved that they were high-demand databases. We began negotiations with DEC and began ordering equipment, including the compact disc drives recommended by DEC for their databases. We had promised Mr. Wiley that we would have the new service ready to go in the fall semester,1986, and we seemed well on the way to fulfilling the promise when we received word from DEC in August 1986 that the technical databases would not be produced. Fortunately, by that time other databases were on the market, and our anxious calls to database producers had alerted them to our interest and readiness for CD-ROM databases. We were asked to try out some products that were still in test phase. So we had databases in place and in use late in the fall semester, in time for the dedication ceremony recognizing Mr. Wiley's generosity.

The early decisions on which databases to purchase were greatly colored by what was available at that time, but we also relied on statistics gathered from mediated and end-user searches. Online databases that are accessed frequently, especially by end-users, are prime targets when we make decisions to purchase CD-ROM databases. At present, the following databases are installed in the Wiley Laser Disk Service:

>ABI/Inform (UMI)
>Agricola (SilverPlatter)
>Applied Science and Technology Index (Wilson)
>Books-in-Print-Plus and Books-out-of-Print-Plus (Bowker)
>Dissertation Abstracts Ondisc (UMI)
>Electronic Encyclopedia (Grolier)

GPI (Government Publications Index from IAC)
Humanities Index (Wilson)
InfoTrac (IAC)
Kirk-Othmer Encyclopedia of Chemical Technology
LegalTrac (IAC)
Life Sciences Collection (Compact Cambridge)
Lotus One Source (formerly Datext)
Periodical Abstracts Ondisc (UMI)
PsycLIT (SilverPlatter)
Science Citation Index Compact Disc Edition (ISI)
SocioFile (SilverPlatter)

Other CD-ROM databases are located in different units of the Library; for example, ERIC and Newsbank are in the Microtext Department; the Marcive government publications index, NTIS, and some Census Bureau databases from Slater Hall are in the Documents Division.

It was known from the first that the Wiley Laser Disk Service would be a part of the Automated Information Retrieval Service which already had several years of experience with end-user searching. The AIRS equipment and the InfoTrac test installation were in a public area close to the Reference Desk, but the area was too small to accommodate the additional equipment needed for the CD-ROM databases. In fact, only a major rearrangement of the Reference Desk, shelving, and index tables, could have cleared a space large enough to hold everything we had planned, and such a massive undertaking was out of the question. A small reading area of about 800 square feet just outside the Reference staff office was the only place large enough for the Service. The tables and chairs occupying it were redistributed in the Reference area so that no seating was lost, and the area was wired with electrical outlets and telephone lines. The major disadvantages of the area are its distance from the Reference Desk (intervening book shelves block it from view of the staff at the Desk) and the fact that it is an open, public area which cannot be enclosed by temporary or permanent walls.

Equipment and Furniture
Workstations

While getting the equipment orders ready, we also looked at furniture to house the equipment and keep it secure. We decided to buy locking, rolltop computer workstations to provide security, although at first we worried about being able to fit everything inside. Since the original purchase, we have tried a few different models of computer workstations and have settled on Highsmith Model CO1A-83417 as our favorite. It has a back access panel that provides access to the cables and connections, making it easy to check or change connections. Without the back panel, one either has to pull all the equipment out of the cabinet or work by feel with the connections. The Highsmith model also has a pull-out keyboard tray; models without the tray require us to stand the keyboard on edge before we can lock the workstation. None of the workstation cabinets are ideal; once they have been loaded with microcomputer, printer and CD-ROM drive there is not an inch of space left for a patron to put down a piece of paper to take a note. One other problem with all the workstations we have tried is the lack of a good quality lock. Several of the locks have broken, forcing us to resort to security cables to tie down the equipment inside the cabinet.

Microcomputers

The original purchase of microcomputers consisted of IBM XTs and ATs. We wanted hard disk machines because we had experienced some tampering with the two disk drive PCs used in the InfoTrac installation. A couple of times someone simply pulled the software out of the floppy drive and walked off with it; another time we found a patron using an InfoTrac computer to run his own software. Our solution, of sorts, to this problem was to put a tight-fitting piece of stiff cardboard into the recessed area over the floppy drives on the PC. Since the InfoTrac software is never removed from the A-drive, and the programming does not permit downloading, the cardboard can stay in place without inconveniencing any but those who are trying to misuse the system. InfoTrac is the only system we run using floppy disks. Our problems convinced us to use hard disk machines for all other systems because the searching software can be loaded onto the hard disk where most people cannot tamper with it. Computer Science students are the exception, and at first we worried about the damage a determined CS student could do to the programming on the hard disk. However, we worried needlessly because most patrons rush to get their searching done in the time allotted to them on a system, and they do not have time to tinker.

Another concern we had regarding hard disk machines was the possibility of patrons downloading searches to the hard disk and thus cluttering it with garbage. Most of the software supplied with the databases allows certain choices during the installation procedure, including the destination of downloaded information. Whenever possible we configure the system to download to the floppy drive, but on a few systems this is not possible and we do occasionally find patrons' searches on our hard disks. Deleting them is not an overwhelming problem, but we did on one occasion fill up a hard disk to the point where the program would no longer run, and we spent a few days fussing over possible solutions until we discovered the cause of the problem. It is something to keep in mind if a system suddenly stops or slows down.

The faster processing speed of an IBM AT or compatible makes a noticeable difference in the time it takes to complete a search, and our latest purchases have been faster machines, when we can afford them. We have also experimented with Compaq IIIs. These small machines fit neatly into a workstation cabinet and leave plenty of space for note-taking. Also, they are light enough to take to classes when we demonstrate CD-ROM databases, which we do several times a year. However, they are not totally IBM-compatible and we have had some problems getting them to work with certain systems' on-screen graphics and highlighting features.

Printers

Hewlett-Packard Thinkjet printers are small enough to fit inside the workstation cabinets, and they are quiet enough to operate in a public area, so they are the printers we use with most of our databases. The major disadvantage of the Thinkjet printer is the cost of the ink cartridge. There are 15 Thinkjet printers in the Wiley area that consume nine to 10 cartridges a week at a cost of around $100 per week. Also, they are slow printers; with databases that have a great deal of text to print, such as Lotus One Source, we have used dot matrix printers. The major disadvantage of fast dot matrix printers is the noise, which can be heard 100 feet away. However, the Thinkjet printers are quite reliable; some have been operating at high volume for nearly three years, and only one has been sent out for repairs (which cost almost as much as the printer). In the future we will probably replace rather than repair the Thinkjets. On the other hand, the dot matrix printers have been repaired several times at a cost of about $1,000.

Thinkjet printers are inexpensive to purchase compared to good quality dot matrix printers, and with their low repair rate we seem to be breaking even on the cost of operating them. Furthermore, the noise of a dozen or so dot matrix printers all operating at once would be unbearable. The paper for all the printers is the cheapest quality we can get, and we use four to five boxes in a week. There have been a few mild complaints about the quality of the paper we use, but most patrons are more than pleased to walk away with a printout that cost them nothing. We do not charge for the use of any of the CD-ROM databases or supplies.

CD Reader

The compact disc drives were usually purchased as a package with the databases from the database producers, such as SilverPlatter and UMI. We have used Phillips, Hitachi, Toshiba and Sony models and have found all of them to be reliable. Only one has been sent out for repair, at a cost of $80. It could not be repaired locally and had to be sent to California. It was gone for about a month. Another defective machine was replaced by the manufacturer. Since then no other CD-ROM drives have needed repair, but if one should malfunction in the future, we would have to consider the cost and the inconvenience of a machine missing for several weeks in deciding whether to repair or replace it. We have not purchased warranties on any of the CD-ROM drives because they have been so reliable, and a one-year warranty on the machine that did malfunction would have expired by the time it needed repair. We have not noticed that one model functions any faster or better than another. We do prefer front-loading CD-ROM drives simply because they can be stacked between a microcomputer's CPU and monitor and thus take up less room inside a workstation cabinet. Microcomputer repairs for the 17 machines in the Wiley area have been less than $500 since the fall of 1986.

When we were considering which databases to buy and how the Wiley area would operate, we decided that each database would have its own workstation and equipment—one database, which may be several discs, per searching station. We have maintained that philosophy although equipment failures have forced us, on occasion, to double up databases on one searching station and we will test a database being considered for purchase on a searching station already being used for another database.

We learned very early that it is nice to have spare equipment—a printer, a CD-ROM drive, and a microcomputer—that can replace equipment out for repair, and to take to classes for demonstrations. We now have a spare searching unit although its status as a "spare" is sometimes difficult to maintain when something goes wrong with a piece of equipment in the Wiley area. Our average cost for a searching station consisting of cabinet, hard disk microcomputer, printer and CD-ROM drive is around $4,000.

Staffing and Instruction
Staffing

The Wiley Laser Disk Service is open to the public from 8:00 a.m. to 10:00 p.m. Monday through Friday, 9:00 a.m. to 6:00 p.m. Saturday, and 1:00 p.m. to 10:00 p.m. Sunday. These are the same hours that the service desks in the Library are staffed for full-service operations. We learned as soon as we opened the area that it too would need to be staffed because "user-friendly" does not mean the same thing to all users. Some people are perfectly happy to sit down at a computer and start a hunt and peck system of self-instruction; others develop sweaty palms at the thought of using a computer. This led to some philosophical discussions in the Reference Division about who should staff the Wiley area. Professional librarians were the first choice because teaching patrons to use indexes and bibliographic techniques is a professional level task. However, librarians in the Reference Division also staff the Reference Desk, provide mediated searches through the Automated Information Retrieval Service, provide tours and lectures through the Bibliographic Instruction service, staff the Library on nights and weekends, and engage in research and publishing activities to meet the faculty status requirements of the University; we did not have enough librarians to staff another service point. Since the Wiley area was located far from the Reference Desk it could not be handled as an appendage of Reference Desk duties with staff from the desk keeping an eye on the area and providing service as needed.

Eventually the Reference Division's classified staff were assigned to the Wiley area during the day, and at night the After Dark staff were expected to handle their usual end-user online searching patrons as well as the CD-ROM patrons. In a short time the After Dark staff complained that they could not provide the level of service needed in both areas, and an extra student worker was assigned to the Wiley area at night. Reality eventually overcame our philosophical discussions, and now the Wiley area is staffed by student workers all the hours it is open to the public.

The student assigned to the first hour of operation unlocks the workstation cabinets and turns on the equipment, usually under the anxious eyes of patrons waiting to use the databases. For most of the databases turning on the machines is all that is required to make them ready for use. InfoTrac takes 20 to 30 minutes to run through its checkout programs before it can be used. The student worker checks ink and paper supplies and also picks up the area. Usually there is only one student worker on duty at a time, and they work one or two hour shifts. The remainder of their shift is spent on other duties in the Reference Division such as assisting at the desk, reshelving, and office duties. The student workers are trained for Wiley area duty by one of the librarians, and a "Wiley Manual" has been developed to answer recurring questions. Furthermore, the student workers are not assisting patrons every minute they are on duty, and in fact there are long stretches of time when patrons are quietly searching or printing, and the student worker can spend the spare moments familiarizing himself or herself with a particular database. The student workers are not allowed to study or read while on duty, so in the time not spent assisting patrons they work with the databases. When a question arises which the student worker cannot answer, a librarian in the Reference Office adjacent to the Wiley area is contacted. The major problem with staffing the area with student workers is the fact that they look like students, and patrons sometimes cannot distinguish the person on duty from the users in the area. To compensate for this, our student workers wear a tag that reads "Reference" to help identify them, and we instruct them to be aggressive in offering help and to approach patrons coming in to the area instead of waiting for the patron to ask for assistance.

One type of student worker is absolutely essential to the success of the operation: the technical troubleshooter. We look for upper level undergraduates who have experience with microcomputer assembly or repair, and some programming experience if possible. They are employed as student assistants for 16 to 20 hours a week, and we pay them an above average hourly wage. These student assistants do not help patrons in the Wiley area. They concentrate on hardware and software matters, repairing equipment when it malfunctions or identifying the problem and explaining it to computer service center repairmen. We believe that our "computer technician" student workers have saved us a great deal of money by performing in-house repairs, and a great deal of down time by identifying and explaining problems to professional repairmen. A librarian may only be able to say to the repairmen, "it doesn't work," but the computer technician can explain what does not work and why, and thus save some of the time and money spent on diagnosing the problem.

Also, the technicians install new equipment and software, write programs that make searching software "boot" automatically when the equipment is turned on, write menuing programs that make it easy to switch between databases when we have more than one database mounted on a microcomputer, write screen-saver programs, and perform routine maintenance on the equipment. When we set up a new database, our technician does the initial installation and testing, and frequently telephones the technical staff of the database producer when there are problems getting the program to work, or questions that are not answered by the producer's manuals. Our technicians have saved the librarians a great deal of heartache and confusion, and have made the databases and equipment easier for everyone to use.

Instruction

Handouts are available for all the databases in the area. They explain the content of the database, simplified "how to search" instructions, function key usage, and printing or downloading instructions. A laminated copy of the instruction sheet is placed at each database workstation and multiple copies are available as handouts for patrons, but, as with our online end-users, we have discovered that most patrons want individualized one-on-one instruction.

Our student workers have been trained to provide "over the shoulder" instructions with the patron's hands on the keyboard while the student worker explains which keys to strike, if necessary. A novice user on a complicated system such as Science

Citation Index can take as much as 20 minutes of instruction before the student worker can feel confident the basics have been learned. On the other hand, patrons who have performed an online end-user search or have already used one of the CD-ROM databases need only a few minutes of instruction, and as a last resort they can be shown the written instructions if the student worker is very busy with other patrons. We have seen a "buddy system" develop whereby one patron who has learned a particular system will bring his friends and show them how it works.

We have experimented with more organized instructional methods, such as offering classes in the Library on particular databases or more generalized classes on computerized searching techniques, and we are frequently asked by classroom instructors to bring a database to the classroom to demonstrate to the students. We are quite willing to demonstrate to classes, and we bought the Compaq III microcomputers expressly because they are portable enough to carry around campus, but we gave up on the classes offered in the Library because the attendance was too disappointing. Furthermore, our experience with end-users has shown that no amount of demonstration and lecture educates as effectively as a few minutes of one-on-one instruction with the patron's hands on the keyboard, and this is exactly what the Wiley Laser Disk Service provides.

Problems

The student workers in the Wiley area troubleshoot the various problems that can arise. For example, some of the systems require a user to strike the "escape" key to back up one step in the searching process. If users strike the escape key once too often they are left with nothing but a C> prompt on the screen. Downloading is the most difficult of the routine procedures available to end-users since there are as many different methods as there are systems, and even the names for downloading vary from system to system.

Disc switching is often bothersome. Many of the big databases are on multiple discs, and some of our searching stations have more than one database assigned to them, thus requiring the user to remove one CD-ROM from the drive and replace it with another. When we first established the Wiley Laser Disk Service we made the decision to keep earlier discs in a filing cabinet and allow only staff members to switch discs, but as the service grew to more databases and more discs and more patrons, we were forced to change that decision because the attendant's time was consumed with fetching and changing discs. Now all discs are in the workstations and patrons are allowed to handle them. This has led to two problems. First is the bewildering situation when an inexperienced patron loads the compact disc into the floppy drive of the microcomputer. Naturally, this does not work and the patron, perhaps realizing too late that he has made a mistake, quietly walks away. We have never had a patron admit to loading the compact disc into the floppy drive but it happens often enough so that we always check the floppy drives whenever a compact disc is reported missing.

More serious is the damage that occurs when patrons do their own disc switching, even when they get the disc in the correct drive. Some of the heavily used discs have been so badly scratched that portions of the data on them can no longer be read. So far the database producers have been willing to replace scratched discs without charge and usually by express mail that gets the replacement disc to us three or four days after we call. Brightly lettered signs on the compact disc cases ask users to handle them carefully to avoid scratches, but the problem still occurs, and there seems to be nothing we can do about it—short of returning to our original policy of removing the discs from the public's hands. Multiple CD drives in a stacked configuration would solve the problem nicely, but at the moment we cannot afford them.

Another challenge has been the creation of an equitable scheduling system. This function is handled by the student workers. All the databases are available on a first come, first served basis; we do not schedule appointments for any of them, but we will sign up users on a waiting list. For example: Patron A is using Database #1. Patron B arrives and also wants to use Database #1. Patron B signs the waiting list and is told to come back in 30 minutes. The Wiley attendant sets a timer located on top of each workstation (an inexpensive kitchen timer) and warns Patron A that his or her search must be completed when the timer goes off. If Patron C wants to use the same database, he too is allowed to sign the waiting list and is told to come back 30 minutes after Patron B is due to start. Meanwhile if Patron A finishes before the 30 minutes elapse, any patron is allowed to use the system but is warned that Patron B will "bump" him at the assigned time. We will allow a patron to be five minutes late but beyond that the patron loses his turn and must sign the waiting list for a later time. This complicated system works, and our patrons cooperate, but it has produced the most complaints of any of the policies or procedures used in the Wiley area. Patrons who miss their turn by being late complain the loudest, and many complain that 30 minutes is not long enough. Patrons frequently suggest we should have multiple copies of a database and the equipment to run it. During the busiest part of the semester, our most popular databases may be booked up with waiting lists for the most of the day's operation.

Effect of CD-ROM on Online Operations

Statistics on various library operations are generated and collected every hour the building is open, but one particular week of the spring semester is declared "Statistics Week" when every reference or directional question is counted, every book circulated or reshelved is counted, and every database use is counted. To record CD use, we designed a half-page form for each of the CD-ROM products in the Library (figure 1) and placed a box of the forms at each workstation.

The Wiley attendants were instructed to be persistent in encouraging patrons to fill out the forms, and signs in the area asked users to fill out a form each time they used a database. We know that many patrons left without completing a form, some used the forms for scratch paper and walked away with them, and others complained, "But I filled out a form yesterday!" Based on our observations, we believe we received forms from about 60 to 70 percent of the users. Using these figures, we averaged over a hundred users a day. Seventy-five percent of the users completed a search in less than 30 minutes and the average search produced 19 citations. Users were invited to make comments, most of which were enthusiastic, complimentary, or grateful to the Wileys for their generous gift. Complaints about having to wait to use a particular database were the most frequent negative comments, and patrons often suggested that we buy more of everything.

DISSERTATION ABSTRACTS

What is your major/department?
Please circle your status:
   faculty/staff graduate   undergraduate   non-university
Please circle the hour you started using this database:
   8am 9am 10am 11am noon 1pm 2pm 3pm 4pm 5pm 6pm 7pm 8pm 9pm
How long did you use this database? Please circle the nearest estimate:
   less than 15 minutes 15–30 min. 30–45 min. 45–60 min. more than 60 min.
How many records did you print/download?
Did you print abstracts?   yes   no
   Was this search done to support: Class assignment faculty/staff research
   Graduate student research Other (please specify)

---

figure 1. "Statistics Week" CD use form.

The statistics collected from CD-ROM databases were compared with statistics from the online services, and some interesting trends emerged. We selected Agricola, PsycLIT, Dissertation Abstracts Ondisc and ERIC for our study because all had been available as compact disc databases for over a year in Evans Library, and all were available for mediated and end-user searches through our online services. The month-by-month use of each online database was figured as a percentage of the total hours of online access for all databases. Percentages were used instead of actual hours to smooth out the seasonal peaks and valleys caused by Christmas holidays, semester breaks, "term paper season," and the dramatic effect of a change in pricing policy for end-user searches instituted in the middle of the year under study.

Our study showed that usage of the online equivalents of the databases began to decline only two or three months after the CD-ROM versions became available. ERIC, Agricola and PsycInfo had always been among the top 10 databases accessed in both mediated and end-user online searches; at present only Agricola is in the top 10 of mediated searches, ranking fourth, and as end-user databases Agricola ranks 18th, PsycInfo is 19th, and ERIC is 22nd based on the number of times a database is accessed.

However, it must be noted that the savings in online costs are not nearly enough to cover the subscription costs of the CD-ROM databases, and in order to avoid paying for the same information twice, we have begun actively discouraging the online use of databases available on CD-ROM by not subsidizing them; in other words After Dark users must pay for connect costs, and graduate students who get one subsidized search per year are told that they must use the compact disc databases rather than the online versions if they want the data without charge. If the patron is willing to pay for the search we are willing to perform the search, but we no longer subsidize the cost of online databases already available in the Library as CD-ROM databases. We used to perform mediated searches in ERIC and Agricola and Dissertation Abstracts quite frequently, and these are relatively inexpensive databases. Now they have been taken out of our repertoire. To make our funds stretch as far as possible it makes economic sense to instruct patrons to use the compact disc database that we have already paid for, rather than pay connect and printing charges for the same data in an online environment.

The search analysts who perform mediated searches are careful to explain all the options, and patrons will frequently decide to perform their own searches on those databases available on CD-ROM or After Dark, and only use the full-service (and expensive) mediated search for other databases. This has resulted in an increase in the average cost of a mediated search. Also, patrons of mediated search services now tell us that they have already performed a search in PsycLIT and SocioFile on CD-ROM, for example, and they want us to search their psychology subject in "any other database" that might be relevant to be sure they have found everything on the subject. The search becomes a treasure hunt through several of the more expensive online databases, thus raising the average cost of a mediated search.

Another interesting statistic is illustrated in Table 1.

Table 1
Users of Computerized Literature Searching Services

	Mediated search	After Dark search	CD-ROM search
Faculty/staff	75%	5%	4%
Graduate students	18%	61%	18%
Undergrads	1%	33%	73%
Others*	6%	1%	5%

*This includes local area residents, middle and high school students from the community, etc.

CD-ROM databases make computerized literature searching available to users who previously were disenfranchised. Before we installed CD-ROM databases, undergraduates accounted for less than thirty percent of the After Dark searches and less than one percent of the mediated searches; now undergraduates have a piece of the action, their own niche. There is a lovely symmetry in the table above that should appeal to any librarian who aims to serve all the patrons of the library.

Conclusions

Comments from users who completed the statistics form are nearly always complimentary. After the first year of operation the comments were compiled and sent to Mr. Wiley as he continues to be interested in providing a service that serves so many students so admirably. In April, 1989, the Texas Library Association recognized his generosity with a Philanthropic Award, and students who have used the CD-ROM databases have written him personal letters of thanks. We hope that more gifts or grants designated for the Wiley area will be forthcoming, but if not, the subscription costs of the databases can be absorbed by the Library's materials budget to continue the service at its present level. Three-fourths of the original gifts were spent on equipment and furniture, and we do not anticipate the need for a similarly large outlay in the future. If necessary, we can mount more than one database on a microcomputer.

We continue to monitor CD-ROM database usage and to examine online database statistics to help us decide which databases to continue and which to add. Many database producers will "lend" a new database for a month's trial, thus allowing a hands-on evaluation by both library staff and patrons. As more databases become available, "comparison shopping" becomes necessary. Such a comparison has convinced us to replace InfoTrac with UMI's Periodicals Abstracts and ABI/Inform databases because they satisfy our patrons' demands for more information and the flexibility of Boolean searching. Using such methods we plan to refine, enhance, and expand the Wiley Laser Disk Service, and to continue a service our patrons have come to expect from us.

"This is great! It makes me feel like Superman!" one undergraduate commented after using Agricola on CD-ROM. There cannot be a better endorsement for compact disc databases. It is true that CD-ROM technology is expensive, the machinery requires extra care and maintenance, and the searching techniques require more explanation than printed indexes, but we at Evans Library think they are worth it. They make us a "Super Library" in the eyes of our patrons.

Vicki Anders came to Texas A&M University Library as the Head of Separates Acquisitions in 1968. In 1978 she became the Instructional Services Librarian, and since 1985 has served as Head, Automated Information Retrieval Service. She received a B.A. in History and an M.L.S. from the University of Oklahoma.

15

The Byte of Electronic Information at Oregon State University: The CD-ROM Reference Center at the Kerr Library

Karen J. Starr

The 1960s were an era of change in American society, and developments occurred which had far-reaching implications. One example was the use of computers by the information industry. Publishers used computers to print newspapers, and, in libraries, indexes and abstracting services migrated from print to electronic format. As the computer became the new publishing and storage medium, organizations such as the Lockheed Corporation, Systems Development Corporation, and the National Library of Medicine developed online systems to access these databases, and individual libraries began to evaluate how computers could be used to manage in-house files. The William Jasper Kerr Library at Oregon State University (OSU) was one such library.

Institutional Context

Oregon State University is a land- and sea-grant university located in Corvallis. Twelve colleges and schools serve approximately 15,000 graduate and undergraduate students. The university emphasizes research and extension services in agriculture, forestry, engineering, home economics, veterinary medicine, education, oceanography, business, pharmacy, the sciences, and the liberal arts. It offers undergraduate degrees in the arts, humanities, social sciences, sciences, and the professions. Graduate programs are concentrated in the sciences and the professional schools. In addition, the university operates the Mark O. Hatfield Marine Science Center (HMSC) in Newport, Oregon. The university's research needs—on the campus, in the state of Oregon, and on an international basis—influence the collection and services provided by the library.

Kerr Library houses slightly more than one million volumes specializing in the areas of agriculture, life sciences, engineering, forestry, oceanography, home economics, education, pharmacy, and business. It is a centralized library with one departmental library at the Marine Science Center in Newport. Special services in Kerr Library include a map library, government documents section, and a micro-forms collection. Linus Pauling, an OSU alumnus, donated his peace collection, which provides the core of a special collections section. The library purchased GEAC's Advance system and brought up an online card catalog and circulation system in 1989.

The library offers reference service through a reference desk and an information desk on the second floor of the library. Sixteen reference librarians work at the reference desk. They are involved, along with the CD-ROM librarian, in including CD-ROM in the collection development process, developing user documentation, and integrating the CD-ROM Reference Center into the bibliographic instruction program.

History of Automation at Kerr Library

Providing access to information through the use of automation has been part of the Kerr Library scene for 20 years. During the late 1960s the staff developed an automated acquisitions system known as LOLITA (Pemberton, 1985) and the library has kept pace as newer information technologies developed, including the automation of reference services. A password to DIALOG was acquired in 1973, and was soon followed by passwords to SDC Search Service and the National Library of Medicine. As other systems, such as BRS Information Technologies, STN International, and the Sponsored Programs Information Network, became commercially available, they too were added to the library's services.

Initially, the staff used a 110 baud teletype machine and offered free online searches to university faculty and students. By 1975, the library administration had formalized the online searching program, assigned a coordinator, named the program the Library Information Retrieval Service (LIRS), and because of budget constraints, made the decision to bill the direct costs of online searching (online time, telecommunications charges, and print charges) to patrons. This limited the use of the service to clientele who worked on grants and contracts, who had access to subsidy monies, or who could afford to pay. Free searches were offered only during the initial stage of the service for promotional and training purposes. OSU's Research Office purchased a prototype computer terminal for LIRS and a 1200 baud modem was also made available.

Before the advent of CD-ROM, about 1,000 faculty and students used the mediated online search service annually. The majority of these patrons were from the areas of agriculture, engineering, pharmacy, education, and the biological sciences.

CD-ROM Planning and Implementation

During the summer of 1986, it became clear that CD-ROM was a new technology in the realm of information retrieval. Keeping with the library's tradition of innovation in the automation arena, the Director of Libraries wanted to implement optical technology in some form at OSU and requested that the Assistant Director of Research and Reference investigate the potential of this technology. Since it is the university's goal to engage in research, and the librarians have faculty rank and status, the library administration viewed the investigation and implementation of CD-ROM technology as a research project. For the next year, the Assistant Director worked with the library's Automation Coordinating Council (ACC) to plan and implement a CD-ROM reference service (the ACC is responsible for reviewing all requests for library automation and evaluating their impact on the library). Other participants in the planning process included the reference staff and members of the university's research and teaching faculty. The process of planning for and implementing any new technology is one of balancing constraints. The factors and variables we considered in planning for CD-ROMs were available time, management support, technical expertise, budget, and staff commitment to the process and the technology.

During the early stages of the planning process, in 1986, the librarian at the Hatfield Marine Science Center branch library obtained a copy of the Aquatic Science and Fisheries Abstracts on CD-ROM. Several librarians visited Newport to familiarize themselves with the technology, and members of the ACC called vendors in order to compile a list of available CD-ROM products. These titles were made available to the reference staff. Teaching and research faculty also reviewed the list and showed a keen interest in CD-ROM products, like MEDLINE, that would support their research. The ACC used the feedback provided by faculty and reference staff, the experiences of the online searching program, and requests from the research and teaching faculty to make the final selection of databases in the spring of 1987. During the summer of 1988, the library ordered additional databases. These databases were added to fill research needs not dealt with during the first selection process or in response to requests by the teaching and research faculty.

The CD-ROM Reference Center

The CD-ROM Reference Center is a collection of 18 databases accessible on 14 workstations. It provides automated access to research information by all members of the user community.

The Center is located on the second floor of the library and is adjacent to the main entrance to the library. It is supervised by an administrative assistant who reports to the Head of Research Services and staffed with eight to 10 student lab monitors. The CD-ROM librarian, reference librarians, and automation staff provide professional support. The Center was opened to the public on November 10, 1987. This chapter will focus on the Center and the various processes, activities, and tasks used to establish and run the center.

In the months prior to the implementation of the CD-ROM Center, the library chose to introduce the Infotrac system as a means of familiarizing both the library's patrons and the staff with the new technology. Two Infotrac workstations were placed between the circulation desk and the reference desk on the second floor of the library, and patrons liked Infotrac so well that the library administration extended the three month trial to a year's subscription (which was not renewed due to the high subscriptions costs initially required to support Infotrac).

During the initial installation of the center, the Assistant Director for Reference and Research formed a CD-ROM task force to serve as a focus for the library staff's concerns about the new technology. The task force's responsibilities were to evaluate currently held and new CD-ROM products, and suggest changes to, and provide input on, other aspects of the Center. That task force has since changed its focus and its membership. Originally composed only of reference librarians, it now includes the Collection Development Officer, the Head of Research Services, the Head of Reference, the Assistant Director for Research and Reference, and the CD-ROM Librarian. Currently the task force evaluates requests for new CD-ROM subscriptions.

The staff selected CD-ROM products from Cambridge Scientific Abstracts, SilverPlatter, H.W. Wilson, and University Microfilms. Equipment and CDs began arriving at the library in June, 1987.

Hardware

The best approach to purchasing any equipment for an automation project includes determining the goals of the project, looking for the software to support those goals, and only then looking for the equipment to support the software.

The ACC analyzed the specifications for each of the selected CD-ROM products. The original purchase included nine IBM PC/XTs with 20MB hard disks, three Leading Edge microcomputers with dual disk drives (one of the two floppy disk drives on each Leading Edge has since been replaced with a 20MB hard drive), 14 Philips players, and 13 Hewlett-Packard Thinkjet printers.

Three of the four publishers required a hard disk to run their product and all four supported the Philips drive. SilverPlatter supported the Leading Edge microcomputer and a two disk drive system. Two of the Leading Edge computers eventually replaced the Infotrac workstations that were located next to the circulation desk. The library added two additional IBM PC/XTs to the CD-ROM collection of supporting equipment. The remaining Leading Edge was also exchanged for an IBM because the Leading Edge is not IBM-compatible and does not consistently support CD-ROM software and equipment. In the library's ongoing game of musical computers, the remaining Leading Edges may eventually be exchanged for IBM PC/XTs.

We modified an existing workstation design from the campus computer center and ordered 14 workstations from a local cabinetmaker. With the arrival of the equipment we began to plan where the workstations would be located. The print version of *Dissertation Abstracts* was shelved in a highly visible alcove next to the main entrance of the library on the second floor. The library administration decided to move *Dissertation Abstracts* and replace it with the CD-ROM reference center. Active publicity was not necessary to advertise the center because of its location, high visibility, and word-of-mouth referral.

Workstation Management

We wanted the configuration and management of the workstations to be simple, practical, and flexible. The processes were developed through the combined efforts of the Online Searching Coordinator (the predecessor to the CD-ROM Librarian) and the Library Automation Coordinator. Some of the techniques used to manage the workstations have stood the test of time and are worth mentioning.

When the CD-ROMs first arrived at the library, there was some concern that the databases offered by the four CD-ROM distributors would be incompatible on the same hard drive. These concerns soon proved to be unfounded, although there were a few glitches as updates arrived over the next year. Often these glitches stemmed from programming changes made by the producer, and a configuration change here or there tended to solve the problem. The staff created no fancy configuration files (Hoffman, 1988; Hensinger, 1989) and extensions were not used—the staff install software updates using each publisher's installation procedures

(Starr, 1988). Twelve of the 14 workstations in the CD-ROM center run all the CD-ROMs in the library's collection. The two remaining stations are dedicated to Business Periodicals Index and Readers' Guide to Periodical Literature, and are located next to the library's circulation desk and near the center.

The appropriate software for each product is selected from a menu (Starr, 1988) consisting of either the name of the CD-ROM publisher, or the name of the index (depending on how many CD-ROMs the library receives from each publisher). By means of a series of batch files, the appropriate software is activated to read the CD-ROM.

When new CD-ROM software arrives, one station is selected to install the update. To prevent transmission of a computer virus, the hard disk at the station used to install the software is reformatted and the previous clean update restored. The new software is then installed, and when the process of installation is finished, all of the other CD-ROM indexes are called up off the menu to insure that they will still operate. The staff backs up the hard drive using a software package called Fastback.

The hard drives on all of the other stations also need to be reformatted. Reformatting the drives cleans out all the user files and old software, along with any viruses, at one time. Once the hard drive begins to format, the DOS floppy disk is no longer necessary at that microcomputer. It can be removed, taken to the next microcomputer, and the format command repeated. This is done until all the workstations are reformatting simultaneously. As each microcomputer finishes formatting the hard disk, Fastback is used to begin restoring the new update. It takes up to one and a half hours to install an update and upgrade 12 workstations.

While workstation security has not yet been a problem for the OSU library, it has been at other institutions. We decided early in the process of managing the center to take a few preventive measures. All DOS commands were removed from the hard drives and the floppy drives were covered. To create mischief or inflict damage, a user would have to come prepared with a DOS operating disk and remove the front computer covers to gain access to the disk drives. Further security meaures have been incorporated into the software installation process.

Despite our smooth operating procedures, the staff knew that it was time for them to change when the latest update for Dissertation Abstracts arrived and required extensions to operate. Some CD-ROM publishers fully support extensions, and some do not. When CD-ROM software that requires extensions is placed on a station with software that does not, different DOS system configuration files must be used. The workstation must be rebooted when a disk from a publisher who uses extensions is exchanged for one published by a company that does not use extensions. The staff chose not to rewrite the system being used in the center to accommodate the lack of industry standardization where MS-DOS extensions are concerned. Instead, a decision was made to wait for the installation of the recently purchased Meridian local area network. The network arrived at the end of June 1989, and at that time the entire configuration of the center was rewritten.

Staffing

The center is open up to 108 hours each week and eight to 10 students staff the center as lab monitors (Appendix 1). They load the compact discs into the microcomputers, answer software questions, deal with hardware problems, and handle as many as 12 patrons at 12 machines. Reference questions which lab monitors cannot answer are referred to the reference desk, while questions dealing with the hardware or the center's operation are referred to the lab supervisor, an appropriate member of the reference staff, or someone from the automation support staff.

During implementation and the first year of its operation, the Online Searching Coordinator supervised the area. Responsibilities for that position included troubleshooting software and hardware problems, hiring and training student monitors, installing software updates, and providing backup for the lab monitors. That same time period saw a reorganization of the Reference Division of the library, and since January 1, 1989, the center has been supervised by an Administrative Assistant (AA) who reports to the Head of Research Services. Supervision of the center by the AA takes about 50 percent of that person's time. The Online Searching Coordinator position was redefined, and a new position has been created, called the CD-ROM Librarian, to work on CD-ROM program development. Fifty percent of the CD-ROM librarian's position involves developing end-user training programs, CD-ROM collection development, and working with CD-ROM publishers. These positions are still new, and their tasks and responsibilites are still being defined.

The process used to manage the workstations is simple enough that the AA or a well-trained lab monitor can complete the work. The automation support staff becomes involved only when the products will not operate and the reason is not readily apparent. This will change with the installation of the LAN. The LAN equipment is housed in a machine room adjacent to the CD-ROM center. The software updates are being dealt with by the automation staff directly rather than being routed to the lab supervisor. The discs running on the LAN are being loaded in the machine room and only those CD-ROM discs not being run on the LAN will be dealt with by the reference department; these will continue to be loaded by the lab monitors as needed.

Cost of Operation

Currently patrons are not charged to use the center. The library has come back full circle to the early 1970s when it provided free access to automated information resources. The initial cost to install the center was $60,320. The library annually spends about $21,384 in student wages, $20,640 in administrative assistant salary, $13,584 in CD-ROM librarian salary, $1,580 for paper, $2,424 for ink cartridges, and $24,640 for subscriptions. This totals $84,252. Of that total $28,644 are direct costs; i.e., paper, ink cartridges, and subscriptions. The ink cartridges used on the Hewlett-Packard Thinkjets last about one and a half weeks during peak usage. The first time the library administration received a $600 bill for ink cartridges, a number of eyebrows went up.

Using direct costs only, this works out to about $1.45 per requester, who may or may not use multiple CD-ROM indexes during one session. At this point in time, the library administration intends to continue offering free access to the CD-ROM products and the mediated online searching program will continue to bill its direct costs back to the patron.

Patron Access

When a patron wants to use an index in the center, that person must sign in with the lab monitor and provide an identification card. The log sheet tracks use of the center and provides statistics for collection development and administrative purposes. The monitor places the identification cards in a folder with the number of the machine the patron will be using. The student monitor loads the appropriate compact disc into the drive, and either the student monitor or the patron selects the appropriate software from the menu. When the patron finishes, that patron signs out and retrieves her/his identification card.

Each patron can work 30 minutes per session. If no one wants the disc, the patron can continue for another 30 minutes or until someone else requests the disc. If there are relatively few people using the center, the patron can continue as long as she/he cares to. Patrons are able to download results to floppy disk after notifying the lab monitor and obtaining instructions. To save the library paper, individuals who wish to print more than 200 citations are asked to refine their search or download the search to disk.

User Statistics

The center has been in operation for 18 months. In early 1988, 150 users each day was considered "out of sight." In early 1989, 150 users each day was considered normal. During the 1988 calendar year, the high day was November 2 with 195 patrons, and the low day was January 17, with one patron. January 17, incidentally, was a Sunday. During the 1988 calendar year, the center was used by 19,666 people. By contrast, the total number of patrons using the Library Information Retrieval Service for online searching in 1988 was 385. There has been a significant drop in the LIRS searches since the CD-ROM center opened.

The most frequently used CD-ROM product during 1988 was Business Periodicals Index with 2,105 recorded uses (this number is an underestimate). The least used index was MLA Bibliography with 61 uses. The indexes and their usages for calendar year 1988 are illustrated in figure 1.

A drop in the number of requests for online searches occurred in the mediated search service (LIRS) where the databases were available on CD-ROM (figure 2). The average cost per CD-ROM search, based on the subscription cost, was substantially lower than those searches completed online for the same database.

User Documentation

Initially, user documentation in the center included only library designed manuals and templates. During the first year's operation the staff found that people rarely read a manual. Most choose not to read the information presented on the screen, and the system tutorials are almost never used. Cheat sheets were subsequently added and an attempt is being made to make the aids for different systems conform in style, with similar information appearing in the same place on the page, regardless of the system being described. User documentation is now being modified to include templates, cheat sheets, and a subject index to the available products.

User Training

The library chose not to offer a formal CD-ROM end-user training program during the first 18 months of the center's operation. Instead, the lab monitors were

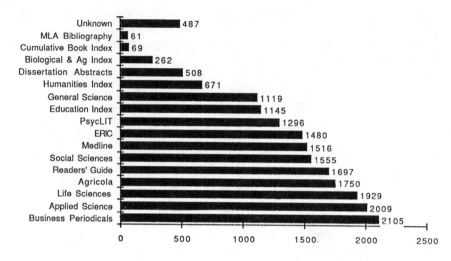

figure 1. CD-ROM Searches by Index for Calendar Year 1988.

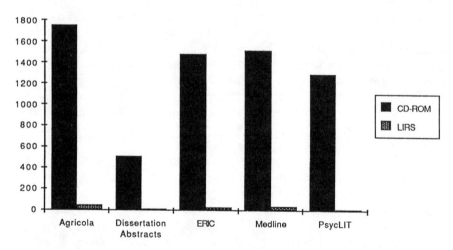

figure 2. Number of Searches on Indexes CD-ROM vs. LIRS, 1988.

trained to use the software and provide one-on-one support to the users. Questions that could not be answered by the lab monitors were referred to the reference desk or to the CD-ROM librarian. This type of teaching works well only when the support staff are highly trained and are supported by skilled reference staff.

The CD-ROM librarian initially spent a great deal of time in the lab working with the lab monitors and the users. Many of the users, however, were computer literate and preferred to work on their own. Peer tutoring occurred among the users as they became familiar with the software.

There are no magic solutions for either staff or user training. Librarians must now deal not only with the information literacy needs of their users, but also with their own computer literacy needs (Herther, 1988). Several projects are underway in order to address these needs for user training. They include: 1) A tutorial utilizing HyperCard may be developed for a bibliographic instruction workstation dedicated to teaching patrons how to use the library; 2) Strategy formulation and system-oriented seminars are in the planning stages. The primary targets of these seminars are graduate students and faculty (the undergraduate students will continue to be reached through the traditional library bibliographic instruction program); and 3) Faculty members on campus, as well, are adding training in CD-ROM searching to their regular class curricula in such departments as English and computer science.

The Collection Management Process

Libraries traditionally have dealt with print and microform, and the collection development process for print materials has a long history with a well-established set of guidelines. Librarians know how to evaluate print products, but in early 1987 they were inexperienced in evaluating both CD-ROM products and online systems. These two forms had not merged with the traditional collection development mindset. Librarians other than online searchers must now understand automated information processes, systems, and products. In particular, they must deal not only with the information content of CD-ROM products, but also with the user interface and the general population's use of the software and Boolean logic.

Our CD-ROM collection evaluation criteria (Appendix 2) has been influenced by a number of sources. OSU has worked with information published in electronic formats since 1973. The mediated search service accesses six mainframe online services and many of the criteria used to deal with mainframe systems can be carried over to optical technology. In addition, recent articles have talked about the selection of CD-ROM products (Herther, 1988; Hoffman, 1989), and Apple Computer, Inc., has developed a set of human interface guidelines that are useful for evaluating software design (Apple, 1987).

The statistics from the log sheets in the center provide the library administration and the reference librarians with information for collection management purposes. The CD-ROM librarian uses one of the reference office microcomputers to introduce new CD-ROM products to the staff. Demonstration discs are actively sought, including competitors of products currently held. If the staff decides the competing product provides a better service, the currently held version is replaced.

The library cancelled a number of print indexes when the CD-ROM versions were ordered. These included the *Bibliography of Agriculture,* the *MLA Bibliography, Aquatic Science and Fisheries Abstracts,* and *Dissertation Abstracts.* The teaching and research faculty in the English department and the modern languages department collectively signed a petition agreeing to the cancellation of the *MLA Bibliography* in order to obtain it on CD-ROM. Most of the indexes were cancelled in part due to funding, but also because they are harder for patrons to use in print format than they are on CD-ROM. The library also cancelled its subscription to Infotrac, but since then, Information Access Company has developed new products and, as part of the collection management process, we are reconsidering that decision.

Initially, the library administration intended to fund CD-ROM technology with year-end monies. When it became clear, in early 1987, that these monies would not be available, the director made the decision to continue with the project. Kerr Library's budget includes $2.6 million for materials, which does not go far toward supporting a growing collection of over one million volumes. The Director chose to support CD-ROMs as a regular part of the library's collection, funded by the materials budget. That decision has not changed.

Keeping Up with the Technology

When the center was installed, the staff looked with interest at the services a local area network could make available. LAN technology is still in its infancy for CD-ROMs. Nonetheless, the library administration made the decision to support the technology. The library purchased a 22 drive Meridian system that arrived in June of 1989. As LAN technology matures the ultimate objective will be to have as many CD-ROMs on a LAN as is financially possible.

A LAN offers a secure environment for CD-ROM access. The discs, software, and network servers can be stored away from the end-user. With the LAN, more than one user can access the same CD-ROM at the same time thereby eliminating queues. The users will be able to access multiple discs, the number of discs loaded by the lab monitors will decrease, as will, we hope, the damage being done to the discs by handling and human carelessness. Our Philips players are top-loading and do not use a caddy; improperly handled discs have resulted in scratches and required replacement of the disc.

The library is currently installing an administrative LAN and the two systems will be consolidated as much as possible. The existing workstations in the Center will be used to access the CD-ROM LAN. When the two LANs are consolidated, all computers in the library will be able to access the CD-ROMs. Eventually, the LAN will be open to the entire campus; an attempt will be made, however, to control how many users access each disc to prevent search time degradation and to meet licensing requirements. The Philips drives at each station will be accessible, along with the drives in the network. These original drives will be used for products which cannot be used on the network.

The decision about which discs will be loaded on the LAN has not yet been made. Some CD-ROM products, like H.W. Wilson's, use most of the RAM to operate. They consequently do not adapt well to Meridian's LAN due to the RAM requirements of the LAN software. Also, since PsycLIT requires an extra fee to run on a LAN, the Science Citation Index (SCI) license agreement states that SCI cannot be run on a LAN, and Dissertation Abstracts requires a license fee for LAN usage, it is unlikely that these products will be run on our LAN unless some agreement can be reached about restrictions on their use. Agricola (SilverPlatter), ERIC (SilverPlatter), NTIS (SilverPlatter), MEDLINE (Cambridge), ASFA (Cambridge), and Life Sciences Collection (Cambridge) are all known to run on Meridian's system, so they are prime candidates for the LAN (also, they do not have license fees at this time). Unfortunately, SilverPlatter and Cambridge do not run together on the same Meridian LAN. The library staff is working on a solution to this problem. How the center will look in six months remains to be seen; if there is anything consistent about CD-ROM technology, it is change.

The Future

Providing access to the library's collection through "free" computer systems has an impact on the library's collection, staff and services. People are willing to use a library when they can easily find information for free. Contact at the reference desk increased and the number of interlibrary loans (ILL) grew with the advent of online searching. At OSU, OCLC, Western Library Network, RLIN, and CD-ROMs gave resource sharing through ILL further impetus. A complete analysis of the impact of CD-ROMs on our library services is being addressed in a separate article by another OSU staff member.

At some future point the collection managers may have to consider locally loading tapes of heavily used databases (Halperin, 1988). A LAN may not be able to keep up with the demand for the CD-ROM resources. Information costs money and accessing information costs yet more money. In a state where higher education budgets are constantly being cut, the library administration must make critical choices about how best to distribute its resources.

With CD-ROM, there are as many questions as there are answers. While the correct answers will only be known in the future, we can safely say that compact disc technology will be with us until a new storage medium replaces it. At the present rate of technological change (Hogan, 1989), one will. Perhaps even by the year 2002.

References

Apple Human Interface Guidelines: The Apple Desktop Interface. 1987. Reading, Massachusetts: Addison-Wesley Publishing Company, Inc.

Brindley, Lynne. 1988. "Online Versus Print Versus CD-ROM: Costs and Benefits." *Serials* 1(2):21–24.

Brunell, David H. 1988. "Comparing CD-ROM Products." *CD-ROM Librarian* 3(3): 14–18.

Halperin, Michael, and Patricia Renfro. 1988. "Online vs CD-ROM vs Onsite: High Volume Searching—Considering the Alternatives." *Online* 12 (6):36-42.

Hensinger, James Speed. 1989. "Using Multiple CD-ROM Databases on One Workstation." *Laserdisk Professional* 2 (2):84–87.

Herther, Nancy K. 1988. "How to Evaluate Reference Materials on CD-ROM." *Online* 12 (2):106–108.

————. 1988. "Microcomputer Technology: Helping Users Cope." *Online* 12(5):120–122.

Hoffman, Jake. 1988. "Creating a CD-ROM/PC Reference Workstation." *CD-ROM Librarian* 3 (2):17–20.

Hogan, Eddy, Tim Jewell, Jean Reese, and Karen J. Starr. 1989. "Seeing is Believing: A Conference Report—Microsoft's Fourth International Conference on CD-ROM." *Library Hi Tech News* 61:1–8.

Littlejohn, Alice C., Joan M. Parker. 1988. "Compact Disks in an Academic Library: Developing an Evaluation Methodology." *Laserdisk Professional* 1(1): 36–43.

Machovec, George S. 1988. "Selection Criteria for Leasing Databases on CD-ROM and Magnetic Tape." *Online Libraries and Microcomputers* 6(3): 1–4.

Miller, David C. 1987. "Evaluating CD-ROMs: To Buy or What to Buy?" *Database* 10(3): 41–42.

Nicholls, Paul Travis. 1988. "Laser/Optical Data Base Products: Evaluation and Selection." *Canadian Library Journal* 45(5): 296–300.

Nissley, Meta. 1988. "Optical Technology: Considerations for Collection Development." *Library Acquisitions: Practise and Theory* 12(1): 11–15.

Pemberton, Jeffery K. 1985. "Database Interviews an Online Pioneer—Fran Spigai." *Database* 8(3):15–21.

Starr, Karen J. 1988. "The Compact Disc at Oregon State University." *The SilverPlatter Exchange* 1(2):10–11,13.

————. 1988. "Taming the CD-ROM Wilderness: Developing and Managing a Workstation." *Laserdisk Professional* 1(4):46–52.

Starr, Karen J., and Karyle S. Butcher. 1989. "Establishing a Compact Disk Reference Center at OSU: Some Considerations." *Laserdisk Professional* 1(2):82–89.

York, Charlene C. 1988. "Optical Disk Products in the Collection Development Policy." *CD-ROM Librarian* 3(8): 16–18.

Karen J. Starr joined the staff at the Kerr Library as the Gifts and Exchange Librarian in 1977. By the middle of 1977, she was assigned part-time as a search consultant for the Library Information Retrieval Service (LIRS). Karen became the LIRS Coordinator in 1982. When the decision was made to install CD-ROM technology, she was assigned the additional responsibility of the center in July 1987. She became the CD-ROM librarian in February 1989. During the 1989–90 academic year, Karen took a leave of absence from Kerr Library to serve as an ALA Library Fellow at the Norwegian School for Librarian and Information Science in Oslo. Karen received a B.A. in history and an M.A. in anthropology from Oregon State University. Her M.L.S. is from Texas Woman's University in Denton. Prior to joining the Kerr Library staff, Karen was a cataloger at Washburn University Law Library in Topeka, Kansas.

Appendix 1

CD-ROM Center Lab Monitor Job Description
Primary Duties

1. Printers: vacuum weekly, maintain paper, maintain ink cartridges.
2. Boot up and shut down micros, drives, and printers daily.
3. Maintain log sheet of all users by name, status, department, and database.
4. Hold patrons' ID cards during their usage of the indexes.
5. Refer patrons to the reference desk for strategy formulation questions.
6. Load disks into drives.
7. Be familiar with Wilson, Cambridge, SilverPlatter, Dissertation Abstracts, and ISI software.
8. Answer software related questions and extract patrons from software related problems.
9. Be familiar with Boolean algebra and answer basic relational questions.
10. Hand out "cheat sheets" for the databases, etc.

QUALIFICATIONS

1. Ability to work with microcomputers (IBM, or compatible, experience preferred).
2. Ability to work with the public.

Appendix 2

Evaluation Criteria for CD-ROM Publications

Accuracy & Documentation

Any information product is only as good as the integrity of the database itself.

—Does the producer use an editorial board or groups of advisors?
—Compare the results and content descriptions with other reference materials.
—Verify producer claims with sample searches.

Appropriateness

Even if the CD-ROM product is a useful source of information, it may not be appropriate for the patrons.

—Is the arrangement, content and approach to the subject matter relevant and useful to the library patrons?
—What are the research needs for the subject area of the product?
—What educational level would use the product?
—What is the sophistication level of the intended user?

Ease of Use/Comprehension

CD-ROM is different than print. The CD-ROM product must be easy for people to use and understand. This requires an evaluation of the basic arrangement of the information.

—How readable is the product?
—If abbreviations are used, are they logical for your average user?
—Is the use of color, windows and other artistic qualities appropriate and valuable?
—Are the screen layouts logical?
—Do the commands make sense?
—What access points are available?
—What are the indexed fields?
—Are the instructions and help menus clear?
—Is the order of events in the search process on the CD-ROM logical?
—Are the number of keystrokes minimal?

—Does the user have the ability to print and to download to a floppy disk?

—What levels of sophistication are available in the searching software; i.e., novice vs expert?

—Is the system user-friendly—particularly if your user group is not computer literate (even more so if your population contains those who are not reading literate)?

Authority & Credibility

Many CD-ROM products are subsets of familiar products either online or in print. If this is the source of the database used, information on this product can be compared and analyzed with the other forms of the products. If not, the qualifications of the contributors, indexers and source documents must be considered.

—What quality control mechanisms are used?

—What is the reputation of the publisher?

Content Analysis

The contents of the CD-ROM product must be taken into account.

—What is the value of the information included in this product?

—How comprehensive is this product?

—How does it compare to other products and to the state-of-the-art for this subject area?

—Does it include all of the major journals, relevant issues, important dates, and significant companies or people?

—Subject specialization is important.

Comparisons to Similar Products

Just as we do for printed reference items, we need to check the literature for reviews and discussions of the product. If possible, do manual or online searches where products are from the same pool of information.

—Are there other CD-ROM products you can compare this product to?

—Compare a complete citation or entry from each—are they the same?

—If not, what is missing?

—How many disks make up the product? Are there other CD-ROM versions with fewer disks?

Revisions, Updates & Other Special Services

CD-ROM in practice is very similar to online systems. Use of Boolean search techniques, downloading and other features of these CD-ROM products requires the same help services that producers of online databases now provide.

—Where currency is critical, are updates or revisions to the disks timely?

—What are the replacement costs for lost/damaged disks?

—If end-users are involved in searching the products, are help menus, manuals or special services available?

—What support and training are available from the producer/vendor?

—For those with free online updates to the CD-ROMs, is the transition to online easy for end-users while being sufficiently well-controlled to prevent patron abuse or misuse of online services?

—Are special help lines available in order to obtain assistance as needed?

16
Fee-Based CD-ROMs at Kent State University

Barbara F. Schloman, Jeffrey N. Gatten, Greg Byerly

Introduction

Librarians at Kent State University (KSU) first became interested in CD-ROMs in 1985. An article about a new company, SilverPlatter, intrigued staff of both the Libraries' Reference Department and Systems Office (Lightbown, 1985). The article summarized issues that KSU would need to address before CD-ROMs could become a reality in the Libraries. Specifically, the article noted that the difficulty in choosing to purchase a CD-ROM product was "exacerbated by the rapid pace of change in information technologies" and emphasized the necessity to "minimize the need for investment by libraries and insulate them from the uncertainties of technological change."

The materials budget at Kent State was already stretched by inflation and serials price hikes. It was clear that funding for new technological products would have to come from other sources. The decision was made, therefore, to assess user fees to recover CD-ROM costs. With CD-ROMs, the KSU Libraries had to address all the standard issues of introducing a new service: product evaluation and selection, equipment purchase and maintenance, staff training, publicity, and policies. The added element was implementation of a user fee.

This chapter discusses the overall process of introducing CD-ROMs in public service areas at KSU with an emphasis on the consideration given throughout to the impact of user fees. While the pace of technological change has not decreased and the amount of uncertainty has not lessened, the CD-ROM experience of Kent State may provide some "insulation" for other libraries about to introduce or expand their CD-ROM operations.

Overview

Kent State University has an enrollment of over 20,000 students and is organized into four undergraduate colleges, three graduate units and three independent schools. The Libraries maintain a membership in the Association of Research Libraries and comprise a main library and five branch libraries. The collections total more than 1.7 million volumes and over 12,000 active serials.

The KSU Libraries' Systems Office was organized in 1986 and formally charged with the responsibility of implementing NOTIS as the Libraries' online integrated system. The charge was expanded later that year, after a three-month trial and rejection of InfoTrac, to "review, evaluate, and recommend new library technologies; implement them as appropriate and financially possible; and introduce CD-ROM technology to the Libraries." By December 1986, a report had been prepared listing the advantages of CD-ROMs and comparing existing CD-ROM products.

In January 1987, a CD-ROM Committee was formed to develop a plan for selecting CD-ROM products and equipment. Included were the systems librarian, the coordinator of the online search service, and two reference librarians. The Committee outlined and later published the primary considerations in acquiring CD-ROMs and goals for CD-ROM collection development (Gatten, 1987).

The ERIC product available from DIALOG was recommended to be the first CD-ROM subscription at KSU. DIALOG's ERIC was chosen because it was judged to be user-friendly and because reference staff were familiar with both DIALOG and the ERIC database. Compact Disclosure from Disclosure, PsycLIT from SilverPlatter, and Impact (GPO Monthly Catalog) from AutoGraphics have since been added.

In April 1987, the KSU Libraries were fortunate to receive special outside funding for CD-ROM equipment. However, no monies were provided for CD-ROM subscriptions. Serious budget problems, including the very real prospect of major serial cancellations, forced the decision to charge users for access to CD-ROMs in order to offer this new technology.

User Fees

A mechanism for charging library users for other services was already in place. KSU used a debit card charging system, VendaCard, to assess photocopy charges. It was relatively easy for the vendor to convert the same hardware to charge a per-minute fee to use a CD-ROM workstation. This allowed users to use the same debit card they had used for photocopying to access a CD-ROM product. The actual mechanism is very simple: a debit unit is connected between the keyboard and the microcomputer (figure 1). An electronic switch nulls the keyboard unless a valid debit card is inserted into the unit. With a valid debit card, the unit deducts a set amount from the debit card each minute.

The objective was to assess user fees only to pay for the annual subscriptions to the CD-ROM products. Since the microcomputers, CD-ROM drives, and printers were purchased with special funding, it was not necessary to recover equipment costs. Consequently, the Committee determined that only a minimal charge of $.15 per minute was needed. This compared quite favorably to the $1.00 per minute fee that the online service at KSU charged for a mediated online search of the DIALOG ERIC database.

Debit units can be used for charging for time on the microcomputer and/or for printing. The cost for printing supplies was not an issue in the initial decision, and the amount to be charged for access time was expected to cover subscription costs.

Because printers for making screen prints were available for free on several of the online catalog terminals in the Reference Center, the decision was made not to charge for printing at the CD-ROM workstations.

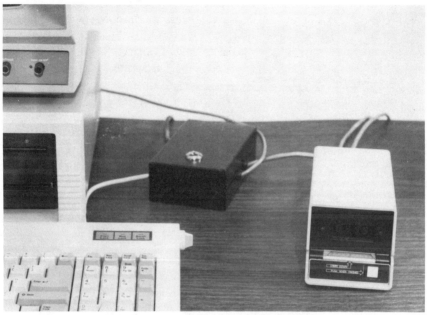

Figure 1. The CD-ROM workstation keyboard plugs into the debit card unit "black box" as does the debit card reader. The "black box" plugs into the keyboard slot on the backside of the microcomputer.

Any revenue collected beyond what was needed for existing CD-ROM subscriptions would be used to subscribe to additional CD-ROM products and to purchase more workstations. It was estimated that a usage rate of six 10-minute searches a day for 250 days would produce enough income to more than cover the actual subscription costs. The experience after the first year proved the original estimates to be correct. Enough revenue was generated from ERIC and Compact Disclosure to allow a modest expansion of the products received (Table 1).

Having decided to make CD-ROMs a fee-based service, the Committee and staff were concerned about user reaction. However, no users complained formally about the fees. Similarly, few complaints are received about the Libraries' other cost-recovery services (i.e., online searches, interlibrary loans). Promotional materials always emphasized that the charge was substantially less than the cost of a mediated online search. At least one academic department on campus began to subsidize the use of the CD-ROMs by providing debit cards to students as course "lab" material.

The extremely low per minute charge undoubtedly contributed to general acceptance of fee-based CD-ROMs. At $.15 per minute a student can use a CD-ROM for 20 minutes for a total cost of $3.00 (or less than the cost of half a pizza, in the economic language of college students). Just as some users are willing to pay significant amounts for an online search, many others demonstrated their willingness to spend a few dollars to facilitate their research with CD-ROM access.

Table 1

Twelve-month Accounting for Fee-Based Access to CD-ROMs (At $.15/minute)

	Dialog ERIC	Compact Disclosure	Row Total
Expenditure			
Subscription[a]	$950	$2,000	$2,950
Hardware[b]	N/A	N/A	N/A
Debit Card Unit[c]	360	360	720
Total	$1,310	$2,360	$3,670
Revenue	$2,772	$2,038	$4,810
Profit[d]	$1,462	($322)	$1,140
Expenditures Recovered (%)[e]	212%	86%	131%

[a] Annual subscription cost.

[b] Hardware (i.e., microcomputer, printer, CD-ROM drive) purchased with outside funding at no cost to the Libraries.

[c] $1,800/unit amortized over five years.

[d] Profit = Revenue – Total Expenditures

[e] Expenditures Recovered (%) = (Revenue / Total Expenditures) x 100

Equipment

In recent years, the General Assembly of the State of Ohio has provided special biennium capital appropriations for instructional equipment to state-supported institutions of higher education. The KSU Libraries successfully convinced the University administration that the necessary equipment for CD-ROM workstations qualified as instructional equipment. The result was that the Libraries could acquire almost all the CD-ROM equipment (i.e., microcomputers, printers, and CD-ROM drives) with these non-library funds. In addition to public workstations, the Libraries also used these appropriations to equip a state-of-the-art classroom within the main library, including a CD-ROM workstation with full-color video projection for bibliographic instruction.

The Philips CM-100 drive was selected initially as the most desirable brand of CD-ROM drive for the public workstations due to its "locking cabinet" feature. This model allowed the staff to lock a CD-ROM disc into the drive, thereby increasing security of the disc. However, the model is apparently no longer available, and the subsequent decision was made to purchase the Hitachi 1503S model. This is a stand-alone model, as opposed to an internal drive, which is mounted inside the microcomputer. This allows greater flexibility in switching drives from microcomputer to microcomputer, if necessary.

IBM-compatible microcomputers were selected based upon the availability of campus service for the particular model. The criteria used to select printers had been used previously to select printers for OCLC terminals and staff microcomputers: a dependable, trouble-free model that requires little attention. The Epson-FX series has proven to be durable and to require minimal maintenance. Mufflers for the printers have since been purchased to reduce the level of printer noise in the Reference Center. The least expensive muffler model (Printer Muffler 80 by Kensington Microware Ltd.) that could be identified was selected and has proven to be quite effective in reducing printer noise in the public area.

The largest library investment in CD-ROM equipment to date has been the purchase of the debit units used to charge users for CD-ROM access. Typically, these units cost as much as a microcomputer. They have been reliable and have required no special attention.

The Systems Office is responsible for installing and maintaining the CD-ROM products and workstations. The actual maintenance of the printers, including the loading of paper and the changing of ribbons, has been assigned to the same library unit, Audio Visual Services, that maintains the Libraries' photocopiers.

Evaluation and Selection

From the first KSU experience with laser disc technology in the spring of 1986 (InfoTrac), the unofficial policy has been to have an in-house trial of each product prior to subscribing. In addition, this informal policy has been extended to include the mandatory return of a CD-ROM product after the trial. This allows library staff an opportunity to make decisions regarding a purchase without the added pressure of the product being on-site.

CD-ROM products are selected for trial by periodically surveying public service librarians to determine their priorities. Each librarian submits a ranked list to the Committee. Preference is given to those CD-ROMs that will serve a large number of users, but consideration is also given to branch library needs. After a strong core of CD-ROMs is established, the Committee plans to review more specialized products.

Once a CD-ROM product has been selected for trial, the methods used to evaluate it vary. Initially, vendor-supplied user surveys were distributed. But staff decided that the questions being asked and the wording used served simply to promote the product at hand. After testing several formats and examining user surveys from other university libraries, a one-page user questionnaire was developed.

The questionnaire collects information regarding user status (e.g., faculty, undergraduate), the extent of the user's previous CD-ROM experience, the purpose for which the information is needed (e.g., paper, thesis), and perceived success of the search. The concept of a "successful" information search has been debated in the library literature. On the Kent State survey, the user is asked to rate the search as "highly successful," "somewhat successful" or "not successful." The user is then asked why a particular ranking was selected. The use of this open-ended question has provided useful information about the problems and needs of CD-ROM users. For example, based on these comments, the value of the database can be contrasted with the effectiveness of the search software. This information can lead the Committee to agree that a particular database is needed, but that it might be better to buy it from another vendor with better search software.

Policies and Procedures

As with most new library services, preparation for the introduction of the first CD-ROMs into the Reference Center included the development of a policy and procedure manual. The manual addressed the ways in which reference staff should respond to problems with the CD-ROM hardware and software. Particular attention was paid to the development of guidelines for problems that might arise because of charging for user access. Guidelines were written on what would constitute a legitimate refund. Typing errors or poor search strategy choices were generally considered "non-refundable." Hardware and software service problems warranted intervention by reference staff.

An "override" debit card was kept at the reference desk to be used by staff to handle service problems. For refundable problems, staff were directed to use the override card to correct the problem and to provide an appropriate amount of compensation time to the user. Users who preferred to have credit applied directly to their debit card were to be directed to the circulation desk, which also handles photocopier refunds. The policy further directed that limited free assistance could be provided to users who became "very upset or discouraged."

In practice, the reference staff has given liberal interpretation to these guidelines. No users to date have requested a credit be applied directly to their debit card. The override card has also been used for staff practice, library staff searches, and reference questions. The amount of use the override card receives can be determined because it is loaded with time units, rather than monetary units as are the user cards. To date, staff use has accounted for approximately 20 percent of total use.

Another initial policy decision was to have each workstation dedicated to one CD-ROM product, and only the current disc of that product. Discs covering an earlier time period would not be offered. This policy was later changed when it was determined that there was a small group of users who would elect to access the earlier discs if they were available. A sign was placed on the workstation informing users of the availability of the other discs and directing them to ask at the reference desk. Staff then make the switch. Experience has been that requests are infrequent.

Staff Training

Training of the reference staff on the CD-ROM products was considered to be critical. Because users would be paying while learning to use the CD-ROMs, staff would need to be able to assist them when necessary to minimize their frustration and help keep their costs reasonable.

For ERIC, the first CD-ROM product acquired, a preview of the search software was given to the entire reference staff in the library classroom. Moreover, each CD-ROM product has been made available first to the reference staff in their office before being installed in the Reference Center. This allows mini-workshops to be given to groups of staff and accords them time for self-instruction and practice. These opportunities have been made available to all desk staff, including librarians, support staff, and student assistants.

Publicity

In order to promote the CD-ROM products to students and faculty, a number of activities were undertaken. Because this was to be a new fee-based service, promotional activities were designed to meet two objectives: inform users that the products were available and give fair warning that there would be a charge.

Fliers publicizing the first products were drafted and distributed to all faculty members in appropriate academic departments. One side of the flier explained the particular CD-ROM product, the dates covered, and where it was available. The opposite side detailed the contents of the database, reviewed the print and online search alternatives, and outlined the advantages of a CD-ROM search over a mediated online search of the same database (e.g., less expensive, available all hours the library is open, no appointment required).

Handouts were also developed that provided step-by-step procedures for using the CD-ROM products. In general, each handout reviewed how to start the search, modify a search, and print search results. The handouts were placed next to each workstation.

Several open attendance workshops were scheduled to introduce the new CD-ROM products to prospective users and provide them with some understanding of the search software. It was thought that this would reduce the anxiety of having to "pay to learn" the first time a product was used. The products were demonstrated, search techniques described, and suggestions given for making the most effective use of one's time (e.g., first checking the thesaurus). However, as was expected, attendance at the workshops was very small. Three workshops were held, each with about five to eight attendees.

Perhaps the most effective CD-ROM promotion occurs during bibliographic instruction for specific classes. The well-equipped classroom in the library allows librarians to incorporate CD-ROM demonstrations directly into the course-related library instruction.

Impact on the Library

Kent State library users are using CD-ROMs despite the fees. Library staff recognize that it would not have been financially possible to have CD-ROMs at KSU without this method of cost recovery. Nonetheless, they believe that the charging policy works against the educational potential of the products. The capabilities of a given CD-ROM can only be explored fully through hands-on, trial and error experience. Charging the user to learn and experiment may discourage some users and possibly places undue pressure on those who do try. There has been no indication that incurring a fee for use has encouraged users to spend more time planning searches before they begin. In addition, several faculty members have indicated their desire to make course-related assignments using the CD-ROMs, but are reluctant to do so if students will directly incur costs.

Another impact has been on staff. Experienced online searchers have had to adjust to using a menu-driven software and accept its limitations. Reference staff who have not been doing online searching have had to develop an understanding of formal search strategy construction, as well as the protocol and techniques of the different CD-ROM products.

All staff have had to be flexible and assimilate the variations presented by each of the products, all of which are presently from different vendors. Staff have also felt restricted in the assistance they have given users because of the pressure of the per minute charge. To some degree the situation parallels fee-based online searching, except that the librarian is not acting as an intermediary. In addition, it has been necessary for librarians to incorporate this new technology into their bibliographic instruction when appropriate.

The most dramatic impact of CD-ROMs has been realized in KSU's mediated online searching service. For the past decade, the two most heavily searched online databases have been ERIC and PsycInfo. The 1986/87 academic year, before ERIC on CD-ROM, shows a high percentage of ERIC searches throughout the year. ERIC on CD-ROM was introduced in February 1988, and the percentage of ERIC online searches began to decline. By 1988/89 there had been a significant reduction in the level of ERIC online searching. A similar pattern has been seen with PsycInfo online searches after the introduction of SilverPlatter's PsycLIT.

Overall, the number of mediated online searches has declined about 30 percent. This has allowed staff to begin looking at other potential users on campus who could benefit from online searching but are unlikely to have their sources available on CD-ROM.

In the meantime, the decline in online search activity has meant a reduction in the level of staffing required for this service. During the summer of 1988, staff that would have normally been assigned to the online search service were relocated to the CD-ROM workstations in the reference area in order to provide assistance to users. This was a successful attempt to provide dedicated assistance to CD-ROM users, as opposed to relying on the staff at the reference desk. However, the practice worked less effectively in fall semester and was discontinued. CD-ROM staff found themselves being drawn more into all of the other reference desk activities by virtue of the close proximity of the CD-ROM workstations to the reference desk. Users during the regular academic term do not have the limited time constraints of summer school students. Therefore, servicing the CD-ROMs with the normal desk staff of one or two reference libarians and a student reference assistant has seemed to work well during fall and spring semesters.

The Future

The CD-ROM Committee has monitored the financial state of the fee-based CD-ROM service and its impact on users and staff. In addition, it has regularly reconsidered the need to charge users directly and has sought other sources of funding. Reference librarians, in particular, acknowledged the economic necessity of charging for CD-ROMs, but continued to be uncomfortable with charging for access to a technology that offers such potential for instructing users about how information is organized and accessed.

Consequently, when a substantial increase in the Libraries' materials budget was announced for 1989/90, the CD-ROM Committee submitted a proposal to eliminate the user fee. Debit card units will be removed from the CD-ROMs in the summer of 1989. A $20,000 budget line has been established which will allow the existing products to be continued with no user charges, plus provide for several new products for both the main library and branches.

The CD-ROM budget line is intentionally kept distinct from the serials and monographic allocations. This will make it possible to monitor the development of a CD-ROM collection and prevent the serials budget from being skewed by costly CD-ROM subscriptions. Because free access to the CD-ROMs can now be provided without cancelling print serial titles, there has been little disagreement about this change in policy.

Summary

As early as 1986, KSU wanted to make CD-ROMs available to users. Online searching had been offered since 1974, and this seemed like a logical extension of quality reference service. However, economic realities at the time necessitated a difficult choice: to offer the service as fee-based or to wait until some unknown time in the future when complete funding might be available.

The KSU Libraries found fee-based CD-ROMs workable, although not desirable. Applying a user fee made it possible for KSU library users to experience this new information technology first-hand. External factors have now made it possible to remove the user fee. However, our experiences with introducing CD-ROMs should help the Libraries meet the future challenges presented by a rapidly evolving information technology.

References

Gatten, Jeffrey N., Judy Ohles, Mary Gaylord, and Harvey Soule. 1987. "Purchasing CD-ROM products: Considerations for a new technology." *Library Acquisitions: Practice & Theory* 11 (4):273–281.

Lightbown, Parke P. 1985. "The I.S.I.S. SilverPlatter Service: Confronting a new technology (Part 2)." *Library Hi Tech* 3 (2):116–120.

Barbara F. Schloman has worked as Reference Librarian at Kent State University since 1977. She presently serves as Coordinator of Computerized Information Services. Barbara received a B.S. degree from Iowa State University and a M.S.L.S. degree from the University of Wisconsin. In July 1989, she assumed the position of Head of Reference.

Jeffrey N. Gatten joined the Library Administration faculty of Kent State University in 1984 as a Reference Librarian. He became the Systems Librarian in 1986. Jeff received his

B.A. degree in Political Science from Ohio State University, and his M.L.S. from Kent State University. He is chair of the KSU Libraries CD-ROM Committee and was the 1988/89 Leader of the RASD-MARS Discussion Group on Disc Technology.

Greg Byerly was a reference librarian and online searcher at Kent State from 1975–1984. Since 1984, he has served as Head of Systems for the University Libraries. He received an M.L.S. in 1975, an M.A. in English in 1976, and a Ph.D. in Higher Educational Administration in 1979, all from Kent State University. Currently, he is also working as a Director of the Ohio Library Information System (OLIS), a statewide project to provide an online union catalog and circulation system for the 15 state-assisted universities in Ohio. Active in ALA, Greg was Chair of the RASD/Machine-Assisted Reference Section (MARS) in 1987–88.

17

The Changing LANdscape of Undergraduate Research: The Rutgers-Newark Experience

Ka-Neng Au, Natalie Borisovets

Until recently, hardware limitations, especially the lack of multi-unit CD-ROM players and the subsequent lack of simultaneous multi-user access, have seriously hindered the acquisition of a wide range of CD-ROM products by academic libraries. Some 300 titles, many of them basic reference sources, are already available in CD-ROM format. Moreover, despite the tremendous storage capacity of CD-ROMs and the increased use of compression software, a number of basic products still require multiple discs. Thus, a library acquiring SilverPlatter's seven-disc version of MEDLINE, for example, would either have to dedicate multiple workstations to access just that product, or would have to change discs every time someone wanted to search a different time segment of the file. The former solution is both costly and inefficient. The latter is cumbersome, inefficient, and, as it might involve the interaction of another party, a limitation to access. Indeed, as both scenarios mandate one-at-a-time usage, access in both is severely limited.

The recent development of CD-ROM local area networks (LANs) promises to have a major impact on the acquisition and use of CD-ROM products by academic libraries. Like many others, the John Cotton Dana Library of Rutgers, the State University of New Jersey, has chosen to integrate optical technology into its traditional range of services. Rather than acquire a burgeoning number of stand-alone workstations, however, the library has decided to concentrate on the implementation of CD-ROM LANs. In the past year, partly in response to the demands of a new undergraduate curriculum, multiple CD-ROM LANs, accessing some 15 bibliographic and non-bibliographic products, have been installed. These new automated reference sources have been physically and conceptually integrated with the existing automated and print resources.

Institutional Background

Rutgers, the State University of New Jersey, has over 47,000 students on its three campuses in Camden, Newark, and New Brunswick. Rutgers-Newark has a student population of approximately 9,500 and a faculty of 500. There are two undergraduate liberal arts colleges on the campus, as well as the College of Nursing, the Graduate School-Newark, the Graduate School of Management, the School of Criminal Justice, and the School of Law. The John Cotton Dana Library serves the Newark campus and all its divisions except the School of Law. It is the primary business research library for the University, and also has substantial holdings to support doctoral programs in behavioral and neural sciences, biology, chemistry, criminal justice, management, nursing, and psychology. The Dana Library's collections currently consist of approximately 353,000 books and bound periodicals, 2,400 periodical subscriptions, 516,000 microform items, and approximately 150,000 government documents. The library has a reference collection of about 19,000 items, and a reference staff of eight librarians, including the Head of Public Services and the Head of Collection Development and Management. All reference librarians are also subject specialists with collection development responsibilities, and most also participate in the bibliographic instruction and online search programs. One of the Business Librarians also has the title of "Microcomputer Coordinator," a designation which presently encompasses everything from software installation, routine hardware maintenance, and troubleshooting to the development of computerized database management programs with library applications.

In addition to its librarian-mediated external search services, which include fee-based access to online databases as well as access to bibliographic utilities such as OCLC and RLIN, the Dana Library provides access to automated reference sources via local or patron-accessible terminals and workstations. These include eight public access terminals for the automated circulation system, which is soon to be upgraded to a full online catalog, and a workstation with free dial-up access to Dow Jones News/Retrieval, which is an online database with corporate and industry information, current news items and a range of consumer services such as the Official Airline Guide. Also available to library patrons are several optical-based systems.

Optical Systems Prior to the Networks

In June 1986, the Dana Library installed a cluster of four workstations from the Information Access Company (IAC). IAC's InfoTrac system, a precursor to "real" networking, used 12 inch optical platters. Each workstation had its own printer but shared access via a distributor unit to the three laser disc drives on the system. IAC's General Periodicals Index and Government Publications Index proved to be very popular and the workstations were constantly occupied. The InfoTrac databases were subsequently upgraded to CD-ROM format in the spring of 1989.

Patrons also had the opportunity to use CD-ROM products at two single-user CD-ROM workstations. The first one provided access to the Modern Language Association (MLA) International Bibliography, a Wilsondisc product from the H.W. Wilson Company. This disc product was far superior to the print version and its acceptance was unprecedented, especially with English Composition and Literature students who lined up to use it at term paper time. This dedicated workstation was packaged by the Wilson Company to include an IBM PS/2 Model 30 microcomputer, an external CD-ROM player, an IBM Proprinter, and a Hayes 1200 baud modem to permit access to the Wilsonline online database at no additional search cost. However, the provision of online access proved problematic as patrons would slip into the online search mode without realizing it. This feature, therefore, was subsequently deactivated.

The second single-user workstation was configured to access a selected number of discs, with the most frequently used title being Compact Disclosure from Disclosure, Inc. Compact Disclosure provides a summary of financial and textual information about public companies, culled from their filings with the U.S. Securities and Exchange Commission. Because of its unusual degree of user-friendliness, and the sheer quantity of information available with minimal effort, Compact Disclosure was also constantly in use. The downloading feature in particular proved very popular with patrons who wished to incorporate data into their own electronically composed documents.

This stand alone workstation also permitted the library to try out new titles and, over the course of a year, six other products were tested to gauge patron response. This meant providing an on-screen menu and using batch files to load the search software for each option. Since all the discs were at the reference desk, the librarian on duty had to manually switch discs to respond to patrons' information needs.

The New Curriculum

In May of 1987, the Rutgers-Newark Faculty of Arts and Sciences endorsed the adoption of a new undergraduate curriculum to be implemented in the fall semester of 1988. Among the major components of this radically revised program was a new emphasis on

1) The interdisciplinary nature of intellectual pursuits. This was to be reflected not only in the content of individual courses, but also in the requirement of a 12-credit, four course program "presenting a coherant explanation in depth of related historical, intellectual and literary culture."

2) The teaching of the methodologies used by the major disciplines. Thus students would be required to take sustained sequences of courses which would introduce them to the comparative, critical, empirical, experimental, and historical methods of inquiry.

3) The synthesis of acquired knowledge within the student's area of concentration. Thus students would be required to complete a senior thesis.

The Response: Multi-User, Multi-Source Access to Databases

The Dana Library considered the new curriculum to be a unique opportunity for the library to innovate and make a positive impact on the campus. The new emphases on problem-solving and the research process were expected to increase undergraduate demand for library resources and services. Easy access to both bibliographic and non-bibliographic data was critical to the successful implementation of the research component of the new curriculum. Unfortunately, existing fee-based online services made much data inaccessible to most undergraduates. Databases on CD-ROM, however, offered greater accessibility at a low per-use cost to the library, and thus could permit the library to make these automated resources available at no charge to patrons.

Furthermore, since access is maximized if the CD-ROMs are shared, in January 1988 the Dana Library began investigating local area network options for multi-source, multi-user access to CD-ROMs. A grant proposal was submitted to the New Jersey Department of Higher Education in May 1988. Subsequently, the Library was awarded $117,385 under the Department's Computers in Curricula Program to install several different CD-ROM LAN configurations.

Local Area Networks

A local area network (LAN) consists of two or more microcomputers connected together in one of several network topologies, i.e., bus, ring, star, etc, within a limited geographical area such as a building or a department. The purpose of a LAN is usually to share information stored on one or more devices such as hard disks or CD-ROMs, and/or to share peripherals such as printers. Each microcomputer must have a network interface board and must be cabled, directly or indirectly via a concentrator, to a device that controls the flow of data. This device, known as the file server, might be another microcomputer on the LAN or a more powerful computer that is dedicated to serving the LAN. The actual sharing of devices and peripherals and the execution of applications software is controlled by a network operating system, such as IBM's PC LAN Program or Novell's Netware, which determines the sequence of data flow from one microcomputer node to another, or to a peripheral. In a typical CD-ROM LAN, one or more CD-ROM drives are attached to the file server. Instead of the device drivers used for the operation of stand-alone CD-ROM drives, each microcomputer requires special device drivers to communicate with the networked CD-ROM drives. These device drivers may be supplied either by the manufacturer of the CD-ROM drives or the CD-ROM publisher. In addition, Microsoft Extensions may or may not be needed, depending on the networking configuration. Under most existing configurations, each microcomputer workstation also has a copy of the search software required for each of the CD-ROM products available on the network.

Acquisitions

Before specific networking choices could be made, the Dana librarians had to decide on the CD-ROM titles to be acquired and the logical configurations in which they were to be grouped. The choice of titles appropriate for the target audience of undergraduates was wide and included both bibliographic and non-bibliographic or numeric databases. Many products were proposed and debated by the librarians, and numerous titles were obtained for review. Among the criteria used in judging the CD-ROM products were: ease of use by end-users, ease of installation, availability for use on a network, compatibility of the access software with network hardware and software, appropriateness for an undergraduate audience in general (and the undergraduate population of Rutgers-Newark in particular), advantages over comparable non-automated products, extent of coverage, and suitability within the library's collection development scope.

The deliberate emphasis in this instance on undergraduate research meant that certain titles which might in other cases have received strong support for acquisition, such as Dissertation Abstracts and Cambridge Scientific's Life Sciences Collection, were excluded from consideration. On the other hand, ABI/Inform OnDisc, which was originally thought to be out of scope, proved to be so popular with undergraduate business students during its trial that it was added to the "core" list of acquisitions.

During the course of our deliberations, the list of possible choices continued to evolve and expand. New CD-ROM titles appeared at an astounding rate while other titles were significantly upgraded and improved, sometimes resulting in the reconsideration of sources that had been previously rejected. Although the development of reference collections is always an ongoing process, the speed of development of new optical disc products meant no decision could ever be considered as "final." While this may be all to the good, it is a little difficult to deal with when working on a project with time limits and deadlines.

Other problems that had to be dealt with included: selection from at least eight different versions of MEDLINE, restrictions on CD-ROM usage precluding networking, and incompatibilities between retrieval software from different publishers. Efforts to resolve incompatibilities continued for many months, and to some extent, the issue has yet to be resolved. Some decisions were made on a purely pragmatic basis. After a review of all currently available MEDLINE products on CD-ROM, there was a clear consensus that Cambridge Scientific had the superior product. However, as MEDLINE was to be networked with PsycLIT and Nursing & Allied Health (CINAHL-CD), both exclusively SilverPlatter products, it was felt that, because of both software installation and user training issues, the SilverPlatter version of MEDLINE should be acquired.

Eventually 13 new titles were chosen: six of the "core" indexes from H.W. Wilson (Applied Science & Technology Index, Biological & Agricultural Index, Business Periodicals Index, Essay & General Literature Index, Humanities Index and Social Sciences Index); four titles from SilverPlatter (Corporate and Industry Research Reports Index, MEDLINE, CINAHL-CD, and PsycLIT); ABI/Inform Ondisc from University Microfilms International; and two non-bibliographic databases from Slater-Hall (Business Indicators and County Statistics). These would then be integrated with the five CD-ROM titles already available at Dana: H.W. Wilson's MLA International Bibliography, Disclosure's Compact Disclosure, and IAC's General Periodicals Index-Academic Version (current and backfile), Government Publications Index, and National Newspaper Index.

The Workstation Cluster

Most academic libraries acquiring multiple CD-ROM workstations have chosen to set up "Electronic Labs," or "Reference Centers," i.e., centralized facilities physically separated from traditional reference collections. These centers, which may also house the online end-user search facilities, are usually staffed by students who provide basic assistance with hardware and software. This centralized solution seems to have come most naturally to libraries, such as those of the University of Vermont and Oregon State University, that are themselves "centralized," with few or no separate branch or departmental libraries to support. Other large, physically decentralized systems, such as those of the University of Washington (20 branches), Vanderbilt University (seven divisions), and Columbia University (23 branches), have selected a decentralized, discipline-integrated approach, placing titles into the appropriate library based on content.

At the Dana Library, the decision was made to apply and expand the discipline-integrated approach to encompass the general reference collection. Thus it was decided that the new automated reference sources should be integrated into the reference collection to the fullest extent possible. The prime consideration was one of philosophy: that these automated reference sources were, and should be readily perceived as, reference tools which happened to be in one particular format, and that content, not format, should determine placement. In line with the instructional objectives of the project, it was vital for students to become aware of both the scope and the limitations of what the new technologies made available, and to understand how the new formats related to other research and reference sources, whether they be in computerized or print formats. Moreover, the routine availability of professional assistance and intervention in the research process was seen as an important consideration. After all, there would seem to be few circumstances in which an academic library would arbitrarily decide to remove from its reference collection the print versions of, for example, the *MLA International Bibliography*, *Psychological Abstracts*, the *Monthly Catalog of Government Publications*, and the *Federal Tax Reporter*, and to place them together in a separate room manned by work-study students who, upon request, were expected to be able to deal with questions of content, scope, and the most effective, and appropriate, use of these indexes. The challenge then became to adhere to the principle of primacy of content while responding to the need for simultaneous multi-user access to individual titles.

It was finally decided that five separate CD-ROM workstation "clusters" would be set up in the Reference Area of the Dana Library. Each cluster would have four workstations at which specific titles could be accessed. The workstation clusters would consist of a logical grouping of database products, and would be arranged so as to emphasize the relationship between the computer-based retrieval systems and related, although not necessarily equivalent, print sources. The clusters finally decided upon were:

Cluster 1 Humanities/Social Sciences: Essay and General Literature Index, Humanities Index, MLA International Bibliography, Social Sciences Index

Cluster 2 Science/Business: Applied Science & Technology Index, Biological & Agricultural Index, Business Periodicals Index, Compact Disclosure, Corporate & Industry Research Reports Index

Cluster 3 Life Sciences: Nursing and Allied Health, MEDLINE, PsycLIT

Cluster 4 Business: ABI/Inform Ondisc, Business Indicators, County Statistics

Cluster 5 General: General Periodicals Index, Government Publications Index, National Newspaper Index

Integration of the CD-ROM Clusters

The intellectual as well as physical integration of the CD-ROM clusters into the Dana Reference Area required extensive planning which ultimately resulted in the relocation of all reference index tables, as well as major shifts of the volumes shelved on those tables (figure 1). While most of the reference collection is shelved strictly on the basis of LC classification, some 100 frequently used indexes and reference serials were divided into broad subject categories and distributed among 10 index tables located throughout the Reference Area. These tables were of various sizes and configurations; some were standing height, and some were sit-down tables. In some instances, the logical division of indexes among tables had been lost with the passage of time. Some titles that were no longer frequently used remained on tables, while potentially heavily used titles remained in the reference stacks due to lack of room on tables. In other words, it was a typical Reference Department.

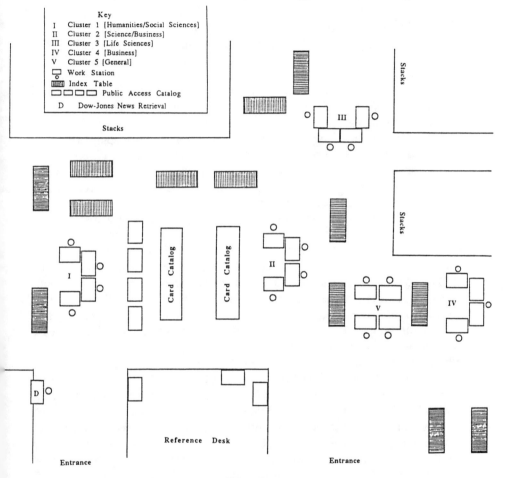

figure 1

Once furniture for the workstations had been chosen, planning for the integration of the CD-ROM clusters meant, first of all, evaluating the appropriateness of current and potential index table titles. Then, as the index tables had to be moved before any workstation furniture could be set up, extensive measurements had to be taken and floor areas marked. Obviously integration is labor-intensive. Certainly it would have been simpler to clear one section of the Reference Department and line up 15 workstations, or to place single workstations in strategic locations. Integration, especially in a networked environment, requires considerable extra work. In the end, however, students searching the MLA International Bibliography on CD-ROM also had, for example, immediate access to earlier years of MLA in print format, selected literary criticism bibliographies, related indexes such as the Arts and Humanities Citation Index, and the CD-ROM version of the Humanities Index on the same cluster.

CD-ROM Multi-User/Networking Options: State of the Art

As the Dana project developed, different networking choices appeared. The individual features and limitations of the various systems changed radically between the time we wrote the grant proposal and when we were ready to acquire the equipment. As of this writing, four separate types of CD-ROM multi-user/networking options exist, most of which were not available when we began our project.

Multi-user Systems

Custom Design Technology's InfoMachine. This system employs a portable 80286-based microcomputer as the host device with a shared printer and up to seven CD-ROM drives connected to it. The host computer supports up to eight dumb terminals (monitor plus keyboard). Networking software, microcomputer workstations, and a file server are not required.

IAC's InfoTrac Reference Center. In this system, customized software is designed to recognize IAC's own titles as well as those from several other publishers: DIALOG, Disclosure, OCLC, and SilverPlatter, but not Cambridge Scientific or H.W. Wilson. The initial product simply daisy-chains dual-drive CD-ROM players to individual IBM PC/AT-compatible workstations. The next "wired" stage will include a file server supporting up to eight workstations. The customized software is now available, while the proprietary multi-user hardware was due to be released in summer 1989. Both options allow libraries to be selective about the databases accessible at each workstation.

Products that Enable CD-ROM Local Area Networks

Meridian Data's CD Net. CD Net consists of proprietary server and workstation software and a multi-drive unit with a 80286 or 80386 CPU in a "tower" much like an IBM PS/2 Model 60. This CD-ROM server is designed to run as a node on a LAN with its own network file server. Network configurations supported include Arcnet, Ethernet, and Token-Ring, running Novell Netware software. The device holds up to five half-height SCSI CD-ROM drives. Additional drives can be attached as separate expansion units. The company affirms that all titles that conform to the ISO 9660 standard will work on the device.

Online Computer System's OPTI-NET. OPTI-NET is a LAN management program that runs on top of a network which supports the Netbios software interface, such as the IBM PC LAN program or 3Com network software, and permits up to 32 CD-ROM drives to be accessed via the LAN. OPTI-NET is available from Online Computer Systems (OCS) which also manufactures multi-drive units and CD-ROM controller cards, as well as integrated CD-ROM systems.

Local Area Network Operating Systems

Artisoft's LANtastic. The LANtastic Network Operating System is an entry level LAN program. According to the manufacturer, LANtastic was designed to accommodate CD-ROM devices, and Microsoft CD-ROM Extensions are not required for individual workstations. This program takes up much less RAM than do the IBM PC LAN or Novell Netware programs. Artisoft also produces its own proprietary LANtastic network interface boards, but the adapter-independent version of their software will run on any NETBIOS compatible hardware.

Integrated CD-ROM Local Area Network Systems

SilverPlatter's MultiPlatter. This system builds on Meridian Data's 5-drive CD Net tower, now renamed a "network server" and bundled with proprietary network management software. Additional drives are housed in an expansion unit (six drives) or a second network server (five drives). The MultiPlatter system supports up to 22 drives and 10 workstations in an Ethernet or Token-Ring hardware configuration, using IBM PC LAN or Novell Netware software. The company will provide support for the software and hardware included.

MultiPlatter systems were tested at several academic libraries, and became commercially available on a "controlled release" basis in the summer of 1989. Currently, all SilverPlatter titles are supported on MultiPlatter, and the company states that other titles conforming to the ISO 9660 standard will run on the network. CD-ROMs from SilverPlatter available on the network appear on a menu within the search software.

H.W. Wilson's Wilson Networking System. A modified version of H.W. Wilson's search software package will run on top of IBM PC LAN software on a Token-Ring network, which allows for networked or local CD-ROM players. An IBM PS/2 Model 30 286 or an IBM PC/AT or compatible serves as a dedicated file server; the network shares a printer and up to 22 native mode (i.e., vendor-specific) or SCSI CD-ROM drives. The network supports up to seven workstations (IBM PC/XT/AT or compatibles as well as IBM PS/2 Model 30s and 30 286s) per multistation access unit (or concentrator) attached to the server. Additional workstations can be supported by adding one or more servers and multistation access units.

Wilsondiscs are accessed via menus within the search software. Wilson is actively working on a feature that will allow other CD-ROM products to run on the same network as Wilsondiscs. Currently, titles from R.R. Bowker, Disclosure, Microsoft, Moody's Investors Service, and SilverPlatter will run along with Wilsondiscs. Wilson's modified search software will not be commercially available until mid-1990.

The Dana Networks

The Dana Library is currently running two different LAN configurations: IBM Token-Ring in an IBM PC LAN environment (two clusters), and LANtastic's own hardware and Network Operating System (one cluster). These particular networking options were not, however, the ones originally chosen. They were selected by trial and error, which, in this case, means we tried other things and got a lot of "ERROR" messages.

Initially, the Library intended to set up two other network configurations. IAC was to supply one, running titles from various publishers. As IAC's proposed network was to exclude access to Wilsondiscs, the other network was to be based on OCS's OPTI-NET and multi-drive units and was to run Wilsondiscs on an Ethernet with Novell software. Due to software incompatibilities, however, preliminary tests with the OCS hardware were not successful. As for IAC, the date of network availability was postponed twice. Thus, new configurations had to be selected.

The next option considered was Meridian Data's CD Net product which also required the separate purchase of network hardware and a networking software package. At that time, the MultiPlatter system had not yet been announced. The library acquired one CD Net tower with the intention of installing an Ethernet network with Novell Netware, but by the time the grant was awarded another possibility presented itself. The H.W. Wilson Company chose the Dana Library to be the beta test site for its new network configuration.

Wilson CD-ROM Network Beta-Test

The apparent inability of Wilsondiscs to run in a networked environment had been a severe blow to project planning. However, discussions with the H.W. Wilson Company revealed that it was in the process of developing its own local area network configuration. After further discussion, it was agreed that the Dana Library would serve as the beta test site for that network. The agreement for site testing was formalized in January of 1989, and the first of Dana's Wilson LANs was installed in early February. Minor software changes were made approximately every three weeks as users and librarians provided the vendor with comments about the system. So far, three different versions of the network software, running both Wilson and non-Wilson products, have been tested.

Network Configurations: Technical Aspects
Cluster 1: Humanities & Social Sciences: H.W. Wilson

The first cluster of workstations is running IBM PC LAN software, version 1.2, on IBM Token-Ring hardware. This networking configuration is rated as having a maximum data transmission rate of 4 megabits per second (Mbps), which is about average for small LANs supporting a work-group or a department. The file server and each of the four workstations are IBM PS/2 Model 30s, equipped with 20MB hard disks and Token-Ring network interface cards. All five machines are cabled to a multistation access unit (MAU) which has a total of eight slots for nodes, which means that another three workstations could be added to this cluster. The file server controls the data flow between the workstations, the CD-ROM drives, and the shared printer. This microcomputer also runs the LAN support programs, one provided by IBM and the other by the H.W. Wilson Company. Wilson's software eliminates the need for Microsoft CD-ROM Extensions to handle the CD-ROM devices.

When the system is powered up at the beginning of each workday, the network support programs automatically initialize all the devices and make the databases on them available to the workstations. These programs can also be called up any time during the day to determine the status of each of the shared devices. Most crucial of all to the LAN operation at the Dana Library is the network printer queue control, which is used to suspend or cancel unwanted or unnecessary print jobs.

Two LMSI/Philips CM132 CD-ROM units, each with two drives, are connected to the file server. The drives are rated at 500 ms average access rate on stand-alone workstations, which is typical of most drives currently available. (The very fastest drives just released by Toshiba are rated at 350 ms.) However, we have found that the average access rate over the first network cluster is 900 ms. This slight degradation in data access is not, however, perceptually apparent to the patron.

The printer on this LAN is a Hewlett-Packard Thinkjet Model 2225C, which uses ink cartridges rather than printer ribbons. The noise level is very low, only about 49 decibels, but printing is relatively slow, rated at about 150 characters per second (cps). Some patrons have commented on this situation, asking for a second printer, but on the whole, most patrons are content to wait in line. Since only four workstations share the printer and, since the indexes on this cluster are all citation-only (without abstracts), the delay is fairly minimal. The search software has been configured to allow up to 100 citations to be printed. Patrons also have the option to download the search results onto a floppy diskette placed in the A drive of a workstation. A standard 720K diskette can hold about 2,400 citations, which can then be printed out on the patron's own printer. The downloaded search results can also be treated as a text file by a word processing program and incorporated into an electronically composed document.

Cluster 2: Science & Business: H.W. Wilson & SilverPlatter

The second cluster of four workstations, also IBM PS/2 Model 30s, runs the same networking software on the same networking hardware. However, the file server, CD-ROM drives, printer, and databases differ from the first cluster. Instead of a fifth microcomputer, the file server on this cluster is a modified Meridian Data 80286-based CD NET. While this device is marketed as a network-sensitive multi-drive unit to be attached to a LAN, we upgraded the device by adding a 20MB hard-disk-on-a-card, a keyboard, and a monochrome display monitor. The unit now serves the network AND the five CD-ROM drives in it. The manufacturer used half-height Toshiba drives rated at 400 ms average access time. On the network, the average access rate is approximately 700 ms. The printer used on this cluster is a newer Hewlett-Packard ink jet printer, appropriately named the QuietJet Model 2227B. This printer is rated at 160 cps and comes equipped with a platen knob to simplify paper feed and removal.

Along with three indexes from the Wilson Company, there are currently two SilverPlatter discs running on this cluster. The technical support people at the Wilson Company provided a software bridge to SilverPlatter's search software so that products from both companies can be run off the same network. This software bridge is part of the enhanced networking software that the H.W. Wilson Company will eventually release. The Dana Library has just signed a network license agreement with Disclosure, Inc. and plans to provide access to Compact Disclosure, another non-Wilson CD-ROM. This cluster epitomizes the concept of multi-publisher, multi-source, multi-user access to CD-ROMs.

Cluster 3: Health & Life Sciences: SilverPlatter

This cluster is also made up of four IBM PS/2 Model 30s and the CD NET device. However, the networking software is LANtastic's Network Operating Software version 2.53u, with the workstations and devices cabled on a bus topology with LANtastic interface cards rated at a maximum of 2 Mbps. Each workstation has its own printer; we chose Panasonic daisy-wheel printers (Model KX-P1091i) which are fairly fast (200 cps) and extremely inexpensive. The noise factor is controlled by the workstation furniture which has a baffled compartment for the printer.

As in the second cluster, the CD Net device was modified with a 20MB hard disk, a keyboard, and a monochrome display monitor. Additionally, we obtained an expansion unit with six drives to provide this cluster with access to a total of 11 CD-ROMs. The reasoning was simple enough: with the thesauri, SilverPlatter's version of MEDLINE resides on seven disks, PsycLIT on three, and Nursing and Allied Health on one. Having so many drives allows us to mount all available discs for each database.

Cluster 4: Business: Stand-alone Workstations

The workstations on this cluster are a mixture of IBM microcomputers for bibliographic and non-bibliographic databases in CD-ROM and other machine-readable formats. Since its retrieval software is slower than most, ABI/Inform is running on an external Toshiba XM 3200 drive (rated at 350 ms) that is connected to an IBM PS/2 Model 50. Another Model 50Z holds statistical data from various government agencies as well as applications software to manipulate the data. The third workstation is an IBM PS/2 Model 30 286 with an LMSI CM 132 dual drive unit for two Slater-Hall titles: Business Indicators and County Statistics. The last machine in this cluster is an IBM PC/XT with another LMSI CM 132 CD-ROM player. This workstation is the original one in the library, and has been modified to hold one 3 1/2" floppy drive and one 5 1/4" floppy drive to facilitate data transfer. The two CD-ROM titles which run on this workstation are Microsoft's Small Business Consultant and Matthew Bender's Federal Tax Service, both of which are full text databases.

Cluster 5: General: IAC

All four stand-alone workstations on this cluster are leased from IAC. Each IBM PC compatible has one floppy drive and two external dual drive CD-ROM modules, which are actually half height Sony drives repackaged by IAC. The current version of the retrieval software accesses only IAC databases. We are considering upgrading the machines on this cluster to the full Reference Center workstation hardware.

Costs

No one said it was going to be cheap. For the first three CD-ROM clusters, costs ranged between $17,000 [Wilsondisc cluster] and $22,000 [SilverPlatter cluster] per four-station cluster. These costs included microcomputers, servers, drives, printers, and networking hardware and software. Workstation furniture and software subscriptions were excluded. Our costs are based on what in some cases were substantial academic discounts and do not reflect list prices (Table 1). While most are one-time costs, subscriptions and supplies, i.e., paper, ink jets, ribbons, etc., will result in an ongoing commitment of approximately $30,000 annually.

Table 1
First Year Costs CD-ROM Workstations Clusters
[Excluding InfoTrac]

Subscriptions:	$26,920
New (13):	$21,225
Existing (2):	$5,695
Workstation/Network Hardware & Software:	$69,212
Printers:	$2,622
Surge Suppressors:	$830
Supplies:	$2,911
Furniture:	$7,923
TOTAL	$110,418

Licensing

Vendor response to the question of licensing requirements for networked use of CD-ROM titles has been extremely cautious, with database producers apparently waiting to see which way the industry would go. Of the titles currently at the Dana Library, only PsycLIT and Compact Disclosure required specific networking agreements. SilverPlatter has announced that there will be an extra charge for multi-user access to Nursing & Allied Health but has not yet set those charges. Currently, SilverPlatter is charging subscribers to Psychological Abstracts an extra $1,700 annually for multi-user access to PsycLIT ($2,000 for non-subscribers), while Disclosure is adding $2,200 to its annual subscription rate for networking Compact Disclosure. In May of 1989 however, the H.W. Wilson Company sent out its challenge to the industry when it formally announced that there will be no extra charges assessed for networking any Wilson CD-ROM title. While it is too early to gauge how this will ultimately affect the issue, Wilson's traditionally dominant position in the library market should have a major impact on both library expectations and optical disc vendor policies.

Security Issues

Microcomputers located in public areas invite attention from many patrons. Sometimes this attention is undesirable, as when patrons tamper with the equipment in the pursuit of knowledge or in pursuit of personal gain. Over the last three years, since microcomputer workstations have been set up to run the automated reference sources, the library has suffered minimal loss. Two hard disks have been wiped clean, one floppy drive accidentally damaged, and one keyboard stolen.

With the addition of so many more machines in the Reference Area, security became a significant issue, especially in light of the networked environment. We had to secure the workstations themselves, the data that resides on their fixed disks, and all of the CD-ROM discs. We also had to ensure the integrity of the LANs.

Since we had standardized on IBM PS/2 machines, one simple solution to workstation security was to employ security cables that looped around the furniture. The Kablit system, available from Secure-It, Inc., includes several steel eyelets that attach to the workstation components with surface-mounted screws and a 10' heavy-gauge steel cable (with a lock) to be inserted through the eyelets. Printers, however, required a different solution: typically, they have recessed rather than surface mounted screws. We had to install a second cabling system that came with steel plates that are glued to the surface of the peripherals. The Universal Security System from ACCO International Inc. comes with a 6' cable, a padlock, and two security plates. One plate goes on to the peripheral device and the other may be fastened to the furniture. After the loss of a keyboard, all keyboards were also tattle-taped for detection by the library's security system. In order to prevent patrons from formatting the C: drive or deleting files essential to the running of the workstation, it was necessary to deny patrons access to the operating system. The fixed disks on workstations that had access to CD-ROMs from only one publisher were easier to protect than workstations which ran products from two or more vendors. Where the retrieval software itself permitted, as was the case with the cluster running only Wilsondiscs, access to DOS was simply disabled. The second cluster, with retrieval software from more than one publisher, required something more sophisticated than a series of batch files invoked from a menu presented at the DOS prompt. The solution was to install a password-protected menuing program which would load the search software with a single keystroke. Our choice was Automenu from Magee Enterprises, a shareware program that is inexpensive and very simple to install. The software was configured so that a patron could also format a diskette in the A: drive or display its directory. The Automenu solution is not fool-proof. One can still reboot a workstation and interrupt the automatic execution file, or reboot from the A: drive with a DOS diskette. However, security programs that eliminate these avenues tend to be much more expensive.

The networks themselves present a different set of security problems. The file server's hard disk is crucial to the operation of the LAN it serves. Password protection through a menuing program was deemed to be insufficient. Instead, the file server is housed in a locked workstation furniture module. The keyboard is kept out of sight, and the display monitor is turned on only when it is necessary to install new discs or to clear the printer queue. CD-ROMs available on the networks are not visible to patrons. In fact, most patrons perform their research in and across many disciplines without ever realizing the storage medium for the information they are accessing. In the case of the Wilsondisc cluster, the two LMSI dual drive units are housed in the workstation furniture module beneath the file server. Optical discs can be inserted and removed only with a special caddy "shell" that is stored inside the locked housing. The Toshiba drives on the CD Net devices serving the other clusters also use caddies (of a different design) to prevent the discs from being scratched. A CD-ROM cabinet was purchased to store older discs; it has three drawers with seven sections in each. Its capacity is 840 CD-ROMs so there is room for us to grow.

Superseded discs from SilverPlatter and Information Access have to be returned since those products are basically leased to the library. Titles which were purchased outright or which are part of subscriptions, such as those from the H.W. Wilson Company and Disclosure Inc., are being archived in the cabinet.

Instruction

At Rutgers, students in many classes are introduced to basic research methods via bibliographic instruction (BI) sessions conducted by the library. These sessions are provided by prior arrangement with faculty members who have assigned their students a term paper or written project for the semester. As the new automated reference sources are added to the collection, instruction on their use is integrated into the regular BI program, and new instructional materials are designed to teach the use of the various titles, especially those on the networks.

An IBM PS/2 Model 30 with a CD-ROM drive has also been set up in the library classroom for use in the instructional program. Screen contents are displayed with the aid of a Sharp Model QA-50 LCD projection panel attached to the computer and placed on top of an overhead projector. This projection panel comes with two cables, one for IBM PC XT/ATs and compatibles and the other for IBM PS/2 machines. Since it is not always possible or desirable to remove discs from the Reference Area to use in the classroom, simulations of search sessions, as well as tutorials, are also being created using Dan Bricklin's Demo II software package. These can then be "played back" during class sessions. The library also purchased a portable computer with a built-in CD-ROM drive to permit demonstrations and training sessions to be conducted away from the library. This computer, from Custom Design Technology, is an IBM PC/AT compatible with a 20 MB hard disk; the CD-ROM drive is a half height LMSI/Philips CM 201 rated at 500 ms average access time.

Patrons are also instructed on the use of the networked workstations as part of the normal reference process. Librarians help with search strategy, explain the network's capabilities, and assist the user in locating the cited sources.

Usage

During the academic year, workstations are continually occupied from the time that the networks are brought up in the morning until they are powered down at closing time. The built-in network statistics maintained by the Wilsondisc network manager show that patrons spent as much as two hours and 49 minutes during a single session on the system, while the average search lasted about 21 minutes. Despite the heavy usage, we have not yet had to restrict patron use time because of the availablity of simultaneous access.

While patron response to the presence of the networks has been extremely enthusiastic, the technology has also raised unrealistic expectations among patrons. Many assume that the indexing covers all subjects without understanding the topical limitations of each database. Some of these patrons are reluctant to go to a print source even after obtaining a printout which clearly indicates that none of the automated sources are appropriate for their particular need. Others assume that all periodicals indexed are available in the library; that the CD-ROM in fact represents the Dana Library's holdings.

From the librarians' point of view, the network represents one more component to be considered as part of regular services and collections. Networking means library staff no longer need to be involved in handing out or switching discs. It also means an increased need for one-on-one instruction, new instructional aids, and revised bibliographic instruction and staff training programs. At the Reference Desk, it means librarians having to perform a myriad of tasks never specified in their job descriptions: initializing the network, adding to printers the reams of paper required by a "paperless society," clearing paper jams, replacing ink cartridges and printer ribbons, and troubleshooting system failures.

Postscript

Not surprisingly in a rapidly changing technological environment, the Dana Library CD-ROM project ran into some initial obstacles which required rethinking and modification of some of the original hardware configurations. As a result, initial progress was disappointingly slow. Once the initial obstacles were overcome, however, and implementation began to proceed at an accelerated pace, all members of the Reference Department were called upon to contribute in one way or another. The tasks associated with the implementation of the automated reference sources were identified, and teams responsible for various aspects, from furniture building to software installation to signage to training, were established. Indeed, without the full cooperation of many individuals, several of whom "earned their screwdrivers" several times over, and the enthusiastic support of the Dana Library Director, there would have been no hope of the project being realized. Nor did the work diminish noticeably once the networks became operational. Much work still remains to be done. Once the seemingly permanent state of flux that we have been operating under for the past year is behind us, more attention can be given to the extensive documentation and training needs resulting from the acquisition of so many new automated reference sources.

Libraries looking to take full advantage of the new technologies must also keep in mind that the integration of automated resources into reference collections and the normal reference process requires a commitment on the part of the entire public services staff. In some cases this may mean having to first convert those who feel that "I'm not responsible for online searching," or "I don't deal with machines." Some degree of computer literacy on the part of Reference Librarians can no longer be viewed as a special skill but must be seen as a minimum professional requirement.

Ka-Neng Au joined the Dana Library as a Reference Librarian and Business Bibliographer in 1986, and became the Microcomputer Coordinator for the Rutgers-Newark libraries as well. He has a B.A. in Management and Economics from the University of Guelph, Guelph, ON, and an M.L.S. degree from Rutgers University.

Natalie Borisovets came to Dana as a Reference Librarian in 1978, after four years as the Librarian at the Rutgers Center for Urban Policy Research. Currently the Head of Public Services, she has served as Bibliographic Instruction Coordinator, Interlibrary Loan Coordinator, and RLIN Coordinator. Natalie has an A.B. degree in Art History from Douglass College, Rutgers University, and an M.L.S. as well as an M.A. in Art History from Rutgers University.

18

INFO-LAN: A CD-ROM Local Area Network in a Public Library

Norma Hill, Joyce Demmitt

Howard County

Howard County is located in the geographic center of the Baltimore/Washington corridor. The county currently is experiencing the fastest growth rate in Maryland. The population of the county increased 90 percent from 1970 to 1980 and growth through the 1980s is expected to be another 49 percent. The population today numbers approximately 172,000.

The County contains 40 office/research parks, many with high-tech facilities. The planned city of Columbia, a population center, has many thriving businesses, ranging from small entrepreneurial firms to national companies. In addition, Columbia is home to more than 55 foreign firms representing 14 countries. Total personal income rose 250 percent from 1970 to 1985, as professional and two-income families moved into Howard County. The county's current average household income is one of the highest in the country; at $44,160 it is one of the highest figures in the Baltimore/Washington Common Market, which itself is the wealthiest consolidated market in the United States.

The county also has a well-educated population. Eighty-three percent are high school graduates and thirty-five percent are college graduates.

Howard County Library System is growing rapidly to match the growth of the County. At present it has a 46,000 square foot Central Library, one major branch library of 23,000 square feet, three small community libraries, and bookmobile service. Two 15,500 square foot branch libraries and a second major branch library of 33,000 square feet will be completed by the mid-1990s. The library system collection numbers 479,656 volumes. Eighty-six percent of county residents are registered library users.

The library has initiated many projects using grant funds from corporations and the federal government. Babywise, a service for children from birth to age three, providing developmentally appropriate toys for loan, programs for parent and child, and family daycare visits by a storyteller, was cited by the U.S. Department of Education as a model library program. Project Literacy has been highly successful and is about to launch a customized literacy mobile resource center (the first of its kind nationally). Easy Access II provides materials and services for the developmentally disabled population. Emphasis is placed on providing meaningful volunteer experiences which will prepare participants for paying positions in the community. These projects have served as models for other libraries in the state and the nation.

Howard County Library's Long Range Service Plan commits us to using "the most relevant technologies developed to meet patron needs and to improve operations and services." An advisory committee of citizens interested in technology has helped guide the library. The library has used CLSI's automated circulation system since 1980 and is adding the online public access catalog now. Dial-up access will be introduced in the 1989/90 fiscal year.

The library has had both Apple and IBM or compatible computers and software available in our major libraries since 1985. In addition, we use Information Access Corporation's (IAC) CD-ROM InfoTrac II as a stand-alone workstation and have InfoTrac II including Magazine Index Plus at our two largest facilities. We have the Health Index from IAC at the Central Library. Response to these products has been consistently high, necessitating a 15 minute time limit on searching during evening and weekend hours. This experience, coupled with our examination of a number of CD-ROMs at professional conferences, caused us to target CD-ROMs as necessary additions to the library's information services. The high cost of many CD-ROM databases and space requirements for individual workstations would have necessitated the gradual addition of these products; however, two corporate grants, one from The Washington Post, the other from Clyde's Restaurant Group of Washington, D.C., allowed us to introduce CD-ROM databases faster and in a more creative environment.

Planning

As we began discussing the addition of CD-ROM databases to the library, a number of issues surfaced. We did not want to purchase single-product workstations which would proliferate non-compatible equipment, nor did we want library patrons waiting in line behind one workstation while others were not in use. Our goal was clear: to develop a network where users could access all databases from any workstation and several users could access a single database simultaneously. We also decided that there should be a variety of databases to meet the needs of the student, the teacher, the business person, and the investor. INFO-LAN, which stands for information on a local area network, became our goal. Our first task was to develop a Request for Proposal (RFP) for the network. We hired a consultant to help us through this phase. Simultaneously, we began contacting CD-ROM publishers for detailed information about their products, including whether they would allow us to use them on a network.

During the initial consulting phase, we discussed how we wanted library patrons to use the network, the security issues necessary to protect both hardware and software, and future development of the network. We needed a systematic approach in the development of the RFP for the hardware components to ensure that the network would perform in a satisfactory manner.

Our first search was for the optical drive. Inquiries and knowledge from ALA exhibits led us to three options—SilverPlatter, as basically a turnkey network,

Meridian Data Products, and Online Products Corporation. The latter two offer multi-platter devices and provide the necessary software to access the CD-ROMs. We then discussed the computer requirements necessary to support the network, including the ability for library users to print or download the results of their searches.

Results of these discussions appear in the RFP (Appendix) developed by our consultant, Howard McQueen, President of CD Consultants. The RFP was sent to Online Products Corporation, Meridian Data Products, and four computer companies. We wanted each company to understand the complexity of the network and how its product would be used in the network environment. Vendors were invited to bid on the section of the RFP applicable to their product. Our time frame was very short; the RFP was sent out in November and we wanted the network available to the public by early April. Responses were reviewed. The SilverPlatter solution was costly and limited us to SilverPlatter products, an unacceptable option. Meridian Data Products chose not to bid, leaving us with Online Products multiple drive units and Optinet as our network software. We selected Acer 900 machines for our workstations, in part because of their expansion capabilities.

We also began a search for workstations for installation in our Reference area. We chose Mohawk-Midland's L-shaped study carrels (figure 1). Mohawk-Midland helped us with wiring both for INFO-LAN and other electrical needs; it even flew a staff person to Howard County to ensure proper installation of its product.

figure 1. Mohawk-Midland's L-shaped study carrels.

Installation

After installation of wiring for the network, we set up the CD-ROM server with the multiple drives and the administrative workstation. We loaded the Optinet software, Netbios, Microsoft Extensions, and search software for some of the products selected to test the network. We experienced immediate problems: the most serious were Netbios errors. We also had problems with Microsoft Extensions and with the databases operating in a consistent manner. This all appeared to be caused by the incompatibility of Optinet with Standard Microsystems' Netbios package. We quickly discovered a problem. We had mistakenly assumed that Netbios support would be provided by Online, and even though we were using one of the most reliable Netbios packages on the market, we had no assurances that a solution to our problems would be speedy or forthcoming. Our short deadline sent us in search of an alternative.

We added a dedicated Novell server and Novell "netware" to our configuration to ensure network performance. This solution provided us with a stable network because Novell's LAN software includes its own Netbios. The final hardware configuration includes a dedicated Novell network server and an Acer 900 with a 70MB hard drive. The server has Netware 2.12 and Netbios software loaded on the hard drive and a CD-ROM server with three four-drive optical units daisy-chained to it. Loaded into the hard drive are Optinet, Netbios, Net 3, and IPX (Novell Netware files) (figure 2). Each workstation has Microsoft Extensions 1.1, Netbios, IPX, Net 3, Optinet, Dos 3.3 plus search software for each of the databases added. In addition, the six public workstations have Direct Access Menu software.

Security Issues

We dealt with our security concerns regarding the CD-ROMs by housing them in multiple drives, behind the scenes, in the computer room which houses our CLSI equipment on the second floor of the Central Library. We decided to purchase hard disks for each of the workstations so that the CD-ROM search software could be loaded onto each hard disk. Therefore, if anyone tampered with a product, only that workstation's hard disk would need to be restored.

We experimented briefly with a high security menu system, "Watchdog," but rejected it because of the amount of staff time required to understand its complexities. We went instead with "Direct Access," which offers safeguards regarding access to file maintenance and DOS. It also provides helpful statistics on workstation use.

Product Selection

In selecting the CD-ROM products for INFO-LAN, we included the titles which met the needs already expressed by our patrons. Under initial consideration were InfoTrac II (IAC), including Magazine Index Plus and Health Index, Newspaper Abstracts (UMI), Microsoft Bookshelf, Microsoft Stat Pack, Magazine Article Summaries (EBSCO), MEDLINE, ERIC, Grolier's New Electronic Encyclopedia, CompactDisclosure, and CIRR OnDisc (Corporate and Industry Research Reports).

We sent a letter of inquiry to each vendor requesting information on the availability of a network version, its cost, additional charges for multiple workstations, and memory requirements (because memory was a critical concern for products

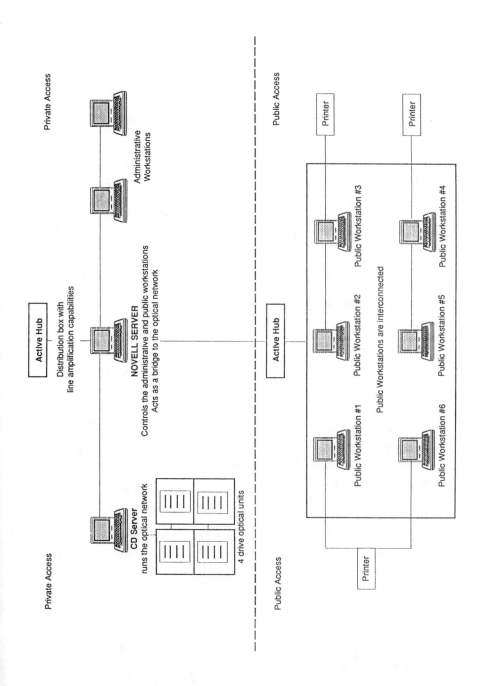

figure 2. INFO-LAN

PUBLIC ACCESS CD-ROMS IN LIBRARIES: CASE STUDIES

with either lengthy abstracts or full text). We also asked how many compact discs we would receive, because we were limited to 12 disc drives, and the length of trial periods for each product.

When responses were returned, we learned that most vendors merely specified that their products would run on a 640K machine, neglecting to tell us exactly how much of that 640K was required. Once we were committed to Novell software, memory became an even larger consideration. Novell's Netware requires approximately 69K; Microsoft Extensions another 18K; Optinet requires 38K; and Netbios another 40K.

After loading the network software, we had only 476K of RAM memory on the network. Given that, we were unable to run EBSCO's Magazine Article Summaries, CORE Medline, and word searches in PDR. InfoTrac II and Compact Disclosure were not available in a network version.

We decided to add Periodical Abstracts Ondisc (UMI) and Microsoft Small Business Consultant and we purchased MEDLINE, instead of CORE Medline.

Vendor support became an important issue. Product incompatibility necessitated numerous calls to vendors, many of whom had never used their products in a network and so were unfamiliar with the problems we were encountering. Salespersons usually cannot answer technical questions and reaching technical support staff is often difficult. We finally pulled Microsoft Stat Pack from the network because of the problems it caused. Products currently running on the network are Periodical Abstracts (UMI), Newspaper Abstracts (UMI), Grolier's New Electronic Encyclopedia, CIRR OnDisc, Microsoft Small Business Consultant, Microsoft Bookshelf, ERIC, PDR Direct Access, MEDLINE, Computer Library, and Peterson's College Database.

We have not yet cancelled any print collection purchases because of INFO-LAN. We see this as a supplemental service, and are able to provide access to the general public to subjects and timely information formerly only available through online searches. We have, however, added several newspapers on microfilm because of demand from Newspaper Abstracts and we are investigating full-text microfiche to complement Periodical Abstracts.

Acquisition and Cataloging

In terms of cost, it is important to consider not just the initial investment in the products, but the ongoing costs as well. Our least expensive product costs $400, our most costly, $3,865. Many vendors add a per workstation cost in addition to the network price. Licensing agreements also needed to be signed for each product. Because our CD-ROMs are housed behind the scenes, there was no need to catalog them. All documentation was property stamped, and originals are housed with the Administrative Workstation. In our online Patron Access Catalog, we hope to have a producer/title/subject entry for each product and indicate that it is available on INFO-LAN.

Staff Involvement

Given our ambitious project schedule—initial discussions with the consultant in October and introduction of INFO-LAN to the public seven months later, in April—intensive staff involvement was essential. We selected the Library's Reference Specialist as the LAN Administrator. It was his responsibility to learn the specifics of LAN management from our consultant, to understand the procedures required in installing new databases, to troubleshoot both hardware and software for the system, to deal with vendors when we encountered problems with their products, and to conduct staff training.

One of the Library's Reference Librarians was appointed his assistant and one of the Library Associates was made the Microcomputer Specialist to assist with hardware and software problems. It should be noted that these individuals still retain the majority of their former responsibilities, although some ongoing duties were deferred during the planning and early implementation stages of INFO-LAN.

These individuals had various levels of technical expertise. It was essential that the LAN Administrator have a good working knowledge of IBM compatible microcomputers, a good working knowledge of DOS, and a strong interest in new technology. Seven additional members of the Library's professional staff were involved in the project. Each spent time working with an individual product to develop a publicity piece, training questions for staff, and a brief and basic search guide for the staff and public to use with each CD-ROM.

Several types of training were provided for staff. The consultant worked with LAN staff for five days, including three days of intensive training on the hardware configuration, bringing the system up and taking it down, Novell basics, Optinet basics, and necessary DOS commands. At the introductory staff training session in February, the Assistant Director, the Head of Information Services, and the LAN Administrator provided background information on the project, explained the upcoming orientations and training, and provided general information about each of the CD-ROM products to be included on the network. Once the initial products were installed on the network in March, we conducted our second staff training session. We discussed changes to the system, reviewed the databases, outlined LAN staff responsibilities, described printing and downloading capabilities, recapped Boolean logic, delineated procedures for introducing patrons to the system, reviewed troubleshooting, and whom to contact for problems. Staff then received the training questions developed for each database. Completed question sheets were to be returned, via supervisors, to the LAN Administrator by the end of March. Each staff person was encouraged to work no more than 8 hours on the questions, and to contact LAN staff or the individuals who had developed the questions if they had difficulty.

Since the system was not yet available to the public in March but the hardware was on the floor, signs were posted on the workstations that staff training was taking place and that the system would be available to the public in April. The workstations were covered when staff was not using them. Patron interest was high, with several individuals asking if they could become staff temporarily just to be able to use the system.

After staff had used the system for a month, we conducted a final training session several days before the official opening of INFO-LAN. At that time we reviewed the completed assignments, answered any questions or concerns about the products, and reiterated procedures. Staff had concerns about age limits for patrons using the system and whether or not time limits would be imposed. We wanted no age limit and deferred the time limit issue until we had a better sense of use.

One staff member is assigned to the INFO-LAN area at all times. It is that person's responsibility to conduct reference interviews with patrons wishing to use the LAN, and those whose questions lend themselves to INFO-LAN are encouraged to use the system. Staff working at the Information Desks use INFO-LAN terminals, when available, to answer walk-in and telephone queries.

Patron Use and Reactions

Patron use has been heavy and reactions have been enthusiastically positive. We introduced INFO-LAN at a reception the evening of April 7, 1989. During National Library Week we conducted special introductory orientations for INFO-LAN three times each day, Monday through Friday. We found that conducting the 15-minute orientations was often impossible at the scheduled times since patrons were already on the system at those times. Many individuals, teenagers and adults alike, sit down because they are interested in anything related to computers.

During the first week more than 300 individuals used the nine available databases. The most frequently used were Periodical Abstracts, Grolier's New Electronic Encyclopedia, and Small Business Consultant. Search topics ranged from televangelism to pay equity, to retail sales figures on microcomputers.

The LAN menu system we are using, "Direct Access," allows us to track workstation use daily and database use within each workstation. From April 10 through April 30, 1989 INFO-LAN was used 545 hours, an average of 51 times per workstation per day.

June 1 through June 30 showed 465 hours of use, an average of 33 times per workstation per day. We know that school summer vacation accounts for this drop during June and anticipate similar statistics through August.

We developed a questionnaire/evaluation for patrons to complete after using INFO-LAN. We ask their level of satisfaction with the products and with the assistance they received from staff. Most have found the products easy to use, but many have requested consistent search software, while acknowledging that this area is beyond our control.

Many individuals have included comments on the questionnaire. One person using Periodical Abstracts and Newspaper Abstracts exclaimed, "This thing is great! I'm really glad I didn't have to go leafing through the *Readers' Guide to Periodical Literature*." Another said, "Helped me to complete my paper, I am forever in debt." Another patron stated, "As always—a positive expenditure of tax funds—keep up the good work!"

Patrons have praised the system, the library and the staff. Many have wondered when they could access INFO-LAN from home, while others want even more sources to be full text (only Small Business Consultant, PDR Direct Access, Microsoft Bookshelf and Grolier's New Electronic Encyclopedia are at present). One gentleman with bifocals asked that the monitor be shifted so he could better read the screen, and one colorblind patron asked that colors on the monitor be changed to improve the contrast.

Our most heavily used databases continue to be Periodical Abstracts, Grolier's New Electronic Encyclopedia, Newspaper Abstracts, and Microsoft Bookshelf, followed by ERIC, CIRR, Medline, PDR, and Small Business Consultant.

If search strategies and printing and downloading commands were consistent, patrons would be delighted. The basic search guides which staff developed are used regularly and have assisted many novices in their searches.

Observations

The CD-ROM publishing industry is volatile. Publishers have recognized the profitability of LANs in the library environment and are scurrying to produce databases and pricing to satisfy this growing market. In many cases quality control has been set aside in order to introduce products. Vendors have not been interested in addressing indexing errors, technical support is often minimal, and response time to calls is often slow.

Product choices in the future will be harder to make, but the industry should also be forced to address issues such as: standardization of search protocols, printing, and downloading commands; attention to memory limitations when writing search software; attention to optical disc space limitations in a network environment; consistent ability to download and print from products; quality control of the products, including misspelled words, inaccurate data, and a general lack of commitment to updating products on a regular basis; and finally, increasing technical knowledge of salespersons or providing easy access to technical staff.

Hardware manufacturers and software developers whose products are interdependent need to create and maintain an open dialogue to keep abreast of, and test, new software releases to ensure compatibility.

Projects such as Caroline County Public Library's LAN (MD), funded by the Maryland State Department of Education, Division of Library Development and Services, which was the first CD-ROM LAN application in a public library setting, will help with this product development. The Library is a test site for LAN development for small libraries, such as new, smaller LAN software which might replace Novell (e.g., Artisoft, Inc.'s "LANtastic"), or extended or enhanced memory which would allow larger databases to run in the network environment, as well as a focal point for testing new CD-ROM products.

Future Developments of LAN

During the upcoming fiscal year we plan to install an updated version of Netbios which should run better with Optinet, work toward remote dial-up access to our network by Howard County citizens, examine the feasibility of removing

Novell from the network and returning to the original configuration if that is possible and consistent with adding remote access, and add additional databases and workstations.

The development of INFO-LAN has been exciting and at times nerve-racking. Positive patron and staff responses continue to affirm the usefulness of INFO-LAN. Patrons are still excited to discover the network. Comments like "What a great idea—The librarian and the computer saved my life!" make it worth the effort.

Norma Hill joined the Howard County Library staff in 1980 as Non-Fiction Department Head. She became Assistant Director in 1981. She graduated from Wheaton College with an A.B. in English literature and received her M.L.S. in 1975. Prior to working for Howard County, she worked as an Information Management Specialist at the Executive Office of the President/White House Information Center after returning from Ramstein, Germany, where she managed an Air Force Library.

Joyce Demmitt joined the staff of Howard County Library in 1970 as a library associate. She graduated from Gettysburg College with a B.A. in English and received her M.L.S. from the University of Maryland, College Park, in 1975. She has worked as Branch Manager of several library facilities, Coordinator of Readers' Advisory Services, Head of Adult Services and, since 1981, as Department Head of Information Services.

Appendix

Howard County Library CD-ROM Network Initial Network Configuration (INC) CD-ROM Server

The initial configuration will include one CPU securely located in the administrative offices. This processor will be a 80286 CPU dedicated to serving the CD-ROM data. Multiple CD-ROM drive units (and/or expansion units) will be attached to this CPU via a CD-ROM disc controller card (or cards) to provide for a total of eleven drives that must be online and simultaneously accessible to all workstations. A network interface card (either Arcnet or Ethernet) will reside in one of the slots of the CPU to allow the corresponding workstation network interface cards to communicate with the CPU and the attached CD-ROM drives. Ample RAM memory will be provided (640K to 3MB) so that your company's proprietary CD-ROM networking software can provide caching of CD-ROM data.

The CPU designated and configured as the CD-ROM server will not use a hard drive. All loading of software will be done from the floppy drive. A "boot" diskette will be prepared which, on one 1.2 MB floppy 5 1/4" diskette must contain all necessary software, drivers and devices to load DOS, Microsoft Extensions, your company's proprietary networking software and any other software required to prepare the CD-ROM server to service workstation requests for CD-ROM data. From the end-user perspective, starting the CD-ROM server at the beginning of each day should entail no more than:

1. Inserting the "boot" diskette described above in drive A.
2. Powering the CPU and CD-ROM drives in a prescribed order as outlined by your manuals.

3. Bringing the individual CD-ROM platters which contain databases of information online and accessible (this should be done via a friendly user interface menu system provided within your network software).

System Requirements Outline

Overview of the INC

A. Exclusive CD-ROM network.
   1. Compatible with industry standards.
      a. MS-DOS extensions.
      b. High Sierra format.
   2. CD-ROM server: One CPU will be dedicated as CD-ROM server.
      a. 286 12 mhz 0 or 1 wait state technology with monochrome monitor and adaptor card with parallel and serial ports and 200 watt power supply with 3 x 8 bit and 4 x 16 bit slots available.
      b. One 1.2 MB floppy drive with controller card and no hard disk.
      c. 640K to 3 MB RAM memory for caching if applicable.
      d. Disc controller card(s) for CD-ROM drive units.
      e. CD-ROM drive units: INC to include 11 drives.
      f. One network interface card.
      g. Your company's CD-ROM networking software: Provides multi-user, multi-tasking processing and file service to all drives and the databases therein; Provides compatibility with Microsoft extensions, High Sierra format and other industry standards; Provides disk caching to minimize the number of times the CD-ROM drives must perform disc reads.
      h. Network interface card compatibility along with standard coaxial cabling compatibility.
   3. Workstations (Seven CPUs will be devoted as workstations: Six public and one Admn).
      a. 286 12 mhz 0 to 1 wait state technology.
      b. One 30 MB hard drive or larger (40 ms avg access or better) for each CPU.
      c. One 1.2 MB floppy drive 5 1/4" for each CPU.
      d. One 360K floppy drive 1 1/4" for three CPUs.
      e. One 720K floppy drive 3 1/2" for one CPU.
      f. Network interface cards for all workstations.
      g. EGA cards for seven workstations.
      h. Color monitors for seven workstations.
      i. One parallel and one serial port for seven workstations.
      j. One 9' centronics parallel printer cable for seven workstations.
      k. DOS 3.3 for seven workstations.
      l. Microsoft extensions for seven workstations.
   4. Printers: Three shared and one dedicated.
      a. The three pairs of public workstations will each share a printer.
      b. Three A/B parallel centronics switch boxes will connect each pair.
      c. Need three special male-to-male cables from A/B box to printer.
      d. All four printers will be H.P. Thinkjet printers.
   5. A standard configuration (which drive has which database) should be able to be saved to the floppy "boot" diskette so that the end-user is not required to add and mount databases during boot each day
   6. Your network software should provide the flexibility to allow a database to span more

than one drive so that a database may occupy 2 or more drives but appear as one contiguous database to the users.

7. Should a workstation lose power, your network software should allow the other network workstations and the CD-ROM server to continue operations without interruption. An individual workstation user should not be able to bring the network down. There will be patrons of the library who will be allowed access to the workstations. The worst case scenario is that a workstation user may only disable their individual workstation.

8. Adding new databases and/or changing databases should be a function provided through your networking software. From the perspective of the end-user, taking one database off the network and adding another database in its place should be easily done by functions such as unmounting and removing the first database and then adding and mounting the next database.

9. The CD-ROM drive units provided by your company should be site reconfigurable by a non-technical staff member of the end-user. In the event a drive unit fails, it should be easy to change the drive configurations so that the other drive units can continue processing during the absence of the malfunctioning unit. This flexibility will allow the end-user to continue using their network while the defective drive is being repaired.

10. Please explain the various alternatives you provide for repairing and/or replacing CD-ROM drives and the CD-ROM drives and the CD-ROM controller cards. Do you offer an extended warranty and what is that annual charge? Can users pay for repairs on a time-and-materials basis? What are your current rates for repairs? How promptly are repairs made?

Flexibility and Expansion

Future plans call for the following known types of expansion with which the INC must remain compatible and expandable with.

Expanding the number of workstations. Based upon reasonable estimates, the number of local workstations could grow to total thirty-five (35). Does your networking software support thirty-five online and simultaneously processing CD-ROM requests? If not, please explain the limitations.

Expanding the number of CD-ROM drives. Please provide the additional items and costs associated with expanding the number of drives to:

A. 15 total drives

B. 20 total drives If additional controller cards, CPUs, CD-ROM drives, additional network software licenses, additional Microsoft Extensions, etc. are required, please note these items and provide costs if you supply these items.

Adding remote workstations. Patrons at home and/or branch library personnel will want to access the CD-ROM databases through standard modem transmission. Please explain how you support remote dial in users. Further explain how all processing is performed in a local workstation with only screen changes being sent over the modem to update the remote workstation.

Adding a Network File Server and Novell/Netware. Future requirements for office automation functionality (word processing, spread sheeting, electronic mail, etc.) must be provided for. Your networking software, controller cards, CD-ROM drives and other items supplied must be compatible with the addition of a file server and Netware Version 2.12. Further, all documentation and user manual literature must be made available to Howard County Library when they add these resources. Users should be able to access the office automation applications and CD-ROM applications using the same network boot diskette and from a network prompt.

Exhibit A

Networking hardware & software & CD-ROM drives and controllers

1. Disk controller card(s) for CD-ROM drive units to support 11 CD-ROM drives.

2. 11 CD-ROM drives and their housing units. Please specify MTBF and average access speed documentation.

3. Your company's CD-ROM networking software.

a. Provides multi-user, multi-tasking processing and file service to all drives and the databases therein.

b. Provides compatibility with Microsoft Extensions, High Sierra format, and other industry standards.

c. Provides disk caching to minimize the number of times the CD-ROM drives must perform disc reads. Please identify if your software can utilize 3 MB of RAM in the CD-ROM server.

Support and Configuration Services

The services that are required are as follows:

1. Provide project management services to assist Howard County Library staff in setting up the CD-ROM network and bringing the network up in satisfactory working condition.

2. Provide specific guidance and support in configuring boot diskettes with proper files, device parameters and to provide adequate documentation so that Howard County Library can become somewhat self-sufficient in the use of the CD-ROM network. Few standards exist today and many CD-ROM software programs operate and behave in a manner inconsistent with each other.

3. Provide specific guidance in the configuration and loading of new CD-ROM subscriptions along with the CD-ROM DOS software that drives the processing of the various CD-ROM databases. This will include work to identify where spill files will reside, optimizing workstation memory issues, and other technical issues specific to CD-ROM networks.

4. Provide guidance and support in setting up the individual workstations so that security problems with the public workstations are minimized with a minimum of effort.

5. Interface directly with the CD-ROM networking companies, the CD-ROM database suppliers and other hardware and software vendors to resolve any incompatibilities and issues that may crop up during installation.

6. Please supply with your RFP previous experience in installing and supporting CD-ROM networking installations. Include the length of time you have been supporting each customer along with the contact person at the customer's site. Outline the type of network they utilize and the hardware and software brands being utilized.

19

The Electronic Information Center at Boston College's O'Neill Library

Marilyn A. Grant

Introduction

Boston College is the largest Jesuit university in the United States, with an enrollment of 14,561 students (10,531 undergraduate students and 4,030 graduate students). Programs of study are offered at the Bachelor's, Master's, and Doctoral level by the College of Arts and Sciences, Graduate School of Arts and Sciences, School of Nursing, School of Education, and Carroll School of Management. The Graduate School of Social Work confers the M.S.W. and D.S.W. degrees, and the Law School confers the J.D. degree. Several combined degree programs are also available.

O'Neill Library, the central research library at Boston College, opened to the public in July 1984. The collection at O'Neill Library covers all areas of the humanities, social sciences, sciences (except engineering), nursing and health sciences, education, and business. The collections and staff that were previously housed in the Nursing Library, Science Library, School of Management Library, and Bapst Library (formerly the Main Library) were incorporated into O'Neill. Other libraries on the Chestnut Hill campus are: Bapst Library (a beautifully restored building with a general and recreational reading collection and student study areas), the John J. Burns Library of Rare Books and Special Collections, the School of Social Work Library (a graduate library), and the Educational Resource Center (primarily supporting the undergraduate education program). The Law Library (Kenny-Cottle Library) and the Newton Study Center (an undergraduate residential collection) are located on the Newton Campus, about two miles away from the Chestnut Hill Campus. The Weston Observatory Library, containing a specialized collection of earth science and seismology materials, is located about twelve miles from Chestnut Hill.

The resources of O'Neill Library are used intensively by the faculty, staff, and students at Boston College, as well as by students and faculty from other institutions in the Boston area. Boston College is a member of the Boston Library Consortium and the Boston Theological Institute. O'Neill Library is also heavily used by local business people and area residents.

CD-ROM databases have been available at Boston College since January 1987. Currently, 10 products are in use: ABI/INFORM (UMI), Books in Print (Bowker), CINAHL (SilverPlatter), CIRR (SilverPlatter), Dissertation Abstracts (UMI), ERIC (SilverPlatter), MEDLINE (SilverPlatter), Oxford English Dictionary (Tri-Star Publishing), PsycLIT (SilverPlatter), and Sociofile (SilverPlatter).

Database Services and Systems

Online searching has been available at Boston College since 1974. The School of Nursing Library became the first nursing library in the United States to offer access to the NLM system. In 1975, Boston College joined NASIC (Northeast Academic Science Information Center), which was funded by the National Science Foundation. NASIC's goal was to introduce online searching into academic science libraries in the New England states by providing online training and administrative support in organizing and managing a search service. The Boston College Libraries added subscriptions to DIALOG, SDC/Orbit, and BRS in quick succession between 1975–1977. When NASIC ceased operations in 1977, training was obtained directly from the vendors and database producers. Today, O'Neill Library also offers these additional online services: VU/TEXT, Wilsonline, STN International, Dow Jones News/Retrieval, and Newsnet. In 1985, BRS/After Dark was introduced as the first end-user service at O'Neill. InfoTrac was also added as an end-user service that same year with the installation of four workstations. In September 1988, O'Neill Library began a subscription to the Dow Jones/News Retrieval academic program and began offering it as another end-user service. The Law Library has offered LEXIS and WESTLAW as end-user services since 1980 and 1982, respectively.

In addition to these online indexes and reference tools, Boston College has used all of the subsystems of the GEAC integrated library system since 1983. The Libraries are migrating to the NOTIS system. The NOTIS cataloging, acquisitions, circulation, and reserves modules are in use, and on August 15, 1989, the NOTIS Online Catalog, which we have named QUEST, became available to the public.

O'Neill Library was the first academic library in the Boston area to have CD-ROM databases. The initial planning and use of CD-ROM at O'Neill Library is described in a case study (Eaton, 1989). CD-ROM databases meet the Reference Department's goal of expanding end-user services to a wider audience during all the hours that the Reference desk is staffed. While the equipment and leasing costs for CD-ROM are not low, they are predictable, fixed costs.

ERIC, PsycLIT, and Sociofile were selected as the first titles for purchase. Statistics for the online search service and for BRS/After Dark indicated that the first two titles were the most heavily used databases, followed by MEDLINE. While Sociofile had lower usage figures, our expectation was that usage would increase in a CD-ROM, no-cost environment. The level of use for ERIC, PsycLIT, and Sociofile in compact disc was expected to, and in fact did, make the cost of each search less than $1.00.

We saw a mockup of a planned product called MultiPlatter designed by SilverPlatter Information, Inc. at the American Library Association Conference in

June 1986. SilverPlatter was looking for test sites for its product; we sent a letter of interest and were selected as a test site in November 1986. The biggest stumbling block for us was obtaining equipment in the current budget year, since no equipment had been requested for this purpose. SilverPlatter provided three workstations for use during testing and O'Neill Library purchased three titles (ERIC, PsycLIT, and Sociofile) to be introduced to our users. Being a test site allowed us to bring this new technology to our users very quickly, while planning for equipment needs in the next budget year.

Location of the Electronic Information Center

The original design plans for O'Neill Library provided for several carrels with electrical power in the area behind the Reference desk. Two public access OCLC terminals were placed in this area shortly after O'Neill opened in 1984. The four InfoTrac workstations are also in this area, as are two fiche readers. It was immediately apparent that this area was also the most convenient spot for the location of the three CD-ROM workstations. The carrels were spacious enough to hold a PC with monitor, CD-ROM drive, and printer. It would be relatively easy for Reference staff to check on users and monitor potential problems. This area, with OCLC, InfoTrac, and CDs, is known as the Electronic Information Center.

Access Issues

MultiPlatter 1, which was installed at Boston College in January 1987, was a compact control unit incorporating four PCs and four CD-ROM drives. The unit was placed near the Reference desk only a few feet away from the desk and from each workstation. Users never handled a disc because discs were inserted into and removed from the MultiPlatter unit by Reference staff. Discs not in use were stored in a cabinet at the Reference desk. When the Reference desk was closed, discs were removed from the MultiPlatter unit and locked in the cabinet.

Initially, no restrictions were placed on the use of CD-ROM databases. Since there were three workstations and six discs and since only one user could access a particular disc at a time, a logbook was kept for scheduling. An interval of one hour was chosen as the length of a search session. This would give users who were new to the technology a chance to take their time and learn the system by trying out one or more search strategies.

The Reference desk is staffed for 85 1/2 hours in a typical week. The first appointment of the day was scheduled for 9 a.m. on Monday-Saturday and for 11 a.m. on Sunday. The maximum number of users per week was 249 (83 hours x 3 workstations). A search session interval of 30 minutes was deliberately rejected in order to restrict the maximum number of users per week during a period of adjustment for staff and users.

As more users became aware of CD-ROM databases, it was decided to restrict an individual user to one hour per day on the system during weeks of peak library use. Users could sign up in advance (up to a week) for a block of time. More and more users did this when they saw how popular the service was. In some cases, they had no other choice because all the appointments were booked for several days in advance.

O'Neill Library has a policy of community open access to the building, collection, and some services for most of the year. Access is restricted during exam periods to holders of Boston College IDs, or Boston Library Consortium, Boston Theological Institute, or Boston College Libraries borrowing cards. All patrons may use InfoTrac or CD-ROM databases. BRS/After Dark, which is subsidized by the Library, is restricted to Boston College students, faculty, and staff.

Each of the three workstations from SilverPlatter came equipped with a Hewlett Packard Think Jet printer. Users were encouraged to review their search results on screen and print only relevant citations. The number of citations printed during a typical search varied tremendously; some undergraduates were only looking for a few current citations whereas many graduate students conducted lengthy searches covering the entire time span of the database and printed hundreds of records.

The amount of paper and Ink Jet cartridges consumed was not an inconsiderable cost and the question of charging users for printing arose periodically at Reference Department meetings. The prospect of counting the number of sheets of paper each person used made this proposal very unattractive, however, and the amount of time it would take to copy citations by hand would be unacceptable to users. In addition, many users wanted copies of the abstract as well as the citation. Printing is now seen as an essential feature of the system for bibliographic databases, and the cost of supplies has been accepted as part of the cost of offering the service.

Downloading was possible with the SilverPlatter system. Users who brought a formatted disk with them to their search session could download search results but few patrons made use of this feature. One reason for the lack of interest in downloading may be that faculty and students at Boston College primarily use Macintosh computers (Boston College is a member of the Apple Consortium and the O'Neill Computing Center has over 140 Macintosh computers available for student use). Most Macintosh users (especially students) did not have or want to take the time to download results from a search and transfer the file from a PC to a Macintosh disk.

CD-ROM Networks

Our experience with MultiPlatter 1 indicated the great popularity of CD-ROM with users but some shortcomings also became evident. More than three workstations would be needed to satisfy user demand. The current discs for ERIC and PsycLIT were in especially heavy demand at certain weeks in the semester. We had only one copy of each disc. Since only one user could use a particular disc at a given time, a user often had to wait several hours or more than a day to complete a search. While many users were somewhat resigned to waiting two to three days for a search appointment at these times, the Reference staff was not happy with this arrangement. Also, Reference staff had to swap discs in the drive unit many times a day. This was not intolerable, but it would be desirable to have a unit in which all the discs could be mounted and which would enable users to access discs without staff intervention. Simultaneous use of the same disc by more than one user would also be very desirable.

There were two readily apparent solutions. One was to mount databases on the mainframe which housed the online catalog. BRS/OnSite was considered but the expected annual cost for the databases desired (approximately $150,000) was too high at the time. The other solution was to configure workstations and CD-ROM drives in a local area network either by building a LAN in-house or by buying a commercially available CD-ROM network.

Dr. Mary Cronin, University Librarian, and Dr. John Stalker, Chief Reference Librarian, wrote a grant proposal to build a CD-ROM network and submitted it to the E.L. Wiegand Foundation. The Wiegand Foundation responded and awarded a grant of $50,000 on condition that Boston College raise $75,000 in matching funds (these were provided by IBM in the form of a hardware grant).

Instead of building a network, the library decided to contract with SilverPlatter for the fall 1988 installation of a CD-ROM network. During that summer, a planning committee consisting of representatives from the Library, Network Services, and SilverPlatter met to discuss specifications, installation, and other issues and procedures.

In September 1988, SilverPlatter installed the first phase of the MultiPlatter CD-ROM network, consisting of four PS/2 Model 50Z workstations and seven CD disc drives on a file server from Meridian Data Corp. The file server was expanded to 11 drives in November 1988, and six PS/2 Model 70 workstations were added to the network in February 1989. Four of the workstations have printers. Each PC in the network is equipped with a security device. There have been no instances of vandalism, tampering, or theft with the network. The MultiPlatter CD-ROM network at O'Neill Library was the first installation in the United States and is discussed in more detail in an article by the author (Grant, 1989).

User Support/Staff Training

When CD-ROM was introduced at O'Neill Library, the Reference staff relied heavily on SilverPlatter Customer Support for assistance whenever system or database problems occurred. As the staff became more familiar with the system, many problems could be fixed without calling SilverPlatter. As a supplement to the printed documentation, screen dumps were made of all the help screens and of the guide for each database. Reference staff were encouraged to read all the documentation and experiment with the system as much as possible. It was expected that early users of CD-ROM would be performing relatively straightforward searches and would learn how to refine their search strategy by working with a Reference Department member. Staff questions or problems were answered in the Reference Log (which everyone reads) or in Department meetings. As new databases with special features (e.g., EXPLODE on MEDLINE) were introduced, they were incorporated into a department meeting with a demonstration using a Kodak Datashow for projection.

User Training and Documentation

Three types of training have been employed for instructing users about CD-ROM: point-of-use instruction, small group or class instruction, and one-on-one research appointment/training sessions. Most of the user instruction is point-of-use instruction at the workstation before a user begins a search. Depending upon the level of activity at the Reference desk, this can be for a brief three minutes or a longer 15-minute period. At very busy times, we suggest that users try out the SilverPlatter tutorial, if the database being searched has a tutorial, or read the Help screens for guidance. Adventurous users will usually just start searching and learn by trial and error, asking questions when they run into a problem. The amount of information given in a typical point-of-use session can vary depending upon the staff person giving the information and the willingness of the user to absorb more or less information. A copy of the main function keys and keyboard layout is pasted on the side of each workstation. We also give users copies of the SilverPlatter Quick Reference Guide to refer to during their search. Each workstation in the network has a guide detailing function keys for SilverPlatter. The UMI titles and the OED run on separate workstations and are not part of the MultiPlatter network, but may be incorporated in the network at a later date. A one page search guide, prepared by Jonas Barciauskas (Reference Librarian for Philosophy and Theology), is available for users of the Oxford English Dictionary. Books in Print was purchased by the Acquisitions Department and is used by Reference staff, but is not currently available to the public at a workstation.

Handouts were developed for each database indicating how to use SilverPlatter's (F4) and (F6) commands, and how to find materials after a search was completed. Each handout displayed a typical full record for the database with field names spelled out, and instructed users on how to find materials in the online catalog. Each handout was also in a different color for easy identification. These handouts are now being revised in accordance with the new logo for all O'Neill Library Reference Department publications.

The experience of teaching thousands of end-users how to search CD-ROM has made the Reference Department more aware of individual differences in learning style. This is constantly stressed in departmental discussions.

Group instruction has been given for small groups (two to six people) working on a joint project or for groups of up to 20 people. With the larger groups, a librarian gives a presentation and groups of three to five people work together at a workstation on different search topics with the opportunity to get immediate feedback. Several faculty members have requested instruction on searching CD-ROM as part of their classes and Monique Lowd, the former Education Librarian (now Educational Resource Center Librarian), prepared an 18-minute video-tape for School of Education students on using O'Neill Library. One section shows how to search ERIC on SilverPlatter. This portion of the videotape has been used in larger classes where hands-on instruction at workstations is not feasible in the class session.

Some users who come for an online search appointment choose to learn CD-ROM instead, as do some users who come for BRS/After Dark training. In these situations, a librarian will do a one-on-one training session at a workstation. Each session usually lasts 30 minutes to an hour. The basic information needed to conduct a search is covered, but more time is devoted to search strategy, other databases of potential use available online, and useful print resource tools. The information presented is tailored to the user.

Impact on Staff, Services and Collections

CD-ROM has had a tremendous impact on the Reference staff. There has been much excitement about this new technology, but it has been a source of stress as well. Everyone on the Reference staff has to be somewhat familiar with each end-user service offered (this was not the case with online searching). Demonstrations and reviews of CD-ROM databases are becoming a standard part of Reference Department meetings as one means of allaying anxiety about new databases, search features, and system changes.

CD-ROM, BRS/After Dark, and Dow Jones accounted for 7,628 end-user sessions between June 1988 and May 1989. In the previous year, there were 2,607 end-user sessions for CD-ROM and BRS/After Dark. This is a conservative count since some users do a quick search during the unused portion of another user's search session. There were 739 mediated search sessions (regular computer search and ready reference) during the period June 1988–May 1989, and 692 mediated search sessions during June 1987–May 1988. The increase was due to a 43.8 percent rise in ready reference searching, which more than offset a 16.8 percent decrease in regular computer searches.

While each of the databases purchased in CD-ROM is still available online and in print format through the Boston College Libraries, O'Neill Library did cancel one of its two print *Psychological Abstracts* subscriptions.

With the exception of the Oxford English Dictionary and Books in Print, both of which were purchased with book funds, all of the other CD-ROM titles leased or purchased were paid for with funds from the Computer Search Service budget. Certain databases (e.g., PsycLIT, ABI/INFORM and Dissertation Abstracts) have an additional annual fee for networking.

To date, there has been a general consensus among members of the Reference Department about which CD-ROM titles should be purchased. As CD-ROM titles proliferate, or in the event that funding becomes less adequate, it may be necessary to conduct a detailed evaluation for each title under consideration for purchase. Littlejohn has an excellent checklist for evaluating CD-ROM titles (Littlejohn, 1988). It has been added as an appendix to the O'Neill Library Collection Development Statement for the Reference Department.

Publicity

The *Biweekly*, from the Boston College Office of Communications, published an article on CD-ROM when it was introduced at O'Neill Library, as did the undergraduate newspaper, the *Heights*. When the MultiPlatter network was installed, a one and one half page press release was sent to each of the campus newspapers. The *Biweekly* and the *Graduate Student Exchange* each ran an article.

CD-ROM is also mentioned in almost every bibliographic instruction session given by the Reference Department. Between June 1988–May 1989, 169 sessions were given for 2,443 people. General library instruction sessions are offered during the first two weeks of each semester, and during the rest of the semester specialized or advanced instruction sessions are given by librarians. Also, BRS/After Dark training classes are given each week and by appointment. Specific CD-ROM training classes are offered only upon request.

Members of the Board of Trustees have seen a demonstration of the MultiPlatter network, as have key University administrators, and the CD-ROM network has been a stop on almost every tour of O'Neill Library given to Boston College visitors. Word-of-mouth, however, has been the primary means of publicity. Often students come in requesting SilverPlatter, even when it may not be their best choice. The marketing of MultiPlatter at Boston College is described in an article by LaRosa (LaRosa, 1989).

CD-ROM Use

CD-ROM databases have been used for ready reference by staff, for term papers by students, for fairly comprehensive searches by graduate students, and for current awareness searches by faculty and administrators. Since most of the CD-ROM titles at O'Neill Library are updated quarterly by the vendor, a combination of CD-ROM and online searching is done when up-to-the-minute information is desired. In the case of a database like MEDLINE, the user may search the CD-ROM file and a librarian may search the most recent and the pre-1980 material online. Occasionally, a user will begin a search on CD-ROM and ask a librarian to perform an online search instead because the search topic has become more complicated than expected.

While the majority of our users have been Boston College undergraduate and graduate students, our CD-ROM databases have also been searched by faculty, administrators, students and librarians from outside Boston College, and by area business people, alumni, and other uncategorized groups of users.

Some users who search a particular database on a regular basis have become very effective searchers. Other users know the basic commands, but require the assistance of Reference staff to refine their search results. The user remains the final arbiter of what constitutes a successful search. While a librarian may feel that a search could have been done better and may make suggestions to the user, the end-user is clearly in the driver's seat.

Evaluation

In April 1989, SilverPlatter installed a statistical package on the MultiPlatter network. Daily usage data for each database is collected on the hard disk at each workstation. By entering a password at any workstation, Reference staff can view a graphical display of usage at the station for the current day, the month to date, or the year to date. The data from each workstation can be downloaded onto a floppy disk and aggregated for monthly and yearly statistics. There has been a substantial increase in usage in 1989. For example, in October of 1988 there were 520 searches on the four workstations in place. The number of searches for October of 1989 increased to 4,744, a more than nine–fold increase! As SilverPlatter makes more refinements to the statistical package, we expect to obtain an even more detailed picture of traffic on the network.

Reflections

Between January 1987 and July 1989, there has been substantial growth in end-user services at O'Neill Library, primarily due to the introduction of CD-ROM. In 1987, there were 11 workstations in the Electronic Information Center (four InfoTrac, three CD-ROM, two OCLC, one BRS/After Dark and/or ready reference, and one Nursearch). Today, there are 19 workstations, 10 of which are in the MultiPlatter CD-ROM network. In 1987, service began with three CD-ROM titles from one vendor. Today we offer 10 databases from four different vendors. Usage has increased dramatically each year and is expected to continue in this vein for the next few years. CD-ROM has allowed the Library to serve many more users than could be handled by a mediated search environment or by the present BRS/After Dark setup.

O'Neill Library was a test site for MultiPlatter 1 and is currently a test site for the MultiPlatter network. This has made implementation of a CD-ROM local area network system an easier process than might be expected. Both SilverPlatter and Boston College Network Services have provided excellent technical support from the very beginning. While it is possible to build a CD-ROM network from scratch, it could be a very daunting task without sufficient in-house technical support or support from a vendor.

It is important to give Reference staff sufficient time to feel comfortable with CD-ROM technology and the searching conventions of each database. One way to do this is to start slowly with only one or two databases or with databases from only one vendor. As staff become more at ease with CD-ROM, the number of databases offered to users can be increased or products from other vendors can be introduced. New CD-ROM databases can be kept "in the back room" for a while until staff feel confident about bringing them out to the public. At O'Neill, this was done with the UMI database for over two months.

If CD-ROM databases are the first end-user service offered by a library, the Reference staff will quickly become aware that end-user training can be a very labor intensive process. Reference staff need a great deal of patience with hardware, software, end-users, and other staff members. The level and type of instruction given should be tailored to the individual's needs. A quick flexible mind that can devise one or more alternate search strategies for a user in a few minutes is certainly an asset.

Future Plans

In the future, the CD-ROM service will include expanding the number of networked workstations. Additional workstations will be located at the Reference Desk, the Reference Office, and the Government Documents Department (located two floors below the Electronic Information Center). As more products are purchased or leased from other vendors, they may be either added to the network, depending upon licensing regulations and prices, or run in a single workstation environment. The Libraries are also planning to mount databases on the QUEST online catalog. These databases will use NOTIS search commands. Selected Wilson databases will be installed early in 1990.

Our experiences at Boston College have shown us that CD-ROM technology can be introduced in a library system as a dynamic new service that grows and evolves over time—a service that keeps pace with the changing information needs of users.

References

Eaton, Nancy L., Linda Brew MacDonald, and Mara R. Saule. 1989. *CD-ROM and Other Optical Information Systems: Implementation Issues*. Phoenix, AZ: Oryx Press, pp. 117–119.

Grant, Marilyn A. and John C. Stalker. 1989. "The MultiPlatter CD-ROM Network at Boston College." *Laserdisk Professional* 2 (5): 12–18.

LaRosa, Sharon. 1989. "Marketing with MultiPlatter." *MLS (Marketing Library Services)* 3 (2): 1–3.

Littlejohn, Alice C. and Joan M. Parker. 1988. "Compact Disks in an Academic Library: Developing an Evaluation Methodology. " *Laserdisk Professional* 1 (2): 36–43.

Marilyn A. Grant is Senior Reference Librarian/Bibliographer and Coordinator, Computer Search Service at O'Neill Library, Boston College. In this position she is involved with reference service (specializing in the sciences), online searching and end-user services, bibliographic instruction, and collection development. She has been active in professional organizations at the regional and national level and was one of the founding members of the New England Online Users Group (NENON). Ms. Grant holds a B.A. in Chemistry from Regis College, an M.S. in Chemistry from Boston College, and an M.S. in Library Science from Simmons College Graduate School of Library and Information Science.

20
CD-ROMs in the High School Library

Errol A. Whelan

This case study addresses how one high school approached the growing problem of information retrieval in the school library environment. In the introduction it describes the library, its clientele, and its institutional context; in the body of the text the issues of access, staff impact, publicity, and evaluation are addressed. The case study concludes with some reflections on the successes and failures associated with the program.

Introduction

Swift Current Comprehensive High School is the largest high school in southwestern Saskatchewan, Canada. Approximately 250,000 people live in the city and surrounding trading area. The school has program offerings in academic, vocational, technical, and special education "streams." For the past 10 years school enrollment has been around 1,000 students. Many of the smaller schools in the area tend to send students with special curriculum requirements to the comprehensive school.

The school library occupies over 6,000 square feet and has a collection of 15,000 volumes and a computer center.

Project Background and Objectives

In the spring of 1986, the Swift Current Comprehensive High School Board of Management obtained special grants from the Saskatchewan Education Development Fund for the development of library computerization and the purchase of electronic resource material. It was decided early in the project that CD databases would be a necessary acquisition to provide large, in-house databases for student research. Over the three years of the project all the evidence has supported this approach.

The thrust of the library computer project was twofold. Our first objective was to create an online catalog that students could use to identify all in-house resources quickly and accurately. The computerized catalog and circulation program was expected to free professional staff from clerical routines and allow them to spend more time with students. The second objective was to provide students with the technological capacity to access remote databases online. Such a service was intended to give students a "window on the world," and the necesssary skills to handle the mass of information now available via telecommunications.

A related but critical rationale behind the project was the recognition of the increasing availability of electronic resource material, and our need to develop the library's capability to handle and store CD sources.

System Configuration: The Hardware and Software

The clarity of hindsight may save some librarians from the pitfalls encountered during the Swift Current project. We were not "computer buffs" and at times we relied on sales representatives for assistance. In retrospect, their knowledge, or lack of it, was on a par with ours.

Expert advice is available from many computer companies, and in our case we contacted Jeff Cauhape, at that time on the technical support staff of ITT Information Systems, San Jose, CA. His list of the requirements for our library system was:

1. Provide access to CDs.
2. Allow four simultaneous users either to access a library database on the main computer or to connect with online databases via modem.
3. Support the use of two serial printers.
4. Support the use of four modems.

Our immediate plan was to provide a computerized catalog and a CD database of the collection. Our experience has taught us that the main computer in the library should be the fastest and biggest you can afford. (The speed of a computer can be easily determined using the Norton Utilities.) The two major factors the librarian should consider are central processor unit (CPU) speed and access time of the hard drive. Random access memory (RAM) should be at least 640K. The majority of local catalog programs developed for libraries with collections of over 15,000 volumes are written to operate under MS-DOS for IBM, or compatible, computers.

In 1986, suppliers suggested installing a computer with a 20MB hard drive and a 360K diskette drive to handle our collection. This configuration is too small. We need a minimum of a fast 40MB hard drive and at least one 1.2MB floppy drive. Even with a 1.2MB drive, over seven disks are required to backup our database. A tape backup system is highly desirable.

Our hardware configuration, in 1989, is as follows:
—one 286 CPU with a 72MB hard drive, two floppy disk drives (one each 1.2MB, 360K), 640K RAM
—four 8088 CPUs with various combinations of hard drives and floppy disk drives, and 640K RAM
—five CD readers
—five modems
—two printers
—three telephone lines

Online Catalog

The first software and CD package we purchased was Bibliofile's LC MARC, together with Any-Book. The software and the five CDs allow for the transfer of the

MARC cataloging information onto the hard drive. This software comes with good documentation (a rarity) and can be installed by anyone willing to follow directions. As an alternative to doing the conversion in-house, there are commercial organizations who convert records. We have no experience with this method, but think it might be cost-effective.

The next step was to load the transferred MARC records into a public catalog software system. We looked at several programs, including Mandrin (from Alberta Book and Novelty, Calgary), Ocelot (Ocelot Software, Regina), Card Catalog (Datatrek, Encinitas), and EPICS (TKM Software, Brandon).

We selected EPICS, because it was the easiest to use and most user-friendly of the systems examined. We were fortunate; the support we received from the staff at TKM over the past three years can only be described as exceptional. A high level of software support is a must for most librarians.

EPICS permits searching by author, title, subject, and keyword(s), single words, phrases, and truncations. In our library environment we are using the MS-DOS version, which sells for $1,000. For larger libraries operating in multi-user mode, the company offers Zenix system programs.

Reference CDs

Our second purchase was Grolier's Electronic Encyclopedia, which contains the full-text of the *Academic American Encyclopedia*. It was easy to install and was a smash hit with the students. We immediately purchased three more copies to handle the high demand.

The combination of software and CD provides for fast, user-friendly searching that appeals to all our students. They are able to find subjects, keywords and truncations anywhere in the text. The material is most appropriate for the high-school level, rather than the university. The system is very competitively priced, and a librarian can easily justify the purchase of the CD when it represents a considerable cost savings over the comparable paper volumes.

A new Grolier's Encyclopedia was released in 1988. The search software is more difficult to use and appeals to more advanced students. We have retained three of the old versions, and have purchased one update.

Our next investment was ERIC from SilverPlatter containing the citations from the *Current Index to Journals in Education* (CIJE) and *Resources in Education* (RIE), 1966 to the present. The company is to be commended for its excellent documentation and directions for updating the software. Its product provides both teachers and students with an introduction to the power of online searching.

We then purchased the McGraw-Hill CD-ROM Science and Technical Reference Set. This disc contains the *McGraw-Hill Concise Encyclopedia* and the *McGraw-Hill Dictionary of Scientific and Technical Terms*. The encyclopedia contains 7,300 articles covering all aspects of sciences from astronomy to zoology. It is designed to present the essential information in a practical, convenient format to give quick, concise answers to frequently asked questions. The dictionary includes 98,500 terms and 115,500 definitions.

The software is powerful and the directions for installation are clear. The student can locate, within seconds, any information about a word or phrase. As with Grolier's, articles may be browsed, read, printed, or copied to a file. HELP is available at all times. For some unknown reason, this disc does not get used as much as the four Grolier's discs, even though approximately 700 of our students are enrolled in science programs.

We acquired the PC-SIG Library on CD to give our computer science and computer applications students an idea of the amount of public domain software available. The CD was purchased in 1987 and has the public domain software disks 1 through 705. Everyone who uses the discs becomes aware of its immense storage capacity in that the contents of over 700 360K floppies are stored on one CD, with enough room left on it to store the full text of the Bible.

The PC-SIG software is very easy to use. Clear directions on installation allow the user to have the program running in a few minutes. Occasional reference to a book called *PC-SIG Library* makes using the CD much more manageable.

Software programs on the CD are either in the public domain or user-supported, so a nominal fee should be paid to the software author if the user is satisfied with the software.

Location and Access

Like most project managers, we see the CD Library as a school resource that should be used as many hours per day as can be arranged. We looked for a software program that would allow students to call the library from any computer in the school or surrounding school community.

The program we eventually selected was from our PC-SIG disc, Remote Bulletin Board System (RBBS), created and maintained by Tom Mack and others. As a remote bulletin board, RBBS offers the library a quick and cheap way to bring users online. (The program can be obtained from the Capital PC User Group, 4510 East-West Highway, Suite 550, Bethesda, MD 20814, for $8.00.)

The documentation for RBBS-PC CPC16-1A (the version currently running in our library) is 210 pages long. This might seem intimidating, but actually a novice can get this software running as a bulletin board in a few hours. One of the RBBS' best features for the small library is its ability to control student use of the online services. RBBS also has several levels of security that make it possible to offer faculty access to school–related files. Tom Mack and his fellow software developers state that no breaches of security have been reported during the long life of this program.

Our plan was to have an entry system that checked the calling computer and decided how communications would take place. RBBS asks all the necessary questions, and controls the caller's online time and access to information. It keeps track of users and stores a report of their activities that the systems operator can view at any time.

RBBS has all the "bells and whistles" of many of the expensive bulletin board programs. But, more importantly, the software, in conjunction with a "doors" program, provides access to other systems, e.g., CD-ROMs. We use Doorway by

Marshall Dudley of Data World BBS (615-966-3574, $15.00). Doorway allows RBBS to function as a "door" to the CD systems. It creates a shell to the program to be run and translates and redirects all video to the required COM port and all COM port inputs to the keyboard buffer.

Students who wish to contact the service use a microcomputer and modem to call one of the three telephone lines we have for library online access. The student must then fill out an online registration form. On subsequent calls students simply give the name under which they have registered and the password they selected. The final step is the opening of the "door" to the CD the student wishes to use. The simple system we operate will not allow the student to do anything with system files that run on the hard drive.

The program allows us to set time limits. In our original set of parameters we allowed the students half an hour online. Based on our experience with the average search time, we have set the limit at 15 minutes so that more students can access the system.

Publicity

A publicity plan was put in place early on in the project. The plan had several components designed to give the project local, provincial, national, and international exposure.

The local plan included exposure in city media, a press release in the annual report of the school board, and an opportunity for students from the elementary schools to visit the library and use the system.

At the provincial level two reports on the project were prepared. One was an evaluation of the project for the funding agency, and the other was a press release for the Annual Report of the Educational Development Fund. A report was also prepared for the Computer User Group of Saskatchewan.

On the national level the project report appeared in two national educational journals. On the international level an article, "Computerizing a High School Library," appeared in *Library Software Review*. Most interest in the project came from the United States. Several school systems and universities requested permission to use the article for in-service training.

Staff Impact

The literature on change often addresses the university and the high school as organizations that are peculiarly resistant to change. Our school was no exception. The new librarian, who put in a great deal of time outside school hours to develop the online catalog, was diligent in developing class presentations for teachers as well as students. Yet it is probably an accurate observation that after three years of operation, students make much more use of the new services than teaching staff. Not all staff members have realized how the library has changed, or the increased amount of resources that are now available for various areas of the curriculum. However, the teachers who are aware of the new resources have higher expectations of what a student can produce in a research essay, or any other assignment that calls for library resources.

Evaluation

During the preparation of the initial proposal it was decided that the critical indicators of success would be that by June of 1987 the online catalog should be fully operational and 100 students should have conducted database searches.

The online card catalog was completed before the end of the 1986–87 school year and has replaced the card catalog. Running on two computers, the online catalog provides all the access necessary for a student body of 1,000 students. School-wide instruction on the use of the system did not take place until the fall of 1987.

Our original goal of 100 students was quickly achieved. By November of 1987 the library had over 350 students per month conducting database searches. Over the years this number has fluctuated between 300 and 500 searches per month. The librarian reports computer use monthly. RBBS tracks all callers and provides reports by the day, week, or month.

It became obvious that in-house databases were not only useful to the academic elite, but were also readily used by students from all across the ability spectrum.

Reflections

Originally, we planned to use the fast (in those days) 286 computer as our network server and bulletin board host so students could call in to the host and be shunted to one of the networked computers to search a database. In fact, the first thing we did was remove the network system and interface cards. Instead of a network, our present operation uses the dedicated computer and phone line concept previously described. In all probability a person with some time and expertise could set up the network to work in a more efficient way than we operate, but installing and maintaining a network is time–consuming and difficult.

A second observation for librarians tackling the creation of an online catalog in a small library is that the catalog is probably best produced by private contractors, rather than in-house. Local production requires the purchase of the Library of Congress card catalog (an expense of about $3,000 in 1986). The conversion is expensive both because of the CD purchase, as well as the long hours staff must devote to the development. A third observation is that librarians considering automation should consider a 386 CPU operating at a minimum of 25mhz. A final observation is that CDs can replace book purchases. Often three or four CDs can be purchased for the price of an encyclopedia in hard copy. Students' preference for CDs over books support this choice.

Conclusions

Shifting from books to CDs is an unsettling task, but the benefits for students and staff are so numerous that the job must be done. There is no easy way to tackle large scale change. Librarians should simply get a computer and a CD player and get on with the job. Those of us who have been there will help you in any way we can.

References

Bardes, D'Ellen. 1986. "Standard reasoning." *CD-ROM Review* 1(1): 40–43.

Beaumont, Jane. 1986. "Retrospective conversion on a micro: Options for Libraries." *Library Software Review* 5(4): 213–218.

Boss, Richard. 1984. "Retrospective conversion: Investing in the future." *Wilson Library Bulletin* 59(3): 173–178.

Chan, Jeannie and Errol Whelan. 1988. "Computerizing a high school library." *Library Software Review* 7(1): 12–16.

DeTray, Jeff. 1986. "CD-ROM standards." *CD-ROM Review* 1(1): 8.

Moynes, R.E. 1984. "Megatrends and education." *The Canadian School Executive* 5(9): 36.

Newcombe, Barbara and Trivedi Harish. 1984. "Newspapers and electronic data bases: Present technology." *Wilson Library Bulletin* 59(2):94–97.

Tenopir, Carol. 1986. "Online searching in schools." *Library Journal* 3(2): 60–61.

Errol A. Whelan is Principal of Swift Current Comprehensive High School in Saskatchewan, Canada. He began the library computer project in the spring of 1986. Errol did his undergraduate work at Saint Francis Xavier University in Nova Scotia. He did his graduate work at the University of Alberta.

21
CD-ROM Technology in a Biomedical Library

Beryl Glitz, Gail A. Yokote

Introduction

The UCLA Louise Darling Biomedical Library began investigating the possible use of CD-ROM technology in the fall of 1986, by experimenting with a trial subscription to Cambridge Scientific's Compact Cambridge/MEDLINE (Glitz 1988). At that time, the library had no online access for end-users to MEDLINE or to any other databases within the library: patrons could either have a search run by staff, for a fee, or use the printed indexes. Work had begun on the programming required to mount a subset of MEDLINE locally, but end-users were not scheduled to have access to this database for another year. Testing Compact Cambridge/ MEDLINE was thus seen as both a means of introducing patrons to end-user searching without incurring costs and as a chance for library staff to gain enough knowledge to embark on a more ambitious program of CD-ROM experimentation and end-user development. Since this initial test, two other versions of MEDLINE, from EBSCO and from SilverPlatter, have been similarly tested and evaluated. As a result of this trial period, the library has developed important skills in CD-ROM technology and has emerged as a test site for relevant CD-ROM products. With the subsequent introduction of a local MEDLINE subset, searchable online through multiple in-house terminals, a dual-level end-user search service is now in place; patrons can try out the new CD-ROM technology while also benefitting from multi-user access to their most important database. Such a service has enabled the library to further its long-standing goal of using innovative technology to provide full and efficient information access for its clientele.

In this case study we will discuss the issues facing an academic, health-sciences library in establishing a CD-ROM search system for patron use. We describe the CD-ROM test environment, the results of tests of various sytems, and the rationale for the decisions which led to the present dual-level end-user searching configuration. Furthermore, the effects of introducing CD-ROM technology into the library are described from the point of view of both staff and patrons.

Background

The Biomedical Library is one of 18 subject specialty branches within the UCLA Library system and serves primarily the Schools of Medicine, Dentistry, Nursing, and Public Health, the UCLA Medical Center, the Departments of Biology and Microbiology in the Life Sciences Division, and various other research institutes in biomedicine. As a state-supported institution, the library system is open to anyone. Hence, the Biomedical Library is heavily used by the general public as well as by students and health care professionals from the Los Angeles area. Moreover, the library also serves as the headquarters for the Pacific Southwest Regional Medical Library Service. The library contains over 450,000 volumes and regularly receives approximately 6,000 serial titles. Its collections are broad in scope and interdisciplinary in nature, designed to support the teaching, research, and patient care needs of its many users. For the past eight years, the library has utilized an online integrated library system, ORION, developed in-house, to perform an increasing number of technical and public service functions, such as acquisitions, serials control, public access catalog, and circulation.

From the beginning of the National Library of Medicine's (NLM) MEDLARS search service to health science libraries in 1972 (Egeland and Foreman, 1982), the Biomedical Library has provided a fee-based, mediated search service for NLM databases, and has added commercially produced databases to the service as they became available. Since late 1987, free access to a subset of MEDLINE, developed through the University of California with a National Library of Medicine grant (G08 LM04466), has been available in the library. This subset, MELVYL MEDLINE, represents the most current two–three years of the MEDLINE database and is available for searching in all campus libraries, as well as through dial-up access for UC staff, students, and faculty. Future plans call for the extension of MELVYL MEDLINE to cover five years of MEDLINE.

Over the years the Biomedical Library has developed a large clientele familiar with computerized search systems in the library, and accustomed to regarding library staff as a technologically advanced information resource group. As microcomputers have become common throughout the academic environment, faculty, staff and students have themselves become increasingly used to the idea of computers as tools to enhance productivity and to further research. A growing number of library patrons have expressed the need for online database access by means of these same microcomputers and have experimented with different search systems, such as BRS and, more recently, GRATEFUL MED, often with advice and instruction from library staff. The major drawback to this type of searching, especially for the student population, has always been the unpredictable costs incurred in online access. The introduction of CD-ROM technology seemed to be a welcome innovation, free from online costs, telecommunications problems, and a ticking clock.

In 1986, when our first CD-ROM trial began, library staff had no experience with this new technology. If we wanted to continue our tradition of providing innovative information services, it was clear that we needed to learn more about CD-ROM systems and to assess their appropriateness for our library users.

Issues To Be Resolved

Library staff faced several important issues in determining which CD-ROM products would best serve the interests and needs of a majority of library users, and what type of search environment would be optimal for both staff and patrons. Choice of databases; location of work stations; ease of searching and the need, if any, for user training; and, the impact on library staff and services, needed to be addressed before a major investment was made in CD-ROM products. Moreover, the future availability of MELVYL MEDLINE, the locally developed subset of MEDLINE, had to be taken into consideration.

Choice of Databases

Since Compact Cambridge/MEDLINE was the best product available within our subject scope when we began our initial CD-ROM test, questions of database selection were temporarily set aside and library staff concentrated on the numerous other questions involved in creating a CD-ROM search environment. After the year of product testing, because the Biomedical Library was now able to provide free in-house access to MEDLINE, we chose CD-ROM products to reflect the broader health and life sciences information needs of our users. Our selections were PsycLIT, Cancer-CD, Chem-Bank, Science Citation Index, and IRL Life Sciences. These databases, along with MELVYL MEDLINE, contribute to a varied repertoire of end-user search options.

Location of Work-Stations

Initially, the single CD-ROM work-station used in experimenting with the Cambridge, EBSCO and SilverPlatter MEDLINE test products was located beside the reference desk so that reference librarians would be available to answer questions and to evaluate user response to these products. Both printing and downloading to disk were permitted during the test phase, though patron searching was restricted when necessary to half-hour time blocks. Reference librarians were kept extremely busy answering search questions, monitoring use, suggesting appropriate subject headings, changing CD-ROM discs, and dealing with recalcitrant printers and other equipment problems. This was in addition to providing the traditional reference service responses to in-person and telephone questions. At times, even scheduling two people at the desk each hour during peak hours was not sufficient to keep up with the number of questions and equipment problems. Clearly, the reference desk environment was not ideal for coping with such a variety of technological and informational demands, especially later in the test period when MELVYL MEDLINE became available from library terminals, also located close to the desk. Still, reference librarians were concerned that the CD-ROM system be widely used, since we wanted to get as much feedback from patrons as possible, and we felt a responsibility to provide producers with relevant usage data on their products.

After these experiments were concluded, it was decided to move the CD-ROM station to the library's Instructional Media Facility (IMF). The IMF, located on the second floor of the library, houses 16 microcomputers, with access to a variety of programs and search services for any registered UCLA student, staff, or faculty member. IMF staff include a division head, a library assistant and several students, all knowledgeable in microcomputer technology.

The decision to move the CD-ROM station was based on several factors: relieving the reference desk staff from the equipment problems (which turned out to be more numerous than search-related problems), maintaining security for multi-disc products, and, providing a quieter search environment than a constantly busy public reference area. Moreover, the later CD-ROM products were clearly becoming more truly user-friendly, and with these improvements in search language it seemed less critical that searching occur in a location where expert assistance was immediately available. Above and beyond these considerations, however, the reference area now provided 10 terminals for patrons to access MELVYL MEDLINE, the database of choice for most of our library users. CD-ROM access to MEDLINE was no longer vitally necessary in the reference environment. The single CD-ROM workstation environment seemed more appropriate for access to less heavily used databases where currency of information and simultaneous multi-user searching were less critical. The IMF was a good location for providing online and CD-ROM access to databases in the basic sciences and other disciplines. It possessed staff with the knowledge needed to handle microcomputer equipment questions, as well as some skill in database searching; and it provided a setting where circulation of discs could easily be controlled. The time restrictions on an individual search session, imposed in the test setting, were no longer necessary, and patrons had unlimited access. The IMF thus provided a less harried environment in which users might develop their skills and more fully utilize the CD-ROM capabilities.

Several disadvantages result, however, from housing the CD-ROM systems away from the main public service area, both for patrons and library staff. Most importantly there is a lack of visibility for the products, since the IMF is away from the main traffic area of the library. Patrons with questions or problems not answerable by IMF staff must travel a considerable distance to secure help at the reference desk. For library staff the move has increased questions for IMF personnel, while distancing reference librarians from familiarity with the products. With little daily contact, reference staff feel less compelled to keep current with product changes and do not develop the familiarity produced from constant use.

Patron Searching Skills and Training Requirements

A critical factor in the choice of products and the location of a workstation is clearly the ease with which patrons can actually search the CD-ROM and get the kind of results they need, preferably with little help from library personnel. When the first product arrived, several staff members explored the search system and designed a short set of instructions to be placed by the workstation. The instructions covered basic patron needs: how to know when the system is functioning properly, how to get help, how to choose menu options and, briefly, what those options mean, how to correct errors, truncate, and return to previous screens, how to print, and how to exit the program. Since this was a test which we hoped, among other things, would reveal just how user-friendly the product was, and therefore how feasible it might be to locate it in a reference area, no further printed instructions were given. More complete instructions were, of course, available on-screen and the printed search manual that came with the product was made available at the reference desk, though few patrons actually consulted the manual. Although training classes were discussed, the decision was made to not provide such classes for the test period. Indeed, given the busy instructional program at the library, which includes classes in searching the online catalog, end-user searching in MEDLINE, class-specific instruction in many disciplines, and more recently, classes in MELVYL MEDLINE, further training sessions could not easily be fitted into the reference division schedule. Moreover, the CD-ROM products being produced were advertised as user-friendly, and presumably could be mastered independently by library patrons.

A formal evaluation form was designed for the initial product, to assess the ease with which patrons could perform searches and how satisfactory their searches proved to be. The form was modified after the first experience with patron responses (figure 1). We hoped to learn several things from the questionnaire: who our users

SEARCHING MEDLINE BY COMPACT DISC
EVALUATION FORM – FALL 1987

Help us assess the value of the system to UCLA faculty, staff and students. Please provide the following information.

A. Answer the questions below: Circle One

1. Is this the first time you have performed   Yes   No
   a computer search yourself?
   If no, what other search systems have you used?
2. Was this search system easy   Yes   No   Don't know
   to learn?
3. Was the compact disc equipment   Yes   No   Don't know
   easy to operate?
4. Were you satisfied with the   Yes   No   Don't know
   results of your search?
5. How many citations did you retrieve?
6. How many of those were relevant?   All   Some   None
7. a. Did you use the "BROWSE"   Yes   No
   option for searching?
   b. Did you use the HELP screens?   Yes   No
8. Would you use this system again?   Yes   No   Don't know
9. Would you recommend that   Yes   No   Don't know
   the library purchase this system? Why?

B. Describe your search topic:

C. Circle One: UCLA Faculty — UCLA Staff — UCLA Graduate/Professional
School Student — UCLA Undergraduate Student — Other
    Department:
    Name (Optional):

D. Additional comments can be recorded on the back of this form.

Thank you for providing an evaluation of MEDLINE on Compact Disc!

figure 1

were, how much previous searching experience they had, and most importantly, their reactions to learning and using the system and the equipment, and their satisfaction with their search results. Copies of the form were placed beside the terminal along with a box for completed evaluations. Reference staff, whenever possible, encouraged users to complete forms, and most users happily complied. Less successful was our request that patrons attach a copy of their search strategy and results to the evaluation form. We had hoped to learn a good deal about user search strategies and the types of results produced from these strategies, but mostly because of printer problems, we received very few.

The results of our first formal evaluation were overwhelming in favor of CD-ROM technology, though it was clear that patrons underutilized the system and produced less than optimal search results. Eighty-one percent of those responding found the system easy to learn, and once learned, 84 percent said it was easy to use. While 56 percent of the respondents indicated that they were satisfied with their searches, and 30 percent were not satisfied, almost everyone (85 percent) said they would use the system again. From the search strategies returned, it was clear that user satisfaction could not have been based on the actual search results. Most searches resulted in huge numbers of citations and no attempt seems to have been made to limit topics in any way. Other searches on subjects which clearly would have had many citations in the database retrieved nothing because of search strategy problems. Yet even patrons retrieving hundreds of citations or no citations at all declared themselves satisfied. Further analysis of search strategies revealed that most patrons never learned how to combine sets, a vital capability in any search system and clearly one of the most basic in terms of online benefits from systems such as CD-ROM. On the other hand, the low retrievals often resulted from the inability to use MeSH headings in the search system, again, a vital capability for any online version of MEDLINE. In the evaluations of later products from Ebsco and SilverPlatter, a similar high rate of satisfaction was expressed and users were more successful in manipulating the search software, though the software capabilities were still underutilized. Thus, although the different products represented a variety of searching capabilities, patron enthusiasm was constant. Because the technology was new and different, patrons viewed CD-ROM products as "better" regardless of what their actual search results were.

Our own patrons' responses were mirrored in those presented at the National Library of Medicine's Evaluation Forum, where health science libraries reported on their evaluations of seven different CD-ROM versions of MEDLINE (Woodsmall, Lyon-Hartmann, and Siegel, 1989). In all the reports, great enthusiasm was coupled with underutilization of software capabilities and a variety of hardware and searching problems, but with a great appreciation for the convenience and potential of this new technology.

Impact on Library Staff and Services

A vital issue in the introduction of public access CD-ROM technology into any library is the impact which such a search service might have on staff and on existing services. The majority of CD-ROM products are in fact reference tools: indexes, encyclopedias, etc. Therefore, the provision of end-user searching of these products is clearly the responsibility of the Reference department (Salomon, 1988). Also, since many libraries wish to locate their CD-ROM workstations in the most visible and accessible part of the library, it is at the reference desk where most of the impact is felt.

At the Biomedical Library, the CD-ROM workstation at the reference desk, presented, above all, a tremendous challenge for desk staff to balance the demands of those wanting to search with the more traditional needs of patrons waiting at the desk for other types of reference assistance. Because online searching with CD-ROM was a totally new experience for most library users, some initially required a great deal of help in overcoming reservations about the new technology or in dealing with the intricacies of search techniques. With other patrons waiting for help at the desk, the traditional reference approaches of providing assistance incrementally and encouraging self-sufficiency proved successful in meeting the needs of this new environment. Staff were careful to provide only sufficient assistance to get searchers started, pointing out the instruction sheet and emphasizing online help features, so that patrons at the desk need not be kept waiting for long. In retrospect, such experience has proved invaluable in anticipating and developing coping skills for patron questions resulting from the introduction of MELVYL MEDLINE.

In order to successfully provide this type of balanced assistance, however, a thorough knowledge of each CD-ROM product and familiarity with the demands of using microcomputers in a public environment were vital for all desk staff. In preparing for product testing, staff clearly needed to understand all the basic features of the system: searching, combining sets, limiting, displaying, etc. They also needed to be comfortable with the work-station so as to help patrons with entering and exiting the system, printing, and using DOS when necessary. The lack of sufficient time for staff to experiment before the test was a serious drawback. The production of "cheat sheets" aimed specifically at staff and which included tips on how to handle patrons questions alleviated this somewhat. Also helpful were demonstrations of each product and informal discussions during regular staff meetings. In these meetings, staff could review the steps in completing a successful search, practice changing discs and paper, and deal with general anxieties over hardware or software. Having one staff member responsible for coordinating each CD-ROM product proved successful. Apart from ensuring the success of the actual test, this person was available to demonstrate the product and act as a guide and resource for other staff. Yet it is clear that beyond the need for understanding the search system, microcomputer literacy for reference librarians and other appropriate library personnel is critical in offering a successful CD-ROM service. This type of expertise has been less critical in previous end-user searching programs, such as teaching MEDLINE through GRATEFUL MED or other user-friendly systems, where traditionally searching has been performed on terminals. Our own Reference staff have since taken classes to enhance their microcomputing skills in DOS, word-processing programs and database management systems. Without such expertise, evaluating CD-ROM products and mounting them on a workstation can prove difficult and time-consuming.

Apart from impact on Reference staff, the use of CD-ROM products has clearly had an effect on other library divisions. The Instructional Microcomputer Facility staff have seen an increase in patron searching and equipment requests. While questions on how to use microcomputers are routine for IMF staff, the demands for help in areas such as search strategy, use of Boolean logic, and suitability of each database are new. In effect, the staff are now being expected to act as reference librarians. While a better understanding of the concepts of online searching and basic search strategy may help IMF personnel provide a minimal level of assistance, they have learned to recognize when referrals to reference librarians are appropriate, and how to deal with the frustrations that the need for referrals can cause. Thus CD-ROM can be seen to have broadened the need for understanding of library staff and the potential services offered by our microcomputer facility.

Collection development is another library department which must cope with the introduction of CD-ROM products, and, as for all other library materials, must establish collection criteria and balance patron needs. Eventually, questions of whether or not to retain print versions of these products will have to be answered. At present, we have too little experience with using CD-ROM to make such decisions. Until CD-ROM networks that allow for many simultaneous users are well established, single workstation access would not permit any such cancellations. To cope with the various problems of adding a new medium of publication to library collections, a committee of librarians from many different libraries on the UCLA campus was formed to discuss the issues raised in acquiring materials in electronic format. Among the issues being examined are: responsibility for subject coverage; use restrictions imposed by producers and/or copyright; hardware specifications; and, general restrictions imposed by product licenses. The committee hopes eventually to provide standardized guidelines for all campus libraries in how to select and acquire these materials.

Of all the issues associated with acquiring CD-ROM products, licensing agreements probably constitute the greatest area of impact for another department within the library, Acquisitions. Such agreements are non-standard and can be very complex. They must be read carefully and kept available, especially for instructions on handling updates. Special notes to remind library staff of procedures for handling update discs should be kept in a convenient location. In the Biomedical Library these notes are found in designated places in the processing fields of our online library information system, ORION. Most importantly, licensing agreements must be signed by an individual who has the authority to represent the institution in legal matters. In some situations, this may in fact be someone outside the library.

The final division affected by CD-ROM products is Cataloging. Here staff must interpret evolving cataloging rules for new formats so as to provide standardized access to these materials through the Library's online public catalog. The challenge to Cataloging staff lies in being able to examine these new types of materials so as to provide appropriate and accurate descriptions and access points. For example, one needs a CD-ROM player available to examine the "title page" of a compact disc if there is no label on the disc or paper insert with the product. Other issues, such as preparing public notes and linking records to print versions of the same work, add to the concerns that CD-ROM brings to catalogers.

Impact on Patrons

Library patrons have been affected by the introduction of CD-ROM searching. By all accounts, the experience has been tremendously positive for them. Searching has proved a novel and exciting experience in spite of minor technical frustrations and, as shown by the evaluations, less than optimal search results. In fact, when equipment was removed after the test period, reference staff had to reassure many disappointed patrons that further CD products would be available at a later time in the library. Doing their own searching has increased users' awareness of library technology and their own microcomputer sophistication, while at the same time developing a greater appreciation and respect for the library.

Implications of Introducing CD-ROM Technology into the Library

What then, are the implications of introducing CD-ROM products that can be deduced from our experience here at UCLA? Product selection, though clearly affected by the total library milieu, is especially dependent on type of users, availability of databases in various media, and financial resources for software and hardware. When an institution provides free access to a popular locally mounted database, the potential use of CD-ROM technology is obviously affected, and one would need to choose appropriate CD-ROM products to complement the locally mounted databases. In a health and life sciences library CD-ROM access to the basic sciences or peripheral subject areas such as psychology seems to satisfy library users in these disciplines. Moreover, the single workstation environment is more nearly sufficient for access to these less highly demanded databases, whereas it is clearly insufficient for such a high-demand item as MEDLINE. Having both locally mounted databases and CD-ROM stations in the same library can thus provide flexibility and versatility, and can be cost effective: locally mounted databases provide simultaneous multiple user access through relatively inexpensive, easy to use computer terminals, without the costs of workstation equipment or dial access; CD-ROMs, with high workstation and product costs, provide single-user access to several databases. Until software and equipment for placing CD-ROM stations on existing local area networks become available and licensing agreements can accommodate many simultaneous users, providing multiple CD-ROM workstations will be a costly proposition.

Whatever means are used to provide access to CD-ROM products, the physical location of the workstations plays a major role in their actual use. If the products are not easily visible to the majority of patrons coming into the library, they will not be heavily used. Publicity is therefore a crucial factor in ensuring that patrons use this technology and justify the library's time and costs in offering the service. Location also affects the staff's response to CD-ROM products and the success with which they can accommodate and exploit this new tool. New technologies such as CD-ROM should be located within the reference desk environment for the reference librarian to learn about user reactions and behaviors, and to be able to provide effective, personal assistance to library patrons. On the other hand, if a library wishes to provide a quiet searching environment which provides knowledgeable help in using microcomputers, as long as search software is sufficiently user-friendly, CD-ROM products may be mounted in the microcomputer laboratory. Staff in such laboratories then need sufficient training and experience to understand the basics of online searching and work effectively with patrons.

Clearly then, the placement of the CD-ROM workstation has implications for staff training and development. For staff in the microcomputer laboratory, this new technology opens up a new challenge in learning more about online searching and patron needs. For reference staff, microcomputer literacy is critical when the work-stations are placed near the reference desk. Since demand for these products to be placed in environments other than libraries will probably increase in the future, staff must be prepared to answer questions regarding the installation of CD-ROM workstations in offices, departments, and perhaps in dormitory settings.

A final implication of providing CD-ROM access to the literature, as with any online system, is the resultant demand on the library's collections. Better access to citations may create problems for users trying to obtain copies of actual documents identified by their searches, especially when libraries have only single copies of important journals. In a public academic library where the primary clientele (faculty, staff, and students) must compete with off-campus users for the same journal titles, the improvement of access to the literature at one level can unwittingly cause obstacles in retrieving that literature at another level. Libraries will need to decide how best to serve their primary clientele by such means as purchasing multiple subscriptions, and limiting or denying the circulation of journals, all of which are difficult decisions in the present era of limited budgets and increasing library usage.

CD-ROM technology is an exciting and important new tool in the growing array of library end-user services. While it provides sophisticated and easy access to an ever growing store of information, and enhances the traditional goals of libraries in the area of information storage and retrieval, it brings with it important and far-reaching implications for library staff and the services they provide. With a thorough understanding of the consequences of these implications, and careful planning on a library-wide basis, CD-ROM products can be integrated into the library and bring added services and benefits to both patrons and staff.

References

Egeland, J., and G. Foreman. 1982. "Reference services: searching and search techniques." In *Handbook of Medical Library Practice. Vol. I, Public Services in Health Science Libraries* 4th ed., ed. L. Darling. Chicago: Medical Library Association, Inc.

Glitz, B. 1988. "Testing the new technology: MEDLINE on CD-ROM in an academic health sciences library." *Special Libraries* 79 (1): 28–33.

Salomon, K. 1988. "The impact of CD-ROM on reference departments." *RQ* 28 (2): 203–219.

Woodsmall, R. M., B. Lyon-Hartmann, and E. Siegel, eds. 1989. *MEDLINE on CD-ROM*. Medford, N.J.: Learned Information, Inc.

Beryl Glitz is Associate Director of the Pacific Southwest Regional Medical Library Service at UCLA. Her prior position was Educational Services Coordinator in the Reference Division of the UCLA Louise Darling Biomedical Library. Before joining the Reference Division, Beryl worked as a cataloger. Beryl received both her B.A. and her M.L.S. from UCLA.

Gail A. Yokote is Associate Biomedical Librarian for Public Services at the UCLA Louise Darling Biomedical Library. Prior to this position Gail held positions as Director of Information Services at the Houston Academy of Medicine–Texas Medical Center Library in Houston, TX; Head of the Information Services Section of the Pacific Southwest Regional Medical Library Service (PSRMLS) at the UCLA Biomedical Library; Assistant Head of the Reference Division at the UCLA Biomedical Library; and Information Specialist for PSRMLS at UCLA. Gail received her B.A. in Biological Sciences from the University of California, Davis and her M.S. in Library Science from the University of Illinois, Champaign-Urbana.

22
CD-ROMs at Carnegie Mellon University

Nancy H. Evans

Introduction

The implementation of CD-ROM services at Carnegie Mellon University is part of the University Libraries' larger program for bringing online bibliographic, numeric, and full-text information services directly to library users, conveniently and without cost. For many academic institutions, CD-ROMs are the only method, other than commercial end-user search systems, available for providing these kinds of information on campus. At Carnegie Mellon, the locally developed Library Information System (LIS) was providing access to several bibliographic and full-text files before the first CD-ROM systems were added to the information service mix. The current mix of services at Carnegie Mellon depends significantly on local community expectations, unique resources and capabilities, and the University's and Libraries' longer-range plans. Consequently, this case study focuses as much on the planning process for electronic information services as it does on particular questions of CD-ROM implementation. Even though Carnegie Mellon's environment differs from that of many other academic libraries, library staff have addressed many of the same questions and problems, particularly those concerning decisions about CD-ROM service implementation, that affect all academic libraries.

The Carnegie Mellon University Community

Carnegie Mellon University, since its founding in 1900, has been known both as an excellent regional technical school and as an educational leader in the fine arts, particularly in drama and architecture. In the past two decades, since its formation by the merging of the Carnegie Institute of Technology and the Mellon Institute for Research, the University has broadened its educational focus to provide a professional/ liberal education for undergraduates in all fields, including a greatly expanded College of Humanities and Social Science. Graduate and research programs in several areas of engineering and the sciences, industrial management, urban and public affairs, and computer science are among top programs in their fields nationally and, in the case of computer science, internationally. Admission to Carnegie Mellon is very selective. The school currently enrolls approximately 6,000 students, of which about 2,000 are graduate students. The full- and part-time faculty of about 600 includes many very active, well-known researchers, including one Nobel laureate.

Carnegie Mellon has defined its niche in the academic marketplace by selecting areas of academic strength and building on those strengths. The University does not offer a comprehensive list of courses in each department. Rather, selected specialities, such as applied history or cognitive psychology, are emphasized. Carnegie Mellon still retains some of the atmosphere of a technical school, including a strong emphasis on quantification, even in such disciplines as history and English. In addition, Carnegie Mellon is highly interdisciplinary, with much overlap of courses and faculty between colleges and schools. The pervasive atmosphere is one of innovation and experimentation, of trying to stay at the leading edge of the specialties emphasized, whether that innovation comes in course offerings or research.

The academic community at Carnegie Mellon has come to expect equally innovative academic support services. The university has a long history of providing wide access to high-level computing services. In particular, since 1982, the Andrew project (a joint development effort with IBM), a new campus data communications network, and the availability of reasonably priced IBM and Apple Macintosh personal computers have created a community of sophisticated and demanding computer users. Many of these users are aware of the possibilities of computers as information management tools, and they expect the university to provide equally sophisticated information services.

Libraries at Carnegie Mellon

Curiously, Andrew Carnegie did not see the need to establish a library when he founded the Carnegie Technical Schools in 1900. Among the consequences of this decision are a smaller library collection (700,000 volumes, 3,500 serials) than one might expect at an institution with a national reputation for excellence in research, or one associated with Andrew Carnegie. Another consequence was that there was no separate library building until 1961, when the Hunt Library was opened. Although library support, and the collections, have grown markedly in the 1980's, it would be impossible to rectify all the collections' historical inadequacies. Consequently, the three Carnegie Mellon libraries are actively seeking to apply new technology, specifically new computing technology, to improve the delivery of information services, including bibliographic access, to materials not held at Carnegie Mellon.

Library facilities include Hunt Library, which now serves primarily the humanities and social sciences, industrial management, urban and public affairs, and the fine arts and music; the Engineering and Science Library, which occupies part of a floor in a classroom/office building and serves engineering, the sciences, and computer science; and the Mellon Institute Library, in the Mellon Institute building, which serves chemistry and biology. Physical facilities are increasingly crowded as collections grow and as the size of both student body and faculty increase.

Although the Libraries have been involved in automated information retrieval since the early days of commercial online services, the first large-scale, generally available online information resource was the LS/2000 online catalog, introduced in 1984. The smaller collection size allowed conversion of essentially all catalog records, so that the online catalog is a nearly complete record of all library holdings. Also in 1984, the Libraries introduced end-user database searching with Search Helper, a product of Information Access Corporation (IAC). Other end-user systems have been added, including EasyNet, WilSearch, Grateful Med, and STN. Since 1986, the chief focus has been the development of the LIS, a campus-based, distributed information retrieval system that includes the library catalog, an encyclopedia, a dictionary, several commercial bibliographic databases, and some local files. (See Evans and Michalak, 1987; Kibbey and Evans, 1988; and Evans, 1989.) LIS can be accessed from terminals and personal computers connected to the campus network, or by telephone from off-campus locations. The ease of access to LIS, coupled with a simple retrieval system and general contents, has increased use of the Libraries; it has also sparked increased user demand for information access.

CD-ROMs in the Libraries

In an effort to broaden bibliographic access, the Libraries have been adding CD-ROM systems since 1987. Currently, Hunt Library provides the following CD-ROM services:
—ERIC (OCLC's Search CD-350), added 1987
—Dissertation Abstracts (University Microforms, Inc.), added 1987
—PsycLIT (SilverPlatter), added 1988
—ABI/INFORM (University Microforms, Inc.), added 1988
The Mellon Institute Library had, since 1988, offered the Kirk-Othmer Encyclopedia of Chemical Technology. However, since John Wiley, the publisher, withdrew Kirk-Othmer from the market in June of 1989, the Mellon Institute Library has dropped it. The Engineering and Science Library has acquired MathSci CD-ROM. Hunt Library had offered the two-user version of IAC's InfoTrac system earlier, when this product was only available as a 12-inch laser disc. InfoTrac has been replaced by the five databases the Libraries lease from IAC (Magazine Index, National Newspaper Index, Management Contents, Trade and Industry Index, and Computer Contents) and distribute through LIS.

Philosophy

For the past few years the Carnegie Mellon Libraries have been building an information service that integrates different information storage and retrieval resources to increase the use of information in all formats. More particularly, the Libraries are attempting to increase the use of existing library collections—whether in print, microform, or machine-readable form—by increasing the ease of access to information about these collections. In addition, the Libraries are attempting to expand bibliographic access to resources held elsewhere and, concomitantly, to provide efficient delivery of these resources. One reason for this approach was mentioned above: since the Libraries' own collections are not limitless, the community needs to be able to find out, quickly, easily, and reliably, what information is available elsewhere. Another, very basic, reason is to encourage users to find out what is available on campus, rather than wrongly assuming that an item is not available. Often a user is too frustrated by a retrieval system—a card catalog, an online catalog, or a printed index—to persist in a search. He may erroneously conclude that what he seeks is not in the library's collection, or he may ultimately stop trying to use the system.

To increase the use of information we are trying to decrease the cost of finding and using it. Part of the strategy of the Carnegie Mellon Libraries is to distribute access to bibliographic tools, such as the library catalog and commercial databases, much more widely across campus. Since 1982, the university has been dedicated to developing a distributed network of powerful personal computing workstations which would provide the individual user with an array of tools to enhance teaching, learning, and research. With the advent of both the campus network and the development of distributed computing, the Libraries undertook to deliver library-type information directly to the workstation, through the campus network. Local distribution, without additional charge to the user, opens up the realm of online searching to the entire community, not just to faculty with research grants that cover the cost of mediated searching of commercial databases. The possibilities for this sort of information delivery are exciting. LIS, mentioned above, is the first stage towards the goal of a widely accessible information resource.

Since the Libraries are focusing on distributed information retrieval, CD-ROMs have not been emphasized as a method of information delivery. Rather, their presence in the Libraries supplements resources available on LIS. CD-ROM systems are less expensive than the corresponding leases of commercial databases, even considering cost of equipment. They do not take up expensive storage space on the LIS system. Such systems also create good publicity for the library, providing an image of a progressive, contemporary information resource adaptive to community needs. And CD-ROMs help achieve the important goal of putting the user in control of his information search.

Planning for CD-ROMs

Since work began on LIS in 1985, the Libraries have pursued several simultaneous tracks to make information available in electronic format. These tracks include LIS development, end-user and mediated database searching, and CD-ROMs. In fact, LIS had been a public resource for a year before the first CD-ROM (ERIC) was introduced. The popularity of LIS demonstrated forcefully that the community prefers electronic database searching to use of print indexes; indeed, some searchers will use a less-than-appropriate electronic database rather than search an appropriate print index.

Given this popularity, and increasing demand from academic departments whose disciplines were not covered in LIS databases, the Libraries were willing to experiment with CD-ROMs. With the exception of the Kirk-Othmer, the current collection of CD-ROM services at Carnegie Mellon has resulted from a combination of opportunity and quick decision making which allowed purchase of relevant CD-ROMs. As these services were being introduced, a library standing committee

(Electronic Information Services Committee, or EISC) has been developing a comprehensive plan and collection policy applicable to all electronic information services. The overall program is the responsibility of one public services staff member (Data and Information Services Manager), with input from the committee. The following discussion describes the selection of the current CD-ROM collection and outlines the selection procedures now in place for future collection development.

Development of Existing Collection

Of the six CD-ROM systems now in the Libraries, one (Kirk-Othmer) was reviewed and recommended for purchase by the EISC. Three (ERIC, Dissertation Abstracts, and ABI/INFORM) were acquired after the Libraries served as beta-test sites for these products. Library staff were willing to undertake beta-testing, which takes extra staff time and attention, because each of these products met an information need for a large group on campus. In the case of Dissertation Abstracts, staff also saw potential for increasing the use of dissertations as an information resource. Beta-test sites were offered attractive pricing, but subscription decisions were not made on price alone. Staff evaluated these services on the basis of potential use, quality of interface, popularity with users, and subscription terms. In each case, decisions had to be made within a few weeks after the completion of testing and thus were made without exhaustive evaluation of all alternatives, such as whether to acquire ERIC from a different vendor. Acquisition of PsycLIT was a similarly quick decision, due to the availability of a favorable price, but staff knew that there was sufficient demand from potential users to warrant a subscription.

Selection Process

The formal selection process is a combination of a long-range plan, collection goals for different time periods, and selection criteria. As mentioned above, the Libraries have a formal strategic plan for electronic information services development over the next two to three years. This plan is rooted in the University's strategic plan, which gives details about projected enrollments, planned changes in academic programs, and research directions for the next three to five years. Conventional assumptions about the community's information needs, such as the assumption that all Carnegie Mellon students want "numbers," were reexamined in light of information developments reported in the strategic plan. The Libraries' plan for electronic services also takes into account projected funding levels, environmental opportunities (such as unexpected opportunities to test new products) and threats (such as changes in vendor contracts, or sharp increases in prices), and service evaluation, as well as the Libraries' mission and philosophy of service. The plan includes goals and objectives for specific time periods, which can be reviewed and altered periodically on the committee's recommendation. Goals and objectives are related to new acquisitions and review of current services.

The planning process did not produce specific recommendations for products or services but rather developed several principles guiding service development. These principles include the focus on widely distributed access to services, a willingness to undertake experimentation, and a commitment to select resources in the format most appropriate for the information and for the potential users. This last principle is difficult to implement, since an LIS-based product is arguably more useful than a stand-alone CD-ROM for most bibliographic and full-text files. However, given that LIS has limited storage space for new files, and an interface more appropriate for bibliographic and full-text files than statistical or numeric data, the choice of an information delivery method must take LIS's limitations into account. At the same time, the EISC must still consider the special equipment, space, and service needs CD-ROMs present. At this point in service development there is an acknowledgement that equity issues, that is, equal access to electronic services for all parts of the community, cannot all be addressed at once. The longer-range plan, however, demonstrates the intention to provide more balance in the collection than exists at this time.

Requests for collection additions come from members of the EISC, from other library staff, and from the Carnegie Mellon community. These requests are considered with reference to both the strategic plan and selection guidelines established as part of the collection development policy. These criteria (Appendix) are consonant with collection policies developed by subject bibliographers and were developed with reference to standard academic library collection development procedures. The Carnegie Mellon policy development process has been greatly aided by guidelines developed by ALA-RTSD for more traditional collections, and a checklist for end-user systems promulgated by the ALA-RASD-MARS Direct Patron Access Committee.

One consideration not specifically addressed in the selection guidelines is the likelihood that a product can be included in LIS within a reasonable time frame. Until now, LIS has been primarily intended as a general reference resource, and thus has left many subjects unserved in an electronic format. The proliferation of standard subject-oriented databases available on CD-ROM creates a temptation to opt for CD-ROMs to fill in these gaps. CD-ROM services generally cost less than an LIS file. LIS costs include not only the price of the annual lease, which can be much higher than the similar CD-ROM product, but also staff time needed to load and maintain the database, to adapt the search interface, and to provide enough disk space for storage (the Libraries are not charged for use of the mainframe computer). In addition, CD-ROMs can be made available more quickly; all that needs to be done is order the subscription and install the software when it arrives. However, particularly for online products expected to be widely used, LIS may be the better distribution mechanism. Decisions on some proposed CD-ROM purchases have been tabled in favor of waiting to see when these or similar products might become part of LIS.

Funding

Funding for electronic information services comes from different sources. For some services, most notably end-user searching and LIS development, the University has provided one-time internal grants of funds, equipment, and/or personnel. A recent grant from the Pew Memorial Trust will help fund acquisitions for approximately three years. The University has also steadily increased library funding for materials acquisitions over the past several years, which makes additional funds available for non-book resources. CD-ROM subscriptions are currently paid from the regular library acquisitions budget. The Libraries were fortunate to have some computing equipment and furniture available, in part because IBM had donated a large number of IBM PCs and IBM PC/XTs to the university. Additional items, such as the CD-ROM readers, were purchased from the regular equipment budget. Supplies, such as printer paper and ink cartridges, are paid for from a general supply budget. In the two years of CD-ROM service, the two systems have consumed approximately two printer ribbons and one box of fanfold paper per month. Supplies and basic maintenance are provided at no charge by agreement with Instructional Technology, a department within the Libraries' division.

Access to CD-ROMs

Since CD-ROM systems were developed for convenient, self-service information delivery, local decisions about access should not detract from this convenience. However, in practice, CD-ROM access becomes a compromise between complete availability and concerns about location, user assistance, and security.

Location

All CD-ROM systems are located in public reference areas, near the reference librarian's desk. In Hunt Library, the four systems share two equipment set-ups, one IBM PC/XT with a Hitachi CD-ROM drive and one NCR IBM clone with a Philips CD-ROM drive; the latter has a color monitor. Search stations have Epson dot-matrix printers. Both systems in Hunt are housed on desks, part of the furniture legacy of the IBM grant. The keyboards are kept locked in a desk drawer when reference staff are not on duty but are left out during normal reference hours. The CD-ROMs and boot-up software are kept at the reference desk; when a user wants to switch from one system to another, the reference staff member trades CD-ROMs.

The location near a reference desk was chosen for several reasons. First, the staff wanted to be easily available to assist users. The three different search systems (ABI/INFORM and Dissertation Abstracts have similar software) create a situation in which users need more help. In addition, since several services share equipment, the reference librarian has to be available to swap discs and start the appropriate search software when a user changes systems. The staff are justifiably concerned about equipment security, and a location near the reference desk permits continuous, if unobtrusive, monitoring. None of the equipment is equipped with an alarm system, nor is it permanently affixed to the furniture, as either measure would inhibit flexibility when equipment needs to be moved.

Availability

For the same reasons as choice of location, service hours for CD-ROM services are limited to those times when a librarian is staffing the reference desk. In Hunt Library, this means that the services are available approximately 73 hours per week during school term, over half the hours the library is open. Systems are available on a first-come, first-served basis, with no sign-up procedures for assigned searching times. When users are waiting, there is a half-hour limit on searching; however, there is no foolproof way to monitor exact times. Reference staff feel that time slot reservation is not yet necessary and would, in any event, increase clerical work and thus decrease the time and attention they have for working with users.

The CD-ROM systems are nominally available only to members of the Carnegie Mellon community—faculty, students, and staff—without charge. Potential users are not screened to ensure that they are affiliated with the university; however, during busy periods users may be asked to provide a university identification card. The Libraries cover the costs of printing references. Downloading is not permitted. In many cases, users would not want to bother with downloading, since Macintosh personal computers are becoming the machine of choice on campus and all current CD-ROM systems are IBM-based.

User Support

User support consists of two basic elements: written documentation, either prepared locally or provided by system vendors, and one-on-one assistance with search strategies and system problems. The written documentation, especially that prepared locally, is generally of the quick-help variety, something the user can glance at to answer a specific question. Quick-help charts are particularly useful for looking up unique commands and search syntax, areas where multiple systems can be particularly confusing. Personal assistance from reference staff addresses more complicated problems or questions.

This approach to providing support, which is consistent with the support provided for LS/2000, LIS and end-user searching, is based on experience with LS/2000 implementation, research on user wants and needs, and empirical evidence that Carnegie Mellon students and faculty prefer to experiment on their own and ask for help if needed. Reference staff have in the past scheduled short classes on both LS/2000 and LIS searching, and although attendees felt the classes were valuable, they were not well-attended. Demonstrations/lectures can be offered on demand as part of library instruction. For written documentation, experience and research have shown that, at least for this campus, users generally read it when they need to correct an error. Since users are near the reference desk, it is easier for the librarian on duty to tell if a user is having a problem and offer help.

Staff Support

The CD-ROM systems are the daily responsibility of reference staff members who also serve as Database Services Coordinators, one in Hunt and another for the Engineering and Science and Mellon Institute Libraries. These staff members see that systems are installed and maintained, including arranging for hard-disk set-up and software fixes if necessary. They also provide documentation for all users and training for staff. Staff usually have had time to use each system for several days before the system is made available to the public so they are familiar with different search commands and procedures.

Security

Demand for the CD-ROM systems warrants greater availability during hours when the library is open but the reference desk is not staffed. However, concerns for security of both equipment and discs are realistic enough to discourage this idea. Carnegie Mellon students tend to think that any publicly available piece of computing equipment is there for them to use in any way they need to use it, including erasing hard drives and installing their own software on the CD-ROM machines. To prevent this, keyboards are removed and locked away when no staff is at the reference desk. Students have also attempted to "play" audio compact discs on the CD-ROM players, and they have been tempted to try to play a CD-ROM on an audio CD player. The CD-ROM discs are also locked up to prevent such misuse. Although theft or damage could usually be remedied within a few hours or days, the staff believe that it is better for service to be more conservative and ensure that the services are reliably available each day than to take the real risk of damage and deprive users of the service while the damage is repaired.

Impact

Addition of CD-ROMs to the Carnegie Mellon Libraries has produced some predictable results for users, reference staff, and information services in general. Perhaps the most predictable result is that users are asking that more subject-specific bibliographic databases be distributed locally and without additional charge to the user. Even without empirical documentation, it appears that availability of both CD-ROMs and LIS has increased the number of library users rather than just increasing the frequency with which the "regulars" come to the Libraries. Some of the anticipated problems, such as user confusion over a plethora of search system interfaces, have not materialized. Instead, effects have frequently been rather more subtle.

On Collections

As mentioned earlier, one goal for information service at Carnegie Mellon is to increase use of existing local collections, and to increase access to collections outside the Libraries. It is difficult to separate the effects of CD-ROMs on local collection and interlibrary loan use from the more general effects of LIS and end-user search systems. In the past two or three years, circulation has increased. Use of the collection of journals on microform has also increased, as evidenced by a 44 percent increase in the number of copies made from microforms between July and December 1987 and 1988. Interlibrary loan volume is also much higher, rising over 70 percent between 1985–86, the period when LIS was introduced, and 1987–88. Access to bibliographic information on CD-ROM, or through the IAC databases, has generated some demand to subscribe to journals not in the collection. This greatly increased use of Carnegie Mellon resources introduces the question of whether the Libraries should continue to subscribe to journals that are not indexed locally. The Carnegie Mellon collections are intended to support current research and teaching interests, rather than providing the depth and breadth of a large research library. Given this collection philosophy, it might make sense to retain items that are used more often, and to replace unused journals with newer or more relevant titles. Journals that are not indexed online will no doubt show a decrease in use, and vice versa. However, this issue cannot be addressed until a much larger portion of the local collection is covered by locally held electronic indexing.

A related question, whether to cancel print indexes where an electronic counterpart exists, has for the present been answered in the negative. Since most services on CD-ROM or magnetic tape are leased rather than owned outright, the Libraries would lose several years' worth of indexing if the electronic service were canceled. Until information vendors, or libraries, work out a satisfactory method to replace indexing so lost, duplicate print subscriptions will no doubt be the norm.

On Other Information Services

Availability of electronic information services has reduced the demand for online search services, both mediated and end-user searching. This decline is more noticeable in subject areas covered by CD-ROMs and LIS than in the sciences and engineering. But it is not possible to completely correlate decreased demand for end-user searching with CD-ROM and LIS availability. End-user searching had been available without charge to students and faculty for two years prior to the introduction of CD-ROMs, but beginning with the 1987–88 academic year students have been allowed only two no-charge searches per semester and faculty are routinely charged. Increased costs and an increase in funding for local resources at the expense of end-user searching necessitated this change in policy.

On Staff

Reference staff have felt the impact of CD-ROMs in several ways. Some of these were anticipated: increased demand for librarians' time to help users get started with their searches, additional local documentation to prepare and update, and related requests for help locating the documents for which users have found references. These additional service demands have been added to the regular work load of the reference staff, without changing other duties or adding staff. These new services, and LIS, have created additional, more subtle changes for the Database Services Coordinators and the reference staff in general.

In the past, the primary responsibility of the Database Services Coordinators has been the day-to-day administration of online search services, both mediated and end-user systems. With the addition of LIS, and more particularly CD-ROM systems, the Coordinators have had to become technically adept with search station hardware and software. In particular, the necessity of having several sets of CD-ROM system software resident on a single search station requires that the Coordinator be able to maintain hard disks and either write programs for switching from one system to another or to hire the work out to a student. This latter solution is not the best choice, since students leave and take with them the understanding of how the system works. Consequently, the Coordinators have of necessity developed the understanding themselves. The key to successful use of outside programming assistance is to require both clear documentation for programs and procedures and to have the programmer teach the Coordinator what he or she needs to know for disaster recovery or regular maintenance.

The reference staff in general have noted an interesting dichotomy in the way users perceive them. Student users in particular apparently see reference librarians both as equipment technicians and as search system experts. This is a distinction from non-electronic days, when a librarian could logically be considered an expert with printed information and the vagaries of a card catalog but not necessarily technically adept. At Carnegie Mellon, where the bulk of the campus community is familiar with things electronic, the staff's expertise with CD-ROMs and LIS no doubt increases their credibility with students. However, the role of equipment technician—the person who can add paper or unfreeze a stuck key—provides no professional fulfillment for the librarian. In the past librarians have been responsible for taking care of simple problems with microform readers, or photocopiers, in public areas. However, the greatly increased use of microcomputers and terminals has increased this association with machines, an association which can frustrate the librarian while, at the same time, it enhances the library's image as a contemporary information service.

Publicity

The most effective publicity for the CD-ROMs has been word-of-mouth from satisfied users. The prominent location of the search stations attracts attention, and each station has a sign inviting users to try the system. As each system is introduced, reference staff have encouraged users with appropriate needs to try a CD-ROM. Systems are discussed in library instruction sessions; and the Libraries' newsletter, *Resources*, has featured new information services. However, there has not been a need to undertake an extensive publicity campaign, since users are finding and using the CD-ROMs extensively.

Evaluation of CD-ROM Services

The Libraries have not yet undertaken any formal post-implementation evaluations of electronic information resources, including CD-ROMs, LIS, and end-user search systems, primarily due to lack of staff time to design and carry out such evaluations. As mentioned earlier, all but PsycLIT and the Kirk-Othmer were tested prior to purchase, both by potential users and by staff. Current evaluation consists of experiential evidence and is limited to perception of user popularity and effectiveness. It is obvious that users like the systems and find their search results useful. One piece of evidence for CD-ROMs' popularity is the necessity of limits on search time. These limits are partly, but not completely, the result of multiple systems sharing two search stations. At the time of this writing the Libraries are testing UMI's combination product of the ABI/INFORM index and full-text articles on compact disc, on a dedicated workstation. Availability of ABI/INFORM on two workstations has increased the number of searchers who can use the index, rather than equalizing demand for the original search stations. As with other schools who have reported on CD-ROM popularity, Carnegie Mellon students like being in charge of their own searches; they apparently trust the computer's results implicitly; and they strongly prefer CD-ROM, or LIS, to paper indexes even when use of a paper index or a different online index would be a librarian's choice. Faculty are also CD-ROM users; PsycLIT in particular is very popular with several departments besides Psychology.

Observational evidence, though, does not answer several more important questions that the EISC will be evaluating in the future. When the Libraries started introducing local electronic information services three years ago, the goal was to get something up and running, and more energy has been expended on this goal than on evaluation. Now that it is time to renew CD-ROM subscriptions, and LIS database leases, the staff are asking questions that cannot be answered by unstructured observation. To ask whether CD-ROM, or LIS, or end-user searching is popular is rather like asking if the user wants more books in the library or extended hours of service. The answer will always be yes. More services, or new services, will be perceived as good unless there is a serious problem with service quality. But user enthusiasm for new services does not mean that the service is the right one for the user.

The questions library staff will be evaluating apply not just to CD-ROMs but to the entire package of electronic services available. First, we must consider whether to continue to offer existing services, LIS-based, CD-ROM, or end-user systems. All services currently offered are popular with some segment of the campus community. LIS files must be chosen carefully, since each one uses limited computer storage resources. CD-ROM services are space- and equipment-intensive. Once offered, some group will protest discontinuation of an LIS file or CD-ROM service. If, however, use declines, it would perhaps make sense to introduce a new resource with greater use potential and revert to paper indexes for the discontinued service. A second possibility might be to change the mix of LIS/CD-ROM/end-user searching, by adding a popular CD-ROM database to LIS, for example. Ideally all bibliographic databases should be available on LIS, since this is the most distributed retrieval system. Space and funding constraints preclude this solution, so an allocation between three service delivery mechanisms must be made. A third question was not even a consideration when initial plans for electronic services were made. In 1985, when LIS development began, very few information vendors were willing to lease their databases to universities. In addition, there were few CD-ROM systems to choose from. Now there are alternative products available both for local database leasing and for CD-ROMs (for example, there are three different vendors for ERIC on CD-ROM). Changing horses in mid-stream could produce some initial negative effects for users. Other considerations, such as lease price, support, or favorable approaches to backup indexing if a subscription is canceled, could outweigh these negatives in the final decision.

These questions can be answered partly on the basis of use, establishing a baseline by current use and measuring future use against the baseline. Another guideline can be cost per use, with an allowance made for the inevitably higher costs of LIS services. Factors that affect cost per use include not just lease or subscription price but also the cost of personnel to support a service. For example, if one CD-ROM system requires that library staff provide more personal assistance, it would be a more expensive choice than another whose subscription price is higher but whose service costs are lower. Such evaluative tools do not include a qualitative measure of value of the information to the user, or the value of an easier interface or a broader selection of journals indexed. Without some sort of qualitative measure, it would be easy to choose a cost-effective but unsatisfactory product.

Another area of evaluation that is of great concern to the reference staff at Carnegie Mellon is the quality of search results users obtain when the user does his or her own searching. This question is the same one librarians have been asking for years, not only about online search services but also about card catalog or print index searching. A limited response to such a question includes comparative studies of different search systems for recall and relevance. Obviously, though, such studies will have to come from facilities with access to the competing services. Another evaluation measure would compare journals indexed in two subject-specific databases, so that the database that indexes more of the local collection, or more of the journals most relevant to local needs, would be selected. Solutions to the problems with user interfaces, and end-user searching, will come from development of improved interfaces and, perhaps, more effective online and printed help.

This discussion of evaluation implies that librarians will be using their own professional judgment about CD-ROM resources rather than relying on the subjective opinions of users. The situation with CD-ROMs is perhaps at base no different than many other collection development decisions, which ultimately rest with the librarian, not the faculty member or student. The librarian in both instances takes a broader view of the collection, whether it consists of books or databases, and must make choices based not only on popular appeal but also quality, potential use, and longer-range plans for collections and services.

Summing Up

CD-ROM service at Carnegie Mellon has expanded, both in the number of products and amount of use, since this technology was introduced two years ago. Changes in the service have been incremental—such as the limitation on search time—rather than monumental. The CD-ROM search stations are as much a part of the Hunt Library Information Center as the online catalog terminals and ready-reference books. Users and staff alike accept these services as part of normal business. The two science libraries expect to increase CD-ROM offerings as well. As with any new service, or any change in service, the addition of CD-ROMs presented some unexpected dilemmas, not all of which could be avoided. The overall experience, though, has been positive for staff and for users. Following is a brief discussion of advice based on Carnegie Mellon's experience and a word about plans for future service.

Suggestions for Service Implementation

Develop a service plan. At Carnegie Mellon, the long-range service plan and collection policy developed simultaneously with selection and implementation of CD-ROM services. There seems to be a great temptation to acquire CD-ROMs because a library does not look progressive without them, without regard to the suitability of the service to the community, or to alternative methods for delivering the same information (such as end-user search services like BRS After Dark or EasyNet). The planning process forces staff to ask these hard questions. It is important to have wide participation in policy development and consensus that the result is reasonable. A plan helps target specific subject areas or service goals. Just as important, when many constituencies cannot be satisfied simultaneously, it is helpful to give concrete evidence that something will be done in the future. The service plan/collection policy should be reviewed and revised regularly to reflect both the changing information marketplace and changes in local needs. Beware of spending too much time planning and not enough time acting, though.

Plan for day-to-day service and upkeep. CD-ROMs do take a somewhat higher level of technical expertise than traditional online searching or even tending to an online catalog terminal. Responsibility for installing and maintaining hardware and software should be agreed upon before the system arrives on campus. It would be even better to have the participation of the responsible party(ies) at the time the system and the attendant hardware is selected. If programming is hired out to students, their work should be clearly documented so that it does not have to be duplicated when they are no longer available. If there are multiple CD-ROM stations available, there should be a decision about whether other stations can be used for back-up. Perhaps most important is to provide a trouble-shooting guide, in very plain English, for all staff members. This guide should say what to do, and when to stop and call for outside assistance.

Plan location of service. Locating CD-ROMs in a library depends on more than just available space and electrical outlets. Library staff also need to consider what effect the level of traffic will have on the location chosen; for example, will users have enough privacy to work, or if the workstation is near the reference desk, will the reference area be too crowded or noisy to answer other users' questions? In addition, if the CD-ROM collection is expected to grow, a location with room for expansion should be chosen. Security questions discussed above should also be very carefully considered.

Ensure that reference staff are comfortable with the system. Never introduce a new service to the public before the reference staff, or whoever is responsible for providing assistance, has had time to use the service in more than a perfunctory way. Granted, it is hard to tell an eager undergraduate that he has to wait a few days to try this new toy. However, service suffers and morale flags when staff are not ready to explain and assist.

Consider impact on other services. The level of impact on other library services, such as increased demand for interlibrary loan, may be hard to predict. However, if Carnegie Mellon's experience is representative, demands both on local collections and interlibrary loan will increase, just as they did when DIALOG searching was introduced. Fee-based or end-user searching may decrease. Since many outcomes will change demands on staff time, planners should be prepared to make adjustments, particularly adjustments in personnel.

Start evaluation plans early. This is advice that is often given and seldom taken. It is important to think of CD-ROMs as no different from other renewable library resources. If a journal subscription no longer fits the community's needs, it is canceled. If a CD-ROM service is not fulfilling its role in library services, it should be canceled. Such decisions should be based on empirical evidence, not just observation. It is equally important to consider decisions to cancel print subscriptions after implementing CD-ROM services. If the CD-ROM is canceled, what will replace it?

The Future at Carnegie Mellon

The Carnegie Mellon Libraries will have more CD-ROM services in the next few years. However, the long-range focus continues to be on campus-wide information delivery rather than services located in the Libraries only. Current crowded conditions in the Libraries will limit the amount of space available for additional CD-ROM workstations. Investment in more equipment will be expensive. Moreover, there is, no doubt, a limit to the number of different search systems users and staff will want to contend with. Since the university has the resources to support distributed information retrieval, it would be folly to stock up with CD-ROMs. Future acquisitions may not be bibliographic databases but rather full-text reference works and numeric and statistical data, which would be less perpetually in demand and which are more difficult to implement on LIS. Although CD-ROMs are not the ideal solution, they will probably continue to play an interim role in campus information delivery for the next few years.

Acknowledgement

The author would be remiss if she did not thank members of the Carnegie Mellon University Libraries staff for their assistance: Patricia FitzGerald, Assistant Director for Public Services, for editorial advice; Dorothea Thompson and Sue Collins, of the Hunt Library Information Center, for thoughtful discussions about CD-ROMs in general and local impact in particular; and members of the Electronic Information Services Committee, who helped write the selection policy.

References

Evans, Nancy. 1989. "Development of the Carnegie Mellon Library Information System." *Information Technology and Libraries*, 8(2):110–120.

———, and Thomas J. Michalak. 1987. "Delivering Reference Information Through a Campus Network: Carnegie Mellon's Library Information System." *Reference Services Review* 15 (Winter):7–13.

Kibbey, Mark, and Nancy Evans. 1988. "The Library Information System: Carnegie Mellon University and Information Access Corporation." *RQ* (Fall):104–108.

Nancy H. Evans has been Data and Information Services Manager for the Carnegie Mellon University Libraries since 1987. She joined Carnegie Mellon as Social Science Reference Librarian in 1981, with responsibilities including bibliographic instruction coordination and government documents collection development. She served as Electronic Information Systems Program Director from 1985 to 1987. Nancy received both her B.A. Degree in Political Science and her Master of Science in Library Science from The University of Tennessee, Knoxville, and she has since earned a Master of Public Management degree from Carnegie Mellon's School of Urban and Public Affairs. She worked as an Information Specialist at Oak Ridge Associated Universities before moving to Carnegie Mellon.

Appendix

Electronic Information Selection Guidelines

These guidelines are an excerpt, "Selection Guidelines," from a larger document, "Electronic Information Resources Management at Carnegie Mellon," developed by the Carnegie Mellon University Libraries.

General Purpose

The Electronic Information Resources Collection includes materials providing basic reference and technical information for the Carnegie Mellon University community, particularly bibliographic access to recent general literature and the scholarly literature of selected fields; basic numeric and statistical data in machine-manipulable formats; and basic full-text reference tools. This includes not only Library Information System (LIS) files but any publicly-accessible information resource.

Contents

Contents of specific information resources must be appropriate to the primary user group(s) targeted. To determine appropriateness, selector(s) should consult with the subject specialist who serves the primary users and with faculty and/or students in the group(s). Aspects of contents to consider include:

Treatment of subject:
—Basic reference materials appropriate to the general reader (including basic bibliographic references to general-interest magazines and newspapers)
—Preference given to scholarly, professional, or special reader for all other subject areas and material types

For *bibliographic databases*, should database be comprehensive for the field or selective? Does database index scholarly literature?

For *numeric/statistical databases*, how should data be collected and aggregated?
Type of material collected:

Primary sources: full-text literary manuscripts; numeric and statistical datafiles (as opposed to tabular data that cannot be used in an analysis package)

Secondary and reference resources: bibliographic databases that index general and scholarly literature (books, journal articles, reports, dissertations); basic reference books including dictionaries, directories, encyclopedias, handbooks. Attempt to avoid redundancy when selecting these resources; e.g. do not duplicate type of material indexed, or content of full-text files.

Language of materials indexed or presented in full text: Prefer English for most fields; justify inclusion of non-English materials when some users request them

Chronological guidelines: Applies to date of publication of material indexed in secondary sources like bibliographic databases; date of publication of full-text reference sources like dictionaries and encyclopedias; dates covered in numerical or statistical time-series data. Guidelines are subject specific but in general prefer recent coverage for bibliographic databases (last 3–5 years); at least 5 years of quarterly data for numeric/

statistical databases; current editions of reference works, with provision for updates

Geographic areas: Applies to numeric/statistical data, prefer United States data but limited European and Canadian material can be collected

Collecting levels:

Applies to all resources. Appropriate collecting levels are partially user-group specific. In all cases, campus or local availability of resources in non-electronic formats must be considered when evaluating the comprehensiveness and depth of the existing collection and how the proposed electronic resource will enhance that collection. Basic reference resources will be collected as a highly selective collection with some standard works and selected current resources. Resources supporting more specific user groups will be collected at either a basic level or at a study level. "Study Level" is defined as supporting undergraduate instruction and providing a general introduction to and current awareness of a particular subject area.

Service Delivery Mechanisms (Format)

One key question for electronic information is whether the advantages of the specific delivery mechanism (local mainframe or file server; remote mainframe; CD-ROM or other optical workstation; microcomputer diskette) outweigh the costs of delivery. Factors affecting comparative advantage over print include the following:

—Initial and ongoing product costs

—Ease of use in machine-readable form versus print or near-print

—Flexibility of use (better indexing; downloading capability)

—Ease of wide distribution, when this is desirable

—Need for multiple copies

—Need to replace paper (space-saving or poor condition)

—More frequent updates

Once the decision is made to acquire a product or service in electronic form the question is which electronic form. Following are guidelines for selecting between delivery mechanisms.

Optical Disc

—For less-used material (used by many people, but seldom, or used by a smaller segment of the community)

—For material that does not change frequently either in print or in other electronic formats (quarterly or annual updates; full-text reference books)

—For material that includes graphics otherwise unreproducible on a computer screen

—When paper counterpart needs replacement

—For material (either bibliographic or numeric) that is downloaded and used in applications packages

—Products that require strict access control

—Products that work better with specialized (commercial) interface

Microcomputer Diskette

—For statistical or numerical material to be downloaded into an applications package

—Allows user to copy entire diskette or portions of same easily

Local mainframe/server storage (LIS, Computing Center, or departmental machine)

—For material of general interest and frequent use by large portion of campus (and thus should be generally available over a network)

—Product of choice unavailable in alternate format (CD, e.g.)

—Usable in conjunction with network software (Andrew document production, e.g.)

—Product is compatible and usable with current or proposed search systems

—Frequent updates (once monthly) necessary for file's most effective use

—Allows one library access to material generally associated with another's clientele
Remote databases: mediated searching (fee-based)
—Unavailable in alternate electronic format
—Available and easy to use in paper
—Too large, too expensive for local online file acquisition
—Infrequent use (once or twice a month) or use by small segment of community
Remote databases: end-user searching
—Same as above, with the additional stipulation that the service be relatively easy for untrained users and appropriate for the type of information the user is seeking.

Product Analysis
This section lists questions selectors should answer when considering specific products and services for purchase.
Product description
—Technology
—Subject area
—Bibliographic data only, enhanced bibliographic, reference manual, full-text, numerical, directory
Description of users
—Primary and secondary groups who will use product
Levels of Access
—Open to all; open to particular classes of users (restricted by password, fee-based, have to be a student not staff).
—Location of service (within library; campus network; remote databases; circulatable)
—Hours that service is available
—Copyright restrictions (stiff restrictions might limit usefulness)
—Ease of use of interface or other access mechanism (appropriate to the information, for primary user group; adequate and appropriate documentation and/or training information)
Levels of support
—Source of financial support (from University Libraries; departments; divisional funds; grants; fees; other)
—Departmental interest, as expressed by willingness to share costs, could be a selection criterion
—Ongoing support requirements? (annual subscriptions, additional equipment; site licenses or other renegotiated use licenses)
Staff support
—Will users have to be trained? How much staff time will it take, and will this staff time be worthwhile?
—Will staff need extensive training?
—How much staff time will it take to get product or service ready to use, and how much ongoing maintenance is necessary ?
—Will we provide differential levels of support for different products and services? e.g. we can make some remote databases available w/out claiming to be expert searchers
Vendor support
—Does vendor provide training, equipment, printed documentation, help line?
—Does vendor provide updates, how often and at what charge?
—Will vendor work with buyers for customized services?
Alternate Formats and Products Available:
—Justification for remote access over in-library access

—Justification for non-print format
—What is already in the library in paper copy?
—What is available through remote services?
—Is duplication is advisable?
Useful Life of Product or Service:
—Will something more appropriate be available in the next 6 months–year?
—Will equipment or software be outdated?
—Will campus interest be sustained over a long enough period of time?
—If subscription is canceled, is there an alternate means of access to the same or information?

Index

247354